RELIGION AND POWER

RELIGION AND POWER

DIVINE KINGSHIP IN THE ANCIENT WORLD AND BEYOND

edited by

NICOLE BRISCH

with contributions by

Nicole Brisch, Gebhard J. Selz, Piotr Michalowski, Paul John Frandsen,
Irene J. Winter, Erica Ehrenberg, Clemens Reichel, Reinhard Bernbeck,
Michelle Gilbert, David Freidel, Michael Puett, Bruce Lincoln,
Greg Woolf, Jerrold S. Cooper, *and* Kathleen D. Morrison

THE ORIENTAL INSTITUTE OF THE UNIVERSITY OF CHICAGO
ORIENTAL INSTITUTE SEMINARS • NUMBER 4
CHICAGO • ILLINOIS

Library of Congress Control Number: 2008920482
ISBN-13: 978-1-885923-55-4
ISBN-10: 1-885923-55-4
ISSN: 1559-2944

The Oriental Institute, Chicago

Second Printing with Minor Corrections, 2012

ORIENTAL INSTITUTE SEMINARS NUMBER 4

Series Editors

Leslie Schramer

and

Thomas G. Urban

with the assistance of

Katie L. Johnson

Publication of this volume was made possible through generous funding
from the Arthur and Lee Herbst Research and Education Fund

Cover Illustration

King Naram-Sin of Akkad in horned tiara near a mountain summit, with soldiers. Rose limestone stele
(2230 B.C.E.). Originally from Mesopotamia, found in Susa, Iran. 200 × 105 cm.
Photo credit: Erich Lessing / Art Resource, NY. Louvre, Paris, France

Digital reprint by The HF Group, North Manchester, Indiana

Printed by Edwards Brothers, Ann Arbor, Michigan

TABLE OF CONTENTS

SECTION FOUR: RESPONSES

LIST OF ABBREVIATIONS

ca.	circa
cf.	*confer*, compare
cm	centimeter(s)
col(s).	column(s)
e.g.	*exempli gratia*, for example
esp.	especially
et al.	*et alii*, and others
etc.	*et cetera*, and so forth
fig(s).	figure(s)
ibid.	*ibidem*, in the same place
i.e.	*id est*, that is
km	kilometer(s)
lit.	literally
m	meter(s)
n(n).	note(s)
n.d.	no date
no(s).	number(s)
obv.	obverse
op. cit.	*opere citato*, in the work cited
p(p).	page(s)
pers. comm.	personal communication
pl(s).	plate(s)
r.	reign
rev.	reverse
viz.	*videlicet*, namely
vs.	versus

LIST OF FIGURES

LIST OF TABLES

PREFACE

This volume contains the proceedings of the Third Annual University of Chicago Oriental Institute Seminars, held February 23–24, 2007. In the tradition of the seminar series, the two-day gathering, entitled Religion and Power: Divine Kingship in the Ancient World and Beyond, combined scholars from various fields and disciplines. Seminar participants came from the field of Assyriology (Gebhard J. Selz, Piotr Michalowski); Egyptology (Paul John Frandsen); art history (Irene J. Winter, Erica Ehrenberg); Near Eastern archaeology (Clemens Reichel, Reinhard Bernbeck); Mayan studies (David Freidel); African studies (Michelle Gilbert); Chinese studies (Michael Puett); religious studies (Bruce Lincoln); and Classics (Greg Woolf). Jerrold S. Cooper (Assyriology) and Kathleen D. Morrison (Anthropology) graciously agreed to serve as respondents.

The seminar was divided into three sections: 1) Divine Kingship in Mesopotamia and Egypt, 2) Iconography and Anthropology of Divine Kingship, and 3) Divine Kingship and Imperialism. The structure of the book follows the seminar sequence as it seems to make most sense.

Series Editors Tom Urban and Leslie Schramer decided, together with Nicole Brisch, to leave the transliteration of personal, geographical, and divine names up to the authors. Hence transliterations are not unified in this volume.

A conference like this cannot go over successfully without the help and support of many people. I am deeply grateful to Gil Stein, Director of the Oriental Institute, and to the members of the Oriental Institute for allowing me to hold this seminar and for being so welcoming and supportive. It was a great experience and I learned a lot from it. I am also grateful to Emily Teeter, Theo van den Hout, and Adam T. Smith for kindly agreeing to serve as section chairs. I would also like to thank Joshua Best for helping so much with making the seminar a smooth and successful experience for all of us, and Kate Grossman for helping out and keeping her head throughout the seminar. I am especially grateful to Tom Urban, Leslie Schramer, and Katie Johnson, from the Oriental Institute Publications Office, for all their help and support throughout the seminar preparations, as well as their dedicated work on putting together what promises to be a fascinating volume. I am very thankful to Carole Krucoff for her help with organizing this seminar and for her kindness in general.

Last but by far not least I would like to express my sincere and deep gratitude to the participants of the conference, without whom this publication would not have been possible. I am grateful for their engaging and thought-provoking contributions, in their papers, in their discussions, and in the final articles.

1

INTRODUCTION

NICOLE BRISCH, UNIVERSITY OF CHICAGO

Who is there that can be compared with him in kingly status,
And can say like Gilgameš, "It is I am the king"?
Gilgameš was his name from the day he was born,
two-thirds of him god but a third of him human.

(The Epic of Gilgameš, Standard Babylonian Version,
Tablet I, lines 45–48, Translation by George 2003: 541)

Kingship is probably one of the most enduring forms of government in the history of hu-mankind and continues to fascinate scholars and lay people alike. The present volume is the result of a two-day seminar held at the Oriental Institute of the University of Chicago on Feb-ruary 23–24, 2007. The topic of the seminar was "Divine Kingship in the Ancient World and Beyond." The following serves as a brief introduction.

The study of kingship goes back to the roots of fields such as anthropology and religious studies (see, for example, Sir James Frazer's famous study *The Golden Bough*), as well as Assyriology and Near Eastern archaeology (for example, Frankfort 1948; Labat 1939). More recently, several conferences have been held on kingship, drawing on cross-cultural compari-sons (Cannadine and Price 1987; Gundlach and Weber 1992; Erkens 2002; Quigley 2005). Yet the question of the divinity of the king — the king as god — has never before been examined within the framework of a cross-cultural and multi-disciplinary conference. Some of the recent anthropological literature on kingship relegates this question of kings who deified themselves to the background (e.g., Quigley 2005: 2; de Heusch 2005a: 25) or voices serious misgivings about the usefulness of the distinction between "divine" and "sacred" kings (Woolf, Gilbert, Winter, this volume). Several contributors to this volume have pointed out the Western, Judeo-Christian background of our categories of the human and the divine (Gilbert, Woolf, Selz, this volume). However, rather than abandoning the term "divine kingship" because of its loaded history it is more productive to examine the concept of divine kingship more closely from a new perspective in order to modify our understanding of this term and the phenomena associ-ated with it.

One of the most influential works on kingship in general and divine kingship in particular is the above-mentioned *The Golden Bough* by James Frazer, which appeared in twelve vol-umes and various editions, among them an abridged one-volume edition, beginning in 1890. While Frazer's study has received strong criticism within anthropology and religious studies,[1] his theories on kingship in various civilizations on the African continent have more recently experienced a revival in anthropological and Africanist literature.[2] In regard to the ancient

---

[1] See, for example, the critique by Lincoln (this volume), with references to older literature.

[2] See especially Quigley 2005; Scubla 2005; de Heusch 2005a. The latter, while rejecting Frazer's evolutionist perspective, still emphasizes Frazer's findings that cer-tain kings drew their power from a "mystical control" they were believed to have had (de Heusch 2005a: 25).

Near East, Frankfort (1948: 287) already had misgivings about Frazer's model of divine king-ship, which revolves around the central, and in Frazer's mind, universal, concepts of the "dy-ing god," sacred marriage, and the scapegoat function of divine kings. Frankfort concluded that ancient Egyptian and Mesopotamian kings were not divine in Frazer's sense. However, it is especially the supposed scapegoat function that has of late instigated heated debates among Africanists (see Scubla 2005; de Heusch 2005b; Gilbert, this volume). This scapegoat func-tion of the king, as well as ritual regicide, are absent from ancient Near Eastern concepts of kingship.[3] Therefore, this Oriental Institute seminar also sought to develop new and alternative theories of divine kingship, theories that move beyond Frazer and the question of scapegoats and regicide.

To my mind, the recent anthropological discourse on kingship is strongly influenced by the findings in the area studied, in this case Africa. While these findings are important for the study of kingship, they are hardly universal or valid for all areas of the world and all periods of history. An example is Lucien Scubla's recent contribution to a volume on kingship, in which he states: "The accumulated ethnographic and historical facts show that kingship is not, in principle, political power. It is an onerous ritual duty which results, more often than not, in the killing of the king" (Scubla 2005: 39–40). While such a statement may be valid for certain forms of kingship in sub-Saharan Africa, it would be misleading to apply this notion to all forms of kingship worldwide, and it is certainly not applicable to ancient Mesopotamia, where the king exerted "real" political power while at the same time fulfilling important ritual func-tions. I should add to this that my own perspective, which infuses the way this introduction is written, is just as biased, albeit in different ways, as I study ancient Mesopotamia.

Another purpose of this seminar was a closer examination of Mesopotamian concepts of kingship. While ancient Egyptian kingship has been studied time and again (for example, O'Connor and Silverman 1995; Gundlach and Weber 1992; Gundlach and Klug 2004), Meso-potamian kingship is often neglected in cross-cultural studies, even though ancient Mesopota-mian kings also deified themselves, albeit for a brief period of time.[4]

In summary, the Oriental Institute seminar had the following goals:

- To examine the term "divine kingship" more closely: What is a divine king? Why does a king become divine? When does he stop being divine and why? For this, it is necessary to scrutinize the different ways in which divine kingship can manifest itself in different geographical and cultural areas and time periods.

- Connected with the first goal is the attempt at developing a new framework for study-ing divine kingship.

- The seminar focused on ancient Mesopotamia. This was due to two reasons. One rea-son is that research on ancient Mesopotamian kingship has changed considerably in

[3] The debate seems to revolve around the question of whether ritual regicide was committed because the king was considered a scapegoat for calamities that befell a society (Scubla 2005) or because it constituted the nega-tive side of the king's function in ensuring prosperity and fertility (de Heusch 2005b). Selz pointed in this connec-tion to the Mesopotamian substitute king ritual, attested in the Neo-Assyrian period, during which a substitute king is first appointed and then killed to avert negative omens threatening the king. However, it seems that a comparison to ritual regicide as visible in some African societies, is problematic.

[4] It is not entirely clear why Mesopotamia is so often ab-sent from comparative studies of kingship. Mesopota-mianists, or more precisely Assyriologists, are partly to blame for this situation, as we ourselves rarely interact with other disciplines. In our defense, however, it should be said that our field is relatively young and that many textual sources are still in the process of being deci-phered, which complicates interdisciplinary cooperation.

the past few decades. The second reason is that, despite this research, there are many aspects of ancient Mesopotamian divine kingship that are in need of more research. The comparative agenda of this seminar was designed to help develop new directions for future research.

Accordingly, the seminar was structured in the following way: The first section dealt with divine kingship in ancient Mesopotamia and ancient Egypt from a historical-philological point of view. The second section focused more on visual and anthropological aspects, with each scholar bringing their own point of view, and included scholars studying ancient Mesopotamia as well as other areas (Akwapim [Ghana]; Maya [Guatemala]). The third section sought to explore the question of a possible relationship between divinization of kings (or its absence) and the emergence of empires. The areas represented in this third section are early China, ancient Persia, and ancient Rome. Scholars were not given any directions or questions in addressing the topic in order to let every scholar develop and present her or his own approach to the topic and then compare these to one another. Therefore, the contributions to this volume are not unified, either in methodology or in theoretical orientation. This is deliberate in order to show the many possibilities — and difficulties — in approaching the topic of divine kingship. Some scholars, for example, chose a philological-linguistic approach, analyzing words or a single word in approaching how the divinity of a king was perceived (Frandsen). Other scholars chose a historical approach (Michalowski, Puett, Woolf), emphasizing the historical and political factors that led to the divinization of kings. Approaches also reflected the specialization of each scholar: art historians reflected on representations of kings (Winter, Ehrenberg), archaeologists on excavations (Reichel, Freidel) or theoretical background (Bernbeck, Freidel), anthropologists on rituals (Gilbert), and historians of religion on religious aspects (Lincoln, Selz). As the topic lies at the confluence of so many disciplines, it is unavoidable that each scholar not only considers information from her or his own specialty but also is as inclusive as possible. Therefore, the lines drawn here are sometimes more blurred. Two respondents were asked to emphasize the salient points of the presentations. One respondent came from the field of Assyriology (Cooper), the other from the field of anthropology (Morrison).

DIVINE KINGSHIP IN ANCIENT MESOPOTAMIA AND ANCIENT EGYPT

The last over-arching study of kingship and religion in ancient Egypt and Mesopotamia was Henri Frankfort's famous *Kingship and the Gods* (1948), a seminal study comparing the different concepts of kingship in these areas to each another.[5] While Frankfort's study was pioneering and admirable for the time, new data and emerging theoretical perspectives make a re-evaluation of some of his statements necessary. For example, Frankfort relied heavily on Thorkild Jacobsen's influential article "Primitive Democracy in Ancient Mesopotamia" (1943), in which he reconstructed an assembly of free men that once had ruled ancient Mesopotamian city-states. Jacobsen's theory, however, is now rejected by most scholars for lack of evidence, and our notions of power, especially in the very early periods of state formation, have changed considerably (Yoffee 2004).

---

[5] Frankfort's study continues to be referenced by authors writing on kingship (for example, Oakley 2006). For an evaluation of Frankfort's study, also see Winter (this volume).

The first three contributions differ strongly as each participant approached the topic in a different way.

Selz uses prototype theory to argue for the need to reconsider our (binary) categories of divine and human, which are ultimately based on "our Aristotelian-based scientific classification system" (Selz, this volume). He contends that Mesopotamian kings, as well as the royal family and in some cases priests can be "composed" of both divine and human elements and need not necessarily belong to either one or the other category or "prototype."

Michalowski pursues a different approach. His central argument is that divine kingship in Mesopotamia should be analyzed in the very specific historical contexts that made its appearance and disappearance possible, even necessary. After a brief historical experiment in the Old Akkadian period sometime in the twenty-fourth century B.C., divine kingship was reintroduced by Shulgi, second ruler of the Ur III empire (2112–2004 B.C.), to bolster his imperialistic expansionist ambitions. A similar historical approach is advocated by Puett (2002; this volume), who emphasizes the importance of analyzing political tensions that were created by the introduction of divine kingship, which may also have led to its abolishment; and by Winter (this volume), who argues that Mesopotamian kingship was always sacred but that the explicit divinization of the king only happened under certain, historically determined circumstances. Michalowski, Puett, Winter, and Woolf (see below) view divine kingship as a punctuated, dynamic phenomenon rather than a static and unchanging concept of government.

Frandsen uses a linguistic approach to present a new view of both the divine and the human nature of ancient Egyptian kingship. By analyzing the way possession is expressed grammatically he observes that it is possible to classify the king's attributes as either intrinsic (inalienable) to his divinity or as acquired and thus separate from the king's divine person. The kingship is also part of the human world. Frandsen illustrates this by providing evidence that teh transfer of the royal office from one generation to the next was governed by the same procedures as those used for the transfer of real world property. As an example, Frandsen isolates one term, which is often translated as "awe" or "fear," that is associated with ancient Egyptian kings. The divinity of ancient Egyptian kings is insofar profoundly different from Mesopotamia as Egyptian kings were always — more or less — divine. Therefore, Frandsen suggests a closer study of the language with which kings are described. In particular, Frandsen isolates one term, often translated as "awe" or "fear," that is associated with ancient Egyptian kings. Interestingly, as Irene Winter remarked during the seminar, this concept can perhaps be compared to the Sumerian me-lam$_2$, Akkadian *melammu*, which describes an aura of fear or awe that emanates from gods as well as kings, although this comparison will require more research.

ICONOGRAPHY AND ANTHROPOLOGY OF DIVINE KINGSHIP

Winter and Ehrenberg approach the subject of visual representation of kings by emphasizing the inclusion of textual and historical sources in their analyses. Winter makes several important observations, among them that visual representations of kings in Mesopotamia often show divine attributes whether the king was explicitly declared divine or not. This attests to the often divine nature of kingship in general, even if the king himself was not deified explicitly. Winter also points to interesting modern examples, in which divine kings have renounced their divinity. This leads her to conclude, "when divine kings do appear, they equally satisfy the requirements of their respective social, religious, and political systems," and she suggests that the driving force for this was political.

Ehrenberg's study adds significant observations coming from a slightly different viewpoint. She focuses on the visual representations of Late Babylonian and Achaemenid kings, who were not explicitly declared divine. Ehrenberg points out that in the relatively few extant visual representations of Late Babylonian kings, "a sense of quiet repose does emanate," and that cultic representations are more frequently attested, as, for example, in the palace decorations of Nebuchadnezzar's famous palace at Babylon. Achaemenid kings are represented in yet different ways. Stressing rather their Iranian/Persian than their Mesopotamian heritage, Achaemenid kings are shown as being the center of the cosmos.

Winter concludes her contribution with the following remark:

> In sum, Mesopotamian kingship was consistently treated as if infused by the divine, "sacral kingship" being the constant in which all rulers participated. At the same time, the literal ascription of "divinity" to the ruler was reserved for times and contexts when that sacral nature needed to be strategically foregrounded, and it is the job of the analyst to determine just what were the determining conditions of that necessity in specific cases (Winter, this volume).

Puett (2002: 234, 258; this volume) argues that deification of rulers appears for the first time with the emergence of empires and is thus also often associated with a sense of appropriation and transgression, as was the case in ancient Greece as well as ancient China. Similarly, for Mesopotamia of the Old Akkadian period (ca. 2334–2193 B.C.),[6] one wonders whether divine kingship may not have been associated with a sense of transgression, as the first ruler to deify himself, Naram-Sin of Akkad, was later decried as an unlucky ruler who was out of favor with the gods.[7] Perhaps it is this sense of transgression that led to the abandonment of ruler deification and may be one explanation for Ehrenberg's observation that the Late Babylonian kings sought to distinguish themselves from their Assyrian predecessors in visual representations, and the Achaemenid kings from their Mesopotamian predecessors (Ehrenberg, this volume).

Reichel discusses the only excavated example of a temple devoted to the cult of a divine king (Reichel 2001; this volume). In this case, the temple — located in the ancient city of Eshnunna (Tell Asmar), which was part of the periphery of the Ur III empire — is associated with a large palace complex. After Reichel's methodical reconstruction of the excavated remains, as well as his analysis of the textual evidence associated with that palace complex, he was able to reconstruct the history of this temple. Reichel shows that the temple was first devoted to the cult of the fourth Ur III ruler, Shu-Sin. After the hold of the Ur III empire slackened, the temple was re-designated to a deified ruler of Eshnunna, Shu-iliya, only to be desecrated afterwards when the rulers of Eshnunna abolished self-deification as well. Reichel also suggests that the deification of Shu-iliya occurred in response to Eshnunna's regaining its independence from Ur and to help the transition of power back to local rulers.

Bernbeck's approach is distinctly more theoretical; he suggests considering the topic by closely examining the practices of governance as well as the conduct of governmental elites (Bernbeck, this volume). He argues that part of a mentality of governing that enabled divine kingship was the religious system, which in Mesopotamia, for example, allowed human kings to be deified in specific historical circumstances. Bernbeck considers deification of rulers as an extreme case of sacralization of "powerful political figures" and emphasizes that historical

---

[6] Dates for the Old Akkadian period are extremely unreliable. See Westenholz (1999) for more information on the Old Akkadian period in general.

[7] This becomes visible in a Sumerian literary work that modern scholars refer to as the "Cursing of Akkade" (Cooper 1983). One would have to re-analyze Mesopotamian literary works according to this new possibility.

factors, such as a charismatic personality, political success, and a rise to power during a historical crisis are of importance for the sacrilization, and therefore, in extension, the deification of kings (Bernbeck, this volume). He continues by discussing the works of Norbert Elias and Mario Erdheim on the one hand, and Clifford Geertz on the other. Bernbeck explains Elias and Erdheim's view of courtly rituals as "a means of reducing potential resistance toward a situation in which a king has exalted himself beyond all reach," whereas Geertz viewed "courtly etiquette [as] part of sustaining a world order" (Bernbeck, this volume). In discussing the case of the first Mesopotamian ruler to deify himself, Naram-Sin of Akkade, Bernbeck favors Elias and Erdheim's interpretations of courtly etiquette and uses this framework to explain the negative reputation that Naram-Sin acquired after his demise. While Bernbeck's approach differs from that of other contributors to this volume, he also emphasizes the importance of historical context as a key factor in understanding the process of deification.

The following two non-Mesopotamian and non-Egyptian contributions add new facets to future paths of research, at least in the area of ancient Mesopotamia.

Gilbert offers an anthropological approach. Her analysis is based on many years of fieldwork in the Akan area of Ghana, studying the Akwapim kingship, in which living kings are sacralized upon installation on the throne. As Gilbert's work makes her part of a very different discourse on kingship, her approach is distinctly shaped by the current discourse on kingship in Africa (see above). In regard to divine kingship, Gilbert argues: "I suggest further that the distinction between 'divine' and 'sacred' kings is a hairline distinction that is Western and Christian, the concern primarily of theology and only relevant to anthropology if the local people make such a distinction. Akwapim people do not" (Gilbert, this volume). Gilbert focuses in her study on the rituals surrounding the installation, de-installation, and maintenance of royal power in Akwapim as well as the roles that some of the courtiers played in the ideology of the divine king. As the royal rites of Akwapim revolve around the notions of purification from evil and negative forces, it is difficult to compare it to kingship in cultures that may not associate kingship with these values. However, studying such rituals relating to kings is a highly neglected topic in Mesopotamian studies, for example, even though it is of great importance in understanding the mechanisms of kingship and the acquisition of power.

Freidel views Mayan divine kingship from a historical perspective as well but adds the important facet of studying the economic history of divine kingship. According to Freidel (this volume), Mayan kings had the ability to be reborn after death, the ability to conjure gods into existence, to manifest as particular deities, to consort with war deities, to manifest the central axis of the cosmos, and to communicate with the dead. This leads Freidel to interpret the basic nature of Mayan kingship as shamanistic: Mayan gods were worshipped through the royal cults.

During the Classic Maya period, so Freidel argues, the cult of the divine king was closely tied to that of the maize gods. This put the king in control of regulating the food supply by means of a "vertically integrated market system" (Freidel, this volume). The importance of this real, economic power that the Mayan divine kings — and possibly kings in other civilizations — held cannot be underestimated and represents an important area of research.

DIVINE KINGSHIP AND EMPIRE

As mentioned above, Puett (2002: 234, 258; this volume) has argued that there existed a link between self-deification of rulers and the emergence of empires in some cultures (ancient

Greece and early China).[8] The third section of the seminar invited scholars who worked on kingship as part of an imperial system.

Puett proposes an approach for studying divine kingship that emphasizes locating "tensions and competing claims of the cultures in question" (Puett, this volume). For early China, he distinguishes two opposing notions of kingship, one that leads to the deification of rulers through sacrifices that break the genealogical tradition, the other, in which the ruler remains human but draws power from sacrificing to ancestors. These notions of kingship competed against each other. In Puett's words: "In China, the interplay of human and divine forms of kingship has been crucial in the development of and reaction to the imperial state" (this volume).

Such tensions can possibly be located in ancient Mesopotamia as well, in which phases of highly centralized power interchanged with phases of decentralization. Thus, as mentioned above, the first instance of divine kings occurred during the so-called "first world empire" of Akkad, which was followed by a breakdown of centralized power structures. The second instance of ruler deification occurred during the Ur III period, another state that showed imperial ambitions, only to be followed by a phase of political fragmentation during the first part of the Old Babylonian (Isin-Larsa) period. Perhaps Mesopotamian kingship knew competing ideologies, similar to early China, although this must remain speculative for the time being.

Lincoln's analysis of the role of religion in the Achaemenid empire illustrates further important points. Achaemenid kings did not deify themselves, nor did they adopt Mesopotamian notions of kingship. However, the king "possessed divine charisma in the most literal sense" (Lincoln, this volume). The king was at the center of the cosmos, and the Persian army was seen not just as mere conquerors but as bringers of peace, whose purpose was "the restoration of primordial happiness and the accomplishment of God's will for humanity" (Lincoln, this volume). It is interesting to note that even though Achaemenid kings did not declare themselves divine, the adoption of Achaemenid court ceremonial by Alexander the Great appeared to some Greeks "to demand honors greater than should be paid to any man" (Woolf, this volume). This is important insofar as it shows how the phenomenon of ruler deification is not only strongly determined by historical circumstances, but also influenced by local traditions and perceptions of power and religion.

Greg Woolf studied the divinity of ancient Roman emperors by analyzing the historical, religious, and cultural circumstances that determine the form of what is termed the "Imperial cult." Woolf's main point is that there was no such thing as *the* imperial cult of Rome. Ruler cult was not an unchanging, homogeneous, and centralized concept throughout the history of the Roman empire, but the opposite. Ruler cult had different morphologies depending on where the ruler was venerated, for example, in Rome itself or in one of the provinces, and was moreover a concept that could change through time and could manifest itself in different ways. Woolf also points out that in some cases it may be difficult to define this imperial cult, as the lines between cult, homage, or veneration cannot always be drawn easily. Woolf begins his contribution by underlining that "'god' is not a concept that can be easily translated from one cultural system to another" and concludes by saying that "it is preferable to imagine a continuum stretching from men to the greatest creator deities" (Woolf, this volume). In this view, "emperors were the lowest of the gods, and the greatest of men" (ibid.). Yet he stresses as well

---

[8] The term "empire" is here substituted with the term "territorial state," which may be equally difficult to define as "empire." As a definition of these terms to describe various forms of political organization was not part of this symposium, they shall remain undefined here.

that these imperial cults flourished in a specific historical context, which focused on the worship of powerful individuals (ibid.).

EMERGING THEMES

Several themes emerged from the conference, as well as some questions that may serve as a starting point for further studies.

Some of the key issues as I see them are the following:

1. Several authors remarked upon the need to rethink our own notions of the categories of the divine and the human (Selz, Gilbert, Bernbeck, Woolf). Our own (Western and Christian) notions of the divine often force us to assign a being to either one or the other category. Some authors therefore suggest abandoning the distinction between divine and sacred kings, as sacred kings often fulfill similar functions (Gilbert), whereas others suggest a continuum on which divine kings may be located somewhere between these two categories (Woolf, Morrison, Winter). Selz argues similarly for the possibility that some humans can be composed of elements of both categories, and Frandsen points out that an analysis of language can help identify characteristics that are shared by divine kings and gods.

2. The most important result is, perhaps, the ephemeral nature of divine kingship. Several authors suggest viewing self-deification of rulers not as a static and permanent institution, but as an anomaly, a "punctuated" (Michalowski) and dynamic phenomenon. In ancient Mesopotamia and in ancient China, divinization of kings only occurs for short periods of time and is replaced by other forms of rulership. This stands in contrast to ancient Egypt and perhaps ancient Maya, where deified kings were the rule rather than the exception. Michalowski, Puett, and Winter suggest studying divinization of kings as a historical phenomenon. Puett proposes analyzing divine kingship by locating political and ideological "tensions and competing claims" that resulted from the deification of rulers. This approach has the advantage of viewing divine kingship within its historical, cultural, and religious context rather than an isolated, but universal phenomenon.

3. Connected with the previous point is the realization that divine kingship manifests itself very differently in varying areas of the world precisely because it is shaped by historical, political, and cultural factors. Many influences within a culture mold the way deified kings are represented. The religious belief system is important for this, as some religions view deification of humans as sacrilegious (Bernbeck). Similarly, there are specific historical (Michalowski, Puett) and "social (...) and political" (Winter) circumstances that make deifications of kings possible. One such context may be a period of crisis that necessitates the creation of a new political system within which the ruler may acquire divine or god-like attributes (Michalowski). Another context may be a connection to the emergence of empires that made divine kingship possible, if not necessary (Puett). Of similar importance are the reasons why divine kingship was renounced or relegated to the background in different historical moments (Winter).

4. If indeed there is a connection between the territorial state[9] and ruler deification, the question arises why some kings that perhaps *should* have been divine were, in fact, not, as, for example, the Achaemenid kings. Clearly, religion plays an important part in this as Achaemenid kings promulgated the cult of Ahura Mazda (Ehrenberg, Lincoln). Yet some of the ancient Greeks seem to have considered Achaemenid kingship more than merely human (Woolf), so perhaps one should consider the possibility that there are different degrees of divine kingship, similar to different degrees of the divine and the human. Woolf clearly shows that the cult of the Roman emperors had very different manifestations throughout the history of the Roman empire *and* throughout the provinces, confirming that ruler cult is culturally, as well as historically, determined.

FUTURE RESEARCH

It is to be hoped that the proceedings of this seminar will stimulate further research in areas in which ruler deification is attested, not only in the ones that are represented here.

Among the most interesting future questions is, perhaps, the possible link between divine kingship and the emergence of empires. This question may be especially interesting for future research in ancient Mesopotamia. Several authors (Michalowski, Winter) have mentioned the possible divinity of some Assyrian rulers, but thus far the question of why the Late Babylonian kings, among them the famous Nebuchadnezzar II of Babylon, or the Achaemenid rulers were not declared divine has to remain subject to further studies.

Related to this is the question, discussed by Winter and Reichel, of why divine kingship was abolished. Puett proposes that competing claims and tensions may have led to its demise in China, but is this the case in other cultures as well? It is, for example, unclear whether divine kingship was truly abolished in ancient Mesopotamia during the Old Babylonian period (ca. 2003–1595 B.C.). Kings such as Rim-Sin of Larsa or the famous Hammurabi of Babylon may have come very close to being deified in their lifetime, but for the time being this question must remain unanswered.[10]

If we assume a "continuum" existed between the categories of divine and human, then what did this continuum look like? Was there a hierarchy of gods? Were divine kings really on the same hierarchical level as lower gods? Winter (this volume) points out that in some representations ancient Mesopotamian divine kings are portrayed similarly to lower-ranked gods, and Woolf describes divine emperors as the "lowest of the gods, and the greatest of men" (this volume). Perhaps further research in the area of religion will help advance our understanding of exactly what position within the religious system of the time a divine king occupied.

---

[9] Or, as Woolf suggested, a rapid territorial expansion, and connected with this, a moment of crisis that may result in changes the ways rulers represented themselves vis-à-vis the divine.

[10] Some scholars would like to add a discussion on the semantic classifier for divinities (the "dingir"-sign) here. However, the significance of adding the divine semantic classifier to a royal name is unclear, and some consider it to be meaningless by the Old Babylonian period.

BIBLIOGRAPHY

Cannadine, D., and S. Price, editors

    1987   *Rituals of Royalty: Power and Ceremonial in Traditional Societies.* Cambridge: Cambridge University Press.

Cooper, Jerrold S.

    1983   *The Curse of Agade.* Baltimore and London: Johns Hopkins University Press.

Erkens, Franz-Reiner, editor

    2002   *Die Sakralität von Herrschaft: Herrschaftslegitimierung im Wechsel der Zeiten und Räume; Fünfzehn interdisziplinäre Beiträge zu einem weltweiten und epochenübergreifenden Phänomen.* Berlin: Akademie-Verlag.

Frankfort, Henri

    1948   *Kingship and the Gods: A Study of Ancient Near Eastern Religion as the Integration of Society and Nature.* Chicago: University of Chicago Press.

George, A. R.

    2003   *The Babylonian Gilgamesh Epic: Introduction, Critical Edition and Cuneiform Texts*, Volume 1. Oxford: Oxford University Press.

Gundlach, R., and A. Klug, editors

    2004   Das altägyptische Königtum im Spannungsfeld zwischen Innen- und Aussenpolitik im 2. Jahrtausend v. Chr. Wiesbaden: Harrassowitz.

Gundlach, R., and H. Weber, editors

    1992   *Legitimation und Funktion des Herrschers: Vom ägyptischen Pharao zum neuzeitlichen Diktator.* Schriften der Mainzer Philosophischen Fakultätsgesellschaft 13. Stuttgart: Franz Steiner Verlag.

de Heusch, L.

    2005a   "Forms of Sacralized Power in Africa." In *The Character of Kingship*, edited by D. Quigley, pp. 25–37. Oxford: Berg.

    2005b   "A Reply to Lucien Scubla." In *The Character of Kingship*, edited by D. Quigley, pp. 63–66. Oxford: Berg.

Jacobsen, Thorkild

    1943   "Primitive Democracy in Ancient Mesopotamia." *Journal of Near Eastern Studies* 2: 159–72.

Labat, Rene

    1939   *Le caractère religieux de la royauté assyro-babylonienne.* Paris: Librairie d'Amérique et d'Orient.

Oakley, F.

    2006   *Kingship: The Politics of Enchantment.* Malden: Blackwell Publishing.

O'Connor, D., and D. Silverman, editors

    1995   *Ancient Egyptian Kingship.* Probleme der Ägyptologie 9. Leiden and New York: Brill.

Puett, Michael J.

    2002   *To Become a God: Cosmology, Sacrifice, and Self-Divinization in Early China.* Cambridge: Harvard University Asia Center.

Quigley, D., editor

    2005   *The Character of Kingship.* Oxford: Berg.

Reichel, Clemens

    2001   Political Changes and Cultural Continuity in the Palace of the Rulers of Eshnunna (Tell Asmar) from the Ur III Period to the Isin-Larsa Period (c. 2070–1850 B.C.). Ph.D. dissertation, University of Chicago.

Scubla, Lucien

    2005   "Sacred King, Sacrificial Victim, Surrogate Victim, or Frazer, Hocart, Girard." In *The Character of Kingship*, edited by D. Quigley, pp. 39–62. Oxford: Berg.

Westenholz, Åge

    1999   "The Old Akkadian Period: History and Culture." In *Mesopotamien: Akkade-Zeit und Ur III-Zeit*, edited by Pascal Attinger and Markus Wäfler, pp. 17–120. Orbis Biblicus et Orientalis 160. Freiburg: Universitätsverlag; Göttingen: Vandenhoeck & Ruprecht.

Yoffee, Norman

    2004   *Myths of the Archaic State: Evolution of the Earliest Cities, States, and Civilizations*. New York: Cambridge University Press.

2

THE DIVINE PROTOTYPES

GEBHARD J. SELZ, ORIENTAL INSTITUTE, VIENNA UNIVERSITY*

In this paper I argue that our usual dichotomy of a human versus divine class is not very helpful in understanding the concept of early divine kingship. In the past, this rather rigid categorization, as well as the general distinction between a sacred versus a divine kingship, rather hampered our understanding of the underlying Mesopotamian concepts. I suggest instead that the concept of prototypes, as formulated by the cognitive sciences and anthropology with special emphasis on various "practices," can help improve our understanding of the role of divine kingship and various sanctification processes in early Mesopotamian history. If we further apply the notion of gradience to the concept of divinity, the riddle of "divine or sacred kingship" may become less puzzling.

In jenen Tagen, so sagt man, lebte Prometheus, von dem man glaubt, er habe Menschen aus Lehm geformt; sein Bruder Atlas, der zur gleichen Zeit lebte, wurde als großer Astrologe betrachtet; Atlas Enkel, Merkur, war ein Weiser, kundig vieler Künste. Deshalb wurde er aus eitlem Irrtum seiner Zeitgenossen nach seinem Tode unter die Götter versetzt.

Erzbischof Ado de Vienne, *Etymologiae*;
Patrologiae cursus completus, series Latina CXXIII, 35

1. PROTOTYPE THEORY AND THE EARLY MESOPOTAMIAN ORGANIZATION OF THE WORLD OF KNOWLEDGE

The hypothesis underlying the following remarks is that the prototype theory, as developed by Rosch, Lakoff, and others and which in the last decades influenced research in cognition and semantic linguistics, can provide a useful incentive for a better understanding of parts of Mesopotamian culture.[1] In fact, our Aristotelian approach toward categorization and hierar-

---

* The following considerations owe much to the COST A 31 project, "Stability and Adaptation of Classification Systems in a Cross-Cultural Perspective," and the many contributions and discussions within the framework of several workshops. My special thanks go to the director of the project, Thekla Wiebusch, and to the Egyptologist Orly Goldwasser, who generously offered their time for numerous discussions. My heartfelt thanks go to Heather Baker for correcting my English.

[1] In this context I may simply remark that Rosch's notion of a given prototype being defined as the best or most representative member of a given category comes not without problems. I quote here briefly from a 2003 article of A. Giannakopoulou, where she states that "[G.] Kleiber [*Prototypensemantic* (trans.), Michael Schreiber (1993)], argues that the prototype should be regarded as a cognitive representation, which is generally associated with a particular word and serves as the reference point for categorization. Therefore, the meaning of a given word is not defined by a concrete prototype, but rather by the mental representation of the prototype. This mental picture is not necessarily the representation of a realistic example of a given category, but rather an abstract entity that involves some combination of related typical features.

These typical features, if considered as prerequisite for the creation of an abstract representation, maintain the idea of the internal structure of a lexical category as a family resemblance structure. Therefore, meanings may cluster or overlap due to the underlying semantic structures. In which case, meanings that show a degree of overlapping involve more structural weight than those that serve as peripheral members of a given category. The mental representation of a prototype, then, should

chization may sometimes turn out to be misleading. To the scholars of ancient Mesopotamian culture it is well known that the application of a *tertium non datur* does not fully match the indigenous Mesopotamian classification procedures which are so well documented.[2] We can observe here that, with some regularity, Mesopotamian classification shows fuzzy boundaries between classes. Nevertheless, classification was a crucial endeavor for the Mesopotamian scholars. As Miguel Civil stated: "the whole of [ancient Mesopotamian] 'science' consists in the enumeration and classification of all natural and cultural entities" (Civil 1995: 2305).

As is well known, lists and classification patterns form the core of the Mesopotamian heritage. Niek Veldhuis has argued that they were used, perhaps even developed, for the purpose of teaching and labeled them therefore as "educational."[3] In reassessing the thematic scope of the earliest lexical texts compared with the traditional labels, Veldhuis provided the following table:

Table. 2.1. Thematic Scope of Earliest Lexical Texts (from Veldhuis 2006, 188)

Subject	*Lexical List (conventional label)*
numbers	"grain" (*Word List D*)
grain and grain products	"grain" (*Word List D*)
fish	fish
birds	birds
domestic animals	animals
wood and wood products	wood
dairy products	vessels
containers	vessels
textiles	vessels
metals	metals
persons	*Lu A*; officials
place names	cities
time indications	"plant"

Veldhuis has further demonstrated that the subjects of these lists match to a great degree the contemporary economic/administrative spheres. He explicitly noted that names of gods and persons are virtually missing, as are "wild animals, stars, and rivers ...; [they] are of little use in this administrative system and they are absent from the lexical lists" (Veldhuis 2006: 187–88). Therefore these lists do not reflect the whole "world" and are of lesser use for any description of "basic level categories" in a Roschian sense, as the author and others had previ-

---

exhibit the greatest degree of overlapping. It could be argued that within category resemblances meaning is not equally distributed among the constituents so that the components — the smaller segments of meaning — can serve different degrees of meaning and are of unequal importance."

[2] On a theoretical level I would like to refer to recent research into fuzzy logical structures; see, for example, Jantzen 2006.

[3] Veldhuis 2006. In this article Veldhuis demonstrates that the recently much-discussed "Tribute List," renamed by him as "Word List C," "is an exercise designed for beginning students in order to tackle the new technique of writing."

ously assumed.[5] It seems more promising, therefore, to turn to the so-called "determinatives" or — better — graphemic classifiers in cuneiform writing, in order to get an impression of early Mesopotamian "basic level classification."[6]

2. CLASSIFYING THE DIVINE

Despite the fact that no early list of deities has been detected so far, it is clear that the concept of divine was perceived as forming such a basic category. In light of "prototype research," the question may be posed, what, by the ancient Mesopotamians, was considered to have been "the best example" of the "divine"? The divine classifier, the DIĜIR-sign, is attested already in the earliest texts from Uruk, and the interpretation that the sign originated as a pictorial representation of a star is generally accepted.[7] However, in the third millennium the use of the DIĜIR-sign for marking divine names is still somewhat restricted. Besides the considerable reluctance to add the divine classifier to syllabically written names of Semitic deities,[8] there are also other instances where the classifier is missing. First of all, the primeval deities, as attested in the texts SF 23, 24 and the parallel from UET VII,[9] lack the divine classifier (I return later to the seeming exceptions AN.INANNA and AN.NISSABA). Second, we note certain divergences in local traditions: the synopsis of SF 57 and IAS 46, 47, 53 provided by Mander (1986: 106–08) shows that, in the Fāra texts, in contrast to Abū Ṣalābīkh, the divine classifier is lacking in several divine names. I mention here ÚR×UD, ŠU.KI.GAL$_2$; nin-gal, il$_x$(KIŠ-la), Ú.ŠUL(-ME)-NANNA(-E) (Fāra: ^{d}ŠUL-nanna), Ú.ŠUL.NANNA, ⌈GIŠ⌉+KAK.GAL$_2$ URU? È GIŠIMMAR KI (Fāra: ^{d}GIŠIMM[AR].x [ś]), SUMAŠ.NU (Fāra: ^{d}GUDU$_4$), TUM.MA (Fāra: ^{d}idigna?), EN.TI, sùd (Fāra: ^{d}RAD), LU:ÚB.KU$_6$, na:rú, gal-x (Fāra: ^{d}PA.GAL.URU×X), nu-saĝ (Fāra: ^{d}NU.SAĜĜA), nu-MUŠ.DU, ŠITA.MU.KISAL. Even more astonishing is the fact that the well-known fire-god gi:bil and the mother goddess li$_9$:si$_4$ are lacking the divine classifier in all these texts, whereas in other lists the expected writing ^{d}gi:bil (kù) and ^{d}li$_9$-si$_4$ are attested. Inconsistent is also the writing of the deified Urukean king Lugalbanda. Roughly a century later both deified heroes, Lugalbanda and Gilgameš, are consistently marked with the DIĜIR-sign. However, even in the late Early Dynastic texts from Lagash a smaller number of deities are still written without the divine classifier.[10]

Returning to the late Uruk situation, the different names for Inana-k, the Lady of Heaven, in offering lists from Uruk, namely ^{d}inana(-k)-húd "Morning Inana-k," ^{d}inana(-k)-sig "Evening Inana-k," and ^{d}inana(-k)-nun "Princely Inana-k," show, by comparison with later philological data, that these are names for a different manifestation of Inana-k as the planet Venus. As a result, there can be little doubt that the astral aspects of Inana-k date back as far as the Uruk IV period. Hence, astral phenomena might provide good candidates for the "best

---

[5] At the same time, Veldhuis draws our attention to the fact that the archaic lists attest "an intellectual and speculative background ... although the intellectual effort builds on the need of an administrative system, not on theology" (Veldhuis 2006: 189).

[6] To a certain extent they nevertheless do correspond to the thematic grouping of the Lexical Lists.

[7] There are, however, traces that the star icon mingled with another iconic depiction, that of a blossom or a bud, which art historians usually name "rosette"; see Moortgat-Correns 1994 and Böck 1994. The "rosette" is one of the major religious symbols referring to vigor or

the power of life, and in Mesopotamia it was used in this meaning right down to the Neo-Assyrian period.

[8] Compare Roberts 1972. Note, however, that the group of (Semitic) astral deities was most important (Roberts 1972: 57).

[9] See Mander 1986: 108–10.

[10] Compare Selz 1995 s.v. en-ki, $^{(d)}$ÈŠ-ir-nun, ^{d}gibil$_6$, $^{(d)}$giríd$^{(ki)}$, lugal-kur-dúb(!), (lum-ma), MÍ.U$_8$-sig, nun-ki, ud$_5$?-kù, $^{(d)}$utu, za-ba$_4$-ba$_4$, $^{(d)}$za-ra. The cultic objects alan, balaĝ, du$_6$, na-rú-a, and ub$_5$-kù are, in contrast to later sources, never marked by the DIĜIR-sign.

examples" of the category of the divine. We may further add that for this early period nothing definite can be said about a possible representation of Inana-k in anthropomorphic guise.[11] Some historians of religion would argue that the celestial phenomena might only reflect a sub-category of the concept of divine, or, as Jan van Dijk has argued, the diĝir-an-na "the deities of heaven" must be supplemented by the diĝir-ki-a "the deities of earth."[12] This hypothesis refers to deified concepts of vital energies, the forces of life behind all natural phenomena. The assumed differentiation according to the divine habitat makes it indeed doubtful if the celestial bodies are correctly considered as prototypes for the divine class. However, it is beyond question that the astralization process did deeply influence religious thought at the time of the invention of writing.

Another, iconic, classifier for deities appears only centuries later. It is the horned crown as a marker of divinity, or rather a divine attribute. First attested in the Early Dynastic II period, the horned crown shows in its earliest attestations a pictographic insertion of some vegetable symbols, perhaps ears of barley, and a kind of bull's mask depicted between the *en face*-turned horns of the crown. The horned crown therefore symbolizes the vigor of life and reproduction and links the concept of divinity specifically to agriculture and cattle breeding. Accordingly, it relates the depicted deities to the animal and vegetal forces of life. We should note, however, that at its beginning the horned crown was evidently not regularly applied when a deity was depicted, much in the same way as the DIĜIR-classifier was not used with the name of every deity. Thus a figure wearing a horned crown surely represents a deity, but the lack of it does not necessarily point to a human being represented.

3. CATEGORIZATION AND FUZZY BORDERS OF CATEGORIES

So far, when discussing the perception of the deified heavenly versus the natural phenomena, I have described combined categories, which together may form a new prototype. The combined categories of the habitat and the divine are, of course, not "basic level categories," and it may remain disputable how much we can deduce from these "secondary prototypes" for any possible identification of the prototype "divine." We should, however, keep in mind that a prototypical structure underlies every category. However, as there might be a prototype of the combined category "white wine," the use of the color term "white" here says little about prototypical color terms. It is not a simple set of features by which prototype categories can be described, and even the number of such features may vary in a given category, inasmuch as the "Mesopotamian locust bird" (bir₅ / buru₅^mušen) has no feathers, or that other birds cannot fly.[13]

Later Mesopotamian traditions show an awareness of the problem of determining rigid categorical borders. Most important in our context is the myth of Atra-hasīs, where humankind's first ancestor, the first human created by the gods, is accordingly named *Ila-we-e-I-la* "god-human." I would even suggest that this expression might reflect a third-millennium tradition with the notion of a partially divine status of its leaders,[14] their functional divinity, to which I return below.

---

[11] See also Seidl 1976–80: 87.

[12] Van Dijk 1957–71: 535 f. J. van Dijk named the latter group "chthonic deities," a term which might be misleading.

[13] In fact, combined categories do pose some difficulties inasmuch as they do not necessarily encapsulate the meaning of each one of its constituents directly and individually.

[14] It is tempting to contrast this with the Neo-Assyrian account of creation VS 24, 92, where the gods created first the *lullû-amēlu* "ordinary human," supplemented in a second creational act by the king (*šarru*), the *māliku-amēlu*.

4. BEYOND NATURAL PHENOMENA

Even if we interpret both aforementioned groups of deities (the heavenly and the earthly divinities) as secondary categorizations or sub-classifications with blurred borders, we have to take into account that, according to prototype theory, category membership can be realized in terms of gradience. Furthermore, from these categorizations all deities are excluded who do not refer to natural phenomena. Nevertheless, such deities do play a major role in the first god lists attested about five hundred years after the earliest texts from Uruk, for example, the god lists from Fāra and Abū Ṣalābīkh.[15] I am not thinking here of such divine entities as the "deified" animals, which would still fit into the described dynamistic notion of the divine; rather I mean the many gods' names which refer to "social phenomena" or which reflect social structures. As proposed in 1997, the pertinent names may be grouped as follows:[16]

  I.   Divine/deified emblems and paraphernalia[17]
  II. Deified professions or offices[18]
  III. "Cultural achievements or properties"[19]

It is of course not the fault of the ancient Mesopotamians that we have difficulties in understanding why divine qualities are attributed to such names, or why they were classified as belonging to the category of the "divine." I propose to see behind this categorization a process of objectification which some would prefer to call sanctification. What does this mean? I am convinced that such objectification processes are everywhere and, indeed, belong to the basic features of thought. This does not necessarily imply that thought must be understood in an objectivist way as a manipulation of abstract symbols, which receive their meaning only via conventional correspondences with things in the external world. Instead I suggest, following and paraphrasing Lakoff 1987, that thought grows out of bodily experience, that it is imaginative, employing metonym, metaphor, and synecdoche, and that thought has "gestalt properties" and is hence "ecological" in the sense that it is related to the structure and meaning of the conceptual systems.[20]

---

[15] Compare Krebernik 1986; see also Mander 1986 and Selz 1997: 170–79.

[16] For the following groups and a discussion of the respective names, see Selz 1997: 173–76.

[17] For example, "the Crown," "the Headband or Turban," "the (Deified) Crown (is) a 'Protective Goddess,'" "the Lady (of) the Crown (is) a 'Protective Goddess,'" "the Princely Ring(?)," "the Staff (of) the Leader," "the Stag-Door"/"Aurochs-Door," "the Lapis Lazuli Necklace," "the Stele," "the Nose-Rope," "the Lady Birth-Brick (is) a 'Protective Goddess,'" "the Saw(?)," "the Holy Foundation Peg," "the Emblem," "the Lady Scepter," and simply "the Scepter."

[18] "A (Divine) Seaman(?)," "the Expert (of) the Temple(?)," "the Brick-Maker (of) the Temple(?)," "the Lord (of(?)) the Granary," "the Temple-Cook(?) (of) Uruk," "a Leading Person in the Dairy Industry," "the Leader of the Land (Sumer)(?)," "the Princely Gudu-Priest(?)," "the Righteous Exorcist," "the True Baker/Cook (of) Uruk," "the Function/Office/Lord (of) the Abzu," "the High Esteem(?)," "the Princeliness(?)," "the 'Lady (of(?) the) Plough,'" "the Lady, the Leading Person of the Pen," "the Lady (of(?)) the Granaries," "the Lady Barmaid," "the Lady (of(?)) the Chisel," "the Lady Jeweler," "the Woman (of) the Sheep-Pen," "the Gardener(?)," "a Priest(?) of Uruk," "the Tax Collector," "the (Divine) Chariot-Fighter(?) (of) Uruk," "the Overseer (of) Uruk," "the Wet-Nurse/Kindergartner," "the (Divine) Writer," "the Shepherd," etc.

[19] "The Bee's Wax," "the Incense," "the Burning Reed, the Fire," "the Warming Fire, the Roasting," "the Brazier," "the Kettle," "the Torch," "the Pot," "the Ex-voto(?)"; to this group also "the Lord: Statue," "the Radiance," "the 'Me' (of) the Lady(?)," "the Lady of (Social) Group(?)," and others could be added.

[20] See Lakoff 1987: xiv f. He further remarks, "Thought has an *ecological structure*. The efficiency of cognitive processing, as learning and memory, depends on the overall structure of the conceptual system and on what the concepts mean."

5. PROCESSES OF OBJECTIFICATION AND SANCTIFICATION

The deified professions or offices just mentioned therefore do not simply reflect an intentional and wilful process of sanctification invented for securing the ruling elite's position or to stabilize the structure of society. These items could only be included in the class of divinities because of an existing *prototypical relation to the divine sphere*. In other words, it was the idea, the model or the prototype of the classes "Seamen(?)," "the Temple Experts," "the Brick-Makers(of) the Temple(?)," "the Lords (of(?)) the Granary"; "the Temple-Cooks(?) (of) Uruk," "Gardeners," "Barmaids," "Tax Collectors," "Overseers," "Wet-Nurses," and so on which qualified them for inclusion in the group of divinities. It is interesting to see that some of these prototypical professions are explicitly personalized. As for the deified items or paraphernalia, the situation has to be judged somewhat differently. Here it is not the office but the item that stands in a synecdochical way for certain concepts: "the Crown," "the Headband or Turban," "the Princely Ring(?)," "the Staff (of) the Leader," "the Nose-Rope" do not only allude to the respective offices and are not only an outward sign for them. Rather, these items were actually thought to contain the respective powers of the respective offices. And, of course, these powers were literally tangible, hence their prototypes qualified also for inclusion in the class of deities. Statements such as that the "crown" and the "staff," the regalia, existed since time immemorial in the heavens / were before the sky-god An, or that "kingship was lowered from heaven to earth" become sensible, even logical. One may still judge such statements as metaphorical, but they are meaningful and precise, much more than wilful traditional literary plays.

It would seem worth following this path and attempting to identify the more precise ideas behind such deified items as "the Lapis Lazuli Necklace," "the Stele," "the Stag-Door" or "the Aurochs-Door," "the Holy Foundation Peg" or "the Emblem." In our context I only remark that, similar to what we observed with the offices, such items were sometimes also personalized, for example, "the Lady Scepter," "the Lady Birth-Brick ((is) a 'Protective Goddess')."

In much the same way, contemporary and slightly later administrative documents focus on officials and offices, not on the persons holding them. Very much like the iconography of this period, the beginning of the third millennium, the images seem to concentrate on prototypes rather than on depicting individuals.[21] The representations of human beings show a kind of statuary stiffness and rigidity that is usually underlined by paratactic and hypotactic arrangement of the individual figures on a given monument. Even when actions are depicted, their ritualization and formalization can hardly be overlooked. The stress lies on the prototypical situation, the model personality behind which all individuality seems to vanish.

The sort of deified offices and functions just discussed show clear connections with the basic Mesopotamian concept of the "ME" (cf. Selz 2003a: 245–46, 251–54). With this term the Sumerians designated physical and mental objects alike. Prototype theory here has the advantage that there is no distinction between a natural sort of category versus artifact as our Aristotelian training inclines us to suppose. And, as indicated above, to the Mesopotamians apparently all these functions and concepts were not only represented by, but were also inherent in, these objects: for instance, rulership is inherent and contained in substance in royal insignia.

---

[21] Compare Selz 2003a. The assumption is certainly plausible that the permanence and ordering displayed by this attitude was of major interest for those who created such objects. However, this statement seems to me as one-sided as Rosch's remark that human categorization "should not be considered the arbitrary product of historical accident or of whimsy but rather the result of psychological principles of categorization" (1978: 27).

In other words, these objects were not mere "attributes"; they were thought to contain "ideas" materially. The concept of rulership is therefore primarily linked to objects like the scepter and the crown, to the "office," and only to a lesser degree to the person holding that office.[22] A result of such objectification processes was the sanctification of rulership.

At first sight, the fact that the very same period can also justly be termed Sumer's Heroic Age seems somewhat to contradict this postulated "formalism." All the heroes, Gilgameš,[23] Lugalbanda,[24] and Enmerkar[25] were, however, conceptualized as prototypes of rulership and only to a lesser degree — if at all — as historical individuals. They were regarded as prototype rulers who had fulfilled their functions in an exemplary way. I return to this shortly.

6. CLASSIFICATION AND EARLY METAPHORS

It fits very well with our brief outline of prototype theory that in the Mesopotamian classification process we do not only observe an interest in "oppositions"; equally important were the borders of semantic features. An eminent interest in the hierarchization of semantic fields also plays an important role. Numerous texts attest to a rhetorical progression from the more general to a more specific meaning. For example, in royal hymns functional or metaphoric "titles" are regularly enumerated before the individual to whom they are applied is mentioned. A related but more complex example can be found in the first lines of Dumuzi-d's Dream.[26] Dumuzi-d, being afraid of his impending death, cries for his sister Geštinana-k with the following words: "Bring my Geštinana-k, bring my sister! Bring my tablet-knowing scribe, bring my sister, bring my song-knowing singer, bring my sister! Bring my skilful girl, who knows the meaning of words, bring my sister! Bring my wise woman, who knows the portent of dreams, bring my sister! Let me relate the dream to her!" This is more than a fine example of literary technique: it shows also a method of hierarchization. In this case, the goddess's is the more general feature, whereas the subsequent descriptions guide us to her contextually most specific function: she is the interpreter of Dumuzi-d's dream.

In the view of the present writer, a similar sort of gradience forms the background of the widely used Sumerian metonymies and metaphors. They are not just similes in the way they are found in modern or even in Akkadian literature;[27] they purport a statement of essentiality. The personal name lugal-anzú[mušen] states that the king under certain circumstances or in certain practices has to be reckoned among the same (sub-)class "thunderbird."

[22] Here we may simply recall the well-known fact that in Mesopotamia permanence has various positive connotations, as can be simply demonstrated by the use of the words gi-na // kīnu(m) "firm, permanent" as opposed to nu-gi-na / lul / lú-IM // sarru(m) "unreliable; false, fraudulent." The impact of the concept of the sanctification of rulership is demonstrated by the secondary sanctification processes of the Akkade and the Ur III periods.

[23] Already from around 2500, there is a votive inscription to the deified Gilgameš that gives no hint as to how one could functionally distinguish him from other deities of that time. Further, the offerings Gilgameš receives according to the administrative documents of this period are much the same as those for other deities; compare Selz 1995: 105–06.

[24] See Wilcke 1987–90; compare Selz 1995: 160–61; further Westenholz 1997: 264.

[25] The hero Enmerkar was never written with the divine determinative and, in contrast to Lugalbanda and Gilgameš, was never venerated. In later literary tradition he was compared with Narām-Sîn and similarly ill-famed. For an explanation that the Mesopotamian tradition provides for this, see Westenholz 1997: 264.

[26] I use Alster's 1972 translation.

[27] See Streck 1999 and compare Selz's 2003b review.

7. DIVINE KINGSHIP, DUMUZI-D AND "SACRED MARRIAGES"

In Ancient Mesopotamian studies the topic of "divine kingship" has somehow gone out of fashion. Even Rene Labat's attempt to differentiate a concept of divine kingship from sacred kingship has not had not many followers. The related concept of the sacred marriage rite, more precisely the somehow problematic marriage between an earthly ruler and a goddess, met with increasing scepticism. This applied especially to the related but somewhat fantastic theories of A. Moortgat, whose 1949 book *Tammuz* was heavily criticized for its biased interpretation or even disregard of data, in short for its methodological flaws.[28] The discussions concerning the concept of the Mesopotamian sacred marriage rite center around the actors' assumed identity, with interpretations reaching from more "realistic" (king, cult personnel), through "symbolic," to purely "fictional" were recently summarized by Lapinkivi (2004, especially pp. 69–77)[29] and Cancik-Kirschbaum (2004).

Dumuzi-d, according to the Sumerian King List, is not only the name of one or two semi-mythological early rulers, but became in later literary tradition also a designation of a role, a metaphor, or a prototype essential for the conception of Mesopotamian rulership. The connection of the Dumuzi-d theme to the so-called sacred marriage is much discussed and both are intimately linked to the concept of sacred kingship. I cannot give here an evaluation of all pertinent sources, as that should be a historian's task. I just mention, more or less at random, a few facts connected with the postulated divinity of Early Dynastic rulers,[30] in order to demonstrate that the process of deification of the ruler started prior to Narām-Sîn: Ur-Nanše(-k), the founder of the Lagash I dynasty, states in one of his commemorative inscriptions that a certain Ur-Nimin[31] was chosen by an omen as "husband (of the Goddess) Nanše." It seems likely that this refers exactly to this sort of "sacred marriage" mentioned above.[32] I leave aside here the more speculative interpretations of the "Royal Tombs of Ur" with their astonishing mass burials. The divine childhood of the Early Dynastic rulers from the city-state of Lagash who call themselves "engendered by the god Ninğirsu," "child borne by the deity NN," or "nourished with the pure milk of the goddess Ninḫursağa," testify to a certain divinity of these kings. Indeed they were (thereafter) considered as belonging to the family of the gods, as En-metena's title "chosen brother of (the god) Nindar" clearly demonstrates. A different but related concept of the ruler's deification is attested by the Stele of Narām-Sîn, where he is depicted with a horned crown, the above-mentioned iconic sign of a deity. Of similar relevance to our topic is an Old Akkadian limestone mold, on which the deified Narām-Sîn is depicted in an intimate scene sitting opposite the astral deity Ištar shown in her warlike aspect (fig. 2.1). Both divinities are sitting on a platform on the top of a tower, above a group of mortal and divine prisoners whom Ištar is restraining by nose-ropes.[33]

---

[28] Compare, for example, the review of Gurney 1962.

[29] It seems, however, quite evident that Moortgat's notions influenced Lapinkivi's 2004 study on "The Sumerian Sacred Marriage," especially when he relates this "marriage" to the "concept of the soul and its afterlife"; compare also Gurney 1962.

[30] For a more extensive account of the sources, see Selz (in press).

[31] The assumption that Ur-Nimin is a variation or a different way of writing the ruler's name Ur-Nanše-k can-

not be confirmed; compare Steinkeller 1999: 118–19 with nn. 41–42.

[32] I refer the reader to the most recent treatments of the sacred marriage by Lapinkivi 2004 and Cancik-Kirschbaum 2004. Also important are the earlier critical remarks by Renger 1972–75, Cooper 1993, and the somewhat speculative reconstruction of the ritual in Steinkeller 1999: 129–36.

[33] See Aruz 2003: 206 no. 133.

The famous Bassetki Inscription attributes Narām-Sîn's divinity to the demand of the inhabitants of several cities he saved in a time of hardship, apparently successfully defending them against an enemy coalition. The deification of king Šulgi-r after his twentieth regnal year certainly draws on this tradition, but the connection of his death with the ascension to heaven was entirely unexpected. The result of this ascension was apparently that Šulgi-r was transformed into a star, a fate that also was ascribed to his father Ur-Namma-k. We may simply add here that this transformation of a deceased ruler into a star, his "becoming a star," is also well attested in the sources of classical antiquity.[34]

This process of deification seems related to a concept called euhemerism, after the Greek philosopher Euhemeros, who taught that the gods are deified heroes. Indeed this sort of euhemerism is attested in the mid-third millennium for the legendary rulers of Uruk, Gilgameš and Lugalbanda. They were, a relatively short period after their deaths, incorporated into the official cultic pantheon.

I cannot give an account here of the various other features that support the notion of a sacred kingship in ancient Mesopotamia. The various election and coronation ceremonies mentioned in different sorts of texts probably do reflect ancient rituals, even when the actual performances are difficult or impossible to reconstruct. Here I cannot avoid returning to the question of the sacred marriage (rite). I believe that in this ritual the ruler did — somehow — perform the role of Dumuzi-Ama'ušumgalana-k. A certain parallelism to divine marriages attested in the Neo-Sumerian period — where they actually were somehow performed — is well established: those of the deities Ninĝirsu and Baba and Nanše and Nindar apparently have a tradition reaching back to the first half of the third millennium. An Old Sumerian deity of the Dumuzi-d type may help to improve our understanding of the relationship between the earthly and the divine. The ruler E'anatum calls himself "the best man (ku-li) of the god ^dlugal-URU×GANÁ-*tenû*, the beloved husband of Inana-k."[35] The deity ^dlugal-URU×GANÁ-*tenû* (another common transliteration is Lugal-URU×KÁR) is a Lagashite Dumuzi(-d) figure playing an important role in the inscriptions of Enanatum I. This ruler (and En-mete-na) does not only claim to be the "child begotten by Lugal-URU×GANÁ-*tenû*,"[36] he even claims to have received the kingship of Lagash and all foreign lands out of the hands of this god. We note that other inscriptions do attribute exactly these deeds to the state-god Ninĝirsu-k.[37] What, then, about the intimate relationship between Dumuzi-d and the king, attested elsewhere, or our interpretation of the king as a Dumuzi-d figure (in given contexts)?

Some years ago M. Krebernik published an article on the "Protohistory of Dumuzi" (Krebernik 2003). In discussing the meanings of the names of the "deities" Ama-ušumgal and Ama-ĝeštin, he proposes that these names were originally just ordinary Sumerian personal names and must be kept apart from other divine names. Tentatively, but rather convincingly, Krebernik interprets Ama-ĝeštin as "the mother is grape-sweet" or the like. By way of parallelism, I suggest that Ama-ušumgal means something like "the mother has the power of

---

[34] For a fuller treatment of this concept, compare Selz 2000.

This tradition, first explicitly attested in Ur III sources, may not have come out of the blue. If we look at the much-discussed victory stele of Narām-Sîn, where the ruler as a warrior fighting in the hostile mountains is separated just by an empty space from the emblem of the heavenly deities Sîn, Šamaš, and Ištar — Moon, Sun,

and Venus — one might get the impression that the ruler himself here is approaching, but not yet incorporated into, the celestial sphere.

[35] Ean. 1, rev. vi 6–9.

[36] In another inscription, En-metena-k claims to be "the child borne by (the goddess) Gatumdu-g" (Ent. 25 9:10).

[37] Cf. Selz 1995: 188 f. 210 f. 231. 236 251. 297 f.

a dragon," the referent being in both cases some divinity, not the name-bearer himself. In Early Dynastic Lagash the name of a deity Ama-ušumgal is attested as an epithet of Lugal-URU×GANÁ-*tenû* and ušumgal // *ušumgallu* is attested as a sort of royal epithet from Šulgi-r down to Neo-Babylonian times. Krebernik further noted that the forms ᵈ(ama-)ĝeštin-an-na-k or ᵈama-ušumgal-an-na-k occur only in later sources. The reason for this is probably an attempt to demonstrate in writing that these beings were now counted among the (heavenly) gods because they became immortal by their deeds, much in the same way as it is attested for Ur-Namma-k and Šulgi-r centuries later. The element an-na "heavenly" makes it very clear that these beings were somehow elevated not only to "the honors of the altar" but also to the *di superi*. In sum, we see that in this deification process the same principles were applied as we observed in the astralization process of the divine in the Uruk period.

Clear are also the astral connections in the pre-posed divine epithet kù-g, "bright, shining," best attested with the Venus-star Inana-k. A similar astral interpretation is suggested here for writings of deities such as AN-ᵈNISSABA, AN-ᵈMAR.TU, and AN-ᵈINANA.[38] Such additional markings became possible or even necessary as soon as spreading use of the divine classifier AN overshadowed its reference to the celestial bodies.

8. HUMAN OR DIVINE?

I now turn to some examples where the notion of difference between the class of deities and the class of humans is blurred. In the ritual contexts two Old Sumerian queens of Lagash are not called by their proper names but bear a sort of religious title. In such contexts dìm-tur, the wife of the ruler En-entarzi, is designated NI-a-a,[39] and bará-nam-tar-ra, Lugal-anda's influential queen, PAP.PAP (or simply munus "woman").[40] Both titles are also well attested in personal names: especially remarkable here are TITLE-ama-da-rí "TITLE (is) the eternal mother" or TITLE-diĝir-ĝu₁₀ "TITLE (is) my deity." The titles are in a position where otherwise theophoric elements occur. The clear consequence arising from this observation is that the titles en, nin, and lugal in personal names do not necessarily refer to high-ranking humans. This conclusion is supported by numerous personal names of this type, where the choice of a deity's name or of a title seems somewhat arbitrary. This ambiguity seems to be intentionally making use of a certain fuzziness of the respective prototype categories.[41] That in the name of a statue of the ruler Lugal-anda, ᵈnin-ĝír-su-ĝír-nun-šè-nu-kúš alan-lugal-an-da, the deity's names are supplemented by the title lugal is then easily explained. I would even argue that a discussion of who is depicted as the central figure on the obverse of the Stele of Vultures, the god Ninĝirsu or the ruler E'anatum, finds its explanation here. It is the ruler in a divine role: as triumphator he, the king, is transgressing categorical boundaries.[42]

A consideration of two similar votive plaques of Ur-Nanše, however, forces us to modify these statements. On one plaque the ruler is shown to carry the working basket, so giving an iconographic account of his building activities. In the text of a fragment from another plaque,

---

[38] See J. van Dijk 1957–71: 536, who writes in this context that the "Zweiteilung führt dazu, daß oft die gleiche Gottheit eine astrale und eine chthonische Erscheinungsform hat"; compare also Krebernik 1986: 192. That ᴬᴺ nin-unug in Fāra II 23:13 or AN.AN-dumu-saĝ in Fāra II 1:20′ belong to this group is doubtful.

[39] Compare Selz 1995: 212.

[40] Compare Selz 1995: 273–74.

[41] We note that the etymology of Inana-k's name as *nin-an-ak "Lady of the Heaven" or "Heavenly Mistress" provokes a similar explanation.

[42] A similar idea is expressed by Steinkeller when he writes: "The ruler of Girsu ... became ... Ninĝirsu's earthly *alter ego*" (1999: 116).

however, it is not the ruler but the god Šul-utul who is said to carry the basket for temple building. What sort of relation, if any, existed between this god and the ruler? Was it just "a bit of humorous scribal fantasy," as J. S. Cooper suggested? As this may not be excluded, in the light of the present arguments it is easier to connect these observations with the intimate relationship between the ruler and his family god. I have argued that the god Šul-utul may be considered as a trans-individual part of the ruler or any other (male(?)) member of that family. According to a "logic of essentialism" (*Substanzlogik*), the god may even be regarded as a mere "double" of Ur-Nanše.[43]

A rather problematic passage from the famous account of Lugalzagesi's plundering of Lagash at the end of URU-KA-gina's reign may support this interpretation. In this inscription URU-KA-gina depicts himself as victim of the outrageous and sacrilegious deeds of the Ummaite ruler Lugalzagesi. The inscription concludes with the statement: lugal-zà-ge-si, ensí umma^{ki}-ka diĝir-ra-ni ^{d}nissaba-ke$_4$ nam-dag-bi gú-na hé-íl-il. Most scholars interpret the verbal form in a causative-factitive sense and translate the passage approximately as "May Nissaba(-k), Lugalzagesi's, the ruler of Umma's deity, make him carry this sin on his neck." Recently, C. Wilcke has observed that there is no grammatical indicator that points toward such a causative interpretation, and indeed there is neither a locative nor a dative infix (Wilcke 2007: 221 n. 45). The resulting translation, "Nissaba-k … may carry this sin on her(!) neck,"[44] seems impossible from the viewpoint of Mesopotamian religious history. Instead, I would argue that — similar to its Akkadian equivalent *našû(m)* — íl has also the basic meanings "to raise, to lift (upon), to load (upon)." Therefore the passage means that Nissaba(-k) may load the sin of Lugalzagesi on his(!) shoulder, that is, may not spare him the severe consequences of his deeds. Consequently, there is no need to assume an unparalleled function for Lugalzagesi's deity, one not attested anywhere else. The passage is, however, an additional example of the intimate relationship between the (family) deities and a person's self.

With the help of the Old Sumerian paradigm outlined above we are also able to improve our understanding of the role of Gudea's family god, Nin-ĝišzida-k. Following Gudea Statue C, his god Nin-ĝišzida-k follows the bridewealth that Nin-ĝirsu-k brings to his divine consort Baba, much in the same way as Gudea might have done in an actual ritual performance. The following passages corroborate this interpretation. In Statue E we read: "(The aforementioned items) are the bridal gifts for Baba for the new house which Gudea, ruler of Lagaš, the house-builder has added (to the former provisions),"[45] and "he let enter his god Nin-ĝišzida-k to Baba in the temple in the Holy City with them (the bridal gifts)."[46]

Let us compare this with a passage from Cylinder B 23: 18–24:[47] "Your (i.e., Gudea's) god is Nin-ĝišzida-k, the grandson of An; your mother goddess is Ninsuna-k, the mother giv-

---

[43] See my article for a reconstruction of the Mesopotamian concept of personal identities (2003a). As noted there, my argumentation shows parallels to earlier ideas of Winter, published in a highly stimulating 1992 article. Focusing on the images, she argues as follows: the ruler's statues have "three simultaneous representational identities ... [which] underscore the absolute aspect of the image" (p. 35). These identities are: "(1) the particular historical personage ...," (2) the representative of a class "ruler" ..., and (3) "a sacred, animate entity identical with its referent" (p. 34). The difference from the present argument is simply due to the different focus, for example, person versus image!

[44] Wilcke 2007: 220: "Des Lugalzagesi ... Göttin Nisaba soll diesen Frevel ... auf ihrem Nacken tragen." This translation implies in fact that the goddess, much in the same way as her protégé, should bear the punishment for his sacrilegious deeds!

[45] Stat. E 7:15–21.

[46] Stat. E 8:11–15.

[47] diĝir-zu ^{d}nin-ĝiš-zi-da dumu-KA-an-na-kam / diĝir-ama -zu ^{d}nin-sún-na ama-gan-numun-zi-da / numun-e ki-áĝ-àm / áb-zi-dè MUNUS(-)ba(-)tu(RÉC 144)-da-me / mes-zi ki-lagaš^{ki}-[ta/a] è-a // ^{d}nin-ĝír-sú-ka-me / ... / ... / ... / ... / [g]ù-dé-a [d]umu-^{d}nin-ĝiš-zi-da-ka / [n]am-ti [ḫ]a-mu-ra-sù.

ing birth to true seed (offspring), who loves her seed (offspring), you are (the one) who the true cow has born, the true mes-tree / youth arisen from Lagaš region, the (one) of Nin-g̃irsu-k ... O Gudea, son of Nin-g̃išzida-k, may for you your life be prolonged."

Here the birth of Gudea is described with words reminiscent not only of the Old Sumerian paradigm of the ruler's divine birth, but especially of similar passages in the literature of Ur III royal hymns. There, Lugalbanda, Ninsuna-k's spouse and the father of Gilgameš, is holding Nin-g̃išzida-k's place. Elsewhere in his inscription Gudea calls himself "child born by Gatumdu-g," once he names the goddess Nanše as his mother.[48] The explanation for this puzzle seems to be that Gudea is referring to different divine prototypes. By mentioning Ninsuna-k as his "mother" he alludes to the concept of the mother goddess per se, Ninsuna-k (and Nin-hursag̃a), and he places himself in Gilgameš's position. By mentioning Gatumdu-g, a (local) Lagašite form of the mother goddess, he establishes himself as heir of divinity or — as later texts would put it — as "god of the land."

In literature and in art we have many examples that establish the parallel roles of rulers and gods. Let us have a look at a statement found in an Old Babylonian copy of a Šū-Su'en text, edited by M. Civil in Šū-Sîn's Historical Inscriptions: Collection B (Civil 1969: A 12: 7–11): "Towards Tummal sailed he (= Šū-Su'en) with Enlil and Ninlil."[49] The interpretation seems clear enough: the king sailed with the (statues of) the gods to this sanctuary. D. R. Frayne, however, provided a different translation: "Towards the canebrake ... the god Enlil, together with the goddess Ninlil sailed" (Frayne 1997: 318). Indeed, such an interpretation seems not to be excluded. In other literary texts, for example, in the hymn Šulgi-r R, the deities are indeed pictured as acting persons.[50] Of course, we might think of statues perceived as "living beings," but an interpretation that the sources allude to the king's and his wife's circumstantial divinity is in the light of the Old Sumerian evidence quite likely.

Rituals such as mouth-opening and naming transferred a statue from the class of material objects to that of the divine.[51] Afterwards they were not only able to transmit prayers and offerings, but also to receive them. It is the same principle we observed already: by ways of objectification and due to the fuzzy borders of categorization they could be included in both groups, either that of artifacts or that of living beings. And since, I would suggest, all living beings share in a gradient way features of divine prototypes, they could have been included in one of these categories.

8. COMPOSITE IDENTITIES

I have argued elsewhere for an emic "Mesopotamian concept of a person as a composite being."[52] Initially, I developed these ideas on the basis of A. L. Oppenheim's remarks on "Mesopotamian psychology," where he concluded that the "protective 'spirits' in Mesopotamia are individualized and mythologized carriers of certain specific aspects of one basic phenomenon, the realization of the self, the personality, as it relates to the ego from the outside

---

[48] Compare Falkenstein 1966.

[49] Sallaberger 1993: 142: "Zum Tummal Röhricht ... fuhr er (= Šū-Su'en) Enlil und Ninlil."

[50] Compare Sallaberger 1993: 141 f.; see also Wilcke 2002 (Šulgi-r F).

[51] The mouth-opening and mouth-washing rituals recently attracted considerable interest; see Dick 1999, espe-

cially Walker and Dick 1999. Similar rituals are widely attested, not only in ancient Egypt, but also in modern India. Compare Waghorne 1999; Hardenberg 1999, and especially Davis 1997.

[52] See Selz 2003a.

world and, at the same time, separates one from the other."[53] Because a human's identity is of composite nature, it is easy to see that under certain circumstances humans could be transferred to the class of gods. And, if for various reasons a ruler is considered of outstanding personal qualities, the perception of him being a divine figure becomes almost unavoidable. The question why this track was not pursued any further in the Old Babylonian period cannot be dealt with here. It is, however, evident that the concepts of rule must have changed considerably at this time.

9. CONCLUSIONS

Using models of the prototype theory, one could also say that humans shared features with other prototypes and therefore might be included in various categories.[54] One might object to such formulations and insist that such statements do not add very much to common descriptions of such features as "metaphors" or "mythologies." Bound to our cultural prejudices, however, such notions still carry an overtone of purely mythological, almost fantastic and nonsensical (priestly), speculations. In my opinion, such an understanding is far too abstract; in early Mesopotamia thought seems much more concrete and precise. It was based on experience, and reasoning was less concerned with possible contradictions than with collecting *possible* "true" explanations: the more a Mesopotamian knew and could say about his world, the greater was his wisdom. Needless to say, the empirical concepts do not correspond to ours, therefore studies of Mesopotamian classification processes are of great importance.

Finally, I return to our central topic, the problems of sacred kingship. Understanding the problem of divine or sacred kingship was, until recently, severely hampered by the fact that the data were reviewed under the premises of our Aristotelian-based scientific classification system. The *tertium non datur*, the so-called binary logic, may have created discussions not always appropriate to our sources.

There can be little doubt that in the third millennium Mesopotamian kings could have had — in varying degrees — divine status. There are several reasons for this: starting from the concept of a human being of a composite nature, the ruler's connection to "eternal," hence deified, functions, which in the course of history became a separate sub-class of deities or secondary divine prototypes, contributed much to his perception of a divine being. This sort of functional divinity need not have been a ruler's prerogative. In varying degree it seems to have affected other members of the ruling elite: priests and holders of other comparable offices, but especially the royal couple (and family) possessed some kind of functional divinity. This concept had, without doubt, a ritualistic corollary, even when our pertinent information is scarce, difficult to interpret, and almost restricted to the upper stratum of the society.

One gets the impression that the ancient Mesopotamians were, in some way, aware of the fact that their explanations had the status of "models," that they were cognitive constructs. It did not bother them that their deities were natural and social phenomena and living beings and, at the same time, they were hypostasised in numerous statues in various cult places. We cannot avoid the conclusion that the Mesopotamian kind of empiricism was basically different from

---

[53] Oppenheim 1964: 199–200; compare Abusch 1999, especially 105 ff.; quote from pp. 106 ff. This differs widely from the position of Edzard 1993: 203 ff., who also summarizes a number of unsolved problems related to the "personal god."

[54] This may also help us understand a salient feature of Mesopotamian material culture. The composite character of many objects, made of different materials, anchors them in a categorial network, in a semantic field of various prototypes.

our own; other cultures may have fewer problems with that. An important corollary of this is the insight "that our successful concepts and theories can never be claimed to be the only ones that work — and therefore they cannot be claimed to be ontologically true." [55]

What I try to demonstrate in this paper is that such concepts as the prototype theories have a salient explanatory force when applied to textual and material data of the earlier Mesopotamian periods. [56] I do not claim to be an expert in cognitive linguistics nor in the history of religion, but I am convinced that many attempts should be made to cross the traditional borders of our specific field. Concepts like the reconstructed prototype concepts of Mesopotamian thought did not simply die out, nor are they restricted to a specific, almost forgotten culture. They are still lingering around, not only in contemporary India, even though they may be modified they are nevertheless influential.

Figure 2.1. Narām-Sîn Shown in Same Position as Ishtar. After Aruz 2003: 206 no. 133

[55] Von Glasersfeld 1999: 285.

[56] In cuneiform studies I know of just one attempt to make use of prototype theory and folk taxonomies (cf. Brown 1984) for the analysis of the lexical texts by Wapnish 1984. To the best of my knowledge she had absolutely no followers.

BIBLIOGRAPHY

Abusch, Tzvi

    1999   "Witchcraft and the Anger of the Personal God." In *Mesopotamian Magic: Textual, Historical, and Interpretative Perspectives*, edited by T. Abusch and K. van der Toorn, pp. 83–121. Groningen: Styx.

Abusch, Tzvi, and K. van der Toorn, editors

    1999   *Mesopotamian Magic: Textual, Historical, and Interpretative Perspectives*. Groningen: Styx.

Alster, Bendt

    1972   *Dumuzi's Dream: Aspects of Oral Poetry in a Sumerian Myth*. Mesopotamia 1. Copenhagen: Akademisk Forlag.

Aruz, Joan

    2003   *The Art of the First Cities: The Third Millennium B.C. from the Mediterranean to the Indus*. New York: Metropolitan Museum of Art; New Haven: Yale University Press.

Böck, B.

    1994   "Zu den piktographischen Zeichen auf der Siegel-Abrollung T.Ch 11/76 vom Tell Chuṣra (Abb. 1a–b)." *Altorientalische Forschungen* 21: 370–71.

Boehmer, R. M.

    1976–80   "Hörnerkrone." *Reallexikon der Assyriologie* 5: 431–34.

Brown, C. H.

    1984   *Language and Living Things: Uniformities in Folk Classification and Naming*. New Brunswick: Rutgers University Press.

Cancik-Kirschbaum, Eva

    2004   "Hierogamie – Eine Skizze zum Sachstand in der Altorientalistik." In *Gelebte Religionen: Untersuchungen zur sozialen Gestaltungskraft religiöser Vorstellungen und Praktiken in Geschichte und Gegenwart; Festschrift für Hartmut Zinser zum 60. Geburtstag*, edited by H. Piegeler, I. Pohl, and S. Rademacher, pp. 65–72. Würzburg: Königshausen & Neumann.

Civil, Miguel

    1969   "Šū-Sîn's Historical Inscriptions: Collection B." *Journal of Cuneiform Studies* 21: 24–38.

    1995   "Ancient Mesopotamian Lexicography." In *Civilizations of the Ancient Near East*, edited by Jack M. Sasson, pp. 2305–14. New York: Scribners.

Cooper, Jerrold S.

    1993   "Sacred Marriage and Popular Cult in Early Mesopotamia." In *Official Cult and Popular Religion in the Ancient Near East: Papers of the First Colloquium on the Ancient Near East; The City and Its Life, Held at the Middle Eastern Culture Center in Japan (Mitaka, Tokyo), March 20–22, 1992*, edited by Eiko Matsushima, pp. 81–96. Heidelberg: Universitätsverlag C. Winter.

Davis, Richard H.

    1997   *Lives of Indian Images*. Princeton: Princeton University Press.

Dick, Michael B., editor

    1999   *Born in Heaven, Made on Earth: The Making of the Cult Image in the Ancient Near East*. Winona Lake: Eisenbrauns.

Edzard, D. O.

1993   "Private Frömmigkeit in Sumer," In *Official Cult and Popular Religion in the Ancient Near East: Papers of the First Colloquium on the Ancient Near East; The City and Its Life, Held at the Middle Eastern Culture Center in Japan (Mitaka, Tokyo), March 20–22, 1992*, edited by Eiko Matsushima, pp. 195–206. Heidelberg: Universitätsverlag C. Winter.

Falkenstein, A.

1966   *Die Inschriften Gudeas von Lagaš*. Analecta Orientalia 30/2. Rome: Pontificium Institutum Biblicum.

Frayne, Douglas R.

1997   *The Royal Inscriptions of Mesopotamia: Early Periods*. Volume 3/2: *Ur III Period, 2112–2004 B.C.* Toronto: University of Toronto Press.

Giannakopoulou, A.

2003   "Prototype Theory: An Evaluation." *Ecloga Online Journal*, Autumn 2003. http://www.strath.ac.uk/ecloga

von Glasersfeld, E.

1999   "Piaget's Legacy: Cognition as Adaptive Activity." In *Understanding Representation in the Cognitive Sciences: Does Representation Need Reality?* edited by A. Riegler, M. Peschl, and A. von Stein, pp. 283–87. New York: Kluwer Academic/Plenum.

Gurney, O.

1962   "Tammuz Reconsidered: Some Recent Developments." *Journal of Semitic Studies* 7: 147–60.

Hardenberg, R.

1999   *Die Wiedergeburt der Götter. Ritual und Gesellschaft in Orissa*. Herodot. Wissenschaftliche Schriften zur Ethnologie und Anthropologie, Vol. 1. Zugleich: Berlin, Freie Univ. Diss. 1998. Hamburg.

Jantzen, J.

2006   "Tutorial on Fuzzy Logic." Technical University of Denmark, Oersted-DTU, Automation, Bldg 326, 2800, Kongens Lyngby, DENMARK. Tech. report no 98-E 868 (logic), revised 22 March 2006.

Koch, P.

2001   "Metonymy: Unity in Diversity." *Journal of Historical Pragmatics* 2/2: 201–44.

Krebernik, M.

1986   "Die Götterlisten aus Fāra." *Zeitschrift für Assyriologie* 76: 161–203.

2003   "Drachenmutter und Himmelsrebe? Zur Frühgeschichte Dumuzis und seiner Familie." In *Literatur, Politik und Recht in Mesopotamien: Festschrift für Claus Wilke*, edited by W. Sallaberger, K. Volk, and A. Zgoll, pp. 151–80. Wiesbaden: Harrassowitz.

Lakoff, G.

1987   *Women, Fire, and Dangerous Things: What Categories Reveal about the Mind*. Cambridge: Cambridge University Press.

Lapinkivi, Pirjo

2004   *The Sumerian Sacred Marriage in the Light of Comparative Evidence*. State Archives of Assyria Studies, 1235–1032, Vol. 15. Helsinki: Neo-Assyrian Text Corpus Project.

Mander, Pietro
    1986   *Il Pantheon di Abū Ṣalābīkh: Contributo allo studio del pantheon sumerico arcaico.* Istituto Universitario Orientale, Dipartimento di Studi Asiatici, Series Minor 26. Naples: Istituto Universitario Orientale, Dipartimento di Studi Asiatici.

Matsushima, Eiko, editor
    1993   *Official Cult and Popular Religion in the Ancient Near East: Papers of the First Colloquium on the Ancient Near East; The City and Its Life, Held at the Middle Eastern Culture Center in Japan (Mitaka, Tokyo), March 20–22, 1992.* Heidelberg: Universitätsverlag C. Winter.

Moortgat-Correns, Ursula
    1994   "Die Rosette ein Schriftzeichen? Die Geburt des Sterns aus dem Geist der Rosette." *Altorientalische Forschungen* 21: 359–69.

Michalowski, Piotr, and Niek Veldhuis, editors
    2006   *Approaches to Sumerian Literature: Studies in Honor of Stip (H. L. J. Vanstiphout).* Leiden and Boston: Brill.

Oppenheim, A. Leo
    1964   *Ancient Mesopotamia: Portrait of a Dead Civilization.* Chicago: University of Chicago Press.

Renger, J.
    1972–75   "Heilige Hochzeit. A. Philologisch." *Reallexikon der Assyriologie* 5: 251–59.

Roberts, J. J. M.
    1972   *The Earliest Semitic Pantheon: A Study of the Semitic Deities Attested in Mesopotamia before Ur III.* Baltimore: Johns Hopkins University Press.

Rosch, Eleanor
    1978   "Principles of Categorization." In *Cognition and Categorization,* E. Rosch and B. B. Lloyd, editors, pp. 27–48. Hillsdale: Erlbaum Associates.

Sallaberger, Walther
    1993   *Der kultische Kalender der Ur III-Zeit.* Berlin and New York: Walter de Gruyter.

Seidl, U.
    1976–80   "Inanna/Ištar (Mesopotamien)." In *Reallexikon der Assyriologie* 5: 87–98.

Selz, Gebhard J.
    1990   "Studies in Early Syncretism: The Development of the Pantheon in Lagaš." *Acta Sumerologica (Japan)* 12: 111–42.
    1995   *Untersuchungen zur Götterwelt des altsumerischen Stadtstaates von Lagaš.* Philadelphia: University of Pennsylvania Museum.
    1997   "The Holy Drum, the Spear, and the Harp: Towards an Understanding of the Problems of Deification in Third Millennium Mesopotamia." In *Sumerian Gods and Their Representatives,* edited by I. L. Finkel and M. J. Geller, pp. 167–213. Cuneiform Monographs 7. Groningen: Styx.
    2000   "Der sogenannte 'geflügelte Tempel' und die 'Himmelfahrt' der Herrscher: Spekulationen über ein ungelöstes Problem der altakkadischen Glyptik und dessen möglichen rituellen Hintergrund." In *Studi sul Vicino Oriente antico dedicati alla memoria de Luigi Cagni,* edited by S. Graziani, pp. 961–83. Naples: Istituto Universitario Orientale.
    2003a   "Die Spur der Objekte: Überlegungen zur Bedeutung von Objektivierungsprozessen und Objektmanipulationen in der mesopotamischen Frühgeschichte." In *Subjekte und*

Gesellschaft: Zur Konstitution von Sozialität; Für Günter Dux, edited by U. Wenzel, B. Bretzinger, and K. Holz, pp. 233–58. Weilerswist: Velbrück Wissenschaft.

2003b   Review of *Die Bildersprache in der akkadischen Epik,* by M. Streck. *Wiener Zeitschrift für die Kunde des Morgenlandes* 93: 268–75.

2004   "Composite Beings: Of Individualisation and Objectification in Third Millennium Mesopotamia." *Archív Orientální* 74: 33–53.

In Press "Götter der Gesellschaft – Gesellschaft der Götter." *Colloquien der Deutschen Orient-Gesellschaft* 5.

Steinkeller, Piotr

1999   "On Rulers Priest and Sacred Marriage: Tracing the Evolution of Early Sumerian Kingship." In *Priests and Officials in the Ancient Near East: Papers of the Second Colloquium on the Ancient Near East: The City and Its Life, Held at the Middle Eastern Culture Center in Japan (Mitaka, Tokyo), March 22–24, 1996,* edited by K. Watanabe, pp. 103–37. Heidelberg: Universitätsverlag C. Winter.

Streck, Michael P.

1999   *Die Bildersprache in der akkadischen Epik.* Alter Orient und Altes Testament 264. Münster: Ugarit-Verlag.

van Dijk, J. J. A.

1957–71 "Gott. A. Nach sumerischen Texten." *Reallexikon der Assyriologie* 3: 532–43.

Veldhuis, Niek

2006   "How Did They Learn Cuneiform?" In *Approaches to Sumerian Literature: Studies in Honor of Stip (H. L. J. Vanstiphout),* edited by P. Michalowski and N. Veldhuis, pp. 181–200. Leiden and Boston: Brill.

Waghorne, J. Punzo

1999   "The Divine Image in Contemporary South India: The Renaissance of a Once Maligned Tradition." In *Born in Heaven, Made on Earth: The Making of the Cult Image in the Ancient Near East,* edited by M. B. Dick, pp. 211–43. Winona Lake: Eisenbrauns.

Walker, C., and Michael B. Dick

1999   "The Induction of the Cult Image in Ancient Mesopotamia: The Mesopotamian mīs pî Ritual." In *Born in Heaven, Made on Earth: The Making of the Cult Image in the Ancient Near East,* edited by M. B. Dick, pp. 55–122. Winona Lake: Eisenbrauns.

Wapnish, P. C.

1984   Animal Names and Animal Classifications in Mesopotamia: An Interdisciplinary Approach Based on Folk Taxonomy. Ph.D. dissertation, Columbia University.

Watanabe, K., editor

1999   *Priests and Officials in the Ancient Near East: Papers of the Second Colloquium on the Ancient Near East: The City and Its Life, Held at the Middle Eastern Culture Center in Japan (Mitaka, Tokyo), March 22–24, 1996.* Heidelberg: Universitätsverlag C. Winter.

Westenholz, Joan Goodnick

1997   *Legends of the Kings of Akkade: The Texts.* Winona Lake: Eisenbrauns.

Wilcke, Claus

1987–90 "Lugalbanda." *Reallexikon der Assyriologie* 7: 117–31.

2002   "Vom göttlichen Wesen des Königtums und seinem Ursprung im Himmel." In *Die Sakralität von Herrschaft: Herrschaftslegitimierung im Wechsel der Zeiten und Räu-*

me; *Fünfzehn interdisziplinäre Beiträge zu einem weltweiten und epochenübergrei-fenden Phänomen*, edited by F.-R. Erkens, pp. 63–83. Berlin: Akademie-Verlag.

2007   "Das Recht: Grundlage des sozialen und politischen Diskurses im Alten Orient." In *Das geistige Erfassen der Welt im Alten Orient: Sprache, Religion, Kultur und Gesellschaft*, edited by C. Wilcke, pp. 209–44. Wiesbaden: Harrassowitz.

Winter, Irene

1992   "'Idols of the King': Royal Images as Recipients of Ritual Action in Ancient Mesopotamia." *Journal of Ritual Studies* 6/1: 13–42.

3

THE MORTAL KINGS OF UR: A SHORT CENTURY OF DIVINE RULE IN ANCIENT MESOPOTAMIA

PIOTR MICHALOWSKI, UNIVERSITY OF MICHIGAN

Assyriologists are at a disadvantage whenever the subject of divine kingship comes up. The issue is not an old one, but it has its lingering ghosts, James Frazer and Edward Evans-Prichard, and it has its favorite haunting ground, the continent of Africa and the island of Madagascar. Ever since Frazer delineated the problem in 1890, the focus of investigation has been on Africa, and the definition has encompassed three central components: duality, regicide, and the mediating role of the king. Of the three, regicide has been the most contentious issue, but it is one that is hardly important outside of the Africanist debates. Moreover, as Kasja Ekholm Friedman (1985: 250) has written, some have viewed divine kingship as "an autonomous symbolic structure that can only be understood in terms of its own internal symbolic structure." Writing about the Lower Congo (Friedman 1985: 251), she undertook to demonstrate that "it is a historical product which has undergone transformations connected to the general structural change that has turned Africa into an underdeveloped periphery of the West." Here, I follow her example and attempt to locate the eruptions of early Mesopotamian divine kingship as historically defined phenomena, rather than as moments in a developmental trajectory of an autonomous symbolic structure.

Most studies of the early history of Mesopotamian kingship concentrate on the development of a specific figure in text and art; the underlying notions are social evolutionary, and the methodology is philological, often relying on etymology and the study of the occurrence and history of lexical labels, as summarized well in a recent article by Nicole Brisch (2006). Much of it is disembodied from a consideration of political and symbolic structures. Thus, for example, the Sumerian terms en, lugal, and énsi are seen by some to have very different symbolic histories and function; in fact, they are just different local words for "sovereign," the first one originally used in the city of Uruk, second in Ur, and the third in the city-state of Lagash. These quasi-synonyms were remodeled within the context of centralized states as part of new political and symbolic languages. Thus, in the Ur III kingdom, around 2100 B.C., there was only one lugal in the world, and that was the king of Ur. In poetic language he combined both the status of en and of lugal, that is, he was characterized by "sovereignty of Ur and kingship of Uruk," and all his governors were énsi, as were all foreign rulers. Like all inventions, this one played with tradition, but it has to be understood not in evolutionary perspective, but within the context of a new language of empire.

Divine kingship has had a similar fate. Although there has been no thorough investigation of the concept since Henri Frankfort's inspired, but now dated monograph (1948), recent studies that mention the phenomenon in passing tend to stress its antecedents and to treat it philologically, rather than as a historical symbolic phenomenon. I argue that episodes of divine kingship were not the apex of a long developmental pattern, but were historically determined events. All kings are sacred and mediate between sacred and profane, but not all kings are gods.

As far as one can determine, the earliest Mesopotamian divine ruler was Naram-Sin (2254–2218 B.C.), the fourth king of the Dynasty of Agade (2334–2154 B.C.).[1] Very little is known of this event; the monarch's divine status is indicated by representational attributes otherwise reserved only for gods and goddesses: a divine classifier before his name, and by the addition of a horned crown in visual representations. His sacred elevation is described in just one royal inscription, which states:

> Because he secured the foundations of his city (Agade) in times of trouble,[2] his city requested of Ishtar in Eana, of Enlil in Nippur, of Dagan in Tuttul, of Ninhursanga in Kesh, of Ea in Eridu, of Sin in Ur, of Shamash in Sippar, and of Nergal in Kutha, that (Naram-Sin) be made a god, and then built his temple in the midst of (the city of) Agade.

This unique statement provides us with the *only* explicit contemporary view of the divinization of Naram-Sin, and its singular nature only serves to draw attention to the limitations of our sources of information. The initiation of the act is attributed not to the king himself, but to the citizens of his city, and is apparently granted in reward for saving the state from an insurrection that nearly toppled it. The phrase translated here as "secured the foundations" is used here for the first time in Mesopotamian history, but will become, in Sumerian as well as Akkadian, a major ideological concept depicting the security of the state and the crown. Moreover, this is done with the approval of all the main divinities of the Akkad kingdom, in Mesopotamia and in Syria as well. It is important to observe that Naram-Sin was not made the god of the whole territory, but of his city Agade, and thus, by implication, joined the goddess Ishtar-Annunitum as divine city ruler, and possibly as her consort.[3] One would like to illustrate this relationship by means of a well-known representation of the couple (Hansen 2002), but there is a good chance that is it simply a forgery. From the passage cited above we learn that Naram-Sin's elevation to city god took place after the Great Rebellion that nearly cost him his kingdom, and which became the best-remembered event of his reign. The length of his reign as well as the chronological placement of this revolt are both uncertain, but one can be fairly certain that Sargon's grandson spent less than two decades as a god on this earth (Åge Westenholz 2000).[4] No details of his cult have survived, but it would seem that the last part of his reign, that is, the period during which he was venerated as the god of Agade, was also a time when the king applied himself to supporting the cults of other deities in various cities of his realm, as argued by Åge Westenholz, something that he had not seen fit to do earlier in his reign. It is

[1] On the period in general, see Åge Westenholz (1999). Wilhelm (1982: 16) considers the possibility that the Hurrians had such an institution earlier, based on an etymology "god" of the Hurrian word for "king" (endan). Buccellati and Kelly-Buccellati (1996: 75) repeat this and make a similar, if cautious suggestion; all of this is based on etymology and a broken seal impression.

[2] Bassetki Statue (E2.1.4.10; Frayne 1993: 113–14) 20–57: *ši in pu-uš-qi-im* SUHUŠ.SUHUŠ IRI.KI-*lí-su ú-kí-nu*. On this text and the divinization of the king, see Farber 1983.

[3] Hence his title DINGIR a-ga-dè[ki], "god of Agade," that alternates with LUGAL a-ga-dè[ki,] "king of Agade," in

some inscriptions. Contrast this with the title dingir (zi) kalam-ma-na, "(effective) god of his land," borne by the kings of Ur and by Ishbi-Erra, the first king of Isin.

[4] Åge Westenholz makes a good argument concerning the placement of the "great rebellion" within the reign of Naram-Sin, but he is too invested in the concept of a shorter reign for the king. The Ur III version of the Sumerian King List, the closest thing we have to a contemporary account, is quite precise: it assigns fifty-four years and six months to the Agade monarch (Steinkeller 2003: 272, 22′–23′).

by no means clear if divinization is part of a restructuring of royal self-representation, or if it is but one symptom of the revival of central authority in a time of state crisis. Because of uncertainties concerning the chronology of his reign, and of the ordering of his surviving inscriptions, it is difficult to correlate acts such as divinization with other changes.

Apparently, Naram-Sin's short time as a god on earth was singular and was neither inheritable nor contagious. His son and successor Sharkalisharri (2217–2193 B.C.) did not aspire to divine status, and neither did his petty successors, who ruled Akkad as the empire crumbled around them. Briefly stated, the divine classifier is absent in Sharkalisharri's year names, except in broken passages where it has been restored by modern editors. A survey of his inscriptions shows that the classifier was also restored by later Mesopotamian copyists of his texts; in contemporary texts it is present in only one inscription, and in dedicatory seals of some of his more enthusiastic servants.[5]

The kingdom of Akkad fell soon after Sharkalisharri's reign, and after a short period of city-state particularism and foreign occupation, the land was reunited under the Third Dynasty of Ur, which ruled Mesopotamia between 2112 and 2004 B.C. (Sallaberger 1999). The founder of the dynasty, Ur-Namma, established his new capital in the city of Ur, but his family probably came from Uruk. Uruk remained important for the next century; it was a ceremonial center and was under rule of the royal family, unlike all other major cities, which were run by state-appointed governors (Michalowski 1987). When Ur-Namma began his state-creation activities, both the north and south of Babylonia were under the rule of ancient Iran. His first order of business was military, but he seems to have handled these matters rather quickly, and then moved on to organize the state and initiate an array of building activities in the major cities of his realm. During his short reign, the founder of the dynasty initiated and perhaps even completed at least four massive multi-level temples (ziggurats) in the most important cities of his realm: Ur, Eridu, Nippur, and Uruk. Such works must have provided fiscal and structural benefits to local elites, but they also refashioned the physical environments of the cities. Wherever one stood, even outside the city walls, one's gaze was attracted to the ziggurat — a symbol of royal patronage and royal mediation between the human and transcendent spheres. But the gods were not placated, and less than eighteen years into his reign, Ur-Namma was mortally wounded while leading his troops in battle.

No comet presaged this death, but by Mesopotamian standards this was a cosmic tragedy. In three millennia of documented history only two kings are known to have been killed in war, Ur-Namma (around 2100 B.C.) and Sargon II of Assyria (722–705 B.C.), fifteen hundred years later. Violent royal death meant only one thing — sin and divine abandonment. Such events, just as military defeats and ends of dynasties, were precipitated by the gods and goddesses, who turned their backs on their favorites and simply walked away. The demise of the Assyrian Sargon led to years of inquiry into the causes for such radical divine displeasure, inquiries pursued by sons who followed him on the throne (Tadmor, Landsberger, and Parpola 1987). No documentation of this kind has survived from the time of Ur-Namma's successors, but we do have a very different, and in its own way even more interesting, composition on the matter: a long poem detailing the king's death and his journey and reception in the netherworld (Flückiger-Hawker 1999: 93–182). It is important to know that this poem is unique; there is

---

[5] Sharkalisharri was an adult when he came to the throne, as he is already attested as a high official during his father's reign. A survey of his inscriptions reveals the following (+/- = presence or absence of the divine classifi-er: 1. *Year Names*: never, except in passages restored by scholars; 2. *Royal inscriptions*: a. contemporary monuments/objects +2/-5; b. contemporary seals/sealings +3/-11; c. later copies: +4/-1).

no other Sumerian literary work on the death of kings. Indeed, it seems that this subject was strictly taboo, and royal demise is never mentioned directly but only alluded to by means of euphemisms.[6]

Royal disaster nearly toppled the young state, but the new king Shulgi (2094–2047 B.C.) managed to hold it together, and this must have been quite an undertaking. Historical sources inform us that he had to face enemies from abroad, and we can surmise that at the same time he needed to repair the ideological foundations of the kingdom, to resist the centrifugal forces that were always there, as local elites were always ready to resist centralization, and would use any opportunity to revert to city-state localism. The second king of Ur ruled for forty-eight years, a long stretch by ancient standards, so it seems that his efforts were successful, and that he managed to pacify the divine wrath that had destroyed his father. How he achieved this is not easy to ascertain, but some clues may be found in the narrative that can be read from the year names that were used to date documents from his reign.[7]

The year names tell a story. They do not describe all the events of Shulgi's reign, but they bring to the fore salient moments, events that were deemed worthy of remembrance and celebration. This story is striking: the first half of the reign, years 1 through 20, mostly reference cultic activities; moreover they concern the central ceremonial cities of the state: Ur, Nippur, and only once Uruk. Years 10 and 11 digress to claim control of strategic border towns on the north and east, but the only significant foreign involvement is the marriage of a princess to the king of the powerful Iranian state of Marhashi. Year name 21 marks a significant new trend: military involvement in the highlands to the east. From now on, until the king's death toward the end of his 48th year, Shulgi's scribes will date almost all the documents in the land with commemorations of military expeditions. It took twenty years of extensive cultic, ceremonial, and organizational activity to secure the foundations of his rule, to overcome the ideological crisis begotten by the curse on his father, and to bring him to the point where he could venture securely into foreign lands, without fear of rebellion at home. There were wars, but this topic was not considered proper for consistent year naming until now. But year name 21 also reveals another radical new development: the name of the sovereign will from now on be preceded by the cuneiform sign for "god," an unpronounced classifier that informs all readers that Shulgi and his successors are no mere mortal kings — they are divine — although, significantly, this divinization was never applied retroactively to his father Ur-Namma.[8]

How does a king become divine? Shulgi may have drawn on the precedent of Naram-Sin (Cooper 1993), but we should keep in mind that the Akkadian king's time as a god was rather brief and had ended more than two generations before the revival of this notion in the middle of the reign of the second king of Ur. It is clear that Shulgi's intentions, as well as the very nature of the new ideology that he and his entourage developed, were not simply antiquarian. Rather, they came as a culmination of the decades of reconstruction that was necessary in the wake of his father's violent death. In order to create his new identity, Shulgi reached back to his family's Uruk origins and inserted himself into the heroic past. The figure of Gilgamesh (George 2003), sired by the union of a mortal royal hero Lugalbanda and the goddess Ninsumuna, provided the perfect model: Shulgi could reflect himself in this poetic mirror by becoming Gilgamesh's brother. Lugalbanda and Ninsumuna became his metaphysical parents,

---

[6] There is also an Old Babylonian Akkadian language "Elegy on the Death of Naram-Sin"; it is not clear which Naram-Sin, of Akkad or Eshnunna, is being lamented (J. G. Westenholz 1997: 203–20).

[7] A full study of the year names of the Ur III kings is long overdue. For now, see Frayne 1997: 92–110.

[8] It is possible that Shulgi's life as a god began earlier; see Sallaberger 1999: 152.

assuring his divinity. There were practical moves that came with this, most importantly the infusion of the power of the Crown into the social, cultural, and above all economic world of the temples, which at this time were massive fiscal organizations. But a dynasty requires continuity and cannot survive by means of a hegemonic ideology that is only good for one generation. Shulgi could not simply become a god, as the illusion would disappear at the moment of his death, leaving his successor without symbolic power. The unique symbolic status of Gilgamesh provided the answer as an ancestor who embodied the central paradox of divine kingship: the inevitable death of kings. Shulgi was worshiped in temples — and so would be his successors — but for the literate classes his divinity was played out in four of the five Gilgamesh poems that we know from later times, although there are other such compositions that did not survive from the Ur III literary world.[9] Together with other tales of mythical Uruk heroes, they illustrated the central metaphors of Ur III royal self-representation: the achievement of eternal fame by means of eastern conquests, conflict, and intimacy with the divine world, wisdom, control over life and death, and, finally, confrontation and management of royal demise. It is obvious, and in some cases even demonstrable, that the versions at our disposal have been remodeled by generations of redactors, and that enigmatic allusions to contemporary events, many of which could no longer be understood, were altered or even eliminated. Some residues remain, including a reference to an Ur III princess, whose name would have meant nothing to the teachers and students in eighteenth-century B.C. schools (Michalowski 2003). Such traces suggest that in their original form the heroic poems, unlike contemporary royal hymns, carried some oppositional messages within the context of a more complex meditation on the social and cosmic role of kings. The documentation that has come down to us offers a stark contrast between the times of the Ur III dynasty and their Sargonic predecessors, who had to face continual rebellion within their realm. One could speculate that the patrimonial state established by Ur-Namma was also quite fragile, but that dissent was erased from the historical record by the self-congratulatory mask of the propaganda of success. The imperfect heroic images in the epic poetry offer a different portrait of the divine and omnipotent rulers of ancient Ur.

For pedagogical as well as structural reasons, these Sumerian heroic poems were never joined into one master narrative, although they were studied in sequence in the eighteenth-century B.C. schools, ending with the emotionally powerful poem that opens with the deathbed scene and then describes the decease and burial of the great hero Gilgamesh and his descent into the netherworld, where he continues to reign as a king (Veldhuis 2001). This text also ennobles the city of Uruk while at the same time explains the lack of a pilgrimage site for Gilgamesh. By divine intervention the Euphrates dries up, his son constructs an elaborate stone tomb, and after the dead king is laid to rest there, the river comes to flow again, forever covering his resting place. His shade may rule the underworld, but in earthly terms he is reborn in the figure of Shulgi and his successors. As a corollary, his immortality is textual, expressed by the survival of his name and deeds in poetry.

Shulgi's transformation and reinvention was a carefully managed affair. As I have already mentioned, his biological father, Ur-Namma, whose fate lay so heavily upon the son, was *never* retroactively divinized, so that the break was well marked. In literature this found expression in the concomitant all-encompassing reinvention of the written tradition, which was now firmly reoriented to represent a new form of charismatic rule designed to overcome the

---

[9] I discuss the "epic" tradition in this context in Michalowski 2010; note that I exclude "Gilgamesh and Akka" from the debate.

ideological crisis precipitated by the martial death of the founder of the dynasty. The centralized, patrimonial state run from Ur required a well-regulated and well-trained bureaucracy
that could be held accountable for all fiscal and organizational activities. Writing was the instrument by which the Crown exercised oversight and control, as documented by the hundred
thousand or so published administrative documents from the period. The hearts and minds of
these literate servants had to be molded through schooling that not only taught them writing
skills but also indoctrinated them into the ideological aspirations of the new state. Although
contemporary evidence is still sparse, it appears that sometime under Shulgi the masters of
the royal academies literally wiped clean the literary slate and discarded all but a few of the
old compositions that went back to Early Dynastic times, that is, more than half a millennium
earlier. They kept most of the basic pedagogical tools such as word lists, but discarded virtually all the old narratives, replacing them with materials written in honor of the contemporary
ruling house.

Some of this also found expression in a composition that we call the Sumerian King List
(Jacobsen 1939; Edzard 1980: 77–84), a largely fictional genealogical enumeration of cities —
and dynasties — that ruled Mesopotamia since time immemorial, when "kingship descended
from the heavens." Now that Piotr Steinkeller (2003) has published an Ur III exemplar of the
text, we can be fairly certain that it was composed under that dynasty, most probably during
Shulgi's reign. This oldest manuscript that we have ends with the reign of Ur-Namma, and
then the scribe added a subscript: "May my king, divine Shulgi, live a life of never-ending
days!" Much can be said about this salutation, but I will let that bide. In this text there were no
divine kings before Shulgi, even Naram-Sin's assumption of the status is suppressed, and he is
deprived of his hard-earned determinative: in this text the divine status of the new king of Ur
is unique!

But there is more. In the middle of his reign Shulgi instituted a number of major structural
reforms; in economic terms this meant the subjugation of large temple estates under some form
of state supervision, the creation of production and redistribution centers, initiation of major
public works, as well as the standardization of bureaucratic means of control (Steinkeller
1987). Local elites were incorporated into the patrimonial royal family by means of intermar-
riage, and the system of local government was revamped to serve the center. A large standing
army took a central role in government activities, and a novel system of taxation included
military colonists in areas of the eastern periphery. One of the new redistribution centers,
Puzrish-Dagan, was used for elaborate royal gift giving to elites (Sallaberger 2003–04); indeed, it appears that at this time ritual gift giving was a royal monopoly. The cult of the living
king spread throughout the state: we know of his temples in Umma, Girsu, KI.AN, and in the
capital of Ur, where he was worshipped, while still alive, as Shulgi-dumu-Ana, "Shulgi-son-
of-the-Heavens (or: of An)."[10] And to the heavens he did return, for, unlike his mortal father
Ur-Namma, divine Shulgi returned to the heavens (or, to An) upon his demise, as we know
from an economic document that mentions this ascent (Wilcke 1988). Thus, as Nicole Brisch
has pointed out to me, upon his departure from the earth, kingship ascended back where it had
come from in the Sumerian King List, which began, in most versions, with the words "When
kingship descended from the heavens...." Presumably, it went back only to be bestowed upon
the successor. Kings come and go, but divinely sanctioned kingship is eternal.

---

[10] Sigrist, Owen, and Young 1984: 73/10 (Š45.ix.13).
This temple is attested as late as Ibbi-Sin 13 (Legrain
1937: 704:7).

I would argue that Shulgi's appropriation of divine attributes was but one element in this elaborate constellation of activities that constituted a virtual reinvention of his state. Hence his divine status had nothing to do with any autonomous symbolic system; it was but one component in a complex fabric of economic, structural, and ideological reformations that took place in a concrete historical context. Some have seen this as the symbolic apex in the process of state building and centralization of power (Steinkeller 1992), but the arguments made here point in other directions. By the time Naram-Sin became a god, his empire had held together for at least a century. Ur-Namma, like the Akkadian king's successors, had eschewed any notions of divine kingship, as far as we know. It may be pure coincidence that both Naram-Sin and Shulgi took tremendous pains to placate local gods and goddesses, as well as local elites, in the process of self-divinization; all of this did not constitute final steps in the rise to power, but rather took place in the aftermath of almost fatal state collapse. And yet, as we have seen, the notion of royal divinity in no way guaranteed everlasting life for any ruler or any state formation. In the words of J. Cooper (1993: 21), "no Sumerian text that is not an immediate product of the court — royal inscription or royal hymn — holds out any hope that sovereignty is forever."

There is a curious sideshow in this short spectacle of divine kingship. East of Sumer, in the highlands of Iran, some contemporary rulers of the Dynasty of Shimashki likewise adopted the divine classifier in front of their names.[11] We know of them primarily from a later list of kings, which survives on a tablet that was found in the city of Susa: the Awan/Shimashki King List (AKL). It is now possible to identify most of these rulers in Mesopotamian documents from the early second millennium, so their historicity is assured. There are a few documents dated to the period and a handful of seals or sealings that mention royal names.

The first five kings of the Shimashki Dynasty were contemporaries of the house of Ur in Mesopotamia. Although apparently related to one another, they did not rule in succession, as the king list would have us believe, but overlapped one another, in charge of different sectors of the so-called Shimashkian state. The details of this complex geo-political order must be left for another occasion; here I only concentrate on the matter at hand.

The second section of the AKL contains the rulers of Shimashki, and it begins with Kirname, fronted by the divine classifier. The names that follow lack this determinative. A similar phenomenon is encountered in the year names of Ebarat; in one case we encounter the classifier, but in the rest we never do. A royal inscription of his grandson Idadu lists three generations of deified Shimashkian monarchs.[12] Thus the first four kings of this dynasty used the divine determinative in their own inscriptions, year names and seals, but not consistently.[13] All four are also mentioned in Ur III administrative texts, but as is to be expected, without a trace of divinity. Some seal inscriptions include the divine determinative before royal names, but others do not. It is difficult to derive any strong conclusions from this limited and inconsistent set of data. We simply do not know enough about the internal structure, modes of royal self-representation, and world view of the Shimashkian state or confederation. Our own view of these matters is filtered through Ur III data, and thus we see early second-millennium Iran as secondary in importance to Sumer. In reality, it is quite possible that the highland states such

[11] On the localization of this land and its history, see Stolper 1982 and Steinkeller 2007.

[12] Steinkeller 2007. One of the two identical copies of the inscription is from Christie's auction house (2001: no. 23).

[13] Ebarat (Iabrat, Ebarti) took over Susa after the third year of Ibbi-Sin. Three different year names of this ruler survive, but only one uses the divine classifier (de Graef 2004). The classifier is also encountered in a seal of Idadu (Lambert 1979; Steinkeller 2007).

as Anshan, Marhashi, and Shimashki were in essence larger, stronger, and geo-politically more important than its lowland Sumerian neighbor to the west, but this is all distorted by the available textual record. As a result, we cannot determine if this highland royal divinization was merely a symbolic answer to the claims of the kings of Ur, or if was something more profound and culturally significant. The former seems more than likely.

It is striking, nevertheless, that divine kingship lost its force when divine Kindattu defeated Ur's last ruler, divine Ibbi-Sin (2028–2004 B.C.), and took him in chains to Anshan, in modern-day Fars, where his remains still lie buried, if we are to believe ancient sources. In Mesopotamia, kingship passed over to Isin, a city north of Ur, and its new king, Ishbi-Erra (2017–1985 B.C.), played a complex ideological game, balancing innovation with purposeful imitation of Ur III traditions, portraying himself as the legitimate successor to their line (Michalowski 2005). In titulature, at least, he retained claims of divinity, but it is impossible to determine how deep this all went. Other Isin successors imitated much of the royal ceremonial of their Ur III models, but there is little evidence for the cult of living kings, and the concept seems to have been alien to other contemporary local rulers who sprung up after the collapse of the Ur III state.[14] To be sure, in poems that to various degrees mimicked or paid homage to the old works dedicated to Ur-Namma and Shulgi, Babylonian kings of the succeeding period carried the divine determinative before their name, but there is little other evidence to suggest that they were consistently worshipped as gods: they were not worshipped in their own temples, nor did they have their own cultic personnel. There is much that we do not know about these matters, but it appears that by now the royal application of the divine determinative was traditional, like most of the titles they bore in texts, but was not meant to signify the kind of heavenly status that was claimed by their Ur III predecessors. These kings were sacred, but not truly divine. The one exception to this appears in the short and relatively insignificant reign of king Naram-Sin of Eshnunna in the eighteenth century B.C., who, for reasons that we cannot recover, apparently assumed both the name and some of the ideological trappings of the great ruler of Akkad (Reichel, this volume).

Perhaps the best example of the poetic representation of the sacred mediating role of an early Old Babylonian ruler is embedded in a hymn that celebrates the goddess Inana (Venus) in her astral role as the morning and evening star, also known under the names Ninsiana and Ninegala. The fourth king of the Isin Dynasty, Iddin-Dagan, takes the role her lover Dumuzi, who is here referred to as Ama'ushumgalana.[15]

> In the River Ordeal Temple of the black-headed people, the assembled population
> Established a chapel for Ninegala.
> The king, as if he were a god, lives with her there.[16]
> ...
> She bathes (her) loins for the king,
> She bathes (her) loins for Iddin-Dagan.
> Holy Inana bathes with soap,
> And sprinkles the floor with aromatic resin.

---

[14] For the first king of Isin, see above.

[15] Iddin-Dagan Hymn A, lines 170–72 and 183–94. The text was edited by Reisman 1970; see also Reisman 1973 for a published translation.

[16] Others would translate "who is a god." There is only one comparable use of dingir-àm known to me, albeit in different semantic and syntactic context: Instructions of Shuruppak 267–69 (Alster 2005: 98) ama ᵈutu-àm lú mu-un-ù-tu ab-ba dingir-a[m (x)] mu-un-zalag₂-e ab-ba dingir-àm inim-ma-ni zi-da "A mother gives one life, just as the Sun, a father brightens [x] just as a god, a father's word is true, just like that of a god."

> The king then approached (her) holy loins with head raised high,
> Iddin-Dagan approached (her) loins with head raised high,
> He approached Inana's loins with head raised high,
> Ama'ushumgalana takes to the bed with her,
> And praised her holy loins.
> After the holy-loined queen had stepped into the bed,
> After holy-loined holy Inana had stepped into the bed,
> She made love with him there on her bed:
> "O Iddin-Dagan, you shall be my beloved!"

I have cited the full passage to provide a flavor of the ritual context. If my translation is true, Iddin-Dagan assumes the role of a god only in the context of the union with the Inana; his sacred character allows him to perform this role and touch the heavens and her loins, but otherwise he remains mortal and fully human and a denizen of the mundane world, even though when his name was written, it was often ceremoniously preceded by the divine determinative. I think the passage speaks for itself.

Much has been made of early Mesopotamian divine kingship, but if the analysis presented here stands, its significance has been highly overstated. The phenomenon had a short shelf life, perhaps no more than a decade or so under Naram-Sin, and just over sixty years during the time of the Ur III kings. The details of all this are hard to pin down, and the trajectory of its short history difficult to trace; for example, we can detect some intensification of royal worship during the reign of Shu-Sin (2037–2029 B.C.), Shulgi's second successor, but the contours of the changes are hard to sketch (Brisch 2006). In the more than three thousand years of written Mesopotamian history, this is but a short moment, although there is a possibility that a rather different form of divine kingship may have taken root in Assyria in the first millennium B.C. (Machinist 2006).

There are reasons to suspect that the divine claims of the kings of Ur were consciously rejected by subsequent generations, but one can only find vague traces of the process. Some of this was liberating, and its benefits are still felt today, as without the abandonment of divine royal attributes we would not have the Babylonian Gilgamesh Epic in the form that we know it (Michalowski 2010). The reasons for this development are never stated explicitly, but can be inferred from the very nature of Mesopotamian kingship. I would propose that Shulgi's invention, or reinvention, of this ideology might have been right for its time and may have played a central role in the political theater of the day, but its future was hardly assured, as the new vision of royalty clashed with a central component of the institution, namely its sacral character. There is a paradox here, as the notions of divine and sacred kingship are often misconstrued as one and the same thing. Mesopotamian kings, similar to monarchs in many other times and cultures, were, first and foremost, mediators between the mundane and transcendent orders. Brute force aside, all other royal attributes derived from this function. Kings were beyond category; they did not combine human and divine aspects, rather they existed above and beyond this fundamental classificatory distinction. When Shulgi — and Naram-Sin before him — moved over to the divine sphere, he disrupted the liminal state of being that provided him with the power to mediate between the heavens and the earth. The new state required a meditation on the dual nature of the divine king, who albeit it a god, nevertheless would have to leave the earth, for only death could lead him to the heavens. This had the undesired consequence of accentuating the mundane nature of the king, even as he claimed membership in the company of those who existed in the transcendent world, and as result, paradoxically, divinization undermined the sacral nature of kingship. As long as the Ur dynasty was in power, political contingencies and institutional developments made up for this imbalance, as the familial nature of the patrimonial state and new economic opportunities, including privileges related to the royal cult, motivated elites to support this ideology. Although there is much that we simply do not know, it does not appear that any of this survived after the collapse of the Ur state. Once all these conditions were gone, kingship reverted to its familiar nature and the monarchs of Mesopotamia were safe to be sacred once more.

Seen in this light, the institution of divine kingship in early Mesopotamia appears to have been highly overrated by modern scholarship, undoubtedly a reflection of tacit fascination with Frazier and his successors. All told, the truly functioning life of the phenomenon amounted to no more than about eighty years in aggregate. The times may have been short, but they were eventful, and perhaps by framing royal self-divinization within the complex shifting roles of ritual, politics, and symbolic representations in specific historical circumstances, we may arrive at a better understanding of the complex dynamics of power in ancient polities.[17] Historicized and freed from being understood as an autonomous symbolic structure, divine kingship becomes interesting once again.

---

[17] Important, in this respect, are the observations of Feely-Harnick 1985: 306–07.

BIBLIOGRAPHY

Alster, Bendt

    2005   *Wisdom of Ancient Sumer*. Bethesda: CDL.

Buccellati, Giorgio, and M. Kelly-Buccellati

    1996   "The Seals of the King of Urkesh: Evidence from the Western Wing of the Royal Storehouse AK." *Wiener Zeitschrift für die Kunde des Morgenlandes* 86: 65–103.

Brisch, Nicole

    2006   "The Priestess and the King: The Divine Kingship of Šū-Sîn of Ur." *Journal of the American Oriental Society* 126/2: 161–76.

Christie's

    2001   *Christie's Fine Antiquities: Wednesday 25 April 2001. Sale Code: ANT-9088.* London: Christie's South Kensington.

Cooper, Jerrold S.

    1993   "Paradigm and Propaganda: The Dynasty of Akkad in the 21st Century." In *Akkad: The First World Empire*, edited by Mario Liverani, pp. 11–23. History of the Ancient Near East 5. Padua: Sargon.

de Graef, K.

    2004   "Les noms d'année du roi simashkéen Ebarat I°." *Akkadica* 125: 107–08.

Edzard, Dietz Otto

    1980   "Königslisten und Chroniken. A. Sumerisch." *Reallexikon der Assyriologie* 6: 77–86. Berlin: Walter de Gruyter.

Farber, Walter

    1983   "Die Vergöttlichung Narām-Sins." *Orientalia*, n.s., 52: 67–72.

Feely-Harnick, Gillian

    1985   "Issues in Divine Kingship." *Annual Review of Anthropology* 14: 273–313.

Flückiger-Hawker, Esther

    1999   *Urnamma of Ur in Sumerian Literary Tradition.* Orbis Biblicus et Orientalis 166. Freiburg: University of Freiburg; Göttingen: Vandenhoeck & Ruprecht.

Frankfort, Henri

    1948   *Kingship and the Gods: A Study of Ancient Near Eastern Religion as the Integration of Society and Nature.* Oriental Institute Essay. Chicago: University of Chicago Press.

Frayne, Douglas R.

    1993   *Sargonic and Gutian Periods, 2334–2113 BC.* The Royal Inscriptions of Mesopotamia, Early Periods 2. Toronto: University of Toronto Press.

    1997   *Ur III Period, 2112–2004 BC.* The Royal Inscriptions of Mesopotamia, Early Periods 3/2. Toronto: University of Toronto Press.

Friedman, Kasja Ekholm

    1985   "'… Sad Stories of the Death of Kings': The Involution of Divine Kingship." *Ethnos* 50: 248–72.

George, Andrew R.

    2003   *The Babylonian Gilgamesh Epic: Introduction, Critical Edition, and Cuneiform Texts.* Oxford: Oxford University Press.

Hansen, Donald
   2002   "Through the Love of Ishtar." In *Of Pots and Plans: Papers on the Archaeology and History of Mesopotamia and Syria Presented to David Oates in Honour of His 75th Birthday*, edited by Lamia Al-Gailani Werr, John Curtis, Harriet Martin, Augusta Mc-Mahon, Joan Oates, and Julian Reade, pp. 91–112. London: NABU.

Jacobsen, Thorkild
   1939   *The Sumerian King List*. Assyriological Studies 11. Chicago: University of Chicago Press.

Lambert, W. G.
   1979   "Near Eastern Seals in the Gubelkian Museum of Oriental Art, University of Durham." *Iraq* 41: 1–46.

Legrain, Leon
   1937   *Business Documents of the Third Dynasty of Ur*. Ur Excavations, Texts 3. Philadelphia: The University Museum; London: British Museum.

Machinist, Peter
   2006   "Kingship and Divinity in Imperial Assyria." In *Text, Artifact, and Image: Revealing Ancient Israelite Religion*, edited by Gary M. Beckman and Theodore J. Lewis, pp. 152–88. Brown Judaic Studies 346. Providence: Brown Judaic Studies.

Michalowski, Piotr
   1977   "Durum and Uruk During the Ur III Period." *Mesopotamia* 12: 83–96.
   2003   "A Man Called Enmebaragesi." In *Literatur, Politik und Recht in Mesopotamien: Festschrift für Claus Wilcke*, edited by Walther Sallaberger, Konrad Volk, and Annette Zgoll, pp. 195–208. Orientalia Biblica et Christiana 14. Wiesbaden: Harrassowitz.
   2005   "Literary Works from the Court of King Ishbi-Erra of Isin." In *"An Experienced Scribe Who Neglects Nothing": Ancient Near Eastern Studies in Honor of Jacob Klein,* edited by Yitschak Sefati, Pinhas Artzi, Chaim Cohen, Barry L. Eichler, and Victor A. Hurowitz, pp. 199–212. Bethesda: CDL.
   2010   "Maybe Epic: The Origins and Reception of Sumerian Heroic Poetry." In *Epic and History*, edited by David Konstan and Kurt A. Raaflaub, pp. 7–25. Malden: Wiley-Blackwell.

Reisman, Daniel David
   1970   Two Neo-Sumerian Royal Hymns. Ph.D. dissertation, University of Pennsylvania.
   1973   "Iddin-Dagan's Sacred Marriage Hymn." *Journal of Cuneiform Studies* 25: 185–202.

Sallaberger, Walther
   1999   "Ur III-Zeit." In *Mesopotamien: Akkade-Zeit und Ur III-Zeit*, edited by Walther Sallaberger and Åge Westenholz, pp. 119–414. Orbis Biblicus et Orientalis 160/3. Freiburg: Universitätsverlag; Göttingen: Vandenhoeck & Ruprecht.
   2003–04 "Schlachtvieh aus Puzriš-Dagān: Zur Bedeutung dieses königlichen Archivs." *Jaarbericht ex Oriente Lux*: 45–62.

Sigrist, Marcel; David I. Owen; and Gordon D. Young
   1984   *The John Frederick Lewis Collection,* Part 2. Materiali per il vocabolario Neosumerico 13. Rome: Multigrafica Editrice.

Sommerfeld, Walther
   2000   "Naram-Sin, die 'Große Revolte' und MAR.TU.ki." In *Assyriologica et semitica: Festschrift für Joachim Oelsner anlässlich seines 65. Geburtstages am 18. Februar*

1997, edited by Joachim Marzahn and Hans Neumann, pp. 419–36. Alter Orient und Altes Testament 252. Münster: Ugarit-Verlag.

Steinkeller, Piotr

1987   "The Administrative and Economic Organization of the Ur III State: The Core and the Periphery." In *The Organization of Power: Aspects of Bureaucracy in the Ancient Near East*, edited by McGuire Gibson and Robert D. Biggs, pp. 19–41. Studies in Ancient Oriental Civilization 46. Chicago: The Oriental Institute.

1992   "Mesopotamia in the Third Millennium B.C." In *The Anchor Bible Dictionary*, Vol. 4, edited by David Noel Freedman, pp. 724–32. New York: Doubleday.

2003   "An Ur III. Manuscript of the Sumerian King List." In *Literatur, Politik und Recht in Mesopotamien: Festschrift für Claus Wilcke*, edited by Walther Sallaberger, Konrad Volk, and Annette Zgoll, pp. 267–92. Orientalia Biblica et Christiana 14. Wiesbaden: Harrassowitz.

2007   "New Light on Šimaški and Its Rulers." *Zeitschrift für Assyriologie* 97: 215–32.

Stève, M.-J.

1989   "Des sceaux-cylindres de Simaški?" *Revue d'Assyriologie* 83: 13–26.

Stolper, Matthew W.

1982   "On the Dynasty of Shimashki and the Early Sukkalmahs." *Zeitschrift für Assyriologie* 72: 42–67.

Tadmor, H.; Benno Landsberger; and Simo Parpola

1989   "The Sin of Sargon and Sennacherib's Last Will." *State Archives of Assyria Bulletin* 3: 3–51.

Veldhuis, Niek

2001   "The Solution of the Dream: A New Interpretation of Bilgames' Death." *Journal of Cuneiform Studies* 53: 133–48.

Westenholz, Åge

1999   "The Old Akkadian Period: History and Culture." In *Mesopotamien: Akkade-Zeit und Ur III-Zeit,* edited by Walther Sallaberger and Åge Westenholz, pp. 17–117. Orbis Biblicus et Orientalis 160/3. Freiburg: Universitätsverlag; Göttingen: Vandenhoeck & Ruprecht.

2000   "Assyriologists, Ancient and Modern, on Naram-Sin and Sharkalisharri." In *Assyriologica et semitica: Festschrift für Joachim Oelsner anlässlich seines 65. Geburtstages am 18. Februar 1997*, edited by Joachim Marzahn and Hans Neumann, pp. 419–36. Alter Orient und Altes Testament 252. Münster: Ugarit-Verlag.

Westenholz, Joan Goodnick

1997   *Legends of the Kings of Akkade: The Texts*. Mesopotamian Civilizations 7. Winona Lake: Eisenbrauns.

Wilhelm, Gernot

1982   *Grundzüge der Geschichte und Kultur der Hurriter*. Grundzüge 45. Darmstadt: Wissenschaftliche Buchgesellschaft.

Wilcke, Claus

1988   "König Shulgis Himmelfahrt." *Münchner Beiträge zur Völkerkunde* 1: 245–55.

4

ASPECTS OF KINGSHIP IN ANCIENT EGYPT

PAUL JOHN FRANDSEN, COPENHAGEN UNIVERSITY

INTRODUCTION*

The notion of divine kingship has always been closely associated with ancient Egypt. In the biblical tradition the Egyptian king appears as the epitome of mortal arrogance and megalomania because of his claims to the status of a demiurge (Ezekiel 29:3–9).[1] This ascription is no exaggeration. In Egypt, the cosmogonic moment, when the undifferentiated chaos or potential existence became differentiated being, also set in motion the cyclical solar journey. This event was called the First Occasion (*sp tpy*) and marked the beginning of an infinity of repetitions, a recurring *creatio continua*. Kingship is seen as a prerequisite for the all important maintenance of creation and exercise of *maat*, the principle of world order (Bergman 1972: 80–102; Assmann 1990). Ancient Egypt was a geo-political and cultural unity and is therefore to be regarded as an early, as well as a good, example of a nation-state. The institution of kingship was crucial to the existence of political and social order and to its integration into the cosmology of the Egyptians. The king was considered to be the incarnation of the creator god, and thus divine kingship, as put by Jan Assmann (1990: 219), was "der geometrische Ort der Konvergenz der anthropologischen und der kosmischen Sphäre." There was a correlation between the ideological position of the king and the immensity of the royal funerary monuments of the middle third millennium, and of the temples that pharaohs of later periods lavished upon their fathers, the gods.

The problem of the king's divinity and its definition has been the subject of Egyptological discussions for more than a century, with the discourse focusing on the divinity of the institution of the kingship and of the king himself. Variations in the views put forth can be directly related to current social and intellectual trends.[2] An important new dimension was added when it was suggested that monarchy in Egypt can only be fully comprehended if seen as a combination of kingship and queenship (Troy 1986). Common to all positions has been the observation that the life of the king was circumscribed and permeated by ritual. The king was the chief ritualist and therefore responsible for the maintenance of the cult in the temples, even though the actual performance of a ritual would be delegated to priests. This also made the building

---

* I am indebted to Lana Troy for correcting my English.

[1] God addresses Ezekiel: "Mortal, set your face against Pharaoh king of Egypt, and prophesy against him, and against all Egypt; speak, and say, Thus says the Lord God: I am against you, Pharaoh king of Egypt, the great dragon sprawling in the midst of its channels, saying, 'My Nile is my own, I made it for myself.'"

[2] Compare this quotation from the introductory pages of Poserner's influential work (1960: XV): "La situation, en égyptologie, diffère de celle qu'on trouve dans bien d'autres disciplines où l'étude du caractère sacré ou divin de la royauté commence à peine, où il convient de la développer. Le thème du pharaon dieu est exploité depuis longtemps; on peut dire que l'élaboration de la doctrine a été poussée jusqu'à ses extrêmes limites; dans ces conditions, pour l'ancienne Égypte, il est plus utile actuellement d'ajouter à l'autre plateau de la balance. J'essaierai donc de montre que l'image courante du pharaon est, par certains côtés, excessive et surtout qu'elle n'est pas la seule que fournissent les sources; les Égyptiens pouvaient aussi avoir de leur souverain et de son rôle des conceptions différentes et plus modérées." For the debate since 1960, compare the following select references: Hornung 1957; Blumenthal 1970; Assmann 1984; Baines 1995; Frandsen 1989.

of temples, mortuary establishments, and other significant construction work one of his most important duties. The king was also responsible for all foreign relations. All these activities were formalized according to detailed ritual prescriptions. The depictions of victory in battles never fought,[3] and royal participation in rituals never performed,[4] provide telling evidence for the ritualization of rulership. Even though there was a great variation in the formulation of the doctrines of kingship, royal and non-royal texts and representations patterned the actions of the king and his elite in accordance with the prevailing literary and artistic conventions. History in terms of the actions of kings therefore comes only refracted through what was perceived as the norms of kingship.[5]

If the problem of the divinity of the kingship is approached from a historical perspective, the millennia-long history of the country may be seen as a process where the internal colonization of the Nile Valley and the increasing contact with the world outside its borders correlate with a process of desacralization of the person of the king. This can be contrasted with the doctrines and the mythology underpinning the king's divinity that remained remarkably stable. Roman emperors, who never set their foot on Egyptian soil, were nonetheless regarded and represented as legitimate successors to the long line of divine kings.

In contradistinction to what seems to hold for studies of theocracy and kingship in the other ancient Near Eastern civilizations, Egyptologists seem to have arrived at a consensus of sorts concerning the general character of divine kingship and its historical manifestation. Our concepts and views still need to be fine-tuned, and the two points that this paper addresses are intended to serve this end.

The discussion has up to now attempted to define kingship through studies of royal iconography, ritual, discursive, and historical texts.[6] It has been suggested, moreover, that the ritualization of rulership is linked to certain grammatical characteristics of the terminology for features connected with kingship. The present paper uses a linguistic approach to examine these aspects of kingship, dealing specifically with so-called constituent elements of the king's person from the point of view of inalienable possession, that is, the grammar of possessives and genitives.[7] The paper concludes with a discussion of an aspect of kingship, where the mediation between its divine and human dimensions is resolved by recourse to legal fiction.

FEAR AND AWE

The starting point of this discussion is provided by the two important publications, Jan Assmann's *Liturgische Lieder an den Sonnengott* and a paper by Siegfried Morenz, entitled "Der Schrecken Pharaos" (Assmann 1969; Morenz 1969 [1975]).

---

[3] The prototypical example is the scene showing the king clubbing a Libyan chieftain in the presence of the latter's wife and children. The oldest source for this particular conflict with the Libyans is dated to the Fifth Dynasty, and the latest version, found on a wall in Nubia (Kawa), to the Twenty-fifth, where the names of the wife and sons of the hapless foreign prince of the Fifth Dynasty are still to be found. It is not known whether the Fifth Dynasty version reflects a real, contemporary conflict, but it probably does not. For the material, see conveniently Osing 1980: cols. 1017 and 1016 with nn. 37 and 38.

[4] Prototypical examples are representations of the so-called *sed*-festival, supposedly celebrated by kings after

a reign of thirty years. These festivals frequently took place only in the representations; see Hornung and Staehelin 2006.

[5] As reflected, for instance, in the genre called "The King's Novel" (*Königsnovelle*), which has been aptly characterized "as a mirror of changing paradigms of royalty, or more precisely of the debate between human and divine dimension in the figure of the king" (see Loprieno 1996: 294–95).

[6] For a succinct overview, see Baines 1997: 128–32.

[7] I have previously discussed aspects of the grammar of the possessives in an article in Danish (Frandsen 1994).

In the latter the great German scholar suggested that some exceedingly common royal (and, one might add, divine) phrases such as *snḏ⸗f* and *šfšft⸗f* [8] should be taken as instances of what is often called the subjective genitive. Instead of interpreting the phrases *snḏ⸗f* (FEAR⸗HIS) as "fear of him" and *šfšft/šfyt⸗f* (AWE⸗HIS) as "awe of him" we should consider *snḏ*, *šfšft/šfyt*, and suchlike to be properties (*Grösse*) belonging to and emanating from the king and render the said phrases as "his fearsomeness" (*snḏ⸗f*) and "his awesomeness or his impressiveness" (*šfšft⸗f*). Thus when it is said about pharaoh that *nrw⸗f* (TERROR⸗HIS) or *snḏ⸗f* has defeated the enemies this must be understood literally:

> Von diesen Eigenschaften oder wohl besser Kräften des Königs, die schon in diesem Zeugnis bis zu einem gewissen Grade verselbständigt erscheinen, wird gesagt, dass sie Scharen der Feinde töten. Ideologisch fassbare Potenzen des Königs und nicht die Praxis in Gestalt von Soldaten Pharaos ringen den Gegner nieder.... Es handelt sich zunächst um das Konkrete: die "Furcht," die als eine seiner Potenzen vom Pharao ausgeht und ihn zu einem Träger der Furchtbarkeit macht.[9]

If this interpretation of the data is correct it would change our view of the personality of the king — or other holders of high offices — because this grammatical construction would indicate that the king is regarded as being endowed with *snḏ* and *šfšft/šfyt* in the same way as he is said to be in possession of a *ka, ba*, name, shadow, etc.[10]

Assmann has twice discussed the interpretation of the concept of fear; the first time in connection with his study of a hymn from Book of the Dead, and later in an article on *Furcht* in *Lexikon der Ägyptologie* (1982). His approach is based on an earlier suggestion by de Buck, who in turn borrowed it from the great German theologian Rudolf Otto's influential book on the concept of the holy. According to Assmann, the notion of fear is to be grouped together with the idea of love, corresponding to Otto's *mysterium tremendum* and *mysterium fascinans*.[11] The words for "fear" and "love" denote affects, for instance, forces and feelings giving rise to emotions and action;[12] they are "construed with the objective genitive" and are

---

[8] Conventionally pronounced senedjef and shefsheftef respectively. *snḏ* means "fear" and *šfšft* means "awe," while *f* is a third-person singular pronoun that is suffixed to substantives, as indicated by the notation ⸗. Depending on the syntagmatic context it may be rendered as he, him, or his. The syntagms may therefore be analyzed as FEAR⸗HIS and AWE⸗HIS.

[9] Morenz 1969 [1975]: 140–41. Compare the following passage from a model letter concerning annual Nubian deliveries: "Increase your revenues every year. Have a care for your head. (…) Remember the day of bringing the products, when you pass into the presence of the king [from the parallel Turin D] under the Window of Appearance, the nobles standing in two rows in the presence of His Person ... you being afraid and shrinking back, your hand being weak and you do not know whether it be death or life that is before you" (pKoller 4,7–5,4 = Gardiner 1937: 119–20). Compare Caminos 1954: 438–39.

[10] Morenz 1969 [1975]: 147: "Wir werden in Betracht ziehen müssen, dass sich die 'Amtsperson König' aus einer Fülle von Elementen aufbaut, die unter gegebenen Umständen im Leben wie im Tode selbständig in Erscheinung treten können. Neben den (schliesslich allgemeinen anthropologischen) Hauptbestandteilen *kȝ, bȝ, šḥ* und *ḥȝt*,

neben Name, Schatten und anderen Elementen sind beim Pharao Potenzen in Rechnung zu setzen, die immer auf ihn beschränkt bleiben und deren eine 'sein Schrecken' ist." In a footnote (n. 34) he adds: "Meine Definitionen lassen es nicht geraten erscheinen, Begriffe wie 'Hypostase' oder 'Personifikation' auf den 'Schrecken Pharaos' anzuwenden."

[11] Otto 1987: 13ff. and 42ff. Otto actually traces the discourse of the relationship between the two notions to Luther: "Gleich wie wir ein Heiligtum mit Furcht ehren und doch nicht davor fliehen sondern mehr hinzudringen."

[12] In the first study, Assmann (1969: 65) states that "[m]it *snḏ* und *mrwt* sind primär nicht Affekte gemeint, sondern Ausdrucksqualitäten ('Strahlkräfte') der göttlichen Erscheinungsform, an der sie eine Art 'dinglichen Sitz' haben (Szepter, Insignien, Amulette, Ornat und vor allem Kronen — [for the association of 'Strahlkraft und dinglichen Sitz' Assmann refers to Cassirer apud Moret 1902], aber nach außen gerichtet sind und einwirken auf (*ḫpr r* nach PT 74a) 'die Herzen' der Menschen und Götter. Mit der Antithese dieser beiden extremen Pole soll die ganze Skala der 'Strahlkräfte,' das semantische Feld dieser vielen, einander teilweise überschneidenden Begriffe bezeichnet werden."

used "transitively." Assmann thus renders *nb snḏ* as "Herr/Besitzer einer Furcht einflößenden Furchtbarkeit" and *nb mrwt* as "Herr einer liebe einflößenden Lieblichkeit." In his terminology the source of such affects is the *Strahlkraft* of the king or a god. The semantic field of *Strahlkraft* is determined by the opposition between attraction (*Anziehung*) and repulsion/repelling (*Abstoßung*). On one hand, properties expressed with words for love belong to the field of attraction, while qualities associated with the vocabulary for terror and fear are subsumed under repulsion/repelling (*Abstoßung*) (Assmann 1977: cols. 360–61). The object is in both cases the same, for instance, the king or the god, but the response differs according to whether the subject is the friend or the enemy. For the friend the experience is love, while the enemy responds with fear.[13]

It appears that for all practical purposes the views of Morenz and Assmann are rather close to each other. Yet the explanations they provide are rather different. According to Assmann, the king is the object (OBJECT) of love from (SUBJECT) his people and of fear from (SUBJECT) his enemies. Morenz says nothing about love, but for the sake of the argument his view may be represented so that the king (SUBJECT) emanates love and fear towards his (OBJECT) people and his (OBJECT) enemies.

The idea that emotions or affects such as "*snḏ*"and "*mrwt*" are inherent properties of kings and gods is an interesting hypothesis that deserves closer scrutiny. I am not convinced that *mrwt* really works the way suggested by de Buck and Assmann, and although I cannot on this occasion fully argue the point, I adduce just one example that illustrates this doubt. In the central scene of the so-called "Birth Legend," a cycle of pictures and texts deal with the *hieros gamos*, the union between Amun and the queen of the reigning king.[14] In the text we are told that the god Amun takes on the appearance of the king, the husband of the queen. He then enters her "bedroom," the *nfrw*-chamber,[15] in order to beget the next king. The queen, however, is fully aware of his true identity and of what is expected of her, and the text describes in no uncertain terms what is going on.

> E.1   He found her resting in the *nfrw*-chamber of her palace. At the scent of the god she awoke, laughing before His Person. He went to her at once, and had an erection towards her. He gave his heart towards her. He caused her to see him in his true form as god after he had come close to her, she rejoicing at seeing his radiant vitality, while his love flowed through her body (*sw rdi mȝn=s sw m irw=f n nṯr m-ḫt iy=f tp-im=s ḥ ͨ.ti* [the text has *y*] *m mȝ nfrw=f mrt=f ḥp(=s) m ḥ ͨw=f*), the palace being flooded with the scent of the god, all his fragrance being those of Punt (Urk. IV 219,12–220,6).[16]

[13] Assmann (1969: 65): "Man kann sich freilich fragen, ob diese Gegensätze wirklich so unversöhnlich sind und ihr Zusammenauftreten nicht vielmehr etwas sehr Gewöhnliches. Beim Anblick von etwas außerordentlich Eindrucksvollem mischen sich Schrecken und Bewunderung. Ein guter Herrscher soll sowohl geliebt wie gefürchtet sein. Aber gerade beim Herrscherbild zeigt sich deutlich, daß Furcht und Liebe zwar im Objekt [i.e., the king or the god] zusammengehen, nicht aber im Subjekt, das sich im Gegenteil dadurch bestimmt, daß ihm die Macht des Königs entweder liebe einflösst (die Loyalen), oder Schrecken (die Feinde). Die Macht des Königs hat ein Doppelgesicht ('Sachmet und Bastet'), das der zwiespältigen, in Freund und Feind (gut und böse) geteilten Welt entspricht."

[14] This particular scene has been preserved in three versions from the Eighteenth Dynasty. The standard study of the texts is still Brunner 1964: 35–58.

[15] The *nfrw*-chamber is the innermost part of certain buildings, such as tombs, temples, and palaces, and the term connotes "creation," "rejuvenation," "regeneration," "end and beginning," "perfection," "beauty," "goodness," etc.; see Frandsen 1992: 53–54, passim.

[16] The version rendered here — that of the birth of queen Hatshepsut, preserved in the temple at Deir el-Bahri (ca. 1460 B.C.) — is the earliest of three. It differs from the slightly later Luxor version in having the phrase "he gave his heart towards her" or even better "that of hers." For the Luxor version, see Helck 1957: 1714,8–16. Compare

The concept of love, as illustrated in this example,[17] is of a different order and complexity, and therefore not considered any further in this paper.

The views of Morenz and Assmann have another feature in common, namely, that they are insufficiently argued. Morenz tried to support his position by adducing certain parallels from the Old Testament, while Assmann's approach is more philological/exegetic in nature. However, the idea that the king is not merely the passive, yet privileged, partner in a relationship of dominance and submission is worth reconsidering. This is truly a case where the interpretation of linguistic data could be of importance for our view of the nature of theocracy or divine kingship in ancient Egypt. And, as I hope to show, my conclusion has even wider ramifications.

SUBJECTIVE (DOMINATING) AND OBJECTIVE (DOMINATED) GENITIVE

At this point it becomes necessary to turn to the notion of subjective and objective genitive, and in order to get a firm basis for what follows I shall briefly recapitulate the basics of this discussion. I use the classical examples from Latin grammar:

> *amor dei* (*nostri*) which means "God's love (for us)," where *dei* is a subjective genitive, while *nostri* is an objective genitive. The meaning corresponds to the sentence *deus amat nos* "God loves us"

and

> *amor noster dei ꜥ*, meaning "(our) love of God," with *dei* being the objective genitive while *noster* is the possessive pronoun/adjective used as a subjective genitive. The meaning corresponds to the sentence *amamus deum* "we love god."

In many, often very different, languages, this phenomenon is correlated to a division of nouns into two classes distinguished by the way in which possession is indicated (Chappell and McGregor 1996; cf. Jespersen 1924: 169–72, 133–39; Rosén 1959). This phenomenon was first noticed by the French philosopher and anthropologist Lévy-Bruhl in a paper from 1914 (1916) entitled "*L'expression de la possession dans les langues mélanésiennes.*" He also realized that this phenomenon had implications that went beyond the realm of linguistics, but was incorrect, I think, in adding that it was likely to contribute to our understanding of only "sociétés inférieures."[18] In the languages that he discussed, one class comprised nouns denoting body parts, objects closely associated with a person such as weaponry and other personal objects, close kin, etc. The other class comprised all other nouns. For members of the first class Lévy-Bruhl

---

also the translation by Bardinet 1995: 146. "(Alors) il (le dieu) alla aussitôt auprès d'elle, éjacula en elle, et son intérieur-*ib* fut placé en elle." See further my discussion of the scene in Frandsen 1997: 84–93. For the role of the heart, compare also Lekov 2004: 70.

[17] Brunner (1964: 52) argued differently: "Man könnte versucht sein, die Aussage 'Seine Liebe, sie trat in ihren Leib ein' als eine dezente Beschreibung des Beischlafs aufzufassen, wobei etwa 'Liebe' für 'Samen' stünde. Das Possesiv-Suffix wäre dann Genitivus subjectivus, nicht, wie in der oben gegebenen Übersetzung, objectivus. Doch ist diese Deutung ausgeschlossen, da der Begattungsakt erst später erwähnt wird." For another interpretation of the passage see however Müller 1966: 259–60.

For a further example in keeping with this hypothesis, compare "You are not to do anything which is in conflict with my precepts which give all the laws of kingship (…) and no one will accuse you (lit., 'there is not your accuser' *nn srḥy ꜥk*). (….) Place your love in the entire land (*imm mrwt ꜥk n tꜣ-tmw*), for a good character is that which is remembered, when the years have gone by" (The Teaching for Merikare, pp. 138–41). Compare also Simpson 1977.

[18] "Leur [certain Melanesian languages] division des noms en deux classes a donc un intérêt sociologique, et une analyse attentive de ce fait linguistique peut contribuer à l'interprétation exacte de certaines institutions des sociétés inférieures" (Lévy-Bruhl 1914/16: 104).

coined the term *inalienable nouns* as opposed to the other class consisting of *alienable nouns*. In the scholarly literature these classes are also known under the label "non-acquirable vs. acquirable nouns." The terminology used is, in fact, of some significance in grasping a phenomenon.[19] In a discussion of possessive constructions in certain Malayo-Polynesian languages, for instance, the Danish Sinologist Søren Egerod noted that there are very clear distinctions between the two types of genitive. In these languages when they talk about "the man's horse" they use a morphologically distinct, subjective, or as the terminology goes, a *dominating genitive*, because the man dominates the horse and can get rid of it. But in a phrase like "the man's arm" the speaker would employ an objective or *dominated genitive* "the arm on the man," as it were, because the arm cannot be got rid of and therefore dominates the man (Egerod 1984; cf. Aikhenvald 2003: 125ff.).

I find both set of terms useful when considering the Egyptian material, and in what follows I concentrate on the marked group of nouns, the inalienable nouns, where possession is expressed in terms of a something corresponding to a dominated genitive. As I stated above, Morenz did not offer any Egyptological evidence for his view that "fear," "awe," and similar notions were properties inherent to the king. Indeed, making this case may appear to be a lost cause, given that the language in which all such phrases were couched, Classical Egyptian, used one and the same set of pronouns to express both "functions" of the genitive.[20] However, the situation is not completely without hope, because during the second millennium B.C. the language — already rich in pronouns — evolved a new set of possessive pronouns that seem to function as indicators of a subjective genitive, while retaining the old set for use in connection with the category of nouns called the inalienable nouns. Thus, in the classical stage of the Egyptian language the third-person singular pronoun *=f* was used to say "**his** house" (*pr=f*) and "**his** head" (*tp=f*). In the later stages the Egyptians would say *p3y=f pr* instead of *pr=f* for "**his** house," while for "**his** head" they would still say *tp=f*. This, as well as another important linguistic feature characteristic of the class — very special rules of determination — has been known for a long time, but to my knowledge no empirical study has ever been made to determine which words were admitted into this class. What the grammars have to say about this is certainly not very accurate.[21] However, there can little doubt that the core of the group of

---

[19] I fully subscribe, however, to the splendid remark of Sottas (1913: 78), who, on the subject of the nomenclature applied to a certain grammatical form, said that "à tout prendre, un non-sens prête moins aux confusions qu'un contresens."

[20] This applies also to inscriptions from the periods, where the vernacular was rather different; see for example, this passage from the main record of the "First Hittite Marriage," where it is said of the king (Ramesses II, ca. 1250 B.C.) as the manifestation of the sun god: "Omniscient like *Sia*, one who searches the bellies like Re, Lord of Heaven (*si3 ib mi si3 d'r htw mi r' nb pt*), it is his terrifyingness who has made people great, his impressiveness which pacifies the evil(?) of this land" (*in nrw=f s'3 rmt šft=f hr shtp dww [] t3 pn*) (Kitchen 1979: 240/14–241/1). Incidentally, the first part of this quotation is probably more than an echo of the famous "The Loyalist Teaching"; see Posener 1976: 62–63.

[21] For some basic observations, see Stern 1880: ch. XI, §195; Erman 1933: §§163–69; Gilula 1976: 170–71;

Černý and Israelit-Groll 1984: 59–66 (= §4.2.9). In the Shenoutean Coptic, *MMO=* is used "to predicate so-called 'inalienable' possession ..., and is selected by a special sub-paradigm of noun lexemes"; see Shisha-Halevy 1986: 37, cf. 21, 237, 24 supra β 2; 32; 33,3–4; 34 with pp. 161 n. 36 and 162 n. 37; 130ff.; idem 2007: 247. See also Stern 1880: §317; Till 1955: 324; idem 1961: §§208 and 296; Westendorf 1965–77: 272 n. 5; Quack 1994: 35–36. The use of the so-called weak plural article, attested in three syntagms, was discussed in Polotsky 1968. According to him the presence of this otherwise "non-existent" article is due to the fact that the three phrases all begin with "an unstressed vowel (i.e., vocalized zero consonant) with which the article forms one syllable, as shown by the constant absence of a point over the vowel" (Quack 1968: 245). This observation is not to be denied, but the explanation for the occurrence of the article is more likely to be that the core of each of the three syntagms would seem to be made up of a word belonging to the category of inalienable nouns.

inalienable nouns is comprised of words denoting parts of the body, and in order to express a phrase like "**his** head" the Egyptians would therefore still use the old set of pronouns.

This is not the place to attempt a detailed review of the evidence for what determines membership of this particular class. Moreover, it is even more difficult to put Morenz's hypothesis to a test. The reason for this is that 99.9% of all texts in which we are likely to find the vocabulary containing the phrases we are looking for, are written in a form of Classical Egyptian. Therefore, they would not normally — if ever — use the new set of possessive pronouns. In inscriptions, hymns, adorations, and suchlike, we only find what we already know from earlier texts. As an example I quote a passage from the great Papyrus Harris I, which contains a catalog of all the goods and personnel that Ramesses III gave to the gods. The text is written in Late Egyptian, or to be more exact, a form of Late Egyptian as close to "high" Late Egyptian (cf. Papyrus Abbott) as would be expected in such a text. This implies the usage of pronouns of the *a-series*. However, when it comes to the vocabulary that we are interested in, this text, which measures more than forty meters, does not contain a single example of the possessive construction that we are looking for — the possessive adjective used to express alienable possession and a possessed substantive.

> E.2   Place his (i.e., the king's) sword and his club over the head of the Asiatics so that they bow down in awe of him (lit., to his awe *šfyt⸗f* AWE⸗HIS) as they do for Baal. Extend for him the borders as far as he desires so that the low lands and the mountain countries tremble for fear of him (lit., fear in dread of him *snḏ tꜣw ḫꜣswt n ḥryt⸗f* DREAD⸗HIS) .... Place his love in the hearts of the gods and the goddesses (*mrwt⸗f m ibw* LOVE⸗HIS) and his sweetness and awe in the heart of the people (*bnr⸗f šfšft⸗f m ḥꜣtyw* SWEETNESS⸗HIS ... AWE⸗HIS) (pHarris I, 22,8–11).[22]

But one word can be put to a test, for instance, the word for destiny *šꜣi - shai*. In order to facilitate the understanding of the ensuing quotations I have decided to use a somewhat unorthodox transliteration of the Egyptian.

THE TALE OF THE DOOMED PRINCE

In the Tale of the Doomed Prince, known from a text written in literary Late Egyptian, a king and a queen are granted a son after many prayers to the gods. At his birth the goddesses of destiny come to decree his fate — *shai*: He is to die by crocodile, snake, or dog. Consequently the prince passes his childhood in splendid isolation. When he has reached adulthood, he obtains permission to go out into the world, because, as he puts it: "I am committed to a certain fate (*pa shai - pꜣ šꜣi*); allow me to leave home so that I may do whatever I want until God does what is his will." The prince sets out and arrives, incognito, at Mitanni, where he eventually is awarded the "princess in the tower" in the shape of the daughter of the King of Mitanni. In the following part of the story the snake is eliminated through the vigilance and care of his wife. Subsequently, the hero is pursued by his dog and in order to escape that destiny, he jumps into a lake, where he is seized by a crocodile. It presents itself to him as his destiny, but it also holds out a prospect of salvation. The crocodile is in a predicament. For two months it has fought a water spirit, and if the prince helps him to kill that creature, the crocodile will let him go.

At this point the papyrus breaks off and the remainder of the tale is lost.

---

[22] Compare the most recent translation into French: "... que ceux-ci [the Asiatics] se prosternent devant la crainte qu'il inspire(ra) .... Place l'amour pour lui ... que la douceur (qui émane de lui), (comme) la crainte qu'il inspire soient dans les poitrines ..." (Grandet 1994: 253–54).

THE LATE EGYPTIAN DESTINY

The problem is now whether destiny had to take its course or whether it could be manipulated. If destiny was unalterable and could not be averted (e.g., an inalienable attribute), we would expect *šʒi* - "shai" to combine with the old suffix pronoun *=f,* giving us **shai=f** - *šʒi =f* "his destiny." Interestingly enough this is not the case. As a matter of fact, I have not been able to find a single example of this combination in the genuinely Late Egyptian texts. We always find this word with the new possessive adjective *pay=f* as will be evident from what follows.

In the account of the Egyptian envoy Wenamun's journey to Byblos at the end of the Twentieth Dynasty (ca. 1080 B.C.), Wenamun succeeds in persuading the local prince to supply the timber for which he has come. When the logs have been delivered, Wenamun suggests that the prince erect a stele with a commemorative inscription on it. He even comes up with a proposal for the text:

> E.3   .... I felled it; I loaded it aboard. I provided him with my own ships and my own crews. I let them reach Egypt to request for me fifty years of life from Amun in excess of my fate (**pay=i shai** - *pʒy=i šʒy*) (...) (*Wenamun* 2,56–58 = *LES* 72,15–73,2).[23]

An unusual and exceptionally interesting letter from the Ramesside period is about destiny, pure and simple, and deserves to be cited almost in extenso:

> E.4   (A says to B): What means your not going to the Wise Woman concerning the two boys who died[24] while they were in your charge? Consult the Wise Woman about the death which befell them: was it their fate or was it their lot (**pay=w shai n tay=w rennet** - *n pʒy=w šʒy n tʒy=w rnnt*)? (O. Letellier [Letellier 1980] = *KRI* VII,257–58).

In the so-called Oracular Amuletic Decrees of the Late New Kingdom, three texts yield pronouncements of the following type:

> E.5   We (the protecting gods) will protect NN from those gods who carry off a human being, even though it is neither its destiny nor its lot (**pay=f shai tay=f rennet** - *iw bn pʒy=f šʒy tʒy=f rnnt*) (pTurin 1984, rt. 18–20 = Edwards 1960 (T. 2), vol. 1: 63 and vol. 2: pl. XXII).[25]

In the Egyptian version of the famous treaty between Ramesses II and the Hittite king Hattusili III the latter briefly recapitulates the accession of the new Hittite king:

> E.6   When Muwatalli, the Great Prince of Hatti, my brother, went to his fate (i.e., died), then Hattusilli took his father's place as Great Prince of Hatti (*ir [m]-dr ḥnn Mtnr pʒ wr ʿʒ n ḥttʒ pʒy=i sn m-sʒ* **pay=f shai** - *pʒy=f šʒy*) (Hittite Treaty, 10–11 = *KRI* II 227,8–10).[26]

---

[23] That this particular example occurs in a passage where Wenamun, as was to be expected from a competent scribe, drafts his proposal in the language of contemporary inscriptions — the Classical Egyptian idiom — is a forceful argument in favor of the point we are making.

[24] *ir mwt!* Perhaps the meaning is a sort of euphemism for being put to death. At any rate, I know of no other example of *mwt* being used in a periphrastic construction.

[25] Similarly, pLouvre E.25354, rt. 55–58 = *op. cit.,* (*P.3*), I, p. 86 og II, pl. XXXIII; pBerlin 10462 rt. 40–42 = *op. cit.,* (*B.*), I, p. 115 og II, pl. XLV.

[26] The phrase "go or run to one's fate" is an Egyptian rendering of a Hittite idiom, which occurs also in line 20 = *KRI* II,228,13, where the verb is *šm* instead of *ḥn*. See also Quaegebeur 1975: 126–27; Spalinger 1981: 314; Edel 1982–85/I: 146; Jasnow 1992: 79–80; Quack 1993.

A literary text, The Instruction of Ani, dispenses advice and warnings. The consequences are clear:

> E.7   God judges the righteous, but (as for the iniquitous) his destiny comes to
> take him away (**pay⸗f shai** - *p ꜣy⸗f š ꜣy*) (*Ani* B 20,12 = pBoulaq 4, VII,11–12).[27]

In the Tale of the Doomed Prince, the wife of our hero renders the snake harmless by getting it drunk and subsequently cutting it into pieces. She then informs her husband about what she has done:

> E.8   See, your god has delivered one of your fates into your hand (*w ꜥ m* **nay⸗k
> shai** - *n ꜣy⸗k š ꜣyw m ḏrt⸗k*) (Doomed Prince 8,5 = *LES* 8,4–5).

The same texts states that the crocodile is (E.9) his fate (*pay⸗f shai* - *p ꜣy⸗f š ꜣy*) (Doomed Prince 7,10 = *LES* 7,2). When the creature seizes the prince it is with these words:

> E.10   I am your fate that has been made to come in pursuit of you (*ink* **pay⸗k shai**
> - *p ꜣy⸗k š ꜣy iryt iw m-s ꜣ⸗k*), (Doomed Prince 8,11 = *LES* 8,15–16).

Finally, in yet another literary text, a love song, we find a passage where the use of metaphors is strongly reminiscent of certain Roman elegies:

> E.11   I passed by her house at night. I knocked, but no one opened to me. I hope
> the doorkeeper had a good night's sleep. Oh door bolt, I will open you, Oh lock, you
> are my fate (*ṯr mntk* **pay⸗i shai** - *p ꜣy⸗i š ꜣy*) (Gardiner 1931: rt. 17,7–9).

These few examples will suffice to show that in Late Egyptian proper the word **shai** - *š ꜣy* always has the status of a possessed noun vis-à-vis a possessor and that the relationship is one of alienable possession. In short, it is always used with the possessive adjective. This implies that man is not a slave of his destiny. It can be altered, as indicated in the example from Wenamun. As it happens the year 1975 also saw the publication of the standard monograph on the concept of destiny, and in this important book Jan Quagebeur made the very same inference — although he did not approach the problem from the angle of inalienable possession.

MORENZ AND AWE

Let us return to Morenz's hypothesis. As will be understood, it is not an easy task to verify or disprove his idea that phrases such as *snḏ⸗f* (FEAR⸗HIS) and *šfšft/šfyt⸗f* (AWE⸗HIS) are properties (*Grösse*) belonging to and emanating from the king, I am, in fact, unable to supply more than a single example of one of "Morenz's" words, but as it happens it comes from precisely the literary Tale of the Doomed Prince. The king of Mitanni is furious at the thought of having his daughter marry an Egyptian fugitive — the prince has at no point revealed his true identity to anyone in Mitanni — but when the young man finally comes into the presence of his future father-in-law things take a different turn:

> E.12   Her father had the young man and his daughter brought before him. The
> young man came before him, and his WORTH entered into the prince (*iw* **tay⸗f she-
> fyt** - *t ꜣy⸗f šfyt ḥr ꜥḳ m p ꜣ wr*), and he [the prince] embraced him and kissed him ..."
> (Doomed Prince, 7,1–7,2 = *LES* 6,3).

---

[27] The passage can also be interpreted differently; see Quack 1994: 109.

The translation "worth" is a pure makeshift because in English words for "fear," "awe," etc. can only be used of emotions experienced, not of the force that gives rise to them. The word *šft* belongs, moreover, to a group of words that, taken together, seem to cover the semantic field HONOR, a field that has never been the subject of any specific study (Assmann 1982: col. 968). Be this as it may, in theory we should be able to render the passage as "his awe entered." The young man — who happens, as the listener/reader knows, to be a king's son himself — is the possessor of awe. It is he who is in control of the emotions/affects, just as he is able to manipulate his fate.

(IN)ALIENABLE PROPERTIES OF THE KING

To my knowledge, the example cited above is the only of its kind. Although any additional examples would be greatly appreciated, this single one will suffice to show what I am driving at. If the evidence, meagre as it is, for the argument presented here is accepted, it shows that the king was in possession of certain properties or attributes — or for that matter *Potenz*, Radiance, or *Strahlkraft* — that inspired feelings of love and/or fear in people and enemies. Morenz and Assmann were obviously on the right track but were incorrect when they suggested that the properties were integral parts of the person of the king. They never used that kind of terminology, of course, but each in his own way argued that the properties were integrated parts of the essence of the king. The present argument shows that we cannot understand the relationship between the possessor/king and "his fear" as an objective genitive, as that would entail identifying "fear" as a non-acquirable or inalienable property of the king. I suggest that the discussion would be better served by considering all this from the point of view of classification. Being a king or defining a king — or any other ontological entity — would thus be based on a catalog, not merely of properties, but of the ways the relevant terms combine with the two forms of possession. Thus, in a true Late Egyptian text we would expect to find instances of pay≠f senedj - *pꜣyꜥf snd*, that is, an affect emanating from the king, something that he controls, and something which is **not** a vital component of his being. The king was in control of qualities or attributes such as fear, etc., but they were not constituent elements on the same level as, for instance, his *ka*. This conclusion will be seen to be in keeping with the evidence considered next.

FEAR AND AWE AS GIFT OF THE GODS

Another perspective on this issue is found by examining the use of these terms in the Coffin Texts. This very comprehensive corpus of funerary texts, inscribed on the interior sides of wooden coffins of private individuals during the so-called First Intermediate Period and Middle Kingdom, was designed to help the deceased cross from this world into the other world. Salvation entailed participating in the solar cycle. The dead wished to be at one with this process, and for this to happen he must be endowed with the properties subsumed in the notion *akh*, transfiguration. Participation in the eternal cycle of death and life implies, however, communication with the gods, and for this to be possible the deceased must be elevated to the status of a god, that is, attain a divine status hitherto the prerogative of the god incarnate, that is, the king. This required the means of attaining royal status. The Coffin Texts are one of those means and it has been suggested that "the ornamentation of the coffin as a whole can now be 'read' as an account of the ceremonies on the day of burial" (Willems 1988: 240;

1996). Kingly status would further imply possession of the appropriate insignia[28] and residence in a palace, and Willems is undoubtedly right when he follows Scharff in interpreting the coffin as such rather than as a house:

> But the whole decoration of coffins of the period concentrates on the representation of rites aiming at investing the deceased with the kingship of the Netherworld. The implication of this is rather that his eternal dwelling symbolizes his *palace* than his house. Something similar may underlie those elements of the decoration by which the coffin is turned into a *miniature of the universe*. The central position of the deceased in this microcosmos may again be a way to indicate his rulership and his role as a creator god (Willems 1988: 242).

Historically speaking, this was a new development by comparison with the prospect for salvation in the Old Kingdom (i.e., the third millennium). This change of outlook for the members of the elite very likely resulted from the bureaucratization of the *central* political and economic power of the state. Decentralization of this power entailed new responsibility for the new elite of administrators, and at the same time made them a vital force in the perpetual and all-important task of doing *maat*. In performing their duties toward the king, and in extension to the state, they became responsible for maintaining *maat*, since, in essence, this was the only proper exercise of power. It could be said that by delegating his sovereign obligations in this matter, the king had conferred upon his officials the potential of integration into the mechanics of the cosmic dynamic. They were called upon for their assistance in this world, but the ultimate consequence was that this also gave them a share in what had previously been exclusively the king's mortuary expectations. And thus this-worldly power became a hope for participation in the life and death cycle of Osiris. By integrating his officials in the eternal task of doing *maat*, the king had endowed them with *maat*, in the same way that it had been done for the priests who performed the cult in the temples on his behalf. The core of the cult is the exchange of Maat between partners who possess *maat* and who are of *maat*, and when performing the offerings the priest is — strictly speaking — not doing this "on behalf" of the king, but rather as someone who has been transposed to the level of royalty and divinity. Consequently, it may be presumed, these officials, and eventually members of their household, sought divine/royal status as well as the necessary means, in the form of, for example, texts, object frieze, in order to obtain it.

In an article on "Furcht und Schrecken in den Sargtexten,"[29] Susanne Bickel arrived at conclusions of great significance for our study. In the Coffin Texts it appears that the vast majority of instances of fear relate to cases where it is the deceased who is the object of fear. "Die Substantive des Begriffsfeldes 'Furcht' sind fast immer von einem Suffix oder indirektem Genitiv gefolgt. In jedem Fall zwingt der Zusammenhang zur Übersetzung mit objektiven Genitiv ('die Furcht von dir')" (Bickel 1988: 20 n. 9). The terms in question are the same as those we

---

[28] See, for example, *CT* VI,285w–x (= Spell 660), where it is said: "Hail to you, Uraeus, what you will receive is your place on the head of this NN."

[29] Bickel 1988. Bickel's interpretation of the genitive is, however, hardly correct. That the dead is the *possessor* of fear comes out quite clearly in examples such as the following cited by her: "I have fetched my dread (which is to be) in my belly and my awe (which comes forth) from my lips, my strength in my gullet … and my fear in my flesh" (*iw in.n=i nrw=i m ẖt=i šfšt=i m spty=y wsrw=i m šbb=i … snḏ=i m iwf=i*) *CT* Spell 469 = V,392e–g. The passage may, in fact, be translated in several different ways (*iw in* as a passive *sḏmw* and the following phrases as circumstantial clauses, for instance), but the point is that the suffix pronouns cannot be interpreted as instances of an objective genitive, because this would make the dead the object of fear and terror of himself!

have been considering so far, that is, *nrw, snḏ,* and *šfsft,* and it appears, moreover, that they are given to the dead in the spells that aim at helping him transcend his mortality so as to be transformed into a god. The properties denoted by these terms "sind somit deutlich göttliche Potenzen, die dem Verstorbenen bei seiner Gottwerdung von einem Gott gegeben werden können" (Bickel 1988: 21). Bickel also notes that the deceased may receive a number of other properties, such as *nḫt, sḫm, wsr, pḥty,* or *ꜣt,* a set of terms denoting power, strength, greatness, etc.

The discovery that "fear" and "awe" are *given* to the deceased is in perfect harmony with our results. These are properties that the possessor controls because they are *alienable* and consequently can be acquired for instance as a gift from the gods. The dead seeks to obtain kingly status, which implies being given the attributes of kingship. This arouses the suspicion that also the king would be given these attributes at his coronation or accession to the throne. Morenz seemed to have had the same view, which is also shared by Susanne Bickel (Morenz 1969 [1975]: 140; Bickel 1988: 22–23). The question, then, is whether this is a "recent" phenomenon, for instance, a corollary to the very comprehensive changes in the Egyptian society during the transition from the third to the second millennium. For our line of reasoning, the material from the Old Kingdom is not very informative. Bickel quotes a spell from the Pyramid Texts, which she takes as evidence for the king having to pray for these attributes. However, the spell in question, which forms part of the king's resurrection ritual, is a hymn or praise to the Red Crown and its curl, and the king does not "pray" for these attributes, but for their continued efficacy. He *is* in possession of *šꜥt* "ferocity," *snḏ* "fearsomeness," *mrwt* "love" as well as other attributes of power such as batons and sceptres, and he uses the spell to assure that his properties or attributes of power will be like those of the crown with which he aspires to merge (Pyramid Texts Spell 221). Owing to the state of the extant material from the third millennium, there is, therefore, no answer to the question as to whether fear of the king in the third millennium might be an *in*alienable property of the king.

CONSTITUENT ELEMENTS, ATTRIBUTES, WIDER IMPLICATIONS

In the following I briefly pursue the line of enquiry presented above in order to demonstrate its wider potential. As mentioned above, Morenz suggested that the "Amtsperson König" was composed of a number of elements that would be actualized under various circumstances. In addition to the properties already discussed, this group would include the *ka, ba, akh, khat* (*kꜣ, bꜣ, ꜣḫ, ḥꜣt*) as well as the name and the shadow.[30] The idea that the Egyptian concept of person is both very complex and radically different from our own is far from novel. A number of nineteenth- and early twentieth-century Egyptologists argued along lines similar to those presented by Morenz,[31] and the matter came on an even firmer footing with the publication of the texts from the Eighteenth Dynasty Theban tomb of the scribe, steward of the vizier, and

---

[30] See n. 10 above.

[31] To my knowledge, Wiedemann was the first to produce a list of components. The list comprised the *ka*, the *ba*, the body (*ḥt*), the two words for "heart," the shadow, and the mummy (Wiedemann 1878). In the same volume, French orientalist Textor de Ravisi added the *name* to Wiedemann's list of components (Textor de Ravisi 1878). Common to both of them was the idea that these components were divisions of the non-material part of the Egyptian person, who in turn was seen as a bipartite being consisting of a "soul" and a body. In the words of Textor de Ravisi (1878: 173): "*L'homme est composé de deux créatures distinctes de natures différentes,* UN CORPS ET UNE AME, intimement unis pendant la vie de ce monde et qui peuvent continuer à l'être dans l'autre vie. L'une *créée* par le dieu Ra, composée d'une seule partie (du limon du Nil), et l'autre *émanation* du principe vital de ce Dieu, composée, comme ce dieu lui-même, de sept parties ...."

grain assessor Amenemhet.[32] Here two scenes depicting the presentation of offerings are accompanied by two legends. The beginning of each is lost, but otherwise both specify that the offerings should be presented to the deceased and to (South Wall) "his *ka*, his stele (ʿ*bꜣ*[33]), this tomb (*is*, emended) (of his) which is in the Necropolis,[34] (his) destiny (*šꜣy*), his life span (ʿ*ḥ* ʿ), his birth brick (*msḫnt*), his lot (or circumstances) (*rnnt*), his Khnum,"[35] and to (North Wall) "his *ka*, his false door offering place (ʿ*bꜣ*), […], his [*ba*], his *akh*, his corpse (*ḫꜣt*), his shadow (*šwt*), and all his forms of existence, transformations and appearances (*ḫprw⸗f*)" (Sethe 1909: 1060,9–1061,6; Davies and Gardiner 1915: 99, pls. 19, 22, and 23). Both lists are headed by the *ka,* which therefore appears to be the principal recipient of the offerings. This inference depends, however, on the overall interpretation of the lists, and here the principle behind their organization is not immediately apparent.[36] Fecht interpreted the first group as consisting of "Schicksalsgottheiten," while the second is composed of "Erscheinungsformen" (Fecht 1978: 24). According to Baines the lists are "revealing for the lack of 'logical' unity" with the only consistent element in the organization being "the relation of the terms to the deceased" (Baines 1985: 24). Herman te Velde divides the text in two series of nine items with "no academic philosopher (being) at work here" (te Velde 1990: 97), while Assmann counts fourteen constituents. Assmann also thinks that this scene is "a unique instance, unparalleled in any other tomb."[37] However, it is precisely this unique character that makes the list so valuable, given the basic truth in Iversen's well-known "general rule," on lexicography that "the more 'out of place'" a word is in a given context, the more likely it is to reveal its basic meaning (Iversen 1955: 6; Harris 1961: 9). The lists do not seem to be based on standard correspondences such as, for instance, corpse (*ḫꜣt*) and *ba*, nor do the presentations seem to exhibit pairs of constituent elements. Given the lack of consensus among scholars concerning the proper understanding of all these elements, Gardiner's view, as expressed more than ninety years ago, is still worth quoting. His starting point is the two passages that conclude the two lists.[38] They mention "these gods," but in that the opening phrases of both legends are missing, it is far from clear who these gods are. Sethe had suggested a restoration of the usual phrases

---

[32] The texts were first published in Sethe 1909. The tomb was subsequently published by Davies and Gardiner (1915); Compare PM I,1², p. 166.

[33] If indeed the text has ʿ*bꜣ*, I suspect that it is a mistake for ʿ*ḥ* ʿ*w*. If not, then the false door offering place occurs twice *in the text*, as does the *ka,* and both would then be the principal recipients of the offerings.

[34] Also, these phrases might be open to other renderings. Gardiner thus translated: "for his stele belonging to this tomb which is in the Necropolis" (Davies and Gardiner 1915: 99), while Fecht (1978: 24) translated: "dieser-seiner-Opferstele, die-in-der-Nekropole-ist."

[35] Meskhenet and Khnum appear as members of the group of gods who in the Late Middle Kingdom literary text pWestcar assist in the birth of three future kings. They appear as a pair in texts from the Middle Kingdom and the Late Period; see, conveniently Assmann 1972: 61 n. 39. From the Nineteenth Dynasty onwards Renenet, Meskhenet, and Shai, the divinities associated with fate and lot, from birth to the end, were present at the Judgment of the Dead; see Seeber 1976: 83–88. Just as *shai* could be manipulated, the power of the two goddesses in determining the future may also have been somewhat

limited. In the often discussed passage in The Instruction of a Man for His Son, §5, it would seem that the power of the king is of greater importance to the success of an individual than the fortune decreed to him by Meskhenet and Renenet, as all they can do is to make him breathe. For this passage, see Fecht 1978: 21ff.; Vernus 2001: 226 with ample bibliography.

[36] The scenes have been discussed by, for example, Bonnet 1952: 675, passim; George 1970: 19–21, c61; Fecht 1978: 24; Gee (2006) presented a new study of the text. Further studies are cited in the following notes.

[37] Assmann 2001: 118; 2005: 88–89. As it happens there is a list of the same character in pBremner-Rhind 29,18–19; see Faulkner 1933: 74.

[38] The text on the South Wall cited above continues: "May these gods grant him to have control thereof, to be rich therewith, to be justified therewith, even as those [gods who are in] his train for ever and ever." And on the North Wall Gardiner renders the text as: "May these gods <grant> him to have superfluity thereof, to partake thereof, to eat thereof and to drink thereof, like the ancients eternally."

by which such scenes are introduced, but Gardiner had misgivings about this and thought that "it seems incontestable" that the legends use the term God to refer to the components found in the list from Amenemhet's tomb.

> Herein consists the truly unique character of these two bands of hieroglyphic inscrip-
> tion, though indeed they merely illustrate the extreme logical consequence of a very
> ancient direction of thought. From the earliest times whence we have written records,
> the Egyptians believed that the human individuality could present itself under a va-
> riety of forms, which are less "parts" of its nature, as vulgarly stated, than shifting
> modes of its being.... These distinctions are the outcome of separate trends of thought,
> not necessarily consecutive yet not the result of a single effort of self-analysis; in the
> earlier times they co-existed in the religious consciousness as almost unperceived in-
> consistencies, being seldom compared or contrasted with one another. The theological
> and mystery-loving tendencies of the Eighteenth Dynasty, on the other hand, seem
> to revel in the variety of aspects under which the dead man could reveal himself, as
> if each additional one of them increased his chances of eternal life and welfare. In
> the older period we seldom hear of other modes of existence than the *ka*, the *bai*, and
> the *ikh* or glorious and illuminated state, with which the shadow, the name, and the
> corpse are not yet quite on a par. The Eighteenth Dynasty adds the destiny (*shay*),
> the upbringing (*rnn*), and the place of origin (*mshnt*). Almost peculiar to the tomb of
> Amenemhēt is the acceptation of a man's life (*'ahe*), his stele (*'b*), and his Khnum,
> as forms of immanence of the soul; the last of these appears to be the ram-headed
> Potter-god personified in the act of moulding the particular image of Amenemhēt out
> of the wet clay. Strangest things of all, these various modes of being (*hprw*) are here
> regarded as gods, spirits distinct from Amenemhēt himself, and jealously vigilant over
> his means sustenance. (...) but the passages we are considering appear to stand alone
> in their qualification of these and the other modes of being as gods distinct from and
> exerting guardianship over the individual to whom the particularly belong.[39]

In light of what is known today about the various elements/"forms of being," it just might be a more fruitful avenue of research to consider the concept of divinity in light of evidence provided by these lists, the more so since Khnum and Meskhenet, as well as Shai and Renenet, might qualify as "gods." In his book on personification, Baines briefly discusses the category of *ntr* "god" as used in this text and remarked "that the most that may be concluded [is] that *ntr* can be used for subdivisions of a non-divine unity that are given independence, if only as an elaborate metaphor" (Baines 1985: 33). However, by analogy with the principle of *Gliedervergottung*, in which each body part is associated with a god and thus itself becomes divine, I would suggest that the lists provide a sort of *curriculum vitae* with the *ka* (-statue?) providing the junction between the two phases of existence. Starting with the South Wall we begin with the fashioning of the embryo and its *ka* – Khnum. Renenet provides the circumstances of the future life as well as the air for the newborn child. Then follows birth, life span, destiny, leading eventually to the tomb with a stele on which we have the autobiography or curriculum of the deceased who has gone to his *ka*. The *ka* (-statue) as well as the offering stone are also the receptacles and intermediaries between this world and the other world where the remaining components become the new forms of "existence." The succession *ba*, *akh*, corpse, and shadow is interesting, but a precise interpreta-

---

[39] Davies and Gardiner 1915: 99–100. Compare also Gardiner (1917: 787), where it is suggested that the various entities have become divine by *analogy* — although it is not said with what this is supposed to have have happened.

tion is hampered by the lacuna preceding the *ba*. The last phrase, *n ḫprw ꞊f nbw*, which Gardiner translated "and for all his modes of being," is also somewhat ambiguous — quite apart from the question of the precise rendering of *ḫprw* itself. Should the phrase be taken to mean "(and) all his *kheperu*," that is, the *kheperu* being different from the members of the preceding list? Or is the phrase to be rendered "(as well as) all the (other) *kheperu* of his," in which case the preceding items are to be regarded as instances of *kheperu*, the phrase *m hprw ꞊f nbw* being almost equivalent to our "and so on"? Or, finally, is it to be understood as "(in short,) all his *kheperu*," implying that the list is exhaustive and consists of *kheperu*? Gardiner's translation and discussion vacillate between the latter two possibilities, but it is quite clear that he regarded *kheperu* as a concept that subsumes all the other items in the list.

The framework of the present paper does not provide space for a discussion of Gardiner's "definition" of the *kheperu*, let alone of the individual items, but some light would be thrown on the problem were we to extend the approach utilized above in order to determine whether the terms listed in the inscription of Amenemhet represent elements that are inalienable properties. No such study has been undertaken so far, and I therefore conclude this part of the paper by a few brief remarks on some of the components. But before I do so I must deal with a methodological question. A priori — if for no other reason — the investigation should treat private individuals and royalty as separate entities. We are, however, fortunate in having evidence at our disposal that shows that at least some of the components mentioned in the tomb of Amenemhet are the same for royalty as for private individuals. On the outer lid of the granite sarcophagus of the Nineteenth Dynasty king Merenptah there is a hymn to the dead king recited by his mother the goddess Neith (Assmann 1972). The theme of the hymn is that form of rebirth known as *regressus ad uterum*.[40] The text describes in great detail how the king appears between the legs of the goddess and how the various parts of her body are instrumental in recreating and rebuilding his body. For our purpose the following passages are relevant:

> E.13   I bring the air to you from my nostrils and breathe for you the northwind from
> my throat, my birth brick (Meskhent), my providence (Renenet) are attached to you,
> while my Khnum fashion your body providing you with a rebirth as a great lotus bud
> (lit., repeating for you birth as a lotus bud) (*iṯḥ ꞊i n ꞊k ṯꞽw m šrt ꞊i nšp ꞊i n ꞊k mḥyt m
> ḥḥ ꞊i msḥnt ꞊i rnnt ꞊i m-ḫt ꞊k ḫnmw ꞊i ḥr skd ḏt ꞊k ḥr wḥm n ꞊k mswt m nḥb wr*) (lines
> 8–9; Assmann 1972: 50–51).

I can do no better than citing the comments of the editor himself: "Die vorliegende Stelle ist ein wertvoller Beleg dafür, daß der Person-Begriff zumindest des NR in diesen Komponenten keinen Unterschied zwischen Göttern und Menschen kannte" (Assmann 1972: 61), the king being subsumed in the category of men. Since the relevance for the king of the other components mentioned in Amenemhet's inscription has never been called in question, we may proceed with our investigation without classifying the material according to the kind of person that it relates to. The task is not impossible, because it is quite clear that some of the components are alienable. This applies beyond any doubt to the stele and the tomb, but also the destiny and the lot, as we have seen above (E.4–5). A search through the *Wb. zetteln* seems to show that *ꜥḥꜥw* "life span" and *ḫ3t* "corpse" are attested only with possession indicated by the suffix pronouns, but true Late Egyptians texts are virtually excluded from the material from which this information is derived. If we turn to the more well-known components, however, we do get an interesting result.

---

[40] For bibliography, see conveniently Frandsen 2007: 101
n. 63.

The *ka* of a person, which unites him with his ancestors, and which is part of his self, his alter ego, is an inalienable component. It always appears with the suffix pronouns, for example, *k₃ꞽf*, a fact that is in perfect harmony with what is known about the concept of the *ka*.

The *ba,* on the other hand, can appear with the possessive article/adjective *pay꞊f ba* (*p₃y꞊f b₃*) and is therefore an element of a different order. This again is not really surprising in that the *ba* is the component that, *inter alia,* enables the deceased to move about and to take on other forms of appearance. The *ba* can be distinct from its owner. The well-known Middle Kingdom text, variously known under the names *Lebensmüde*, The Man Who Was Tired of Life*, and Le dialogue du Désespéré avec son Ame, provides additional insight into this question, as it contains a debate as to whether the *ba* should be allowed to separate itself from the man.

The shadow (*ḥ₃ybt*) would seem to combine with the possessive adjective used to express alienable possession. The word for shadow, however, is a bit tricky, because it [41] is used for what in English is denoted by the terms shadow and shade — a distinction not necessarily found in other languages. Unfortunately — once again — examples of the shade/shadow of, for instance, a tree and the shadow of a person occur rarely in genuine Late Egyptian texts. As an example of the first we have the following:

> E.14   I (i.e., the king) made the entire country flourish with trees and plants and I enabled the people to sit in their shade (**nay꞊u shubu** - *n₃y꞊w šwbw*) (*pHarris* I 78,8).[42]

These three remarks must suffice to show the direction and the possibilities of this type of investigation. The analysis explores what in cognitive linguistics is called the pre-conceptual level and, as I hope to have shown, it is likely to yield results of some interest.

A NEW FACET IN THE MECHANISM OF ROYAL SUCCESSION AND REGENERATION

I conclude this paper with a short remark on another approach to the problem of the king's divinity.

Royal succession in Egypt may be seen as a system of inheritance in which several forms of divine and social actions converged. On the one side, we have divine intervention in the form of divine selection and decision making, the idea of predestination, as well as the institution of theogamy. On the other side, within the predominantly collateral descent system of the Egyptians, succession to office was determined by masculine primogeniture and patrilineal devolution. In practice, however, the system gave the eldest son of the reigning king automatic accession to the throne when his father died.

In Egypt transfer of property generally required a deed of transfer called an *imyt-pr*, literally, "that which is in the house." Depending on the type of transaction, the term may be rendered as will, donation, sale, or contract (Mrsich 1968). During the late New Kingdom, royal suc-

---

[41] Two words, in fact, are used about the shadow/shade: *ḥ₃ybt* and *šwt*. According to the authoritative study by George (1970: 6–11), the former of these two terms replace the latter, with a number of hybrid forms such as *šwbw* showing the development.

[42] Similarly, pLansing 12,11 = Gardiner 1937: 112,2–3: *iw꞊k m n₃y꞊sn ḥ₃bswt iw꞊k wnm n₃y꞊sn dkrw* "while you sit in their shades and eat their fruit." As soon as we go into the realm of poetry, the scribe returns to the older set of pronouns. The sycamore tree speaks to the girl: *mi iry꞊t p₃ hrw m nfr dw₃ (ḥr) – s₃ dw₃ r hrw 3 iw꞊t ḥms. tw n šwbt (꞊i)* "Come that you may spend a perfect day, tomorrow, the day after tomorrow and a third day sitting in my shade" (pTurin 1996, rt. 2,11 = Mathieu 1996: pl. 16).

cession began to have recourse to such deeds, and the procedure may thus be seen as a new and interesting phase in that gradual process of desacralization that kingship went through during its millennia long history. The use of this legal concept adds a new facet to the interpretation of the interplay of the divine and human dimensions of kingship, which not only constitutes a hitherto unnoticed aspect of what it takes to become a king, but also became an instrument in that process of *regressus ad uturum* whereby the king was reborn.

Thus when Sety I followed his father Ramesses I on the throne in the early Nineteenth Dynasty, the process of succession was described in terms of a piece of legal fiction. In Abydos, the principal place for the worship of the god Osiris and therefore the prototypical locale of father-son relationships, Sety erected a shrine for the cult of his late father. The structure is very dilapidated and the texts on the walls, doorjambs, stele, and statue have therefore been only partly preserved. Almost two-thirds of the text of the great dedicatory stele, which stood in front of the doorway to the chapel proper, have disappeared, but in the extant part there is a section describing the accession of Ramesses followed by another giving us an account of his death and the subsequent accession of Sety:

> He (Ramesses) joined heaven. Then I arose upon his throne and it is I who keeps his name alive. I am like Re at dawn now that I have received my father's regalia. I am the king on the seat which he enlarged and on the throne which he occupied. This land is in my hand as (it was in) my father's. He, on the other hand, has (now) begun to function as a god (*ntf pw šꜝ ꜥ irt nṯr*), and (therefore) I protect him from whom I came forth and cause his body to appear as a god (Schott 1964: pl. 2, lines 7–8 = *KRI* I 111,15–112,3).

Sety is Re in the morning, that is, the young god. Egypt belongs to him as it used to belong to his father, and as the new ruler he honors his obligations toward his father the god by establishing a cult for him. The details of what he did are specified in the rest of this long text and we are fortunate in also having the statue that was at the center of the cult.

His father, Ramesses, on the other hand, who had now begun to act as a god, responded to the arrangements by providing his son and successor with a divine, legal decree. The text is found on the right doorjamb of the shrine, that is, to the right of the text of the stele. Accompanied by the remains of a representation of Ramesses, the text appears to tell of the king's presence at a meeting of the

> entire Ennead of the Gods. I heard their statement and they handed over to you the throne of Atum and the years of Horus to be the protector. They (further) gave to you this land by way of a deed of transfer and curbed the Nine Bows for you (*sḏmꜗi tp-rꜝꜗsn swḏꜗw nꜗk nst tm rnpwt ḥr r nḏty dïwꜗw nꜗk tꜝ pn m imyt-pr wꜥf nꜗk psḏwt*) (Schott 1964: pl. 9 = *KRI* I 110,6–8).[43]

What is novel here is the clear distinction between two levels or degrees of divinity and the use of the instrument of *imyt-pr* to bring about devolution and to regulate what always was *and is* a give-and-take relationship between king and god, variously characterized as a *do ut des* or *do quia dedisti* relationship (Frandsen 1989).

---

[43] Given that the *-t* in *imyt* may be merely graphic, one might perhaps take *wꜥf* as referring to the deed and translate: "which curbs." Compare Schott 1964: 11: "Vereinigt war für mich die Neunheit insgesamt. Ich habe ihre Aussprüche gehört, die Dir den Thron des Atum und die Jahre des Horus überweisen [die dich] zum Schutzherrn [bestimmen, die Dir dies Land testamentarisch übergeben und Dir die neun Bogen bändigen]."

There is another contemporary example that illustrates the role of the *ỉmyt-pr*. In the great temple of Sety I in Abydos there is a scene where the king offers frankincense to Osiris and Isis. The latter says to the king that she gives him the country by an *ỉmyt-pr*.[44] From the reign of Merenptah of the same dynasty comes yet another example of the same kind. On a stele in Hermopolis Thoth tells the king that he has informed Re that the "life span of heaven in the form of kingship has been written down" for the king. This decision is expressed through an "*ỉmyt-pr* committed to writing by Thoth with his own fingers at the right hand of Amun" (*KRI* IV 29,1–2). The introduction of this mechanism is not, however, confined to the devolution of kingdom. The use of the *ỉmyt-pr* also emerges in the Book of the Dead, a compilation of funerary texts made in the New Kingdom, and it is interesting to note that here it is used about divine succession. In the New Kingdom version of the well-known aetiological section of chapter seventeen, which explains how Re came to be called the great cat, there is an addition which goes: "Another saying: This is Shu making an *ỉmyt-pr* concerning Geb for the benefit of (his son) Osiris" (Lapp 2006: 198–201). Thoth is also the manufacturer of an *ỉmyt-pr* which puts Shu on the throne of his father, as related in another late New Kingdom text, the magical Papyrus Harris (pMag. Harris I 15–18 = Lange 1927: 14–15). The late New Kingdom is also the period in which we first encounter royal endowments for the gods made in the form of an *ỉmyt-pr*. A famous case is that of Ramesses II, who in his account of the battle of Kadesh rebukes Amun for seemingly having abandoned him despite the fact that Ramesses has transferred "all my property by an *ỉmyt-pr*" (Kadesh §100).

The increasing use of legal means in the mediation of the human and divine aspects of kingship finds a supreme expression in the fact that an *ỉmyt-pr* is instrumental in the king's rebirth — even when this is done through the so-called *regressus ad uterum*. The evidence comes from the Nineteenth Dynasty hymn of the goddess Neith to her son Merenptah. The text is found on the outer lid of his granite sarcophagus from which I have cited a passage above. At the beginning of the hymn the goddess welcomes the king and tells him that she is his mother who nurses him, who is pregnant with him in the morning and gives birth to him as Re in the evening:

> I carry you, ... I lift your mummy, my arms being under you, ... you step into me, ...
> I being your mother/sarcophagus (𓎡𓉐𓏏𓀗) which hides that form of yours that is ready for the rite de passage (*bs*).

And then it comes:

> my heart belongs to you through a deed — *ỉmyt-pr* (𓄣𓈖𓏏𓂝𓊗) (lines 2–4).[45]

A deed is here the crucial means of solving what, according to Egyptian ontology, was a cosmological crisis. Instead of having recourse to ritual politics, a legal instrument was brought in.

It is not admissible, I think, to infer from the increasing use of this juridical instrument that the human dimension of the king had gained ground at the expense of the divine. The evidence

---

[44] Mariette 1869–80/1, Appendix B, pl. 29 = Wb. DZA 20.669.510.

[45] Assmann 1972: 48–49. It is immaterial for the present argument that the beginning of the passage seems to confuse the timing of the various phases of rebirth. Assmann has this comment: "Die Aussage ist höchst paradox. Re ist als Sonne von allen Himmelskörpern der einzige, der gerade nicht 'am Morgen empfangen und am Abend geboren wird,' sondern umgekehrt. Eine versehentliche Verwechslung anzunehmen, geht wohl nicht an. Es muss sich entweder um eine jenseitlich-unterweltliche Geburt des Königs als 'Nachtsonne' handeln, womit möglicherweise der Mond gemeint ist ... oder um eine bewusst paradoxe Formulierung (coincidentia oppositorum), ..."

happens to emerge in the sources at a time, the Ramesside period, when other evidence takes on the form of occasionally megalomaniac protestations to the contrary. While the reigning king builds gigantic temples in which he offers to deified forms of himself (Wildung 1973), evidence from a variety of other sources bear witness to a development, where the theocracy no longer has the king as its focus. Society had, by that time, become more complex and this in itself is likely to have contributed to the significant inclusion of legal terminology in theological contexts.

SUMMARY

The Egyptological debate on the character of rulership in Egypt has oscillated between emphasizing two positions: the king as a deity and the king as human. The preceding pages have adduced two new arguments in favor of each of the two positions. The divine aspect of the king is clarified using his names and describing his appearance, his actions, etc. in the form of statements and epithets. Linguistic analysis is used to determine whether those attributes ascribed to the king are regarded as inalienable (inseparable) from his divine nature and thus shared by king and god alike. Given that the discussion of kingship within Egyptology has its focus on how to delineate the divine nature of the king as an individual human being, this approach is useful in that it allows us to chart those characteristics that were inherent to the king as god. The discussion of, *inter alia*, the terms for fear and awe were examples used to illustrate this argument.

An argument in favor of the human character of the kingship concludes the paper. It shows that during the Ramesside period, when the displays of the king's divinity were at its most ostentatious (Abu Simbel is only one example), the transfer of royal power in the succession was subject to procedures identical to those used in ordinary property transactions. This indicates that, despite its divine character, the office of the king was treated as transferable property that was separate from the person of the king.

ABBREVIATIONS

CT	Coffin Text
CT V	de Buck 1954
CT VI	de Buck 1956
E.	Example
KRI I	Kitchen 1975
KRI II	Kitchen 1979
KRI IV	Kitchen 1982
KRI VII	Kitchen 1989
LES	Gardiner 1932
p	papyrus
PM I,1^2	Porter and Moss 1960
PT	Pyramid Text
Urk. IV	Sethe 1909

BIBLIOGRAPHY

Aikhenvald, Alexandra Y.

2003   *Classifiers: A Typology of Noun Categorization Devices*. Oxford Studies in Typology
            and Linguistic Theory; Oxford Linguistics. Oxford: Oxford University Press.

Assmann, Jan

1969   *Liturgische Lieder an den Sonnengott: Untersuchungen zur altägyptischen Hymnik*,
            Volume 1. Münchner altägyptische Studien 19. Berlin: Bruno Hessling.

1972   "Die Inschrift auf dem äußeren Sarkophagdeckel des Merenptah." *Mitteilungen des
            deutschen archäologischen Instituts Abteilung Kairo* 28: 47–73.

1977   "Furcht." *Lexikon der Ägyptologie*, Vol 2: *Erntefest–Hordjedef*, edited by Wolfgang
            Helck and Wolfhart Westendorf, columns 359–67. Wiesbaden: Harrassowitz.

1982   "Persönlichkeitsbegriff und -bewußtsein." *Lexikon der Ägyptologie*, Volume 4:
            Megiddo–Pyramiden, edited by Wolfgang Helck and Wolfhart Westendorf, columns
            963–78. Wiesbaden: Harrassowitz.

1984   "Politik zwischen Ritual und Dogma: Spielräume politischen Handelns im pharao-
            nischen Ägyptens." *Saeculum* 35: 97–114.

1990   *Ma'at: Gerechtigkeit und Unsterblichkeit im Ägypten*. Munich: C. H. Beck.

2001   *Tod und Jenseits im Alten Ägypten*. Munich: C. H. Beck.

2005   *Death and Salvation in Ancient Egypt*. Ithaca: Cornell University Press.

Baines, John

1985   *Fecundity Figures: Egyptian Personification and the Iconology of a Genre*. Modern
            Egyptology. Warminster: Aris & Phillips.

1995   "Origins of Egyptian Kingship." *Ancient Egyptian Kingship*, edited by David B.
            O'Connor and David P. Silverman, pp. 95–156. Probleme der Ägyptologie 9. Leiden:
            Brill.

1997   "Kingship before Literature: The World of the King in the Old Kingdom." In *Selbst-
            verständnis und Realität* (Akten des Symposiums zur ägyptischen Königsideologie in
            Mainz, 15–17 June 1995), edited by Rolf Gundlach and Christine Raedler, pp. 125–
            74. Beiträge zur altägyptischen Königsideologie 1; Ägypten und Altes Testament
            36/1. Wiesbaden: Harrassowitz.

Bardinet, Thierry

1995   *Les papyrus médicaux de l'Égypte pharaonique: Traduction intégrale et commen-
            taire*. Penser la médecine. Paris: Fayard.

Bergman, Jan

1972   "Zum 'Mythus vom Staat' im Alten Ägypten." In *The Myth of the State*, (Based on
            Papers read at the Symposium on the Myth of the State held at Åbo, 6–8 September,
            1971), edited by Haralds Biezais, pp. 80–102. Scripta Instituti Donneriani Aboen-
            sis 6. Stockholm: Almquist & Wiksell.

Bickel, Susanne

1988   "Furcht und Schrecken in den Sargtexten." *Studien zur altägyptischen Kultur* 15:
            17–25.

Blumenthal, Elke

1970   *Untersuchungen zum ägyptischen Königtum des Mittleren Reiches*, Volume 1: *Die
            Phraseologie*. Abhandlungen der Sächsischen Akademie der Wissenschaften zu Leip-
            zig, Philologisch-historische Klasse 61/1. Berlin: Akademie-Verlag.

Bonnet, Hans

    1952   *Reallexikon der ägyptischen Religionsgeschichte.* Berlin: Walter de Gruyter.

Brunner, Hellmut

    1964   *Die Geburt des Gottkönigs: Studien zur Überlieferung eines altägyptischen Mythos.* Ägyptologische Abhandlungen 10. Wiesbaden: Harrassowitz.

Caminos, Ricardo A.

    1954   *Late-Egyptian Miscellanies.* Brown Egyptological Studies 1. London: Oxford University Press.

Černý, Jaroslav, and Sarah Israelit-Groll

    1984   *A Late Egyptian Grammar.* Third edition. Studia Pohl, Series Maior 4. Rome: Biblical Institute Press.

Chappell, Hilary, and William McGregor

    1996   "Prolegomena to a Theory of Inalienability." In *The Grammar of Inalienability: A Typological Perspective on Body Part Terms and the Part-Whole Relation*, edited by Hilary Chappell and William McGregor, pp. 3–30. Empirical Approaches to Language Typology 14. Berlin and New York: Mouton de Gruyter.

Davies, Nina de Garis, and Alan Henderson Gardiner

    1915   *The Tomb of Amenemhēt (No. 82).* Theban Tomb Series 1. London: Egypt Exploration Fund.

de Buck, Adriaan

    1954   *Egyptian Coffin Texts,* Volume 5: *Texts of Spells 355–471.* Oriental Institute Publications 73. Chicago: University of Chicago Press.

    1956   *Egyptian Coffin Texts,* Volume 6: *Texts of Spells 472–786.* Oriental Institute Publications 81. Chicago: University of Chicago Press.

Edel, Elmar

    1982–85   "Der ägyptisch-hethitische Friedensvertrag zwischen Ramses II. und Hattusili III." In *Texte aus der Umwelt des Alten Testaments*, edited by Riekele Borger and O. Kaiser, pp. 135–53. Gütersloh: Gerd Mohn.

Edwards, I. E. S.

    1960   *Oracular Amuletic Decrees of the Late New Kingdom.* 2 volumes. Hieratic Papyri in the British Museum, Fourth Series. London: Trustees of the British Museum.

Egerod, Søren

    1984   *Østasiatiske sprog: Forelæsning den 1. marts 1984 i anledning af 25 års jubilæet som professor ved Københavns Universitet.* Copenhagen. Københavns Universitets Østasiatiske Institut.

Erichsen, Wolja

    1933   *Papyrus Harris I: Hieroglyphische Transkription.* Bibliotheca aegyptica 5. Brussels: Édition de la Fondation égyptologique Reine Élisabeth.

Erman, Adolf

    1933   *Neuaegyptische Grammatik.* Second edition. Leipzig: Wilhelm Engelmann.

Faulkner, Raymond Oliver

    1933   *The Papyrus Bremner-Rhind* (British Museum No. 10188). Bibliotheca aegyptiaca 3. Brussels: Édition de la Fondation égyptologique Reine Élisabeth.

Fecht, Gerhard
    1978   "Schicksalsgöttinnen und König in der 'Lehre eines Mannes für seinen Sohn.'" *Zeitschrift für ägyptische Sprache und Altertumskunde* 105: 14–42.

Frandsen, Paul John
    1989a   "*BWT* — Divine Kingship and Grammar." In *Akten des Vierten Internationalen Ägyptologen-Kongresses* (Munich, 1985), edited by the International Congress of Egyptology, pp. 151–58. Studien zur altägyptischen Kultur, Beihefte 3. Hamburg: Helmut Buske.

    1989b   "Trade and Cult." In *The Religion of the Ancient Egyptians: Cognitive Structures and Popular Expressions* (Proceedings of Symposia in Uppsala and Bergen, 1987 and 1988), edited by Gertie Englund, pp. 95–108. Acta Universitatis Upsaliensis, Boreas 20. Uppsala: S. Academiae Upsaliensis.

    1992   "On the Root *nfr* and a Clever Remark on Embalming." In *The Heritage of Ancient Egypt: Studies in Honour of Erik Iversen*, edited by Jürgen Osing and Erland Kolding Nielsen, pp. 49–62. Carsten Niebuhr Institute Publications 13. Copenhagen: Museum Tusculanum Press and Carsten Niebuhr Institute of Ancient Near Eastern Studies.

    1994   "Prinsen og skæbnen og sprogvidenskaben." In *Fra dybet: Festskrift til John Strange i anledning af 60 års fødselsdagen den 20 juli 1994*, edited by Niels Peter Lemche and Mogens Müller, pp. 63–83. Forum for bibelsk eksegese 5. Copenhagen: Museum Tusculanums Forlag.

    1997   "On Categorization and Metaphorical Structuring: Some Remarks on Egyptian Art and Language." *Cambridge Archaeological Journal* 7/1: 71–104.

    2007   "Menstrual 'Taboo' in Ancient Egypt." *Journal of Near Eastern Studies* 66: 81–105.

Gardiner, Alan Henderson
    1917   "Personification." In *Encyclopedia of Religion and Ethics*, Volume 9, edited by James Hastings, pp. 787–92. New York: Scribner's.

    1931   *The Library of A. Chester Beatty: Description of a Hieratic Papyrus with a Mythological Story, Love-Songs, and Other Miscellaneous Texts*. The Chester Beatty Papyri 1. London: Oxford University Press.

    1932   *Late-Egyptian Stories*. Bibliotheca aegyptiaca 1. Brussels: Édition de la Fondation égyptologique Reine Élisabeth.

    1937   *Late Egyptian Miscellanies*. Bibliotheca aegyptiaca 7. Brussels: Édition de la Fondation égyptologique Reine Élisabeth.

Gee, John
    2006   "A New Look at the Conception of the Human Being in Ancient Egypt." Lecture given at the Copenhagen conference on *Being in Ancient Egypt: Thoughts on Agency, Materiality and Cognition*, 29–30 September 2006.

George, Beate
    1970   *Zu den altägyptischen Vorstellungen vom Schatten als Seele*. Habelts Dissertationsdrucke, Reihe Klassische Philologie 7. Bonn: Rudolf Habelts.

Gilula, Mordechai
    1976   "An Unusual Nominal Pattern in Middle Egyptian." *Journal of Egyptian Archaeology* 62: 160–75.

Grandet, Pierre
    1994   *Le Papyrus Harris I (BM 9999)*, Volume 1. Bibliothèque d'étude 109/1. Cairo: Institut français d'archéologie orientale.

1994   *Le Papyrus Harris I (BM 9999)*, Volume 2. Bibliothèque d'étude 109/2. Cairo: Institut français d'archéologie orientale.

1999   *Le Papyrus Harris I*, Volume 3: *Glossaire*. Bibliothèque d'étude 129. Cairo: Institut français d'archéologie orientale.

Gundlach, Rolf, and Christine Raedler

1997   *Selbstverständnis und Realität* (Akten des Symposiums zur ägyptischen Königsideologie in Mainz, 15–17 June 1995). Beiträge zur altägyptischen Königsideologie 1; Ägypten und Altes Testament 36/1. Wiesbaden: Harrassowitz.

Harris, John R.

1961   *Lexicographical Studies in Ancient Egyptian Minerals*. Deutsche Akademie der Wissenschaften zu Berlin, Institut für Orientforschung 54. Berlin: Akademie-Verlag.

Helck, Wolfgang

1957   *Urkunden der 18. Dynastie,* Part 20: *Historische Inschriften Amenohis' III.* Urkunden des ägyptischen Altertums 4/6. Leipzig: Hinrichs.

Hornung, Erik

1957   "Zur geschichtlichen Rolle des Königs in der 18. Dynastie." In "Festschrift zum 80. Geburtstag von Professor Dr. Hermann Junker," special edition of *Mitteilungen des Deutschen Archäologischen Instituts, Abteilung Kairo* 15: 120–33.

Hornung, Erik, and Elisabeth Staehelin

2006   *Neue Studien zum Sedfest*. Aegyptiaca Helvetica 20. Basel: Schwabe.

Iversen, Erik

1955   *Some Ancient Egyptian Paints and Pigments: A Lexicographical Study*. Det Kongelige Danske videnskabernes selskab, Historisk-filologiske meddelelser 34,4. Copenhagen: I komission hos Munksgaard.

Jasnow, Richard L.

1992   *A Late Period Hieratic Wisdom Text (P. Brooklyn 47.218.135)*. Studies in Ancient Oriental Civilization 52. Chicago: The Oriental Institute.

Jespersen, Otto

1924   *The Philosophy of Grammar*. London: Allen & Unwin.

Kitchen, Kenneth A.

1975   *Ramesside Inscriptions: Historical and Biographical*, Volume 1: *Ramesses I, Sethos I, and Contemporaries*. Oxford: B. H. Blackwell.

1979   *Ramesside Inscriptions: Historical and Biographical*, Volume 2: *Ramesses II, Royal Inscriptions*. Oxford: B. H. Blackwell.

1982   *Ramesside Inscriptions: Historical and Biographical*, Volume 4: *Merenptah and the Late 19th Dynasty*. Oxford: B. H. Blackwell.

1989   *Ramesside Inscriptions: Historical and Biographical*, Volume 7: *Addenda and Indexes*. Oxford: B. H. Blackwell.

Lange, Hans O.

1927   *Der magische Papyrus Harris*. Kongelige Danske videnskabernes selskab, Historisk-filosofiske meddelelser 14/2. Copenhagen: A. F. Høst & søn.

Lapp, Günther

2006   *Totenbuch Spruch 17*. Totenbuchtexte 1. Basel: Orientverlag.

Lekov, Teodor

     2004   "The Formula of the 'Giving of the Heart' in Ancient Egyptian Texts." *Journal of Egyptological Studies* 1: 33–60.

Letellier, Bernadette

     1980   "La destinée de deux enfants, un ostracon ramesside inédit." In *Livre du Centenaire 1880–1980*, edited by Jean Vercoutter, pp. 127–31. Mémoires publiés par les membres de l'Institut français d'archéologie orientale du Caire 104. Cairo: Institut français d'archéologie orientale.

Lévy-Bruhl, Lucien

     1914/16   "L'expression de la possession dans les langues mélanésiennes." *Mémoires de la Société de Linguistique* 19: 96–104.

Loprieno, Antonio

     1996   "The 'King's Novel.'" In *Ancient Egyptian Literature: History and Forms*, edited by Antonio Loprieno, pp. 277–95. Probleme der Ägyptologie 10. Leiden: Brill.

Mariette, Auguste

     1869–80   *Abydos: Description des fouilles exécutées sur l'emplacement de cette ville.* 2 volumes. Paris: Imprimerie nationale.

Mathieu, Bernhard

     1996   *La poésie amoureuse de l'Égypte ancienne: Recherches sur un genre littéraire au Nouvel Empire.* Bibliothèque d'étude 115. Cairo: Institut français d'archéologie orientale.

Morenz, Siegfried

     1969 (1975) "Der Schrecken Pharaos." In *Liber Amicorum: Studies in Honour of Professor Dr. C. J. Bleeker*, pp.113–37, Leiden: E. J. Brill, 1969. Cited after the reprint in Siegfried Morenz, *Religion und Geschichte des Alten Ägypten: Gesammelte Aufsätze*, edited by Elke Blumenthal and Siegfried Herrmann with the assistance of Angela Onasch, pp. 139–50. Weimar: Hermann Böhlaus Nachfolger, 1975.

Moret, Alexandre

     1902   *Du caractère religieux de la royauté pharaonique.* Annales du Musée Guimet, Bibliothèque d'études 15. Paris: Ernest Leroux.

Mrsich, Tycho Q.

     1968   *Untersuchungen zur Hausurkunde des Alten Reiches: Ein Beitrag zum altägyptischen Stiftungsrecht.* Münchner ägyptologische Studien 13. Berlin: Bruno Hessling.

Müller, Dieter

     1966   "Die Zeugung durch das Herz in Religion und Medizin der Ägypter." *Orientalia* 35: 247–74.

O'Connor, David B., and David P. Silverman

     1995   *Ancient Egyptian Kingship.* Probleme der Ägyptologie 9. Leiden and New York: Brill.

Osing, Jürgen

     1980   "Libyen, Libyer." *Lexikon der Ägyptologie*, Volume 3: *Horhekenu–Megeb*, edited by Wolfgang Helck and Wolfhart Westendorf, columns 1015–33. Wiesbaden: Harrassowitz.

Otto, Rudolf

    1987   *Das Heilige: Über das Irrationale in der Idee des Göttlichen und sein Verhältnis zum Rationalen.* Beck'sche Reihe 328. Munich: C. H. Beck.

Polotsky, Hans Jakob

    1968   "The 'Weak' Plural Article in Bohairic." *Journal of Egyptian Archaeology* 54: 243–45.

Porter, Bertha, and Rosalind L. B. Moss

    1960   *Topographical Bibliography of Ancient Egyptian Hieroglyphic Texts, Reliefs, and Paintings,* Volume 1: *The Theban Necropolis,* Part 1: *Private Tombs.* Second edition. Oxford: Clarendon Press.

Posener, Georges

    1960   *De la divinité du Pharaon.* Cahiers de la Société asiatique 15. Paris: Imprimerie nationale.

    1976   *L'enseignement loyaliste: Sagesse égyptienne du Moyen Empire.* Hautes études orientales 5. Geneva: Librairie Droz.

Quack, Joachim Friedrich

    1992   *Studien zur Lehre für Merikare.* Göttinger Orientforschungen, 4th Reihe, Ägypten 23. Wiesbaden: Harrassowitz.

    1993   "Ein neuer ägyptischer Weisheitstext." *Die Welt des Orients* 24: 5–19.

    1994   *Die Lehren des Ani: Ein neuägyptischer Weisheitstext in seinem kulturellen Umfeld.* Orbis Biblicus et Orientalis 141. Freiburg: Universitätsverlag; Göttingen: Vandenhoeck & Ruprecht.

Quaegebeur, Jan

    1975   *Le dieu égyptien Shaï dans la religion et l'onomastique.* Orientalia Lovaniensia Analecta 2. Leuven: Leuven University Press.

Rosén, H. B.

    1959   "Die Ausdrucksform für 'veräusserlichen' und 'unveräusserlichen Besitz' im Frühgriechischen." *Lingua* 8: 264–93.

Schott, Siegfried

    1964   *Der Denkstein Sethos' I. für die Kapelle Ramses' I. in Abydos.* Nachrichten von der Akademie der Wissenschaften zu Göttingen, Philologisch-historische Klasse 1964/1. Göttingen: Vandenhoeck & Ruprecht.

Seeber, Christine

    1976   *Untersuchungen zur Darstellung des Totengerichts im Alten Ägypten.* Münchner ägyptologische Studien 35. Munich and Berlin: Deutscher Kunstverlag.

Sethe, Kurt

    1909   *Urkunden der 18. Dynastie: Historisch-biographische Urkunden.* Urkunden des ägyptischen Altertums 4. Leipzig: J. C. Hinrichs.

Shisha-Halevy, Ariel

    1986   *Coptic Grammatical Categories: Structural Studies in the Syntax of Shenoutean Sahidic.* Analecta Orientalia 53. Rome: Pontificium Institutum Biblicum.

    2007   "Determination-Signalling Environment in Old and Middle Egyptian: Work-Notes and Reflections." In *Studies in Semitic and General Linguistics in Honor of Gideon Goldenberg,* edited by Tali Bar and Eran Cohen, pp. 223–54. Alter Orient und Altes Testament 334. Münster: Ugarit-Verlag.

Simpson, William Kelly

1977   "Amor dei: *nṯr mrr rmṯ m tꜣ wꜣ* (Sh.Sai. 147–148) and the Embrace." In *Fragen an die altägyptische Literatur: Studien zum Gedenken an Eberhard Otto*, edited by Jan Assmann, Erika Feucht, and Reinhard Grieshammer, pp. 493–98. Wiesbaden: Reichert Verlag.

Sottas, Henri

1913   *La préservation de la propriété funéraire dans l'ancienne Égypte*. Bibliothèque de l'École des Hautes Études, Sciences philologiques et historiques 205. Paris: Librairie ancienne Honoré Champion.

Spalinger, Anthony

1981   "Considerations on the Hittite Treaty between Egypt and Hatti." *Studien zur altägyptischen Kultur* 9: 299–358.

Stern, Ludwig C.

1880   *Koptische Grammatik*. Leipzig: T. O. Weigel.

Textor de Ravisi, Anatole Arthur

1878   "L'âme et le corps d'après la théogonie égyptienne." In *Congrès Provincial des orientalistes français: Compte-rendu de la première session, Saint-Étienne, 1875*, Volume 2: *Égyptologie*, pp. 169–420. Saint Étienne: Théolier.

Till, Walter C.

1955   "Zum Sprachtbau im Ägyptischen." In *Ägyptologische Studien*, edited by Otto Firchow, pp. 322–37. Deutsche Akademie der Wissenschaften zu Berlin, Institut für Orientforschung 29. Berlin: Akademie-Verlag.

1961   *Koptische Grammatik (saïdischer Dialekt) mit Bibliographie, Lesestücken und Wörterverzeichnissen*. Second edition. Lehrbücher für das Studium der orientalischen Sprachen 1. Leipzig: Verlag Enzyklopädie.

Troy, Lana

1986   *Patterns of Queenship in Ancient Egyptian Myth and History*. Acta Universitatis Upsaliensis, Boreas 14. Uppsala: Universitet; Stockholm: Almquist & Wiksell.

te Velde, Herman

1990   "Some Remarks on the Concept of 'Person' in the Ancient Egyptian Culture." In *Concept of Person in Religion and Thought*, edited by Hans G. Kippenberg, Yme B. Kuiper, and Andy F. Sanders, pp. 83–101. Religion and Reason 37. Berlin: Mouton de Gruyter.

Vernus, Pascal

2001   *Sagesses de l'Égypte pharaonique*. La salamandre. Paris: Imprimerie nationale.

Westendorf, Wolfhart

1965–77   *Koptisches Handwörterbuch*. 2 volumes. Heidelberg: Carl Winter/Universitätsverlag.

Wiedemann, Alfred

1878   "L'immortalité de l'ame chez les anciens égyptiens." In *Congrès Provincial des orientalistes français: Compte-rendu de la première session, Saint-Étienne, 1875*, Volume 2: *Égyptologie*, pp. 159–67. Saint Étienne: Théolier.

Wildung, Dietrich

1973   "Göttlichkeitsstufen des Pharao." *Orientalistische Literaturzeitung* 68: 549–65.

Willems, Harco

   1988   *Chests of Life: A Study of the Typology and Conceptual Development of Middle King-
               dom Standard Class Coffins.* Mededelingen en verhandelingen van het Vooraziatisch-
               Egyptisch Genootschap 'Ex Orinte Lux' 25. Leiden: Ex Oriente Lux.

   1996   *The Coffin of Heqata (Cairo JdE 36418): A Case Study of Egyptian Funerary Culture
               of the Early Middle Kingdom.* Orientalia Lovaniensia Analecta 70. Leuven: Uitgeverij
               Peeters en Departement Oriëntalistiek.

5

TOUCHED BY THE GODS: VISUAL EVIDENCE FOR THE DIVINE STATUS OF RULERS IN THE ANCIENT NEAR EAST

IRENE J. WINTER, HARVARD UNIVERSITY

From the very first inscriptional evidence, all Mesopotamian rulers are said to have been touched by the gods in one way or another, although only some Mesopotamian rulers were explicitly accorded divine status, and only in some periods. In order to explore this association with the divine with respect to the moments/modes/metaphors of visual representation of the ruler across the Mesopotamian sequence, it is important to rehearse some of the issues surrounding "kingship" itself; and it is also important to pose the question of the commonalities and/or divergences between visual and verbal representation. It may be useful to anticipate conclusions at this point as well: that if one distinguishes between the sacred inscribed within notions of rule — that is, sacral kingship — from the explicit ascription of divinity to the ruler — that is, divine kingship — then the Mesopotamian ruler was *never not* accorded special status sanctioned by the gods. From earliest attestations, he participated in and was touched by the divine, and so occupied a space, if not co-terminus with that of a god, then at least that of an intermediary between god and man.

There are at least four useful categories of textual evidence related to kingship upon which we may draw in Mesopotamian studies to inflect readings of royal imagery:

1. those dealing with the origins of the institution of rule
2. those articulating criteria for recruitment
3. those describing the necessary attributes of the effective ruler
4. those designating the signs by which such effectiveness could be recognized

These text categories make clear that the institution of kingship was said to have originated with the gods (Jacobsen 1939; Klein 2006), and individuals ultimately designated to rule then claimed, or were accorded in official text, special qualities that led to their selection — including purposeful shaping by the gods — and manifest physical signs that indicated both their appropriateness for selection and their ability to govern.[1] The texts further permit one to explore the relationship between the ruler and the divine sphere, as well as between "divine kingship" and imagery. In the paper that follows, I shall not confine myself to images associated with periods in which rulers were explicitly accorded divine status — the Akkadian and the Neo-Sumerian periods of the third millennium B.C. — but rather, starting from there, will look at a wide range of images and periods in which rulers were described and treated as if they were born of the gods and/or manifested divine signs. My proposition is that, even when not explicitly accorded divinity per se, rulers nevertheless could be represented verbally and visually as if they occupied a place in society that merited divine attributes, qualities, and status;

---

[1] See "Königslisten und Chroniken" in Edzard 1980a and Grayson 1980; and "Königtum" in Edzard 1980b and Seax 1980; also Jacobsen 1939 and Klein 2006.

and furthermore, that the ascription of divine power within the religious system was a necessary component of the exercise of rule, whether or not the ruler was himself considered divine.

In general, I am interested in the nature of kingship in Mesopotamia not as a frozen category, but as one marked by the tensions between continuity and change within the developing
polities attested by the historical record. In this regard, I would stress the importance of the
socio-political as well as religious forces that may be said to explain the association of rulers
with divinity, the hesitation in certain periods to reify the ruler as a god, and the necessity in
other periods to identify the ruler as a god. The dialectic between these two forces plays itself
out in interesting ways from the third to the first millennium B.C. and can be observed in the
artifactual record no less than the textual. It should be stressed from the outset that the visual
and the verbal interact with complexity: sometimes in parallel harmonies, sometimes in coun-
terpoint, sometimes with apparent subversion of one by the other; and for this reason, there is
progress to be made by observing the variances as well as the homologies in both rhetoric and
representational strategy.

To pursue these patterns, it is useful to begin with historical moments in which there is an
explicit association of the ruler with divine status: the reigns of Naram-Sîn and his son Šar-ka-
li-šarri of the Akkadian period, and the reigns of the post-Ur-Namma rulers of Neo-Sumerian
Ur: his son Šulgi, and the latter's successors, Amar-Sîn, Šu-Sîn, and Ibbi-Sîn.

Naram-Sîn of Agade (ca. 2254–2218 B.C.)[2] was the first ruler to assume the divine deter-
minative/cuneiform sign for dingir/god in Sumerian before the writing of his proper name in
inscriptions. Scholars responding to his Victory Stele, found displaced at Susa and apparently
originally erected in Sippar (see Harper et al. 1992: 166–68), have tended to see in his wearing of a horned helmet on campaign a visual indicator of the king's divinity — echoing the
multi-tiered horned crown worn by the gods as depicted on contemporary monuments (fig.
5.1). I have argued elsewhere, however, that the stele should not be read as the king acting as
sole agent, as if fully divine (Winter 1996). His physical body reflects the perfection of one
accorded divine status. However, emblems of deities were carried with him into battle; the
neck bead he wears was probably a protective ornament invoking divine protection; and his
headdress with its single tier of horns echoes, if anything, the status of a minor deity rather
than a fully established member of the high pantheon. In text, Naram-Sîn was the first to take
on the title, "King of the Four Quarters" along with that of "God of the Land," in denoting his
elevated status — fully consonant with the expansionist tendencies of the Akkadian period that
have led some colleagues to refer to this period as one of "empire." I would resist this term, arguing instead for the establishment of a "nation-state" (see Fallers 1974; Bhabha 1990), unifying formerly autonomous polities under a centralized rule. The confluence of political change
and title/status changes (plural) suggests a fusion of the political and the religious. Whether
consciously, as an overtly political act, or unconsciously, motivated by culturally generated
requisites, the move was likely to have been driven by engines not unlike those marking the
shift from Republican to Imperial Rome.[3]

[2] Note: I have used dates consistent with those published
by J. A. Brinkman in Oppenheim 1964: 335–47, which
follow the "Middle Chronology." In actuality, the "Low
Chronology" is presently thought to be more accurate;
however, it has not yet been standardized with approximate dates for all rules.

[3] Fishwick 1987; Price 1987; and the essays in Small
1996. Note that here, too, Augustus was elevated not
only to supreme ruler, but also to the status of a god. See
also Wengrow 2006 and Hamilton 2006 for the importance of the royal body.

Conclusion: Visual strategies were needed to mark this important shift in the conceptualization of the ruler no less than verbal ones. The two seem to affirm each other, indicating a difference from previous rulers, but with some attempt not to overstate status. Even so, the visual strategy developed by Naram-Sîn seems not to have been sufficiently successful to be continued into later periods.[4]

Ur-Namma of Ur (2112–2095 B.C.) was accorded divine status after his death by his son and heir Šulgi (2094–2047 B.C.), who also took on this status for himself and laid the foundations for its assumption by succeeding Neo-Sumerian rulers.[5] A major monument is associated with Ur-Namma, in the form of a bifacial stele that includes a fragmentary inscription naming the ruler.[6] I tend to believe that Šulgi was in fact the commissioner of the Stele of Ur-Namma found at Ur; but whether or not this is so, it is interesting to note that the representational strategy employed for a major monument does not follow the model of the Stele of Naram-Sîn, despite the fact that the earlier stele was likely to have still been visible at Sippar, since it was available for capture well into the second millennium B.C. when carried off to Susa. Instead, quite traditional modes of spatial division into sequential narrative registers and an iconography of divine service grounded in earlier periods were employed on the obverse of the Stele of Ur-Namma to show the ruler clearly subservient to his god(s) (e.g., fig. 5.2), following Sumerian monuments of the mid-third millennium. This may simply reflect regional/cultural difference between Sumerians and Akkadians; however, I am inclined to think it is more subtle and more important than mere imprinting of ethnic/linguistic identity. On the reverse of the stele (fig. 5.3), a figure at the lower left is dressed in royal cap and garment yet seems to be the object of a libation (Canby 2001: pl. 41; Börker-Klähn 1982: pl. H). This figure may represent the living ruler subject to cultic action; it may represent a deceased ruler undergoing rites appropriate to the replenishing of the commemorative royal image ("mouth washing"/Sumerian ka luḫ; Akkadian *mīs pî*) in the chapel dedicated to rulers known as the ki-a-nag; or, as suggested by Mogens Larsen (pers. comm.), it could represent an image of the hero Gilgamesh as eponymous divine ruler, who was declared to have been two-thirds god, one-third human (George 1999: 2 I 48). Each possibility raises interesting questions, especially why, if the epic was first composed in the Neo-Sumerian period as is commonly assumed, Gilgamesh should have taken on such representational power. Conceivably, the heroic is stressed precisely in a period in which charismatic leadership becomes an essential rhetorical and practical tool of governance (Michalowski 1991). For the period marks not only a return to Sumerian cultural and linguistic dominance, but is also situated *after* the fall of Agade at the hands of foreign invaders, which in some later literature is cited as retribution for Akkadian hubris.

The state governed by the Third Dynasty of Ur was marked by territorial expansion and an increasingly complex bureaucracy consolidating, even improving upon, the governance structures established for the nation-state in the Akkadian period. For this system, I have argued elsewhere that a fourth tier of authority was required in the central administrative and social hierarchy, subsuming the three-tiered hierarchy of the earlier autonomous city-state (fig. 5.4; Winter 1991). Neo-Sumerian rulers at Ur permit themselves/are permitted to take on the divine determinative, after a gap reflecting both the Gutian phase of control and a return to indepen-

---

[4] Unfortunaltely, Naram-Sîn's son and successor, Šar-ka-li-šarri (2217–2193 B.C.), has not left sufficient material traces to permit us to address this issue with other than textual data for his reign.

[5] See Hallo 1957 for an early study of this phenomenon.

[6] Canby 2001 is the most recent study of this monument. See also Winter 2003 and Suter 2005 for reviews.

dence on the part of a number of city-states, such as Lagash and Uruk. They also permitted themselves verbal representation in literature, such as the Šulgi hymns, congruent with this divine status (Klein 1981). However, with respect to formal monuments such as the Ur-Namma stele and statues of Šulgi bearing a sacrificial animal or a libation vessel, visual emphasis seems rather upon traditional religious service.[7]

At the same time, one of the Sumerian Temple Hymns recorded in the Old Babylonian period is dedicated to the "Ehursag of Šulgi" at Ur (Sjöberg 1969: 24; discussed in Klein 2006). While a number of tomb structures and a royal palace were discovered within the sacred precinct of Ur itself, including one tomb containing a fragment of a stone vase inscribed with the name of Šulgi (Woolley 1974: 9), no consecrated temples to any of the Ur III rulers has been identified archaeologically (see discussion below, however, and by Reichel, this volume, for textual evidence). Klein has suggested that the "Ehursag" may therefore have been a reference to the royal palace, not a temple per se, despite the fact that its description in the hymn is not unlike that of other temples; and he further notes that the kings of Ur "never had a shrine erected for them in Nippur, seat of the supreme god Enlil," although their votive statues were placed in the deity's shrine (Klein 2006: 121; see also Klein 1991; Kutscher 1974).

The distinction between temple and royal palace may be ours, not theirs, for both are written using the same Sumerian sign: É, signifying "house/dwelling/seat." The architectural remains of the Neo-Sumerian-phase "Palace of the Rulers" at Tell Asmar/ancient Eshnunna in the Diyala region with its attached temple/shrine intended for worship of Šū-Sîn of Ur (2037–2029 B.C.) constitutes the one concrete example of a cultic locus for the worship of a deified Ur III ruler. Its plan with a niched cella on straight axis from a central court is distinctly *not* that of the building referred to as the Ehursag in the Nanna precinct at Ur, which instead resembles the central quarters of the Eshnunna palace itself, with its great hall and throne room (cf. Frankfort, Lloyd, and Jacobsen 1940: 9–42, pl. 1; Reichel 2001: discussion 28f.; Woolley 1974: pl. 56). It is difficult to generalize from such meager archaeological information, especially when the cultic calendar of Ur records festivals related to the royal cult (Hallo 1988; Cohen 1993; Sallaberger 1993), but these festivals could well represent commemorative ceremonies to deceased, not living, rulers.

Should the absence of royal shrines to living kings in the center and their presence in the absorbed polities of the periphery reflect a pattern, as Frankfort noted, then one could conclude that strategies of control including cultic activities directed to the (divine) ruler were more actively deployed in the periphery of the polity, and not, or less so, within the center. However, syntheses of Ur III rulership (e.g., Barrelet 1974; Sallaberger 1999) suggest that in a tradition in which there was no separation between church and state, cultic activity directed to the Ur III rulers would have been appropriate both in the center and in the periphery, albeit for different reasons.

Conclusion: On the basis of preserved monuments, visual strategies in Ur III may have been more conservative and traditional than verbal strategies, possibly reflecting a controlled manipulation of the medium so as *not* to be considered stepping beyond the bounds of appropriate decorum in articulating the rulers' relationships to the gods. Whether the intended audience for such a hedged visual strategy was the gods themselves or the viewing public cannot

---

[7] See, for example, works discussed in Civil and Zettler 1989. The role of the ruler as cultic officiant/priest and his divine status in the Ur III period is too complex to summarize here. Elevation to deity was once thought to have been an artifact of the performance by the king of the "sacred marriage" ritual; for more recent discussions, see, among others, Wilcke 1974, Cooper 1993, and Steinkeller 1999.

be determined; however, it is important to note the *in*-congruence and lack of homology in text and image in this case, and to see in it the possibility that different media may be deployed differently in a given period, not necessarily as contradictions, but as carefully choreographed strategies when the communication act has different goals or different audiences within a single socio-cultural-political system.

Furthermore, the apparent association between political strategies of control and worship of the deified king in the Third Dynasty of Ur strengthens the hypothesis of fusion between the political and the religious in the elevation of the ruler to the status of divine and the ensuing cultic activities surrounding the person of the ruler.

DISCUSSION

A great deal has been written about individual Mesopotamian kings, and about the institution of kingship, since Henri Frankfort published his monumental *Kingship and the Gods* in 1948. The book offered perspective on Mesopotamian man's search for integration between the forces of nature and the human spirit as he reached toward his gods — a process understood to have been mediated through the office of the king.

Frankfort dealt with aspects of the "sacred marriage," as performed by the ruler with or as divinity, the divine parentage claimed by individual rulers, and the worship of the ruler in temple shrines (Frankfort 1948: 295–312). By suggesting that the Mesopotamian kings actually deified were "worshipped only in the shrines of cities which they dominated," and not in their state centers, he implied the political connotations of the process, but suggested that this was a function of one period only: the Third Dynasty of Ur (ibid., p. 301). Focus overall was on the role of the king as mediator with respect to divine control over the forces of nature.

It is useful to see this study in light of the scholarly generation to which it belonged: contemporary with work on divine kingship in the ancient Near East by C. J. Gadd (1948) and Ivan Engnell (1943), but also contemporary with the writings of theologians Paul Tillich, Reinhold Niebuhr, and Martin Buber. Frankfort's approach echoed that of the theologians in particular, seeing ancient religion and man's relationship to the gods as the driving force in the construction of institutions of rule.[8] Insightful though *Kingship and the Gods* was for its time, implicit throughout was a focus on cosmogony and an evolutionary model of early, mythopoetic man, who would eventually develop into the spiritually-questing Judeo-Christian monotheist. Left out was a complex exploration of the political relationship between the institution of kingship and the formation, development, and maintenance of the early state; and while this aspect has been explored in more recent discussions of Mesopotamian kingship (see, e.g., Heimpel 1992; Lambert 1998; Westenholz 2000; Wilcke 1974), the degree to which a semiotics of imagery can contribute to the discussion remains less examined.

I would like, therefore, to examine the visual and verbal representations of a sample of Mesopotamian rulers not accorded the divine determinative before their written name — for example, Eannatum and his contemporaries of the Early Dynastic period, Gudea of Lagash of the Neo-Sumerian period preceding the "deification" of the rulers of Ur, Hammurapi of Babylon in the Old Babylonian period, Tukulti-Ninurta I of the Middle Assyrian period, and

---

[8] This focus is evident throughout Frankfort's work, made especially clear in the subtitle of his typological, chronological, and iconographical study: *Cylinder Seals:* *Essay on the Art* and Religion *of the Ancient Near East* (1939; emphasis mine).

a variety of kings of the Neo-Assyrian period — in order to pursue the hypotheses that a) there was *no* historical phase within the Mesopotamian sequence in which the ruler was not closely aligned by ascribed birth, attributes, or privilege with the gods; b) there *is* a correlation between periods in which the divinity of rulers was explicitly acknowledged or claimed and periods in which political demands of the state seemed to call for a central and transcendent authority figure; and c) there is not always a perfect homology between text and image.

Eannatum of Lagash (ca. 2500 B.C.) and the "Royal Tombs of Ur": The Early Dynastic period, of the second half of the third millennium B.C., marked the consolidation of the city-state as it had developed in the former Uruk period. In the course of the third millennium, whether in the "Sumerian King List" or the so-called "Eridu Genesis," we see the origins of kingship preserved in text as an artifact of divine agency (Jacobsen 1939, 1991: 116; Klein 2006). We are told that kingship descended from on high — that is, via the gods — and was transmitted to man along with other attributes of civilization. Identifiable by three distinctive and exclusive insignia — the scepter, royal headgear, and the throne — the king was to advise his people, oversee labor, build and administer cities, protect the land, provide abundance, and perform ritual services to the gods.

Unlike ancient Egypt, the king was not ontologically defined as divine, but he was clearly at the top of the social and bureaucratic hierarchy. Although the origination texts themselves significantly post-date the origins of the institution of kingship, and might therefore best be understood as sanctioning, if not rationalizing, the hierarchy, it is still clear from reform texts, such as that of Uru-KA-gi-na of Lagash toward the end of the Early Dynastic Lagash ruling dynasty (Steible 1982), that negotiations/tensions concerning the degrees of appropriate authority and power of the ruler continued for some time.

What seems clear is that a single office of the highest decision-making authority is an absolute requisite of a complex bureaucracy, such as is needed to run an urban state (Wright 1977; Johnson 1978). That the Sumerian term for king, lugal, is derived from two cuneiform signs/words — lú "man," + gal "great/big" — has led some scholars to suggest an evolutionary development from the "big men" of societies manifesting incipient stratification to rulers of archaic states (Johnson and Earle 1987: chapters 8–11; and see also Hallo 1996: 190).

Into the Early Dynastic historical phase of state consolidation fall the assemblages of the "Royal Tombs of Ur," particularly the inlaid panels belonging to the work known as the Standard of Ur, and large, free-standing monuments, particularly the Stele of Eannatum, also known as the Stele of the Vultures, found at Girsu, within the city-state of Lagash. Although the title "king" is attested at Ur and not at Lagash, where the term used to designate authority is énsi, meaning literally "steward" or "governor," in both cases the words represent the highest political office, of which there is only one title holder at a time.[9]

On the upper register of both the "battle" and "banquet" sides of the Standard of Ur (Woolley 1934: pls. 91–92), the principal figure is represented larger in scale than the rest of the actors in the two narratives — receiving prisoners as the result of victory on the one, seated alone facing a group of males at banquet on the other. In accord with the correlation between "rank" and "size" discussed by Meyer Schapiro (1969) for Western Medieval art, and known to pertain in ancient Egypt, this visual strategy suggests that ways of signaling the lú gal as a

---

[9] See Jacobsen 1991; see also Klein 2006; Heimpel 1992: 7–8 for the occasional use of the title lugal in Lagash, and its relationship to concepts of rule.

literal "big man" had been developed in composition along with favored motifs in iconography, allowing for visual recognition of his status.

For the stele, it has been argued that the visual program negotiated between depiction of the god Ningirsu as agent of the victory on the obverse and the narrative of that victory through the ruler on the reverse (fig. 5.5) reflects the emergence of the ruler as agent into the public sphere (Winter 1985). The text inscribed on the stele proclaims Eannatum to have been sired by a high god and suckled by a goddess (Steible 1982). These attributes at the practical level may be said to constitute a way of stressing the divine legitimacy of royal power (Winter 1985: 26), in order to strengthen his earthly authority. At a more cosmic level, however, this ascription can also be said to reflect the special, nearly divine status of the ruler in the very first period in which we also have the title "king" preserved in text and royal palaces identified archaeologically.

Conclusion: From the beginning of the attestation of the royal title in the consolidated city-state, well before the determinative for "god" and divinity were officially and explicitly ascribed to rulers, we have both text and imagery suggesting that the ruler/king was literally represented as a "big man," larger in scale than others, and in filial relationship to the gods, implying thereby his higher-than-human, if not explicitly divine, status.

Gudea of Lagash (ca. 2110 B.C.): Close homologies can be demonstrated between the royal hymns of Gudea and those of Šulgi of Ur, as well as the hymns' regular performance in temple ritual (Klein 1989: 299). Indeed, it has been suggested that royal hymns were probably initiated in the reign of Gudea (or one of his Lagash predecessors, ibid., p. 301). In addition, it is clear from statuary inscriptions as well as longer texts that sculptures of Gudea were installed in temples and intended to be the focus of cult offerings in commemorative chapels (e.g., fig. 5.6), a process carried on well after death, and, in the case of Gudea, into the hegemony of Ur.[10]

In recruitment for office at the practical and local level, Gudea was supremely eligible as he had been married to a daughter of the prior ruler. At the rhetorical level, however, Gudea refers to the goddess Nanše as his "mother" (Edzard 1997: 70, cylinder A, col. i, 29). It is further stated that he had been selected for rule because he was physically outstanding, his personal god Ningišzida making his "head stand out in the assembly" (see discussion, Winter 1989: 578). Simultaneously, various physical properties of the ruler — including breadth of body/chest, full-muscled arm, and width of ear signaling inner qualities of fullness, strength, and wisdom — were declared to have been gifts of specific gods. These properties were simultaneously stated in text and represented in sculpture, as on the well-known seated "Statue B" of Gudea (fig. 5.6). Epithets and body shape thus functioned together as part of a code, allowing viewers/readers/subjects to perceive him as an ideal ruler bearing divinely-apportioned qualities which, by implication, were *not* legible in others.

And yet, as argued by Louis Marin with respect to images of Louis XIV, the king is only truly ideal *in his image* (Marin 1988: 13; emphasis mine)! That is, the rhetorical construction of the royal image was intended to convey the ruler's supra-human qualities, making of him one literally constructed by the gods, hence *of* the gods. I would argue that this is no less true of Gudea than it is of the ideal and "deified" rulers who preceded him in the Akkadian period (e.g., Naram-Sîn of Agade), or of the following Ur III rulers, who shared with him praise hymns and ritual attention associated with divinity and a royal cult of commemoration. Indeed,

---

[10] See discussion in Perlov 1980 and Winter 1992; texts in Steible 1991 and Edzard 1997.

the redating of Gudea and his dynasty to an overlap with the beginning of the Third Dynasty (Steinkeller 1988) brings this shared cultic practice into much closer cultural and historical unity.

Conclusion: Ernst Renan asserted more than a century ago (1882) that "of all cults, that of the ancestors is the most legitimate" in the organization of the nation-state, for "the legacy of memories" is what permits the nation to take on a past, as well as a unified present (reprinted 1990: 19). Given the evidence for cultic observance directed toward the images of Gudea in commemorative chapels, and the importance of ancestral observances in the period (Sallaberger 1999: 259), the bestowal upon Gudea of various divinely accorded physical correlates of authority and rule, and the designation of him as "outstanding" among all citizens of Lagash, one may suggest that the behaviors (and beliefs?) associated with divine status accorded the royal person were *de facto* if not *de jure* maintained in the interim between the formally marked/ deified rulers of Agade and those of Ur in the Neo-Sumerian period. And yet, on monuments, again, as for the rulers of Ur, iconographic focus was upon ritual service by the ruler to the gods.[11] In short, even in a period of rhetorically emphasized piety on the part of the ruler and the absence of an explicit divine determinative, Gudea remains one shaped by the gods, with privileged access to the divine and to cultic observance, and so distinct from ordinary humans.

Hammurapi of Babylon (ca. 1792–1750 B.C.): The same may be said of the rulers following upon the Third Dynasty of Ur: those of the phases of the hegemony of Isin, Larsa, and Babylon. Foundation cones and royal hymns emphasize the cultic service and temple-building activities of post-Ur III rulers.[12] Their titularies only rarely include a divine determinative. Yet, Rīm-Sîn, whose name was written with the divine determinative from year 22 onward (ibid., p. 40 n. 10), is referred to as "our sun-god" in an Old Babylonian copy of a text thought to have been composed for his performance in the "sacred marriage" (Brisch 2006: 40 n. 10; van Dijk, Hussey, and Götze 1985: 28, #24, line 17); and Hammurapi, in a tablet originating in Sippar, is referred to as "god of (his) land" (Frayne 1990: 344–45, #10, line 1; implied also, perhaps, in ibid., 333–36, #2, lines 70–81).

For our purposes, it is regrettable that we do not have a larger corpus of royal imagery to work with from this period, particularly for the Isin and Larsa rulers. To the extent that Rīm-Sîn seems to have been modeling himself on Naram-Sîn of Agade (P. Michalowski, pers. comm.), one would want to know whether the literary references could also have been reflected in the visual sphere.

The Old Babylonian period rulers, Hammurapi in particular, are slightly better attested. Two recent studies are devoted to the historical person of the well-known ruler (Charpin 2003; Van De Mieroop 2005), the former devoting a chapter to the relationship between the king and the gods. If the rhetorical stress is on divine service in text, this is surely reflected in the votive bronze said to be from Larsa and dedicated to the god Marduk for the life of Hammurapi (fig. 5.7; Moortgat 1969: fig. 218). The image (referred to by the Sumerian term alam in the text inscribed on the base; indeed, alam ša_3-ne-ša_4, translated as "suppliant statue" by Frayne 1990: 360: 2002, line 8) shows the kneeling ruler with right hand raised before his face/nose, in a devotional attitude.[13] The same arm gesture is seen on a stele fragment of unknown prov-

---

[11] For example, the steles of Gudea: Börker-Klähn 1982: pls. 35–92; Suter 2000: 161–275 and figs. 16–19.

[12] For example, Frayne 1990: 270–80 for Rīm-Sîn of Larsa and pp. 345–46, 352–55 for Hammurapi; also Van De Mieroop 2005: 12–13; Brisch 2006: 40, 43.

[13] For the inscription, see Frayne 1990: 360, 2002: line 8; for the gesture, see Magen 1986: 104–08.

enance in the British Museum dedicated to a goddess for the life of Hammurapi by one Itur-Ashdum, and on the upper portion of the diorite stele containing the Laws of Hammurapi (fig. 5.8), where the ruler is shown before the seated sun-god Shamash, although in these cases, the king is depicted standing (Moortgat 1969: figs. 208–09). One must be careful not to generalize royal subservience and servitude from this corpus, however, reminded of similar devotional imagery deployed by the kings of the Third Dynasty of Ur (discussed above) at the same time as they were celebrated as divine.

On the Law Stele (fig. 5.8), Hammurapi is depicted making direct eye contact with (the image of) the deity as he receives the authority to promulgate his laws. His head is actually slightly higher than that of the seated sun-god, and the compositional balance suggests a relationship born not of subservience but of almost parity. The image serves as testimony to the king's special relationship with the god, legitimizing his role and special status as righteous ruler (Akk. *šar mīšarim*).[14] It thus corresponds well to the verbal references to the king in the prologue of the text inscribed on the stele. There, he is said to have been called/named by the gods to rule, and to "rise like the god Shamash over all humankind" (Roth 1997: 76–77: i.27–49). In the epilogue, we find the king described as one whose role has been granted by Enlil, who has been charged by Marduk to be the shepherd of his people, and bestowed with weapons/might by the gods Zababa and Ishtar (ibid., 133: xlvii.9–58) — all corresponding to the textual tropes of divine recruitment and endowment mentioned at the beginning of this paper.

These same qualities and attributes are to be found in others of Hammurapi's royal inscriptions, as well as those of his successor, Samsu-iluna, where emphasis is placed on the ruler as "favorite" of one god (^{d}Enlil) or "beloved" of another (^{d}Ninlil); looked upon with favor by a third (^{d}Shamash); and endowed with an awe-inspiring radiant aura/*melammu* by a fourth (^{d}An) (Frayne 1990: 337: #3, lines 7–8; 335: #2, lines 1–3; 344: #10, line 2; and see discussion Brisch 2006: 42). The social and political implications of being favored by/beloved by deity (Sumerian ki-áĝ, Akkadian *râmu*) have been discussed recently by Jaques (2006: 123–45), suggesting that the term is used to demonstrate not only an emotional relationship, but also — conjoined with or independent of emotion — one of partnership. At the same time as this partnership has implications of obedience, loyalty, and cultic service on the part of the recipient of (divine) love, it nonetheless serves to mark the beloved as one of special standing.

Conclusion: The favor shown to Hammurapi by the gods and his special position as a result of that favor, along with the occasional references that suggest a status verging on divine, seems to outweigh the absence of consistent use of the divine determinative in the writing of the royal name. Brisch has noted (2006: 40 n. 10) that "it is not clear how far-reaching the consequences" of the attested instances of divinization were in the Isin-Larsa and Old Babylonian periods, and she has argued that the topic of divine kingship in the Old Babylonian period is in need of re-examination. For the present, it would seem that by implication kingship was no less sacral in the early second millennium B.C. than it had been in the third, even if only rarely explicitly marked as divine.

Tukulti-Ninurta I of Assyria (1243–1207 B.C.): Peter Machinist has recently demonstrated (2006: 160–64) that a number of the ambiguities implying the blurred boundaries between the ruler and the gods that we have seen in earlier periods are also evident in the Middle Assyrian period (Machinist 2006: 160–64). His analysis follows upon that of Kirk Grayson (1971), who had noted an increase in the textual rhetoric claiming the special relationship of the king to the

---

[14] On this image and its role on the stele, see Winter 1997; also Slanski 2007: esp. 49.

gods in the reign of Tukulti-Ninurta I. Machinist cites the text known as the Epic of Tukulti-Ninurta in order to demonstrate instances in which the ruler's "unequalled status before the gods" is articulated. Ascribed aspects and/or qualities include the radiant aura said to surround the ruler (*melammu* and congeners), as a manifest sign of properties and powers held by the gods and conferred at their discretion upon the king. Assertions of divine engendering similar to those of Eannatum and Gudea also pertain. In addition, the king's body is described as "the flesh of the gods" (Akkadian *šēr ilāne*). It is noted that there is no explicit "deification" of the king as demonstrated by the divine determinative, suggesting some hesitation at perpetuating the Akkadian and Ur III models discussed above (Machinist 2006: 163). But at the same time, the king's titles and associated attributes — especially when he is called the "sun(-god) of all the people" — convey a sense of his specially elevated status.

Representations of Tukulti-Ninurta I are few; the two primary examples being relief images of the ruler on two stone altars found in the Ishtar temple at Assur (Moortgat 1969: figs. 246–47). On one, the ruler is depicted in low relief facing right, first standing, then kneeling before an altar similar in shape to the actual object on which the panel is carved. Upon the altar stands a symbol consisting of a rectangular block divided vertically, which has been identified with the god Nusku, a deity associated with light (Moortgat 1969: 120; Sjöberg 1969: TH 4, 48). On the second altar (fig. 5.9), the ruler is shown standing, facing left, with the same garment, absence of headgear, and greeting gesture as on the first. He is situated between two standard-bearers, each holding a pole topped by an emblem of radii within a surrounding circle; and each of the standard bearers carries the same symbol/form upon his own head. This emblem has been associated by Moortgat with the sun-god, Shamash.[15] A dado relief frieze depicting a battle scene over mountainous territory on the same altar (studied by Moortgat-Correns 1988) is unfortunately badly eroded; what can be made out are chariots and soldiers traversing rocky terrain. A figure of the king is identifiable in the center of the frieze (ibid., fig. 2), again without headgear, but holding his mace and a rope tied to subservient prisoners. This would fit well with later, Neo-Assyrian imagery, and with Machinist's discussion of the importance of epithets and titles reflecting the ruler's divinely protected and sanctioned abilities in war in this period, including the resurrection of titles hitherto known best from the Akkadian period (Machinist 2006).

I emphasize this association because it is precisely in such military situations (e.g., in the Epic of Tukulti-Ninurta as well as in annalistic texts like those of Tiglath Pileser I) that the royal attribute of the divinely endowed radiant aura (*melammu*) is stated to be manifest and operative (Machinist 2006; Grayson 1991: 13). As a luminous surround conveying awesome power, this is the paramount quality attributed to rulers (along with deities and powerful works or objects), noted above for rulers of the Old Babylonian period as well. In later representational strategies, such as Roman, Buddhist, or Christian art, such divine splendor is often indicated visually as a halo or nimbus.[16] For Mesopotamia, apart from the rays that often emanate from the shoulders of astral deities on early, third-millennium cylinder seals and on the Law Stele of Hammurapi, discussed above (e.g., Moortgat 1969: fig. 209; Frankfort 1939: pls. 18–19), no such convention for light or radiance is apparent, its textual importance notwithstanding. I would suggest, despite the fact that strategies have not yet been developed to represent

---

[15] See argument in Winter 2004, with respect to the difference between radial disks associated with Shamash and Ishtar. The same emblem occurs in the upper corner of the altar.

[16] See discussion in Winter, in press, as relevant to visual representation in the ancient Near East.

this aspect visually, that such textually ascribed attributes should not be omitted as evidence for the kings' status with respect to the divine. For, as Françoise Brüschweiler has shown, such luminous properties are associated with the sacred in Mesopotamia, reserved for both persons and things *in contact with the divine* (Bruschweiler 1987: 187–89; emphasis mine). In such cases, light serves as the visible form of the vital life-force infused *by* the divine.

Conclusion: In the Middle Assyrian period, roughly from the fifteenth through the eleventh centuries B.C., the titles assumed and attributes ascribed to rulers were consistent with those attested in preceding periods and indicated special status and ascribed attributes verging on the divine, although without explicit attestation of divinity.

Assurnasirpal II (890–884 B.C.)–Assurbanipal (668–627 B.C.) of Assyria: More has been written on Neo-Assyrian kingship than for any other period, so that the visual components of the office can simply be summarized here. A typology of motif, gesture, and meaning was established by Ursula Magen (1986), outlining the various genres of representation and their associated qualities of ideal leadership. This has been followed by a number of studies, all of which have stressed the combination of text and image that contribute to a picture of the ruler's access to power through his formation and endowment, and by his proximity to the divine sphere (e.g., Ataç 2007, Bachelot 1991, Cancik-Kirschbaum 1995, Machinist 2006, Pongratz-Leisten 1999, Winter 1997, among others).

Machinist has laid out the specific role of the king as representative of the gods (2006: 153–59) through his exercise of the office of (chief) priest (Akkadian *šangû*) — consistent with a role articulated for the ruler since the third millennium.[17] This association of the ruler with priestly office (Akkadian *šangûtu*) complements his identification with the office of kingship (Akkadian *šarrūtu*), the combination of the two articulating his agency in mediating between and acting in both the heavenly and the earthly domains.

At the same time, the Assyrian ruler often identifies himself in paternity and in likeness *to* the gods, as in a text of Adad-nirari II (911–891 B.C.), who declares that the gods perfected his features, making him manifestly identifiable as one fit to rule.[18] Such allusions continue through the Neo-Assyrian period, including quite explicit statements that, in his perfection, the king is the "perfect likeness of the god," "the very image of Bel (Marduk)," as noted in letters to the ruler Esarhaddon (680–669 B.C.; see discussion of this in Cole and Machinist 1998; Winter 1997: 374–75; Machinist 2006: 171–74). This mirroring of the god(s) in the king's body finds close parallels in Egyptian texts from the Old Kingdom to the Roman period, where the king was explicitly identified *as* divine (Mysliwiec 1984; Wengrow 2006). The Assyrian case, if more implicit than explicit, is still striking. The ruler, as many of his predecessors, is said to be possessed of that divine attribute, a radiant and powerful aura, *melammu*, discussed above (see Cassin 1968: 71; Machinist 2006: 169; and most recently, Ataç 2007: 308–09). But on occasion, texts go even further in declaring the king *as* a god. In a hymn supposedly composed for the coronation of Assurbanipal, for example, the ruler is stated to be the sun(-god), Shamash (Arneth 1999: 45; Machinist 2006: 172–73); and similarly, in a text describing the departure of an Assyrian king to battle, it is said: "The king who stands in the chariot is the warrior king, the lord (god) Ninurta" (Livingstone 1989: 100–02).

---

[17] Machinist 2006: 153–59; for the third millennium, see Glassner 1993.

[18] Grayson 1991: A–N II.A.0.99.2, ll. 6–7, discussed with respect to "portraiture" in Winter 1997: 372.

Through all this, the Assyrian king does not take on the divine determinative before his name. However, the royal image associated with a temple *can* take on the prefix — [d]*salam šarri* — as in the list known as the "Götteraddressbuch" (discussed by Machinist 2006: 178). The prefix suggests some sanctification of the image, if not of its royal subject. Such images could conceivably be three-dimensional statues, known to have been placed in temples in the Assyrian period (e.g., the Assurnasirpal II statue from the Ishtar Sharrat-niphi temple at Nimrud; Hall 1928: pl. 12), and so probably subject to sanctifying installation ritual. However, they could as well refer to steles, as the Ninurta temple stele of Assurnasirpal II, also found at Nimrud, was installed with an offering table placed directly in front (fig. 5.10; Hall 1928: pl. 13; see also Machinist 2006: 180–81). Similarly, a scene marking the erection of a stele containing a royal image at the shores of Lake Van in Armenia, depicted on one of the bronze door bands of Shalmaneser III from Balawat, shows offering tables and divine symbols placed before the image, the recipient of devotional activity by musicians, a possible priest, and a figure in royal garb, presumably the king himself.[19]

In pursuing the relationship between kingship and divinity in Assyria, Peter Machinist has suggested that the king's image is "both votive and venerated at the same time" (2006: 182). He concludes, further, that the attributes of the ruler seem to imply "some kind of divine status for the king" (Machinist 2006: 184), despite the absence of the divine determinative before the writing of the royal name. A related conclusion is reached by Tallay Ornan with respect to the representation of Sennacherib on a rock relief at Maltai, where the depicted king and god are virtually identical, emphasizing, she argues, the "divine-like nature of the king" (Ornan 2007: 169). And the same might be said of the wall painting depicting the standing ruler and a second male figure before a deity installed upon a podium, presumably Aššur, from Room 12 of Residence K at Khorsabad, dated to the reign of Sargon II (fig. 5.11; Loud and Altman 1938: pl. 88). Here, too, the king is shown virtually identical to and of the same height as the deity, with only the podium elevating the god to a higher level. In visual rhetoric, this suggests that the king not only had access to the god, but was also more or less on a scale of parity, excepting only the elevated/installed status of the god as exemplified by the podium.

Conclusion: As noted by Steven Holloway (2002: 178), the question of the divine status of Neo-Assyrian kings has not received much attention, and this is echoed by Machinist (2006: 185–86), who adds that the royal-divine relationship in the Neo-Assyrian period was extremely complex. The divine status of kings clearly had limits; and at no time is the king invested with the visual attributes of the god (Holloway 2002: 183). At the same time, within the representational code of the period, the god-*like* properties and resemblances of (images of the) ruler had to have been recognizable by viewers, just as the consecrated status of the royal image itself as well as royal texts and correspondence worked both sides of the divide between earthly and divine. What this suggests is that, just as the king was not depicted in sculpture as a personal likeness, but rather as an ideal semblance — bearing signs of the ruler "in the office of kingship" (Winter 1997), so also the sacral aspects of *kingship*, rather than the individual divinity of the king, were what was foregrounded in the Neo-Assyrian period, no less than in earlier phases of the Mesopotamian sequence.

---

[19] King 1915: pl. 1. This scene fits nicely with the text discussed by S. Cole (Cole and Machinist 1998: xxiii, cited by Machinist 2006: 180 n. 102) with respect to VAT 10464, where in the New Year ritual at Assur, the king is described as offering sacrifices before the royal image.

CONCLUDING HYPOTHESES

Inquiry into the divinity of kings and divine aspects of kingship in ancient Mesopotamia cries out for cross-cultural comparison. A number of traditions, both near and far in space and time, manifest similar status associated with offices of rule (e.g., Abitz 1995; Beidelman 1966; Bonatz 2007; Feeley-Harnik 1985; Fischwick 1987; Gilbert 1987; Gonda 1966; Gurukkal 1987; Puett 2002; Small 1996). One case — that of the Yoruba ruler who actually renounced his divinity in 1993 — is especially instructive for our purposes. Noting the most famous instance in which the Japanese Emperor Hirohito renounced his divinity following defeat in World War II, Jacob Olupona (2006) has reported on the Yoruba king's stated desire *not* to be associated with the biblical Nebuchadnezzar, who was described as having forced subjects to bow down before him. The king's decision to renounce his divine status was related to his acknowledgment of a change in understanding of royal authority in the wake of modernization and exposure to the monotheism of Christianity and Islam, especially the new evangelical movements introduced into Nigeria in recent years, along with pressure from the diasporic communities of Nigerians abroad. In short, the king is said to have argued that the social, religious, and political system(s) in which he now operated would no longer sustain his divine status.

What this suggests is that, under new conditions — particularly in the context of religious systems that do not brook multiple authority and/or political systems that no longer allow for absolute power over complexly organized subsystems — divine kings may not satisfy the conditions required by the cultural surround. I would argue, therefore, that, conversely, when divine kings do appear, they equally satisfy the requirements of their respective social, religious, and political systems.

If the ruler in his office clearly had sacral aspects throughout the Mesopotamian sequence, I feel I must stress the political parameters of the explicit ascription of divine status to rulers when it does occur (contra Hallo 1996: 196). Just as the turn from republic to empire in Rome occasioned an elevation of Augustus not only to emperor, but to god (Price 1987), so also at other moments in history, certain political and authority structures require such elevations, especially at the time of the political system's inception, in order to lend force to new authority structures. I would argue that the emergence and consolidation of the nation-state in the Akkadian and Neo-Sumerian periods toward the end of the third millennium B.C. constituted just such a moment, congruent with the need to establish new tiers of socio-political authority and hierarchy. That this formal mechanism was short-lived, petering out in the early second millennium, can then be understood as an artifact of the development of alternative mechanisms of control within the state bureaucracy, however many of the ascribed properties of the ruler negotiating the space between the earthly and the divine remained in place as part of the state apparatus.

Whether kings are designated/understood retrospectively to have been born gods (as in ancient Egypt; Abitz 1995; Wengrow 2006), or elevated to divine status upon installation (as in some Akan kingdoms of Ghana; Gilbert 1987), they must, on the one hand, create or have created around themselves an ideological system that will sustain such status; and they must, on the other hand, be accepted as divine by at least some of those over whom they reign.

Once one can document a porous membrane between the sacred realm and the domain of rulership in a given social system, an additional aspect of exchange is frequently identified: the god is/gods are often reciprocally invested with titles and attributes of kingship. Pursuit of such instances is beyond the scope of the present paper, but it is my sense that parallel inquiry would yield interesting information about the construction of kingship, not just divinity. For medieval India, it has been argued that at such moments, both divinity and kingship are conceived and expressed in mutual terms, both textually and materially (Gurukkal 1987: 120). This is precisely what has been explored by Holloway (2002) with respect to the use of religion in the exercise of political power when the god Aššur is declared "king" in the Neo-Assyrian period. Holloway's claim (2002: 57) that reference to the god as king is largely a political tool of Assyrian imperial strategy is useful for the present inquiry, as support for the argument that the exchange of metaphors and practices of authority speak to the porous membrane and the blurring of boundaries between the identities and attributes of deity and ruler, the two often meeting in a realm of the heroic, beyond the scope of the present paper.

This said, one may note the following correlates with respect to the visual record. First, while imagery may have maintained a system of signs distinguishing gods from rulers by detail and attribute (i.e., horned crown from round brimmed cap or tiara) from earliest attestation well into the Neo-Assyrian period, rulers simultaneously partook of some attributes and qualities shared with/ascribed by and to the gods, whether or not they were formally described or indicated by determinative *as* gods. Second, that the rhetorical strategies employed for verbal representation do not always co-vary with those strategies devised for visual representation. And third, when rulers *were* formally recognized as gods, it would seem that, the lack of separation of church and state in ancient Mesopotamian polities notwithstanding, the culturally driving force necessitating such recognition/elevation was no less political than theological. In sum, Mesopotamian kingship was consistently treated as if infused by the divine, "sacral kingship" being the constant in which all rulers participated. As such, kingship itself was always "divine." At the same time, the literal ascription of "divinity" to the ruler was reserved for times and contexts when that sacral nature needed to be strategically foregrounded. It then becomes the job of the analyst to assess the determining conditions of that necessity in specific cases, such that the boundaries between sacral and divine kingship may be clarified.

ACKNOWLEDGMENTS

I had seen neither the 2006 paper of P. Machinist nor the 2007 papers of T. Ornan and M.-A. Ataç when the first draft of this article was written and given as a talk at the Oriental Institute, Chicago, in February 2007. I am delighted to acknowledge congruence between the conclusions reached in those two papers, now duly cited, and my own thoughts on related subjects. I am grateful to Ari Winitzer and Mehmet-Ali Ataç for comments on the spoken paper. And finally, I would also note a happy congruence of perspective with other participants in the Oriental Institute Seminar, particularly Piotr Michalowski, Jerrold Cooper, and its organizer, Nicole Brisch, for whose efforts in bringing us all together I am most grateful.

Figure 5.1. Detail, Stele of Naram-Sîn, Found at Susa, 2250 B.C.; Sandstone
(Département des antiquités orientales, Musée du Louvre, Paris)

Figure 5.2. Detail, Obverse of Stele of Ur-Namma of Ur, ca. 2110 B.C., Register 2; Limestone
(University of Pennsylvania Museum, Philadelphia)

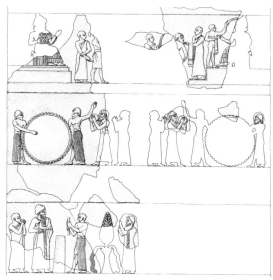

Figure 5.3. Detail, Reverse, Drawing of Stele or Ur-Namma of Ur, Bottom Register
(after Börker-Klähn 1982)

Figure 5.4. Diagram, Four-tiered State Hierarchy of the Ur III Period (after Winter 1991)

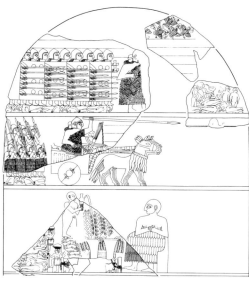

Figure 5.5. Drawing, Reverse, Stele of Eannatum of Lagash, Found at Tello, ca. 2560 B.C.;
Limestone (Drawing by Elizabeth Simpson, Winter 1985)

Figure 5.6. Statue "B" of Gudea of Lagash, Found at Tello, ca. 2115 B.C.; Diorite
(Département des antiquités orientales, Musée du Louvre, Paris)

Figure 5.7. Votive Statue Dedicated for Hammurapi of Babylon, Larsa(?), ca. 1760 B.C.;
Bronze with Gold Overlay (Département des antiquités orientales, Musée du Louvre, Paris)

Figure 5.8. Detail, Top of Law Stele of Hammurapi of Babylon, Found at Susa, ca. 1760 B.C.;
Diorite (Département des antiquités orientales, Musée du Louvre, Paris)

Figure 5.9. Altar of Tukulti-Ninurta I, Found at Ishtar Temple, Assur, ca. 1230 B.C.; Limestone
(Archaeological Museum, Istanbul)

Figure 5.10. Drawing of Placement of Ninurta Temple Stele of Assurnasirpal II,
Found at Nimrud, ca. 850 B.C. (after Layard 1853)

Figure 5.11. Detail, Drawing of Wall Painting, Room 12, Residence K, Khorsabad, ca. 710 B.C.
(after Loud and Altman 1938)

BIBLIOGRAPHY

Abitz, Fredrich
    1995   *Pharao als Gott in den Unterweltsbüchern des Neuen Reiches*. Orbis Biblicus et Ori-
            entalis 146. Freiburg: Universitätsverlag; Göttingen: Vandenhoeck & Ruprecht.

Arneth, M.
    1999   "'Möge Šamaš dich in das Hirtenamt über die vier Weltgegenden einsetzen.' Der Krö-
            nungshymnus Assurbanipals' (SAA II, 11) und die Solarisierung des neuassyrischen
            Königtums." *Zeitschrift für altorientalische und biblische Rechtsgeschichte* 5: 28–53.

Ataç, Mehmet-Ali
    2007   "The *melammu* as Divine Epiphany and Usurped Entity." In *Ancient Near Eastern Art
            in Context: Studies in Honor of Irene J. Winter*, edited by Jack Cheng and Marian H.
            Feldman, pp. 295–313. Culture and History of the Ancient Near East 26. Leiden and
            Boston: Brill.

Bhabha, Homi K.
    1990   "Introduction: Narrating the Nation." In *Nation and Narration*, edited by Homi K.
            Bhabha, pp. 1–7. London and New York: Routledge.

Bachelot, L.
    1991   "La fonction politique des reliefs néo-assyriens." In *Marchands, diplomates et empe-
            reurs: Études sur la civilisation mésopotamienne offertes à Paul Garelli*, edited by
            Dominique Charpin and Francis Joannès, pp. 109–28. Paris: Éditions Recherche sur
            les Civilisations.

Barrelet, M.-Th.
    1974   "La figure du roi." In *Le palais et la royauté, archéologie et civilisation: Compte
            rendu*, (19th Rencontre Assyriologique Internationale, 1971, in Paris), edited by Paul
            Garelli, pp. 27–38. Paris: P. Geuthner.

Beidelman, T. O.
    1966   "Swazi Royal Ritual." *Africa* 36: 373–405.

Bonatz, D.
    2007   "The Divine Image of the King: Religious Representation of Political Power in the
            Hittite Empire." In *Representations of Political Power: Case Histories from Times of
            Change and Dissolving Order in the Ancient Near East*, edited by Marlies Heinz and
            Marian H. Feldman, pp. 111–36. Winona Lake: Eisenbrauns.

Börker-Klähn, Jutta
    1982   *Altvorderasiatische Bildstelen und vergleichbare Felsreliefs*. Baghdader Forschun-
            gen 4. Mainz am Rhein: Philipp von Zabern.

Brinkman, J. A.
    1964   "Appendix: Mesopotamian Chronology of the Historical Period." In *Ancient Mesopo-
            tamia: Portrait of a Dead Civilization*, by A. Leo Oppenheim, pp. 335–48. Revised
            edition. Chicago: University of Chicago Press, 1977.

Brisch, Nicole
    2006   "In Praise of the Kings of Larsa." In *Approaches to Sumerian Literature: Studies in
            Honour of Stip (H. L. J. Vanstiphout)*, edited by Piotr Michalowski and Niek Veld-
            huis, pp. 37–45. Cuneiform Monographs 35. Leiden and Boston: Brill.

Brüschweiler, Françoise

1987   *Inanna: La déesse triomphante et vaincue dans la cosmologie sumérienne: Recherche lexicographique.* Les Cahiers du Centre d'Étude du Proche-Orient Ancien 4. Leuven: Editions Peeters.

Canby, Jeanny V.

2001   *The "Ur-Nammu" Stela.* University Museum Monograph 110. Philadelphia: University of Pennsylvania Museum of Archaeology and Anthropology.

Cancik-Kirschbaum, E.

1995   "Konzeption und Legitimation von Herrschaft in neuassyrischer Zeit: Mythos und Ritual in VS 24,92." *Welt des Orients* 26: 5–20.

Cassin, Elena

1968   *La splendeur divine: Introduction à l'étude de la mentalité mésopotamienne.* Civilisations et Sociétés 8. Paris: Mouton.

Charpin, Dominique

2003   *Hammu-rabi de Babylone.* Paris: Presses universitaires de France.

Civil, Miguel, and Richard L. Zettler

1989   "The Statue of Šulgi-ki-ur₅-sag₉-kalam-ma, Parts One: The Inscription and Two: The Statue." In *DUMU-E²-DUB-BA-A: Studies in Honor of Åke W. Sjöberg*, edited by Hermann Behrens, Darlene Loding, and Martha T. Roth, pp. 49–78. Occasional Publications of the Samuel Noah Kramer Fund 11. Philadelphia: University of Pennsylvania Museum.

Cohen, Mark E.

1993   *The Cultic Calendars of the Ancient Near East.* Bethesda: CDL.

Cole, Steven W., and Peter Machinist

1998   *State Archives of Assyria,* Volume 13: *Letters from Priests to the Kings Esarhaddon and Assurbanipal.* Helsinki: Helsinki University Press.

Cooper, Jerrold S.

1983   *Reconstructing History from Ancient Inscriptions: The Lagash-Umma Border Conflict.* Sources from the Ancient Near East 2/1. Malibu: Undena.

1993   "Sacred Marriage and Popular Cult in Early Mesopotamia." In *Official Cult and Popular Religion in the Ancient Near East* (Papers of the First Colloquium on the Ancient Near East in Tokyo, 20–22 March 1992), edited by Eiko Matsushima, pp. 81–96. Heidelberg: Universitätsverlag.

Edzard, Dietz Otto

1980a   "Königslisten und Chroniken. A. Sumerisch." *Reallexikon der Assyriologie* 6: 77–86. Berlin: Walter de Gruyter.

1980b   "Königtum. A. III. Jahrtausend." *Reallexikon der Assyriologie* 6: 140. Berlin: Walter de Gruyter.

1997   *Gudea and His Dynasty.* Royal Inscriptions of Mesopotamia, Early Periods 3/1. Toronto: University of Toronto.

Engnell, Ivan

1943   *Studies in Divine Kingship in the Ancient Near East.* Uppsala: Almqvist & Wiksell.

Fallers, Lloyd A.

1974   *The Social Anthropology of the Nation-State.* The Lewis Henry Morgan Lectures 1971. Chicago: Aldine.

Feeley-Harnik, Gillian

1985   "Issues in Divine Kingship." *Annual Review of Anthropology* 14: 273–313.

Fishwick, Duncan

1987   *The Imperial Cult in the Latin West: Studies in the Ruler Cult of the Western Provinces of the Roman Empire*. Études préliminaires aux religions orientales dans l'Empire romain 108; Religions in the Graeco-Roman World 148. Leiden and New York: Brill.

Frankfort, Henri

1939   *Cylinder Seals: A Documentary Essay on the Art and Religion of the Ancient Near East*. London: Macmillan.

1948   *Kingship and the Gods: A Study of Ancient Near Eastern Religion as the Integration of Society and Nature*. Oriental Institute Essay. Chicago: University of Chicago Press.

Frankfort, Henri; Seton Lloyd; and Thorkild Jacobsen

1940   *The Gimilsin Temple and the Palace of the Rulers at Tell Asmar*. Oriental Institute Publications 43. Chicago: University of Chicago Press.

Frayne, Douglas R.

1990   *Old Babylonian Period (2003–1595 BC)*. Royal Inscriptions of Mesopotamia, Early Periods 4. Toronto: University of Toronto Press.

Gadd, C. J.

1948   *Ideas of Divine Rule in the Ancient Near East*. Schweich Lectures 1945. London: Oxford University Press.

George, A.

1999   *The Epic of Gilgamesh: A New Translation*. London: Penguin.

Gilbert, Michelle

1987   "The Person of the King: Ritual and Power in a Ghanaian State." In *Rituals of Royalty: Power and Ceremonial in Traditional Societies*, edited by David Cannadine and S. R. F. Price, pp. 298–330. Past and Present Publications. Cambridge: Cambridge University Press.

Glassner, J.-J.

1993   "Le roi-prêtre en Mésopotamie." In *L'ancien proche-orient et les Indes: Parallélismes interculturels religieux* (Colloque franco-finlandais, Paris, 10–11 novembre 1990), edited by Suomen Itälaimen Seura, pp. 9–19. Studia Orientalia 70. Helsinki: Finnish Oriental Society.

Gonda, Jan

1966   *Ancient Indian Kingship from the Religious Point of View*. Leiden: Brill.

Grayson, Albert K.

1971   "The Early Development of Assyrian Monarchy." *Ugarit Forschungen* 3: 311–19.

1980   "Königslisten und Chroniken. B. Akkadisch." *Reallexikon der Assyriologie* 6: 86–135. Berlin: Walter de Gruyter.

1991   *Assyrian Rulers of the Early First Millennium B.C., Volume 1: 1114–859 B.C.* Royal Inscriptions of Mesopotamia, Assyrian Periods 2. Toronto: University of Toronto Press.

Gurrukal, Rajan

1987   "From the Royalty of Icons to the Divinity of Royalty: Aspects of Vaisnava Icons and Kingship in Medieval South India." In *Vaisnavism in Indian Arts and Culture: Na-*

tional Seminar on Impact of Vaisnavism on the Indian Arts: Papers, edited by Ratan Parimoo, pp. 119–24. New Delhi: Books and Books.

Hall, H. R.
 1928   *Babylonian and Assyrian Sculpture in the British Museum*. Paris and Brussels: Les Éditions G. van Oest.

Hallo, William W.
 1957   *Early Mesopotamian Royal Titles: A Philological and Historical Analysis*. American Oriental Series 43. New Haven: American Oriental Society.
 1988   "Texts, Statues, and the Cult of the Divine King." In *Congress Volume: Jerusalem 1986*, edited by John A. Emerton, pp. 54–65. Vetus Testamentum Supplement 40. Leiden and New York: Brill.
 1996   *Origins: The Ancient Near Eastern Background of Some Modern Western Institutions*. Leiden and Boston: Brill.

Hamilton, Mark W.
 2006   *The Body Royal: The Social Poetics of Kingship in Ancient Israel*. Leiden and Boston: Brill.

Harper, Prudence O.; Joan Aruz; and Françoise Tallon, editors
 1992   *The Royal City of Susa: Ancient Near Eastern Treasures in the Louvre*. New York: The Metropolitan Museum of Art.

Heimpel, W.
 1992   "Herrentum und Königtum im vor- und frügeschichtlichen Alten Orient." *Zeitschrift für Assyriologie* 82: 3–21.

Holloway, Steven W.
 2002   *Aššur is King! Aššur is King! Religion in the Exercise of Power in the Neo-Assyrian Empire*. Culture and History of the Ancient Near East 10. Leiden and Boston: Brill.

Jacobsen, Thorkild
 1939   *The Sumerian Kinglist*. Assyriological Studies 11. Chicago: University of Chicago Press.
 1991   "The Term Ensí." *Aula Orientalis* 9: 113–21.

Jaques, Margaret
 2006   *Le vocabulaire des sentiments dans les textes sumériens: Recherche sur le lexique sumérien et akkadien*. Alter Orient und Altes Testament 332. Münster: Ugarit-Verlag.

Johnson, Allen W., and Timothy Earle
 1987   *The Evolution of Human Societies: From Foraging Group to Agrarian State*. Stanford: Stanford University Press.

Johnson, Gregory
 1978   "Information Sources and the Development of Decision-Making Organizations." In *Social Archaeology: Beyond Subsistence and Dating*, edited by Charles L. Redman, pp. 87–112. Studies in Archaeology. New York: Academic Press.

Kantorowicz, Ernst H.
 1957   *The King's Two Bodies: A Study in Medieval Political Theology*. Princeton: Princeton University Press.

King, Leonard W.
 1915   *Bronze Reliefs from the Gates of Shalmaneser, King of Assyria, B.C. 860–825*. London: The British Museum.

Klein, Jacob

    1981   *Three Šulgi Hymns: Sumerian Royal Hymns Glorifying King Šulgi of Ur*. Bar-Ilan Studies in Near Eastern Languages and Culture. Ramat Gan: Bar Ilan University Press.

    1989   "From Gudea to Šulgi: Continuity and Change in Sumerian Literary Tradition." In *DUMU-E²-DUB-BA-A: Studies in Honor of Å. W. Sjöberg*, edited by Hermann Behrens, Darlene Loding, and Martha T. Roth, pp. 289–301. Occasional Publications of the Samuel Noah Kramer Fund 11. Philadelphia: University of Pennsylvania Museum.

    1991   "The Coronation and Consecration of Šulgi in the Ekur (Šulgi G)." In *Ah, Assyria …: Studies in Assyrian History and Ancient Near Eastern Historiography Presented to Hayim Tadmor*, edited by Mordechai Cogan and Israel Eph'al, pp. 292–313. Scripta Hierosolymitana 33. Jerusalem: Magness Press.

    2006   "Sumerian Kingship and the Gods." In *Text, Artifact, and Image: Revealing Ancient Israelite Religion*, edited by G. Beckman and T. J. Lewis, pp. 115–31. Providence: Brown Judaic Studies.

Kutscher, R.

    1974   "An Offering to the Statue of Šulgi." *Tel Aviv* 1: 55–59.

Lambert, W.

    1998   "Kingship in Ancient Mesopotamia." In *King and Messiah in Israel and the Ancient Near East: Proceedings of the Oxford Old Testament Seminar*, edited by John Day, pp. 54–70. Journal for the Study of the Old Testament, Supplement 270. Sheffield: Sheffield Academic Press.

Layard, A. H.

    1853   *The Monuments of Nineveh I*. London: J. Murray.

Livingstone, Alasdair

    1989   *Court Poetry and Literary Miscellanea*. State Archives of Assyria 3. Helsinki: Helsinki University Press.

Loud, Gordon, and Charles B. Altman

    1938   *Khorsabad*, Volume 2: *The Citadel and the Town*. Oriental Institute Publications 40. Chicago: The Oriental Institute.

Machinist, Peter

    2006   "Kingship and Divinity in Imperial Assyria." In *Text, Artifact, and Image: Revealing Ancient Israelite Religion*, edited by Gary M. Beckman and Theodore J. Lewis, pp. 152–88. Brown Judaic Studies 346. Providence: Brown Judaic Studies.

Magen, Ursula

    1986   *Assyrische Königsdarstellungen, Aspekte der Herrschaft: Eine Typologie*. Baghdader Forschungen 9. Mainz am Rhein: Philipp von Zabern.

Marin, Louis

    1988   *Portrait of the King*. Theory and History of Literature 57. Minneapolis: University of Minnesota Press.

Michalowski, Piotr

    1991   "Charisma and Control: On Continuity and Change in Early Mesopotamian Bureaucratic Systems." In *The Organization of Power: Aspects of Bureaucracy in the Ancient Near East*, edited by McGuire Gibson and Robert D. Biggs, pp. 55–68. Studies in Ancient Oriental Civilization 46. Chicago: The Oriental Institute.

Moortgat, Anton
    1969   *The Art of Ancient Mesopotamia: The Classical Art of the Near East.* London and
                    New York: Phaidon.

Moortgat-Correns, Ursula
    1988   "Zur ältesten historischen Darstellung der Assyrer: Tukulti-Ninurtas I. Sieg über das
                    Land der Uqumeni(?)." *Archiv für Orientforschung* 35: 111–16.

Mysliwiec, Karol
    1984   "Iconographic, Literary and Political Aspects of an Ancient Egyptian God's Identifi-
                    cation with the Monarch." In *Monarchies and Socio-Religious Traditions in the An-
                    cient Near East: Papers Read at the 31st International Congress of Human Sciences
                    in Asia and North Africa,* edited by Prince Mikasa No Miya Takahito, pp. 44–50. Bul-
                    letin of the Middle Eastern Culture Center in Japan 1. Wiesbaden: Harrassowitz.

Olupona, Jacob
    2006   "When the King Renounces His Divinity: Kingship, Religion and Ritual in Ife, Nige-
                    ria." Public lecture, Harvard University, 1 November 2006.

Ornan, Tallay
    2007   "The Godlike Semblance of a King: The Case of Sennacherib's Rock Reliefs." In *An-
                    cient Near Eastern Art in Context: Studies in Honor of Irene J. Winter,* edited by Jack
                    Cheng and Marian H. Feldman, pp. 161–75. Culture and History of the Ancient Near
                    East 26. Leiden and Boston: Brill.

Perlov, B.
    1980   "The Families of the Ensis Urbau and Gudea and Their Funerary Cult." In *Death in
                    Mesopotamia: Papers Read at the 26th Rencontre Assyriologique Internationale,* ed-
                    ited by Bendt Alster, pp. 77–81. Mesopotamia 8. Copenhagen: Akademisk Forlag.

Pongratz-Leisten, Beate
    1999   *Herrschaftswissen im Mesopotamien: Formen der Kommunikation zwischen Gott und
                    König im 2. und 1. Jahrtausend v. Chr.* State Archives of Assyria Studies 10. Hel-
                    sinki: Neo-Assyrian Text Corpus Project.

Price, S. R. F.
    1987   "From Noble Funerals to Divine Cult: The Consecration of Roman Emperors." In
                    Rituals of Royalty: Power and Ceremonial in Traditional Societies, edited by David
                    Cannadine and S. R. F. Price, pp. 56–105. Past and Present Publications. Cambridge:
                    Cambridge University Press.

Puett, Michael J.
    2002   *To Become a God: Cosmology, Sacrifice, and Self-Divinization in Early China.* Har-
                    vard-Yenching Institute Monograph Series 57. Cambridge: Harvard University Press.

Reichel, Clemens D.
    2001   Political Changes and Cultural Continuity in the Palace of the Rulers at Eshnunna
                    (Tell Asmar) from the Ur III Period to the Isin-Larsa Period (ca. 2070–1850 B.C.).
                    Ph.D. dissertation, University of Chicago.

Renan, E.
    1990   "What is a Nation?" Edited and translated by M. Thom. In *Nation and Narration,* ed-
                    ited by Homi K. Bhabha, pp. 8–22. Reprint of 1882 edition. London and New York:
                    Routledge.

Roth, Martha T.
1997   *Law Collections from Mesopotamia and Asia Minor*. Writings from the Ancient World 6. Atlanta: Scholars Press.

Sallaberger, Walther
1993   *Der kultische Kalender der Ur III-Zeit*. 2 volumes. Untersuchungen zur Assyriologie und Vorderasiatischen Archäologie 7. Berlin: Walter de Gruyter.
1999   "Königtum und Kult in der Hauptstadt Ur unter den Herrschern ihrer III. Dynastie (21. Jh.)." In *Von Babylon bis Jerusalem: Die Welt der altorientalischen Königsstädte*, Volume 2, edited by Wilfried Seipel and Alfried Wieczorek, 255–60. Milan: Skira.

Schapiro, Meyer
1969   "On Some Problems in the Semiotics of Visual Arts: Vehicle in Image Sign." *Semiotica* 1: 223–41.

Seux, M.-J.
1980   "Königtum. B. II. und I. Jahrtausend." *Reallexikon der Assyriologie* 6: 140–73. Berlin: Walter de Gruyter.

Sjöberg, Åke
1969   *The Collection of the Sumerian Temple Hymns*. Texts from Cuneiform Sources 3. Locust Valley: J. J. Augustin.

Slanski, K. E.
2007   "The Mesopotamian 'Rod and Ring': Icon of Righteous Kingship and Balance of Power between Palace and Temple." In *Regime Change in the Ancient Near East and Egypt: From Sargon of Agade to Saddam Hussein*, edited by Harriet E. W. Crawford, pp. 37–59. Proceedings of the British Academy 136. Oxford: The British Academy.

Small, Alastair, editor
1996   *Subject and Ruler: The Cult of the Ruling Power in Classical Antiquity: Papers Presented at a Conference held in the University of Alberta on April 13–15, 1994, to Celebrate the 65th Anniversary of Duncan Fishwick*. Journal of Roman Archaeology Supplement 17. Ann Arbor: University of Michigan Press.

Spycket, A.
1968   *Les statues de culte dans les textes mésopotamiens des origines à la 1re dynastie de Babylone*. Cahiers de la Revue Biblique 9. Paris: Gabalda.

Steible, Horst
1982   *Die altsumerischen Bau- und Weihinschriften*. 2 volumes. Freiburger altorientalische Studien 5. Wiesbaden: Steiner.
1991   *Die neusumerischen Bau- und Weihinschriften*. 2 volumes. Freiburger altorientalische Studien 9. Stuttgart: Steiner.

Steinkeller, Piotr
1988   "The Date of Gudea and His Dynasty." *Journal of Cuneiform Studies* 40: 47–53.
1999   "On Rulers, Priests and Sacred Marriage: Tracing the Evolution of Early Sumerian Kingship." In *Priests and Officials in the Ancient Near East* (Papers of the Second Colloquium on the Ancient Near East, Tokyo, 22–24 March 1996), edited by Kazuko Watanabe, pp. 112–16. Heidelberg: Universitätsverlag C. Winter.

Suter, C.
2000   *Gudea's Temple Building: The Representation of an Early Mesopotamian Ruler in Text and Image*. Cuneiform Monographs 17. Groningen: Styx.

2005   Review of *The "Ur-Nammu" Stela*, by J. V. Canby. *American Journal of Archaeology* 109: 301–03.

Van De Mieroop, Marc

2005   *King Hammurabi of Babylon: A Biography*. Blackwell Ancient Lives. Malden: Blackwell.

van Dijk, J. J.; M. I. Hussey; Albrecht Götze

1985   *Early Mesopotamian Incantations and Rituals*. Yale Oriental Series, Babylonian Texts 11. New Haven: Yale University Press.

Wengrow, David

2006   *The Archaeology of Early Egypt: Social Transformations in North-East Africa, c. 10,000 to 2,650 BC*. Cambridge: Cambridge University Press.

Westenholz, Joan Goodnick

2000   "The King, the Emperor, and the Empire: Continuity and Discontinuity of Royal Representation in Text and Image." In *The Heirs of Assyria: Proceedings of the Opening Symposium of the Assyrian and Babylonian Intellectual Heritage Project Held in Tvärminne, Finland, October 8–11, 1998*, edited by Sanna Aro and Robert M. Whiting, pp. 99–125. Melammu Symposia 1. Helsinki: Neo-Assyrian Text Corpus Project.

Wilcke, Claus

1974   "Zum Königtum in der Ur III-Zeit." In *Le palais et la royauté, archéologie et civilisation: Compte rendu*, edited by Paul Garelli, pp. 177–232. Paris: Librairie Orientaliste Paul Geuthner.

Winter, Irene J.

1985   "After the Battle Is Over: The 'Stele of the Vultures' and the Beginning of Historical Narrative in the Ancient Near East." In *Pictorial Narrative in Antiquity and the Middle Ages*, edited by Herbert L. Kessler and Marianna S. Simpson, pp. 11–32. Center for Advanced Study in the Visual Arts 4. Washington, D.C.: National Gallery of Art.

1989   "The Body of the Able Ruler: Toward an Understanding of the Statues of Gudea." In *DUMU-E²-DUB-BA-A: Studies in Honor of Å. W. Sjöberg*, edited by Hermann Behrens, Darlene Loding, and Martha T. Roth, pp. 573–83. Occasional Publications of the Samuel Noah Kramer Fund 11. Philadelphia: University of Pennsylvania Museum.

1991   "Legitimation of Authority through Image and Legend." In *The Organization of Power: Aspects of Bureaucracy in the Ancient Near East*, edited by McGuire Gibson and Robert D. Biggs, pp. 59–100. Studies in Ancient Oriental Civilization 46. Chicago: The Oriental Institute.

1992   "Idols of the King: Consecrated Images of Rulers in Ancient Mesopotamia." *Journal of Ritual Studies* 7: 13–43.

1996   "Sex, Rhetoric and the Public Monument: The Alluring Body of the Male Ruler in Mesopotamia." In *Sexuality in Ancient Art: Near East, Egypt, Greece, and Italy*, edited by Natalie B. Kampen, pp. 11–26. Cambridge Studies in New Art History and Criticism. Cambridge and New York: Cambridge University Press.

1997   "Art in Empire: The Royal Image and the Visual Dimensions of Assyrian Ideology." In *Assyria 1995: Proceedings of the Tenth Anniversary Symposium of the Neo-Assyrian Text Corpus Project, Helsinki, 7–11 September 1995*, edited by Simo Parpola and Robert M. Whiting, pp. 359–81. Helsinki: The Neo-Assyrian Text Corpus Project.

2003	Review of *The "Ur-Nammu" Stela*, by J. V. Canby. *Journal of the American Oriental Society* 123: 402–06.
2004	"The Conquest of Space in Time: Three Suns on the Victory Stele of Naram-Sîn." In *Assyria and Beyond: Studies Presented to Mogens Trolle Larsen*, edited by Jan G. Derksen, pp. 607–28. Uitgaven van het Nederlands Instituut voor het Nabije Oosten te Leiden 100. Istanbul: Nederlands Instituut voor het Nabije Oosten.
In press	"Images of Mesopotamian Gods and Kings: Light, Radiance, and the Limits of Visual Representation." In *Proceedings of the Second International Congress on the Archaeology of the Ancient Near East: Copenhagen*, edited by Ingolf Thuesen. 2 volumes. Winona Lake: Eisenbrauns.

Woolley, C. Leonard

| 1934 | *The Royal Cemetery: A Report on the Predynastic and Sargonid Graves Excavated between 1926 and 1931*. Ur Excavations 2. London: The British Museum. |
| 1974 | *The Buildings of the Third Dynasty*. Ur Excavations 6. London: Trustees of the British Museum; Philadelphia: The University Museum. |

Wright, Henry T.

| 1977 | "Recent Research on the Origin of the State." *Annual Review of Anthropology* 6: 379–97. |

6

DIEU ET MON DROIT: KINGSHIP IN LATE BABYLONIAN AND EARLY PERSIAN TIMES

ERICA EHRENBERG, NEW YORK ACADEMY OF ART

The motto of the British monarch's coat of arms, *Dieu et mon droit*, could equally have served as the catch phrase of the Late Babylonian and Achaemenid kings. The sentiment espoused, the divine right to rule, was a defining tenet of greater Mesopotamian kingship and seems to be a universal and enduring one. Unlike a select number of their royal predecessors (and their compatriots in Egypt), Babylonian and Persian rulers of the sixth, fifth, and fourth centuries B.C. did not deify themselves; rather, they followed the more traditional Mesopotamian custom of arrogating to themselves, and themselves alone, divine favor. While visual representations of Babylonian and Persian kings rely heavily on established Mesopotamian iconographic conventions, they nevertheless betray distinct understandings of sovereignty, as revealed through a comparative consideration of these representations with reference as well to royal inscriptions and to the ideology of their predecessors, the Assyrians.

Continuity across cultures, an oft-cited hallmark of Mesopotamian civilization otherwise noted for its recurrent political fluctuations, is particularly remarkable in the transition between the Late Babylonian and early Achaemenid periods, when Semitic control over Mesopotamia passed to Indo-European, Aryan rule. Aspects of this continuity have been discussed regarding social, political, textual, and visual traditions. It has also been pointed out that a liminal period persisted for about fifty years before Persian culture crystallized into unique form, sometime during the reign of Darius I.[1] The bulk of evidence for this period is provided by Late Babylonian and Persepolitan cuneiform tablets, whose texts elucidate administrative, bureaucratic, and socio-economic norms, and whose seal impressions illuminate stylistic and iconographic tendencies.[2] These archival texts, however, do not yield data for constructing hypotheses regarding principles of kingship. Although found in a major Achaemenid royal capital and written by its administration, the Persepolis texts do not concern major matters of state[3] while the Late Babylonian archives stem either from private or temple sources; no state archives are extant.[4] The artifacts that do allow for an inquiry into royal ideology are the monumental ones, from Late Babylonian times primarily the extremely limited remains of Babylon, and from

---

[1] See Ehrenberg 2000 and 2007 for an overview concentrating on iconography, and Jursa 2007 on the texts.

[2] Studies on sealing practices have investigated relationships between iconography and sealers, offices and ethnicities in Late Babylonian and Achaemenid archives. Most often, choice of sealing imagery seems to have been guided by personal predilection. For the Late Babylonian Eanna archive from Uruk, see Ehrenberg 1999: 37; for the Late Babylonian Ebabbar archive from Sippar, in which there is evidence that imagery may be associated with certain offices, see MacGinnis 1995: 170. For the Achaemenid period Murašû archive from Nippur,

in Babylonia, see Bregstein 1993: 206–07, 260–66. The Persepolis Fortification archive is undergoing full publication, but see for now Garrison and Root 2001: 41, who find that sealing praxis can only be determined for two varieties of text.

[3] These texts, written in the Elamite language, are administrative in nature.

[4] The Eanna archive from Uruk and Ebabbar archive from Sippar are temple archives; the Egibi archive from Babylon records the business dealings of the eponymous family.

early Achaemenid times most significantly the structures and carvings of Persepolis, created at a time when the Achaemenid style had come into its own.

An expedient launching point for a study of the visualization of kingship lies in the written equivalent, namely the royal epithets adopted by the kings, enunciating verbatim their perceptions of their role and status. Underlying literary traditions thread through the titulary and royal inscriptions of the Late Babylonian and Achaemenid kings, with pedigrees that trace back to the earliest royal writings in Mesopotamia.[5] Here, reference also to Neo-Assyrian fashions in royal texts helps throw the character of the Late Babylonian and early Achaemenid texts into greater relief. Late Babylonian royal titles and inscriptions, unlike representative Neo-Assyrian inscriptions, are generally acknowledged for their lack of militaristic, political, or heroic interest and language.[6] Inscriptions of the Old Babylonian kings particularly served as models in the Late Babylonian period and titles revived from inscriptions of Hammurabi himself include: humble, wise, judicious, suppliant, who brings expensive gifts (to the temples). Titles taken from the reign of Nebuchadnezzar I of the Isin II period, another earlier Babylonian source of emulation, include: pious, submissive, who constantly seeks the sanctuaries of (god's name).[7] Whereas in Neo-Assyrian inscriptions the gods exhort the king to expand the domain and conquer the enemy in order to "Assyrianize" the lands beyond, the motivation for expansion given the Late Babylonian kings is to create new cult centers.[8]

In this insistence on empire, the Neo-Assyrian inscriptions bear closer similarity with the Achaemenid inscriptions. Royal Achaemenid titles such as: great king, king of kings, king of all countries, king of the world, king in this great earth far and wide, king of the multitude, and king of countries containing all kinds of men, emphasize the enormity of the realm.[9] Attributing his acts to the favor of the god Ahuramazda, Darius enumerates the countries beyond Persia that he defeated and even instructs the reader to look also at the relief carvings showing his throne being borne by the array of conquered peoples (inscription DNa). Well-known is Darius's Susa foundation inscription (DSf), listing the peoples from all over the empire who imported foreign products and built his palace. Like the Neo-Assyrian kings who catalog their impressive physiques and repute as warriors, Darius proclaims his warrior abilities, noting he has a strong body, is a good horseman, bowman, spearman, and fighter of battles and exercises sound judgment. But like the Late Babylonian kings, he relegates to himself qualities of wisdom and justice, he is a friend of the righteous, rewards those who are cooperative and controls his own impulses.[10] Cyrus, the king who conquered Babylonia and took pains to win voluntary

[5] Similarities between Assyrian/Babylonian and Achaemenid royal inscriptions were commented upon already by Gray (1901). Garelli (1981) discusses royal titles, and more recently Vanderhooft (1999) has taken a comprehensive look at Babylonian inscriptions.

[6] It must be kept in mind, however, that extant Late Babylonian inscriptions are mainly building inscriptions; there are no known state archives, as there are in Assyria. The Babylonian Chronicles are later compilations. Garelli (1981: 4) provides a comparative chart of Assyrian and Babylonian royal epithets.

[7] Vanderhooft (1999: 17–19, 17 n. 29) observes that many royal inscriptions of Hammurabi were copied at the time.

[8] Vanderhooft 1999: 41–49. As he further points out, it is only in the inscriptions of the Late Babylonian Nabonidus that language more customary to Neo-Assyrian royal

inscriptions can be found, perhaps resulting in part from his familial ties to the Aramaic west and his mother's place in the court of Assurbanipal. Among the titles chosen by Nabonidus are: great king, mighty king, king of the universe, king of the four corners; see Vanderhooft 1999: 51–58, 57 n. 206.

[9] Briant (2002: 178–79), who also notes that the unconquered lands beyond the realm were uninhabitable and thus "relegated to nonexistence." Frye (1964: 36) remarks that the title "king of kings," while not used by Neo-Assyrian or Neo-/Late Babylonian kings, was invoked once during the reign of the Middle Assyrian Tiglath-Pileser I.

[10] Root (2000: 20) writes that the Achaemenid conceptualization of empire resonates with the teachings of Zoroastrianism, which stress truth, justice, individual responsibility, and righteousness.

acceptance of the populace, cleaved to Mesopotamian fashion and style in his inscriptions, even invoking Assurbanipal and taking his title: king of lands.[11] Beginning with Darius, the Achaemenid kings emphatically stress their Persian, Aryan ethnicity. Whereas earlier, Cyrus had emphasized his Elamite heritage and connections, giving Anshan as his homeland even while calling himself an Achaemenid, Darius calls himself an "Achaemenian, a Persian, son of a Persian, an Aryan having Aryan lineage," highlighting his Iranian and ancestral heritage.[12] Although the title "king of Babylon" is not completely abandoned and can be found in inscriptions of Xerxes and Artaxerxes I, the locus of kingship had shifted to the Persian world.[13]

The kings' verbal self-delineations find counterpart in their visual self-expression. Avoidance of martial reference in the titulature of the Late Babylonian kings seems to correspond to its absence in the royal monuments which portray the king as worshiper of the gods or omit the king altogether in favor of repetitive friezes of divine acolytes. The Achaemenid monuments, on the other hand, focus on the figure of the heroic able-bodied king as the fulcrum of an immense empire. Before analyzing the iconography, a word about style is in order as this, too, seems to reflect conceptualizations of the king's role on earth. Comparison with Neo-Assyrian remains is instructive. Assyrian carvers were masterful in a range of carving techniques from modeled to linear styles, as evidenced primarily in the glyptic. For the palace narrative reliefs, a planar, two-dimensional style was employed, thereby divorcing the scenes from the reality of the three-dimensional world. Perhaps this approach was construed as an appropriate visual companion for the textual annals that lie behind the reliefs and recount that the king acts at the behest of the gods. What the king performs is thus visually as well as symbolically removed from the mundane world. The body itself is more akin to a flat-form mannequin on which is draped the royal robe and regalia.[14] By contrast, the Late Babylonian royal monuments are deeply carved; the higher degree of modeling and "portliness" of figures have often been cited as hallmarks of Neo- and Late Babylonian style. In the British Museum stele of Nabonidus, the king's accouterments and regal trappings are kept to a minimum while the body is given palpable form (fig. 6.1). The king here is first and foremost a human, of this earth. Achaemenid royal carvings are similarly modeled in relief, a trait that has been attributed to the influence of Greek carvers, who took an optical rather than mental approach to their sculptures. But these Achaemenid works could easily be a further development of the Late Babylonian precedent and also betray the notion of a living-and-breathing king, the king as "man." It was Darius, after all, who stated in a building inscription from Susa that the god Ahuramazda "chose me as his man in all the earth" (DSf, 15–18).

A common refrain about Late Babylonian art, often treated as a postscript to general studies on Mesopotamian art because of the exceedingly limited amount of remains, is that it is something of a dull, characterless coda to a distinguished three-millennium run of Mesopotamian art history. Commenting on royal reliefs, Dandamayev remarks that, "In contrast to

---

[11] Kuhrt (1990: 180) notes that Cyrus recognizes Assurbanipal in particular since the latter oversaw many building projects in Babylonia; Högemann (1992: 330–33) remarks on Cyrus's formulation of his kingly ideology based on Babylonian models; according to Beaulieu (1989: 45), Cyrus tried to "pose as legitimate heir to the great empires of Akkad and Assyria" and to "present himself in the garb of a native Babylonian ruler."

[12] On Cyrus, see Waters 2004; on Darius, see Briant 2002: 182. Soudavar (2006: 170–72, 176–77) disputes this translation of the title and would replace the reading

"lineage" for the term čiça with "brilliance" in the sense of luminosity, that is, having a power derived from light, equivalent to khvarnah (for which, see the discussion below) but avoiding the use of the term because of its Mithraic connotations.

[13] See Stolper 1990: 561; 1989: 294; Kuhrt and Sherwin-White 1987: 73.

[14] As Winter (1997) has discussed, relief and sculptured images of the Neo-Assyrian kings are portraits of office rather than of individuals.

Neo-Assyrian and Achaemenid art where kings are pictured as victors of numerous enemies and wild animals or monsters, there are only a few Neo-Babylonian royal reliefs and in them kings appear in some aenemic posture worshipping gods."[15] A sense of quiet repose does emanate from the Late Babylonian imperial monuments, but one that seems to suggest an empire held firm by its position at the heart of the cultic universe and its consequent alignment and unity with the sacred realm. Along with the British Museum stele of Nabonidus are two duplicate steles of the king from Harran, with the king holding his long staff and lifting an arm in prayer before three divine symbols.[16] Nearly identical is one of the two panels of Nabonidus's Teyma stele, showing the king holding the staff.[17] A unique stele of Nebuchadnezzar not only extols in writing the reconstruction of the Etemenanki, the ziggurat of Marduk in Babylon (as well as that of the ziggurat in Borsippa), but also illustrates the temple in elevation and ground plan, before which stands the king, staff in hand. The caption next to the temple plan leaves no doubt concerning the temple's identity: "The house, the foundation of heaven and earth, ziggurat in Babylon."[18] Depiction of the king as temple builder has a hoary tradition in Mesopotamia, dating back to the Early Dynastic period in which Urnanshe, on his wall-plaque, carries a basket for bricks on his head, and retains relevance through Neo-Assyrian times, in which Assurbanipal, on his British Museum stele, is portrayed with building basket.[19] More specifically, the Mesopotamian ruler is pictured along with temple plan in the Neo-Sumerian period, witness the famous Louvre Gudea, seated with architect's blueprints in lap and cognate of the Schøyen stele.[20] In intent, this imagery reinforces the king's role as commissioner and facilitator of the gods' manifestations on earth.

The closest Achaemenid parallel to the Late Babylonian steles in terms of format are the doorjamb relief scenes at Persepolis, which are delimited to a narrow, vertical rectangular field and focus on the figure of the king.[21] Aside from scenes of the king battling wild animals and monsters addressed below, are iconic images of the king walking forward under a parasol and being carried aloft on his throne, beneath the winged disk with human bust, potentially of Ahuramazda, discussed later (fig. 6.2). The king, figuratively larger than life, is delineated literally larger than his whisk- and umbrella-bearing attendants who shade him. Neo-Assyrian kings, regularly more in scale with their attendants, are also depicted on their thrones whose side-beams could be ornamented with atlantid figures holding up the struts, simulating those carved in wood or ivory on the actual throne. On the Achaemenid throne, however, the atlantid figures stacked in rows beneath the platform of the king's throne are meant to be read as actual representatives of the nations of the empire, symbolically and physically supporting

---

[15] Dandamayev (1997: 43) in remarking on Assyrian as opposed to Babylonian traits in Achaemenid art.

[16] Magen (1986: 24–25) believes the staff held by the king is the *palû*, mentioned in texts, granted by Marduk as a staff of rulership. The significance of the "mappa," or small curved object that can be held in the hand of the king, is debated and could perhaps denote kingly favor; see Seidl 1989: 209–10; see also Brinkman and Dalley 1988: 95–97, for a history of opinion on the mappa; and also Reade 1977: 35. Illustrations can be found in Börker-Klähn 1982: #263–64.

[17] Whereas the British Museum stele inscription seems to refer to a revolt, the Harran steles mention the construction of cultic buildings and the Teyma stele contains a text concerning a ritual. Illustrated in Börker-Klähn 1982: #265.

[18] The stele was found in Babylon in 1917 and subsequently divided into three parts, two of which are now rejoined in the Schøyen Collection. This stele will be published by A. George in the series *Manuscripts in The Schøyen Collection*; currently it is published online.

[19] Illustrated, respectively, in Moortgat 1969: pls. 109, 282.

[20] The Louvre Gudea is illustrated in Moortgat 1969: pl. 167.

[21] Jamb reliefs are encountered in various Persepolitan structures including the Palace of Darius, Palace of Xerxes, Apadana, Throne Hall, Council Hall, and Harem of Xerxes.

their king and lifting the entire framework of the platform off the ground, as visible in the cliff tomb facade carvings of the Achaemenid kings at Naqsh-i Rustam and at Persepolis on the Kuh-i Rahmat (fig. 6.3). Horizontally rather than vertically aligned like the doorjambs, the tomb carvings and the famous Treasury panels offer vignettes of royalty in context. In the Treasury reliefs, once adorning the Apadana, the enthroned king, probably Darius, with crown prince and courtiers behind, sits before two censers and receives an official who introduces the row of tributaries from all over the empire, originally marching up the Apadana stairs (fig. 6.4). The king thus metaphorically resides at the center of the world. In the tomb facade scene (fig. 6.3), common to the Achaemenid rulers, the king stands on a pedestal before an altar and the winged disk with human bust above, all atop a platform raised high by the subject nations. As in the stele of Nabonidus (fig. 6.1), the divine symbol at top of the tomb facades and the doorjambs witnesses the motion of the king. But there is only this one deity present and a direct connection between the one king and the one god, not a pantheon, is rendered unequivocal. Furthermore, it has been remarked that the identical gesture, of upraised arm with open palm, of the Persian king and the divine figure in the winged disk is revealing of the basic equality of the relationship between the two. While this gesture is made as well by the Late Babylonian kings and by worshipers on Late Babylonian seals and thus taken for a prayer gesture, it may be more aptly read in the Achaemenid context as a greeting or blessing gesture because the god would not be expected to make a prayerful gesture himself.[22]

Of the few extant works that service a discussion of Late Babylonian royal imagery, only the Wadi Brisa rock relief in Lebanon has a martial dynamism and, indirectly, martial reference: the accompanying inscription, concerning the construction of a road for the transport of cedars to build the palace at Babylon, was likely written on the occasion of the acquisition of Lebanon into the empire (full text in Weissbach 1906). The carving shows Nebuchadnezzar in hand-to-hand combat with a lion (Börker-Klähn 1982: #259). King battling lion is an age-old topos in Mesopotamia, with a history extending back to the Uruk period; later it became the royal seal type for the Neo-Assyrian kings. Chosen to extol the might of the king, who successfully wrangles the king of the beasts, the motif bears kinship with the theme, just as ancient, of the bearded hero contesting animals and imaginary beasts. Commonplace among the seals of the Neo-Assyrian/Neo-Babylonian and Late Babylonian periods, the hero is usually dressed in a robe or kilt and can have the wings of the genius-figure; the figure bears no royal connotations. The contest scene is one that traverses the Assyro-Babylonian and Persian divide, adopted by the Achaemenids for their seals and reliefs as well. In the Achaemenid seals, a royal figure in Persian garb and crown may play the role of the Assyro-Babylonian type of hero and

---

[22] Root (1979: 174–76) makes this observation about the identical hand gesture of the Persian king and god and notes also that the Neo-Assyrian kings, when standing before a deity, raise the arm but with hand clenched and index finger pointed toward the deity, rather than with open palm. Soudavar (2003: 92–94, 41–45) and Soudavar (2006: 160–64) describes this equivalence of gesture made by king and god as manifesting the same type of relationship between the two that is found in the Sasanian era. He would translate the phrase that often follows the Sasanian king's name in royal inscriptions, *ke čihr az yazadān*, as "in the image of gods" rather than "whose seed is from the gods," noting that Middle Persian *čihr* can mean face/appearance as well as seed/origin, that the Sasanians do not otherwise indicate divine ancestry, and that the translation of seed/origin results from the accompanying Greek translation on investiture rock reliefs (of Ardashir I at Naqsh-i Rustam and of Shapur I at Naqsh-i Rajab) which were, however, written from a Greek understanding of the term and of Sasanian royal ideology. In addition, the kings and gods in the Sasanian investiture scenes are shown as equal in size and on the same ground. The phrase would then emphasize the king's god-given power or reflection of divine power, rather than a divine origin.

winged genius, and engage both real and mythical animals.[23] On doorjambs of a number of structures on the Persepolis Apadana, the figure grappling with a lion or monster wears Persian dress and a fillet (fig. 6.5). His identity as hero or the king himself is ambiguous because in all regards except for a crown and footwear he looks like the royal figure in combat.[24] But perhaps the ambiguity is intentional, to underscore that the king's role as supernatural hero is subsumed as an integral aspect of his royal stature.[25]

Contest scenes aside, Achaemenid monumental art is also devoid of scenes of might and aggression, with the exception of the Behistun relief (Root 1979: #6). The prototype for this scene, in which Darius is shown in the divine presence with conquered enemies representing the peoples who rebelled against him, lies in the late third-millennium Stele of Naram-Sin which had been brought to Susa in the twelfth century (Moortgat 1969: pl. 135). A more indigenous model is the late third-millennium Annubanini rock carving at Sar-i Pul (Börker-Klähn 1982: #31). But unlike these reliefs and the Neo-Assyrian battle narratives, the Behistun carving does not capture a precise historical moment; it is a summary tableau, overseen by the figure in the winged disk, of a number of independent revolts that Darius quelled at different times in forging the empire, and, in that regard, an atemporal statement of imperial dominion.[26] In a similar vein, the Persepolitan reliefs of endless tribute-bearers personifying the inhabitants of the empire convening on the imperial capital express the result rather than literal moment of martial expeditions, that is, the timeless, universal kingdom. In her exhaustive study of the Achaemenid carvings, Root discusses the visual program of Persepolis as being designed to illustrate the cooperative, harmonious, and voluntary support of the empire by its constituents and the "sacral covenant" between them, in distinction to the Neo-Assyrian visual program broadcasting empire as achieved through forceful annexation. Similarly, the king's throne is nimbly raised off the ground and borne by the interlocked arms of his subjects.[27] Lincoln would read these scenes instead on a cosmogonic-religious level, as Darius's testimony to his fulfillment of sacred directive, the re-establishment of peace in and the reunification of the universe (symbolized by tributaries arriving cooperatively from across the empire), that had been fragmented in primordial time by the "Lie" which had sown discord and undermined the totality of Ahuramazda's original creation.[28] In either regard, the contrast with both Neo-Assyrian and Late Babylonian palatial visual programs is clear.

---

[23] In her review of Root and Garrison, Ehrenberg (2003–04: 439–40) postulates a gradual increase in the popularity of the Persian hero over the Babylonian-type hero in the early Achaemenid period and suggests the figure may have been developed as a means to adapt a foreign character by endowing it with a native appearance. Ehrenberg (2003–04: 440–41) also notes the penchant for Persian heroes to combat lions (and winged lions) rather than the bulls (and winged bulls) more often paired with the Babylonian hero.

[24] Root (1979: 304–05) observes that these heroes wear strapped shoes like non-royal Persians in sculpture instead of the strapless shoes worn by kings.

[25] Root (1979: 305–08) believes the hero is a depiction of the king as a "Persian man" correlating to Darius's inscriptions wherein he calls himself a Persian man, perhaps illustrating an Indo-Iranian concept of kingship placing the king on a cosmic level. Garrison and Root (2001: 57) identify the "Persian man" as a "generic figure symbolizing the collective force of Persian power."

[26] Root (2000: 22) discusses Achaemenid avoidance of historical narrative and preference for allegorical or metaphorical representations of the ideology of empire, noting that the Behistun relief delineates events in an emblematic manner.

[27] Root 1979: 131, 153. Heed, though, the remarks of Kuhrt (1984: 159) that comparisons of Persepolitan reliefs, found on the external walls of the structures, with Neo-Assyrian narrative reliefs on the interior palace walls, may be ultimately misleading, since they were intended for different audiences, public versus private. Jacobs (2002: passim) takes issue with the reading of monumental Achaemenid art as a tool of imperial propaganda, except under Darius I, countering Root's understanding of the Achaemenid artistic program and writes of the general Achaemenid avoidance of monumental sculpture other than in regions of the empire where such had a long historical tradition.

[28] Lincoln publishes these ideas elsewhere in this volume.

As for the Late Babylonian palace program, it is unique for its utter lack of the royal image; in comparison to Persepolis, the visual landscape of Babylon was something else altogether. All that remains of the original facade décor of Nebuchadnezzar's Southern Palace in Babylon are sections of glazed brick displaying passant lions, palmette stalks, and floral bands (fig. 6.6). The royal residence is thus tied to the glazed brick program of both the Processional Way, also with passant lions, and the Ishtar Gate, with its repetitive rows of bulls and lion-dragons.[29] Had there existed any monumental stone wall reliefs carrying images of the king and his court or exploits, it would be expected that some evidence of such, no matter how small, would have appeared among the remains of the palace.[30] Ritual texts reveal that in Late Babylonian times, priests enacted cultic roles during the New Year's festival, while the king remained somewhat in the background and was subject to humiliation before the gods.[31] The lions and fanciful trees on Nebuchadnezzar's throne-room facade may well have royal connotations, the lion serving as king of the beasts and worthy contender of the king, and the palmette trees perhaps corresponding to the palm-based fanciful trees central to Neo-Assyrian reliefs of palace cultic rites and perhaps referring to the king's assurance of the fertility of the land and its people. The lions patrolling the Processional Way, however, would seem to carry divine significance, as the avatar of Ishtar, from whose gateway the Processional Way cuts through the city to the ziggurat of Marduk. These lions are complemented by the gods' acolytes on the gate itself, Adad's bulls and Marduk's lion-dragons. Babylon's parade of creatures, symbolic of the cosmic sphere and set against the resplendent lapis-colored background of the celestial realm, lies at great remove from Persepolis's pageant of tributaries, symbolic of the imperial sphere and set against the building terraces of the royal realm (fig. 6.7).

The divergence between the visual programs of Babylon and Persepolis is consonant with the distinctive natures of the two cities. By the time it became the Late Babylonian capital, Babylon had a long history not only as the political capital of Babylonia but also the cultic capital, as the city of the national god Marduk, and the intellectual capital, as the ancestral home of Hammurabi. Differing from Neo-Assyrian urban patterns that separated imperial cities like Nineveh and Nimrud from the cult city of Assur, in Babylon political and religious functions were united.[32] In a holistic "reading" of Babylon, Van De Mieroop characterizes the city as a microcosm of the universe, its walls rising up from the surrounding moat like the primordial mound emerging from the sea; and like a Russian *matryoshka* doll, within the city, the platform in the Marduk temple courtyard is also the "pure hill" which arose at creation, a fitting allusion since it is Marduk, according to the Babylonian creation story, who organized the universe and founded Babylon. In the re-enactment of the New Year's festival, the gods descend on Babylon, thereby rendering it the cosmic center as well as the political center.[33] Persepolis,

---

[29] Illustrated in Moortgat 1969: pls. 289–91.

[30] Koldewey (1969: 21) records that fragments of basalt sculptures of lions and bulls were discovered on the Hauptburg/North Palace of Nebuchadnezzar at Babylon, indicating the existence of some monumental stone sculpture in a royal context. Beaulieu (2003: 356, 363) cites a Late Babylonian text from the time of Nebuchadnezzar II referencing guardian animals on the gates of the Esagil temple in Babylon, and a text of Cambyses year 5 from the Eanna in Uruk referencing a *Mischwesen* flanking the temple gate.

[31] Pongratz-Leisten (1994: 109, 147) observes that, in contrast, the Neo-Assyrian kings were central actors in rituals.

[32] Pongratz-Leisten 1994: 128. This observation concerning the intertwined religious and political aspects of the city is reinforced by the remark of Van De Mieroop (2003: 267) that the Ishtar Gate, through which Marduk enters the city during the New Year's festival, is also called the "entrance of kingship," thus affirming both cultic and imperial power.

[33] Van De Mieroop 2003: 262–63, 271, and passim for a complete interpretation of the city of Babylon.

on the other hand, was a new Achaemenid foundation with no landed heritage to supply historical directive to its realization, the situating of the king as the quintessence of empire. Its ceremonial center with soaring columns dominates the site, raised high above ground-level.[34] But it should also be noted that even at an age-old city such as Susa, that becomes an Achaemenid capital, what is known of palace ornamentation coheres to the Persepolitan precepts. Although the facades of Darius's palace are ornamented with glazed bricks as at Babylon, the figurative content consists of Persian archers who form the king's guard, and fantastical creatures who may carry royal rather than, or along with, overt divine association; winged lions and bulls elsewhere contend with the royal hero, while the sphinxes presumably have royal connotations as they do in Egypt.[35]

Albeit subtle, the differences between Late Babylonian and Achaemenid ideologies of kingship seem to result from a gradual transformation of established belief systems, modified to suit new imperial circumstances and tempered by the variant inherent cultural leanings of different ethnic groups. Modifications of Babylonian norms in the Mesopotamian areas of the Achaemenid empire were probably the product of progressive attempts to exert increasing control over the realm (Ehrenberg 2000: 315). In Iran itself, indigenous Median norms were synthesized into a new, Achaemenid, package. Material culture from the reigns of Cyrus and Cambyses is not plentiful, but no radically new initiatives can be assigned to their reigns; instead, it is during the reign of Darius, the king who first accentuates his Iranian, Aryan, heritage, that a unique Achaemenid brand emerges, likely with Ahuramazda at its cultic center. The date of the codification of Zoroastrianism is debated, but it has been theorized that, while Cyrus and Cambyses were adherents of Mithraism as practiced in Iran by the Medes, Darius elevated Ahuramazda to supreme place in the pantheon, accommodating extant Mithraic beliefs in order to ensure the loyalty of the local base, while subtly promoting the fundaments of a new religion in an iconographical form at home in the Babylonian regions of the empire.[36] This masterful maneuvering of sacral credence for political expedience explains the carefully crafted Achaemenid visual program that closely associates the sole king with the sole god and also accounts for its distance from the Late Babylonian program in which the king is almost a non-presence in an empire seemingly under divine control.[37] It has been suggested that the decorative program of Persepolis is a visual encyclopedia of Zoroastrian tenets. Along with the figure in the winged disk he takes for Ahuramazda (see below), Soudavar theorizes that the repeated floral motif, seen, for example, on Persepolis brick panels and that he describes as sunflower emerging from lotus (fig. 6.8), represents the rise of the sun, or Mithra, the sun-god/day/sunflower, from the waters of Apam-Napat, the aquatic god/evening/lotus. Although these two deities were marginalized with the rise of Zoroastrianism, they are nevertheless designated as *ahura* along with Ahuramazda in the *Avesta*.[38] Further, he would identify the roundel at the base of the lotus-sunflower motif as the pearl (native to the sea bed), the essence of aquatic

[34] Root (1980: 7) notes that little is known about the palaces and structures of the city of Persepolis at the base of the terrace.

[35] But note the observation of Azarpay (1987: 198) that the Babylonian bricks are glazed terra-cotta whereas the Achaemenid bricks are glazed siliceous faience, or frit, like earlier Elamite bricks.

[36] Soudavar (2010: 9–10, passim) opines that kingly ideology conditioned developments in Zoroastrianism.

[37] Soudavar (2003: 91–92) remarks that Darius's inscriptional insistence on Ahuramazda rather than a larger pantheon was a political rather than religious move, to promote the idea of one unifying and universal rule in the empire.

[38] For a more complete analysis and discussion, see Soudavar 2003: 53–55.

khvarnah, or sacred radiance/glory, protected underwater by Mithraic Apam-Napat (and later inherited by Zoroastrian Anahita), and a symbol of the sun that sets into the sea at night.[39] The monumental lion-and-bull combat motif ornamenting the Apadana and palaces of Persepolis (fig. 6.9) can perhaps also be ascribed to Zoroastrian beliefs. By commonly held theory, the lion represents Leo and the bull Taurus, and their combat the succumbing of spring to summer. According to Soudavar, the lion symbolizes the sun/Mithra, and the bull the moon and sea/ Apam-Napat, and their eternal struggle with no apparent conclusion thus represents the day/ night periodicity.[40]

Another symbol ubiquitous in Achaemenid reliefs is the winged disk, which has been tied to Zoroastrian beliefs but also has a long pre-Achaemenid history in Mesopotamia and ultimately in Egypt, where it functioned as a solar emblem and from whence it was adopted but subsequently adapted to the new environment.[41] The Mesopotamian and Iranian form of the symbol consists of a disk that may contain a human bust and from which extend horizontal wings and at bottom, a tail; ribbons or streamers may emanate from the base of the wings and may end in pincer-like forms, perhaps reminiscent of bird talons (figs. 6.2, 6.10). The meaning of the device in Mesopotamian and Achaemenid settings, where it can house the bust of a deity, has been widely argued. In the Achaemenid context it has been taken for the god Ahuramazda or the Iranian concept of *khvarnah*, the radiance of divine glory/good fortune.[42] It seems as if it is likely both: Ahuramazda (or deity), particularly where the human figure of the god is present; and *khvarnah* where the winged disk is uninhabited. Soudavar, who makes this case, sees the Ahuramazda symbolism of the winged disk as deriving from an Achaemenid ideology and its *khvarnah* symbolism as deriving from a pre-Achaemenid source, appealing to non-Zoroastrians holding Mithraic beliefs for whom *khvarnah* was the fundamental aspect of kingship.[43] Solar radiance of Mithra, the sun-god, defines *khvarnah* and thus the winged disk, a solar symbol in Egypt and associated with the skies/heavens through its wings, constituted a perfectly embraceable motif.[44] Possession of *khvarnah* sanctioned the king's rule but could be granted, increased, or revoked.[45] In the Mesopotamian context, the winged disk was first identified with Assur, the national god of Assyria, as a result of its prominence in

---

[39] As a whole, then, the scene expresses the journey of *khvarnah* from the water to the sky (Soudavar 2003: 59, 102–03); the notion of *khvarnah* is discussed below.

[40] Soudavar (2003: 118–19), who makes a connection as well to the indigenous Iranian belief of the day's division between Mithra and Apam-Napat and cites the *Bondahesh*, the Zoroastrian book of creation, in which water is associated with the moon on account of the seas' rising at night.

[41] Seidl (1994: 125) opines that the winged disk was adopted by the Achaemenids directly from Urartian representations.

[42] Opinions are divided. Calmeyer (1979, 1984) and Shahbazi (1974, 1980) argue for *khvarnah*, and Calmeyer suggests that the winged disk has kingly (and solar) connotations. Shahbazi (1980) distinguishes the winged disk from the winged disk with bust, describing the former as the *khvarnah* of non-royal people and the latter as that of the king. Lecoq (1984) finds that the winged disk with or without the human bust represents Ahuramazda

but can at the same time signify the power of the king. See also Kaim 1991: 33, who remarks that the winged disk without the bust is found in a greater variety of scenes than the winged disk with bust, but both are tied to sun symbolism and kingly propaganda.

[43] See Soudavar 2003: 3–4, 95–96, and further, 123–24, in which he cites the *Farvardin Yasht* which relates how *khvarnah* was associated with the pre-Zoroastrian *ahuras* Mithra and Apam-Napat, before the promotion of Ahuramazda and Anahita.

[44] The wings of the disk are most probably to be interpreted as falcon wings. The *Avesta* makes mention of bird/falcon feathers possessing *khvarnah*, and the *Shahnameh* speaks of *khvarnah*-bearing falcons. See Soudavar 2003: 22–24.

[45] Soudavar (2003: 26) references *Yasht* 10, sections 16, 27, concerning Mithra's power to grant and revoke *khvarnah*. *Khvarnah* could also be secured through victory or inheritance, (Soudavar 2003: 80).

Neo-Assyrian reliefs in association with the king. Later studies identified the motif with the sun-god Shamash.[46] Based on analogy with the theory mooted for the Persian winged disk, perhaps the Mesopotamian version can be taken not as a specific deity but rather the divine radiance in the abstract, that can be populated by various deities. Although the concept of *khvarnah* is a Persian one, the Mesopotamian notion of *melammu* may serve as something of an equivalent. The conceit of *melammu* was discussed by Oppenheim, who describes it as the radiance that surrounds the sacred but is also given to the king, as the representative of the gods, to legitimize him; it can, however, be given and taken away by the gods, like *khvarnah*.[47] If the winged disk is *melammu*, then there is no conflict concerning the deity within it, which could be Assur in the Neo-Assyrian reliefs, or Shamash in scenes in which this god would be expected.[48] The winged disk is occasionally depicted elevated by atlantid figures. It would be unusual to envision that a deity itself be physically supported, but perhaps not that its abstract aura be lifted.[49] An interpretation of winged disk as *melammu* would also explain instances in which a crescent rather than ring is winged. It is assumed that the deity in the crescent is the moon-god and therefore the reading of the winged symbol as a solar one would be in conflict. If the winged device is understood to be *melammu* and the god within to be interchangeable, then the moon-god's crescent can just as easily bear the wings.

Associated with the deity in the winged disk in the Achaemenid reliefs is the enigmatic ring, held in the hand of the deity as if being proffered to the king. This motif of a deity handing a ring, often accompanied by a rod, to the king, already employed in Iran in the Middle Elamite period on the stele of king Untash-Napirisha,[50] survives through the Parthian and Sasanian periods, in which it is central to compositions of imperial investiture, in which the deity hands the king only a ring, who may grasp it in reception (fig. 6.11).[51] The ring symbol has a long history in Mesopotamia as well, where it is usually paired with the rod, making its

[46] For example, Calmeyer 1979: 358 n. 25; idem 1984: 146 n. 73; Mayer-Opificius 1983: 19; idem 1984: 200; Seidl 1957–71: 485 s.v. §4d Flügelsonne; Unger 1965: 463–65. Dalley (1986: 98–99) posits a connection between the winged disk and the king.

[47] Oppenheim 1943: 31. Winter (1994: 127, passim) has written about *melammu* as depicted in art, where it appears as an enveloping physical emanation, an "affective aura" around the head of person or surrounding objects, which may also possess *melammu*. Soudavar (pers. comm.) takes issue with an analogy between *khvarnah* and *melammu* because in the Babylonian version of Darius's inscriptions, the Aryan *čiça*, which he reads as Ayran brilliance/*khvarnah*, for which, see footnote 12, was not translated.

[48] In instances in which it is inscribed with a "Kassite" cross, it could symbolize Marduk, if the cross is understood as this god's symbol; see Ehrenberg 2002. Ornan (2005a: 207–18) opines that the first-millennium winged disk holds celestial significance and can represent various deities and offers Assur or Marduk for Neo-Assyrian representations, depending on the context in which it appears, and Marduk in Late Babylonian representations.

[49] On a Neo-Assyrian seal, a god standing on his animal mount is winged with the same horizontally extended wings with pendant ribbons as the winged disk, although the actual disk is not present. Atlantid figures hold up a

horizontal beam beneath the wings, indicating that it is this element, the wings (of the disk), or *melammu*, rather than the body of the god, that is being supported. For an illustration, see Ornan 2005b: fig. 134.

[50] On this fragmentary fourteenth-century stele in the Louvre, a section of the uppermost register shows the seated god Inshushinak holding a snake as well as the rod and ring, in front of a standing figure who must be Untash-Napirisha. It is illustrated in Börker-Klähn 1982: #124.

[51] For example, the Sasanian investitures of Ardashir I and Narseh at Naqsh-i Rustam; Ardashir I and Shapur I at Naqsh-i Rajab; Bahram I at Bishapur; and Ardashir II, Shapur III (probably), and Khusrow II at Taq-i Bostan. For a discussion of Sasanian rock reliefs with bibliography, see Harper 1986: 586–88. Parthian examples include, for example, the stele of Artaban V and Kwasak from Susa. Kawami (1987: 164–67, pl. 7) suggests that the seated figure extending the rod and ring is the king Artaban, who holds them out to Kwasak, satrap of Susa, who grasps the ring; however, the seated figure wears a horned crown and this would indicate divine rather than kingly status. Rock relief II at Tang-i Sarvak showing, among other figures, a reclining male holding the ring, serves as another Parthian example. The reclining figure may represent the ruler Orodes, although this is not clear; see Kawami 1987: 196–98, pl. 44. For further bibliogra-

first known appearance in the late third-millennium Ur III period on the stele of Ur-Namma (Moortgat 1969: pl. 194), but manifesting itself perhaps before that in the form of the combined semicircular ring and rod in fourth-millennium Uruk period glyptic, discussed later. As in Iranian scenes, the Mesopotamian deity extends the ring and rod toward the figure of the king and the action may also signify investiture, as in the early second-millennium wall mural of the palace of Zimrilim in Mari.[52]

In the literature, the Iranian ring, often beribboned, is generally agreed to be the ring of investiture or a diadem given in investiture, with comparison made to a head fillet with ribbons. Much ink has been spilled regarding the Mesopotamian rod and ring. Theories are mostly variations on the theme of their representing surveying or measuring tools, a hypothesis stemming from the depiction on the Ur-Namma stele in which the king, granted the rod and ring, is engaged in architectural construction. It is argued, by extrapolation, that the rod and ring symbolize justice that is granted the king by the gods so that he may wisely measure and dispense of it.[53] An alternate explanation, drawing on the rope that is associated with the ring on the Ur-namma stele, holds that that the ring is a nose-ring attached to a rope, for leading bound prisoners or oxen, or for symbolically leading the people, and that the motif later morphs into the rod and ring.[54] Based on comparison with the winged disk, however, it seems as if a completely unrelated explanation is likely, for the ring is the visual equivalent, on small scale, of the disk of the winged disk. Can this ring/disk be taken as the cosmic essence of the divine radiance, perhaps the cosmic circle?[55] The ring/disk of the Mesopotamian and Iranian winged disk is unlike the central form of the Egyptian winged disk, which is truly a disk or orb, and thus actually representative of the spherical sun. Why would the disk have been modified to a ring if not to denote something different. Cross-culturally, the circle can embody the visual understanding of city and by extension cosmic city or celestial world. In Neo-Assyrian reliefs, military camp cities are shown as circular in plan, divided into four quadrants, thus resembling the Egyptian hieroglyph *niwt* or city. Some cities were laid out with circular perimeters, for example Sasanian Firuzabad.[56] The so-called Babylonian world-map tablet depicts a circular world with Babylon at its center, surrounded by the sea and, according to the accompanying cuneiform text, the beyond-lying regions (fig. 6.12). An analogous rendition of the world map is illustrated in the mid-thirteenth century A.D. Bible Moralisée, whose frontispiece shows god as architect with compass in hand, delineating the circular perimeter of the cosmos in which are contained, apparently, the seas and planets.[57] On a more abstract level, the circle, with no

phy on the Tang-i Sarvak reliefs, see Downey 1986: 581 col. 2.

[52] Illustrations and extensive citations of examples of the rod and ring in Mesopotamian art can be found in van Buren 1949; Spycket 2000; Slanski 2007.

[53] For the most recent analysis of the rod and ring summarizing previous theories, see Slanski 2007: 41ff., 51.

[54] This view is held by Hallo (2005: 151, 160–61), who notes that in Sumerian royal hymns there are words for royal staff, nose-rope, and scepter given to the king to guide the people, but no word for ring, and feels that the rope lent its name to the rod and ring. Cooper (1990: 46), commenting on the lack of correspondence between text and image in the third millennium, writes that there are no contemporary references to measuring line and cord and that these objects "metamorphose" into rod and ring

in later eras, with confusing references to both "scepter and ring" and "weapon and ring." Lambert (1984: 90 n. 13) remarks that the words rod and ring never appear together in texts. This serves to underscore the difficulties inherent in identifying iconographic motifs on the basis of textual referents both synchronically and particularly diachronically, and the need to take the larger iconographic context into account. If the third-millennium ring references a nose-ring, it cannot be ascertained that this meaning held for the Babylonians or Persians in the first millennium.

[55] Lecoq (1984: 322) raises the possibility of the ring being a *khvarnah* equivalent.

[56] Firuzabad, founded by Ardashir I, has four gates, north, south, east, and west, with a temple at the center.

[57] Codex Vindobonensis 2554, Vienna National Library.

beginning or end, symbolizes infinity or eternity, hence the cosmic universe. Thus, the octagonal/circular form of the Christian baptistery: its eight sides recall the eighth day, the time beyond earthly time and of new creation, of the resurrected Christ and therefore the eternal life in Christ achieved through baptism. Conceptually cognate, mausoleums, as resting places for the eternal afterlife, were also conceived as circular structures.[58] Soudavar takes the disk of the Iranian winged disk to be the underwater pearl of *khvarnah*, and the ring, when alternatively rendered as a band of drilled dots rather than a solid band, to be a roundel of pearls.[59] The dotted ring in Mespotamian contexts should perhaps be interpreted as composed of precious gems. In the Neo-Assyrian period, a deity is occasionally shown within a circular nimbus of stars which may correspond to the ring both in shape and nature, that is, as a cosmic, celestial ring surrounding the deity.

The ring can also appear in contexts other than its being handed from the god to the king. In Achaemenid seals, a human bust, probably of a deity, can appear within a disk or ring in the center of the field (fig. 6.13).[60] In a Neo-Assyrian cylinder seal, the image is inverted, and the winged and tailed bust of the god sits within the surrounding disk, from which radiate what appear to be small rays (Ornan 2005b: fig. 78). Hence, the *khvarnhah*/Ahuramazda dwells within the cosmic universe. In Mesopotamia, the ring can be found as an independent icon atop a standard, thus, a ring-standard. Standards functioned as substitutes for deities, in their symbolic rather than anthropomorphic guises.[61] Although not a deity per se, the ring as a standard would be emblematic of the divine realm; an iconic standard of a measuring tool or nose-ring (if those readings of the ring symbol are accepted) is not to be expected. Further, the ring of the ring-standard, or the ring alone, can enclose a figure, thus similar to the ring of the winged disk encircling a bust, and deifying or making cosmic that which appears inside it.[62] Ribbons may flutter from Mesopotamian standards and also feature as an adjunct of Sasanian "investiture" rings. Perhaps they parallel, on some level, the banners that often stream from the winged disk (and derive from the uraei that coil down from the Egyptian winged disk) and contain aspects of *melammu/khvarnah*.[63] In a published lecture on comparative research in human culture, in particular cosmic kingship in the ancient world delivered in 1946, L'Orange already hypothesized that the ring in general symbolizes the "world ring of cosmocrator," the universe, the rotating wheel of the zodiac. Examples he provides included a Mithraic relief showing Mithra in the ring of the zodiac that he spins into motion; Roman sarcophagi portraying the bust of the (apotheosized) deceased in a ring/medallion supported by winged victories, and the ubiquitous image of Christ pantocrator in a ring/medallion at the apex of church domes, often

---

[58] An example is the sixth-century A.D. Mausoleum of Theodoric near Ravenna, Italy. Naturally, as a result of form following function, observatories are also circular buildings, for example, the early fifteenth-century A.D. Ulugh Beg observatory in Samarkand.

[59] Soudavar 2003: 18, 39, 102–03. Commenting on a coin of Khosrow II (ibid., p. 18), he remarks that *khvarnah* can be represented by rings, solar disks, sunbursts, and pearl roundels.

[60] In sealing PFS 68, on a Fortification Tablet, the entire body of the figure is depicted, but the ring encloses only the bust; see Garrison 2000: fig. 21.

[61] Deller (1992) discusses the divine status of standards.

[62] Consider the Neo-Assyrian Bavian relief or Neo-Assyrian seals, in which gods are depicted within the rings or ring-standards; for an example of a seal, see Ornan 2005b: fig. 140.

[63] Soudavar (2003: 13–14; 2006: 173–75) connects the ribbons to the Iranian term *dastar* (a word not encountered in pre-Islamic texts), which may be interpreted as "an agent for conveying victory," and notes that in Sasanian rock carvings, ribbons are carried to the king by winged figures, thus embodying the concept of increasing *khvarnah*.

with the four winged evangelists directly below in the spandrels (winged victories and evangelists reminiscent of the aura of the winged disk?).[64]

If the ring is interpreted to be the cosmic or celestial circle, it would be fitting that the deity would literally be handing the universe to the king, and the power to rule it. What, then, of the rod? Assurnasirpal, in his Nimrud palace reliefs, is portrayed holding a shallow vessel and a bow. Winter has demonstrated that the cups/vessels held by rulers in Mesopotamia represent divination bowls (for reading oil omens) and signify the king's ability to interpret the will of the gods and mediate between heaven and earth.[65] The bow, on the other hand, refers to the king's power over the temporal domain, the war-hero and defender of the land. If the vessel-and-bow metaphor is transferred to the symbols of ring and rod which the gods hand the kings, and the ring encapsulates the cosmic/sacred realm, then the rod must embody the terrestrial/secular realm. When full-length, a rod is a staff, often held in the hands of kings and likely marking out the ground on which they stand and over which they preside. Creation myths of numerous cultures envision a primeval separation of sky and earth, with a pillar/pole (or tree) acting as the axis that unites these realms also to the underworld.[66] A rod, when depicted two-dimensionally, translates into a rectangle. Just as the circle/ring must be cosmic, the rectangle/rod must be earthly. The Babylonian world-map tablet, referred to above, delineates the cosmic universe as a circle, within which is a rectangle, identified as the city of Babylon. Analogously, perhaps the rectangular layout of the traditional Mesopotamian temple cella can be thus explained: the temple embodies the manifestation of god on earth and the god's room of appearance, or throne room, on earth is envisioned as the earthly rectangle. The traditional Mesopotamian palatial throne room is also rectangular, reflecting the god's earthly throne room and therefore the king's status as the god's representative on earth. A variant form of the rod and ring mentioned above, in which the two forms are joined, has been identified with the Mesopotamian emblem for temple-door.[67] Such a reading of the motif would be in keeping with the interpretation of the rod and ring as heaven and earth, since the door to the temple marks the boundary between the two. Lending greater credence to this theory of the ring as a cosmic disk and rod as earth pillar is the observation by van Buren that in the Mari wall painting the ring is painted red and the rod white, indicating that the actual objects were of different materials.[68] In Neo-Assyrian reliefs, the color red simulated golden objects (like jewelry) and would be fitting for a heavenly disk; white may have evoked silver or rock crystal.

Again, a cross-cultural comparison serves to strengthen the proposed rod-and-ring theory. In China, carved jades known as *pi*-disks and *tsung*-pillars were fashioned as early as Neolithic times. Although their original meaning is unknown, later tradition associated the *pi*-disk with heaven and the *tsung*-pillar with earth. A scientific explanation for this assignation has been offered, whereby the two forms are considered to be the two elements of Neolithic astronomi-

---

[64] For discussion and illustrations, see L'Orange 1982: 90–102. His notion of the "world ring" is taken up by Segall (1956: 75).

[65] This is discussed in the context of Ur III presentation sealings (Winter 1986: 260–62).

[66] See Seidenberg 1983: 194–95. On a microcosmic scale, the city of Babylon symbolized the center of the world and the axis that joined heaven, earth, and subterranean sea, as its walls rose out of the waters of the surrounding moat and its temples extended to the heavens; see Van De Mieroop 2003: 263–65.

[67] See Spycket 2000: 651–52. This symbol may have derived from the Uruk "bundle" motif that may imitate the doorframe of a typical marshland *muhdif* [construction]. Curiously, a ribbon often hangs from the bundle motif, perhaps related to the ribbons adorning later standards, as discussed above. For an illustration of the Uruk bundle motif, see Moortgat 1969: pl. A, #5.

[68] Van Buren 1949: 450 and passim for other observations on the physical qualities of the symbols.

cal instruments which marked the rotation of the stars around the axis of the earth. According to this hypothesis, the disk, used to track the motions of the heavens, rotated around the pillar with hollow core, used as a sighting tube and earth-axis.[69] Tantalizing, also in the Chinese context, is an early twelfth-century A.D. Chinese scroll on the topic of strong leadership, commissioned by an emperor asserting his legitimacy to rule, by narrating a seventh-century B.C. tale about a prince similarly seeking to establish himself as duke.[70] One scene illustrates a follower of the duke handing him a *pi*-disk, an analog then of the Mesopotamian and Iranian compositions in which the king is handed the disk/ring to affirm his right to rule, and reinforcing the ring's identification as a symbol of the cosmic universe.

Both the Babylonians and Achaemenids partook of an adopted tradition of kingly ideology yet modified and augmented its expression with nuances derived from unique heritages and religious belief systems. The king's role and the hierarchy of his rule reflected and replicated that of the gods in heaven but did not substitute for or replace the celestial establishment. Visually, this is manifested in Persia through explicit royal tableaux, displaying the centrality of the king to world empire under god, and in Babylonia, seemingly through the absence of such, in favor of iconography emphasizing the cultic order maintained by the king. Just as Darius recognized his human servility before his god, who chose him as his "man in all the earth," Nabonidus referred to himself as his god's "humble servant" and worshiper. Divinely appointed, the kings were charged with protection of the corporeal realm and communication with the celestial realm; in the end, they were flesh and blood.

---

[69] Lee 1997: passim for illustrations and further scientific explanation.

[70] The scroll is known as *Duke Wen of Jin Recovering His State* and is pictured in *The New York Times*, October 8, 2006, Arts, p. 30.

Figure 6.1. Stele of Nabonidus. British Museum (Photo: HIP/Art Resource, New York)

Figure 6.2. Relief Showing King and Attendants with Winged Disk Above, from Council Hall, West Jamb, South Doorway of Main Hall, Persepolis (Photo: The Oriental Institute)

Figure 6.3. Tomb Facade of Artaxerxes I, Top Register, Naqsh-i Rustam (Photo: The Oriental Institute)

Figure 6.4. Treasury Relief, from Treasury, South Portico of Courtyard 17, Persepolis
(Photo: The Oriental Institute)

Figure 6.5. Hero/King Contending with Lion, from Palace of Darius, West Jamb, South Doorway,
Room 5, Persepolis (Photo: The Oriental Institute)

Figure 6.6. Brick Facade of Throne Room, Palace of Nebuchadnezzar, Babylon. Vorderasiatisches Museum, Staatliche Museen Berlin (Photo: Erich Lessing/Art Resource, New York)

Figure 6.7. Relief Showing Tribute-bearing Delegates, from Apadana, East Stairway, Persepolis
(Photo: The Oriental Institute)

Figure 6.8. Brick Panel, from Apadana, Persepolis (Photo: The Oriental Institute)

Figure 6.9. Lion-and-Bull Combat, from Apadana, East Stairway, Persepolis
(Photo: The Oriental Institute)

Figure 6.10. Cylinder Seal Impression on Clay Tablet, from Treasury, Room 33, Persepolis
(Photo: The Oriental Institute)

Figure 6.11. Investiture of Ardashir I, Naqsh-i Rustam (Photo: The Oriental Institute)

Figure 6.12. Babylonian World Map, Sippar(?). British Museum (Photo: HIP/Art Resource, New York)

Figure 6.13. Cylinder Seal Impression (enlarged), from Treasury, Persepolis. PT4-759.
(Photo: The Oriental Institute)

BIBLIOGRAPHY

Azarpay, Guitty
 1987   "Proportional Guidelines in Ancient Near Eastern Art." *Journal of Near Eastern Studies* 46: 183–213.

Beaulieu, Paul-Alain
 1989   "Agade in the Late Babylonian Period." *Nouvelles Assyriologiques Brèves et Utilitaires* 1989/3: 44–46.
 2003   *The Pantheon of Uruk during the Neo-Babylonian Period.* Cuneiform Monographs 33. Leiden: Brill.

Börker-Klähn, Jutta
 1982   *Altvorderasiatische Bildstelen und Vergleichbare Felsreliefs.* 2 volumes. Baghdader Forschungen 4. Mainz am Rhien: Philipp von Zabern.

Bregstein, Linda B.
 1993   "Seal Use in Fifth Century B.C. Nippur, Iraq: A Study of Seal Selection and Sealing Practices in the Murašû Archive." Ph.D. dissertation, University of Pennsylvania.

Briant, Pierre
 2002   *From Cyrus to Alexander: A History of the Persian Empire.* Winona Lake: Eisenbrauns.

Brinkman, John A., and Stephanie Dalley
 1988   "A Royal Kudurru from the Reign of Aššur-nadin-šumi." *Zeitschrift für Assyriologie* 78: 76–98.

Calmeyer, Peter
 1979   "Fortuna-Tyche-Khvarnah." *Jahrbuch des Deutschen Archäologischen Instituts* 94: 347–65.
 1984   "Das Zeichen der Herrschaft ... Ohne Šamaš wird es nicht gegeben." *Archäologische Mitteilungen aus Iran*, n.F., 1: 135–53.
 1994   "Babylonische und assyrische Elemente in der achaimenidischen Kunst." In *Continuity and Change* (Proceedings of the Achaemenid History Workshop in Ann Arbor, 6–8 April 1990), edited by Heleen Sancisi-Weerdenburg, Amélie Kuhrt, and Margaret C. Root, pp. 131–47. Achaemenid History 8. Leiden: Nederlands Instituut voor het Nabije Oosten.

Cooper, Jerrold S.
 1990   "Mesopotamian Historical Consciousness and the Production of Monumental Art in the Third Millennium B.C." In *Investigating Artistic Environments in the Ancient Near East*, edited by Ann C. Gunther, pp. 39–51. Washington, D.C.: Arthur M. Sackler Gallery, Smithsonian Institution.

Dalley, Stephanie
 1986   "The God Ṣalmu and the Winged Disk." *Iraq* 48: 85–101.

Dandamayev, Muhammad
 1997   "Assyrian Traditions during Achaemenid Times." In *Assyria 1995* (Proceedings of the 10th Anniversary of the Neo-Assyrian Text Corpus Project, Helsinki, 7–11 September, 1995), edited by Simo Parpola and Robert M. Whiting, pp. 41–48. Helsinki: The Neo-Assyrian Text Corpus Project.

Deller, Karlheinz

1992 "Einleitung." In "Götterstreitwagen und Götterstandarten: Götter auf dem Feldzug und ihr Kult im Feldlager," by Beate Pongratz-Leisten, Karlheinz Deller, and Erika Bleibtreu, pp. 291–98. *Baghdader Mitteilungen* 23: 291–356.

Downey, Susan B.

1986 "Art in Iran IV: Parthian." In *Encyclopedia Iranica*, Volume 2, Fascicle 6, edited by Ehsan Yarshater, pp. 580–85. London: Routledge and Kegan Paul.

Ehrenberg, Erica

1999 *Uruk: Late Babylonian Seal Impressions on Eanna Tablets.* Ausgrabungen in Uruk-Warka, Endberichte 18. Mainz am Rhein: Philipp von Zabern.

2000 "Babylonian Fortleben and Regionalism in Achaemenid Mesopotamia." In *Variatio Delectat: Iran und der Westen; Gedenkschrift für Peter Calmeyer,* edited by Reinhard Dittmann, pp. 313–20. Alter Orient und Altes Testament 272. Münster: Ugarit.

2002 "The Kassite Cross Revisited." In *Mining the Archives: Festschrift for Christopher Walker on the Occasion of His 60th Birthday, 4 October 2002,* edited by Cornelia Wunsch, pp. 65–76. Babylonische Archive 1. Dresden: ISLET.

2003–04 Review of *Seals on the Persepolis Fortification Tablets,* Volume 1: *Images of Heroic Encounter,* Oriental Institute Publications 117, by Mark B. Garrison and Margaret C. Root. *Archäologische Mitteilungen aus Iran und Turan* 35–36: 435–42.

2007 "Persian Conquerors, Babylonian Captivators." In *Regime Change in the Ancient Near East and Egypt: From Sargon of Agade to Saddam Hussein,* edited by Harriet E. W. Crawford, pp. 95–103. Proceedings of the British Academy 136. Oxford: Oxford University Press.

Frye, Richard N.

1964 "The Charisma of Kingship in Ancient Persia." *Iranica Antiqua* 4: 36–54.

Garelli, Paul

1981 "La conception de la royaute en Assyrie." In *Assyrian Royal Inscriptions: New Horizons in Literary, Ideological, and Historical Analysis* (Papers of Symposium in Siena, 26–28 June 1980), edited by Frederick M. Fales, pp. 1–11. Orientis Antiqui Collectio 17. Rome: Istituto per l'Orient.

Garrison, Mark B.

2000 "Achaemenid Iconography as Evidenced by Glyptic Art: Subject Matter, Social Function, Audience and Diffusion." In *Images as Media: Sources for the Cultural History of the Near East and the Eastern Mediterranean (1st Millennium BCE),* edited by Christoph Uehlinger, pp. 115–63. Orbis Biblicus et Orientalis 175. Fribourg: University Press.

Garrison, Mark B., and Margaret C. Root

2001 *Seals on the Persepolis Fortification Tablets,* Volume 1: *Images of Heroic Encounter.* Oriental Institute Publications 117. Chicago: The Oriental Institute.

George, Andrew R.

2007 Manuscripts in The Schøyen Collection. http://www.schoyencollection.com/history-Babylonian.html.

Gray, Louis H.

1901 "Stylistic Parallels between the Assyro-Babylonian and the Old Persian Inscriptions." *American Journal of Semitic Languages and Literatures* 17: 151–59.

Hallo, William W.

2005   "Sumerian History in Pictures: A New Look at the 'Stele of the Flying Angels.'" In
                *"An Experienced Scribe Who Neglects Nothing": Ancient Near Eastern Studies in
                Honor of Jacob Klein*, edited by Yitzhak Sefati, pp. 142–62. Bethesda: CDL Press.

Harper, Prudence O.

1986   "Art in Iran V: Sasanian." In *Encyclopedia Iranica*, Volume 2, Fascicle 6, edited by
                Ehsan Yarshater, pp. 585–94. London: Routledge and Kegan Paul.

Högemann, Peter

1992   *Das alte Vorderasien und die Achämeniden: Ein Beitrag zur Herodot-Analyse*. Bei-
                hefte zum Tübinger Atlas des Vorderen Orients, Reihe B 98. Wiesbaden: Ludwig
                Reichert.

Jacobs, Bruno

2002   "Achämenidische Kunst – Kunst im Achämenidenreich." *Archäologische Mitteil-
                ungen aus Iran und Turan* 34: 345–95.

Jursa, Michael

2007   "The Transition of Babylonia from the Neo-Babylonian Empire to Achaemenid
                Rule." In *Regime Change in the Ancient Near East and Egypt: From Sargon of Agade
                to Saddam Hussein*, edited by Harriet E. W. Crawford, pp. 73–94. Proceedings of the
                British Academy 136. Oxford: Oxford University Press.

Kaim, Barbara

1991   "Das geflügelte Symbol in der achämenidischen Glyptic." *Archäologische Mitteil-
                lungen aus Iran*, n.F., 24: 31–34.

Kawami, Trudy S.

1987   *Monumental Art of the Parthian Period in Iran*. Acta Iranica 26; Textes et mé-
                moires 13. Leiden: Brill.

Koldewey, Robert

1969   *Die Königsburgen von Babylon*, Volume 2: *Die Hauptburg und der Sommerpalast
                Nebukadnezars im Hügel Babil*. Wissenschaftliche Veröffentlichungen der Deutsche
                Orient-Gesellschaft 55. Osnabrück: Otto Zeller.

Kuhrt, Amélie

1984   "The Achaemenid Concept of Kingship." *Iran* 22: 156–60.
1990   "Achaemenid Babylonia: Sources and Problems." In *Achaemenid History*, Volume
                4: *Centre and Periphery* (Proceedings of the Groningen 1986 Achaemenid History
                Workshop), edited by Heleen Sancisi-Weerdenburg and Amélie Kuhrt, pp. 177–94.
                Achaemenid History 4. Leiden: Nederlands Instituut voor het Nabije Oosten.

Kuhrt, Amélie, and Susan Sherwin-White

1987   "Xerxes' Destruction of Babylonian Temples." In *Achaemenid History*, Volume
                2: *The Greek Sources* (Proceedings of the Groningen 1984 Achaemenid History
                Workshop), edited by Heleen Sancisi-Weerdenburg and Amélie Kuhrt, pp. 69–78.
                Achaemenid History 2. Leiden: Nederlands Instituut voor het Nabije Oosten.

Lambert, Wilfred G.

1984   "The History of the muš-ḫuš in Ancient Mesopotamia." In *L'animal, l'homme, le
                Dieu dans le proche-orient ancien* (Actes du colloque de Cartigny in Geneva, 1981),
                edited by Phillippe Borgeaud, Yves Christe, and Ivanka Urio, pp. 87–94. Les Cahiers
                du Centre d'Étude du Proche-Orient ancien 2. Leuven: Peeters.

Lecoq, Pierre

1984 "Ahura Mazda ou Xvarnah." In *Orientalia J. Duchesne-Guillemin emerato oblata,* edited by Jacques Duchesne-Guillemin, pp. 301–26. Acta Iranica 23; Deuxième série, Hommages et opera minora 9. Leiden: Brill.

Lee, Tsung-Dao

1997 "The Origins of Pi, Tsung and Xuan Ji: A Theoretical Suggestion." *Chinese Journal of Physics* 35: 943–46.

L'Orange, Hans Peter

1982 *Studies on the Iconography of Cosmic Kingship in the Ancient World.* Institute for Sammenlignende Kulturforskning, Series A 23. New York: Caratzas Brothers.

MacGinnis, John

1995 *Letter Orders from Sippar and the Administration of the Ebabbara in the Late-Babylonian Period.* Poznan: Bonami.

Magen, Ursula

1986 *Assyrische Königsdarstellungen: Aspekte der Herrschaft: Eine Typologie.* Baghdader Forschungen 9. Mainz am Rhein: Philipp von Zabern.

Mayer-Opificius, Ruth

1983 "Die geflügelte Sonnenscheibe, ein Jahrtausende altes Motiv." In *Antidoron: Festschrfit für Jürgen Thimme zum 65. Geburtstag am 26. September 1982,* edited by Dietler Metzler, Brinna Otto, and Christof Müller-Wirth, pp. 19–24. Karslruhe: C. F. Müller.

1984 "Die geflügelte Sonne: Himmels- und Regendarstellungen im alten Vorderasien." *Ugarit Forschungen* 16: 189–236.

Moortgat, Anton

1969 *The Art of Ancient Mesopotamia: The Classical Art of the Near East.* London: Phaidon.

Oppenheim, A. Leo

1943 "Akkadian pul(u)ḫ(t)u and melammu." *Journal of the American Oriental Society* 63: 31–34.

Ornan, Tallay

2005a "A Complex System of Religious Symbols: The Case of the Winged Disc in Near Eastern Imagery of the First Millennium BCE." In *Crafts and Images in Contact: Studies on Eastern Mediterranean Art of the First Millennium BCE,* edited by Claudia E. Suter and Christoph Uehlinger, pp. 207–41. Orbis Biblicus et Orientalis 210. Fribourg: Academic Press; Göttingen: Vandenhoeck & Ruprecht.

2005b *The Triumph of the Symbol: Pictorial Representation of Deities in Mesopotamia and the Biblical Image Ban.* Orbis Biblicus et Orientalis 213. Fribourg: Academic Press; Göttingen: Vandenhoeck & Ruprecht.

Pongratz-Leisten, Beate

1994 *Ina Šulmi Īrub: Die kulttopographische und ideologische Programmatik der akītu-Prozession in Babylonien und Assyrien im 1. Jahrtausend v. Chr.* Baghdader Forschungen 16. Mainz am Rhien: Philipp von Zabern.

Pongratz-Leisten, Beate; Karlheinz Deller; and Erika Bleibtreu

1992 "Götterstandarten: Götter auf dem Feldzug und ihr Kult im Feldlager." *Baghdader Mitteilungen* 23: 291–356.

Reade, Julian E.

1977   "Shikaft-i Gulgul: Its Date and Symbolism." *Iranica Antiqua* 12: 33–44.

Root, Margaret C.

1979   *The King and Kingship in Achaemenid Art: Essays on the Creation of an Iconography
                of Empire.* Acta Iranica 19; Textes et mémoires 9. Leiden: Brill.

1980   "The Persepolis Perplex: Some Prospects Borne of Retrospect." In *Ancient Persia:
                The Art of an Empire,* edited by Denise Schmandt-Besserat, pp. 5–13. Invited Lec-
                tures on the Middle East at the University of Texas at Austin 4. Malibu: Undena.

1994   "Lifting the Veil: Artistic Transmission beyond the Boundaries of Historical Peri-
                odisation." In *Achaemenid History,* Volume 8: *Continuity and Change* (Proceedings
                of the last Achaemenid History Workshop in Ann Arbor, 6–8 April 1990), edited
                by Heleen Sancisi-Weerdenburg, Amélie Kuhrt, and Margaret C. Root, pp. 9–37.
                Achaemenid History 8. Leiden: Nederlands Instituut voor het Nabije Oosten.

2000   "Imperial Ideology in Achaemenid Persian Art: Transforming the Mesopotamian
                Legacy." *Bulletin of the Canadian Society for Mesopotamian Studies* 35: 19–27.

Segall, Berta

1956   "Notes on the Iconography of Cosmic Kingship." *Art Bulletin* 38: 75–80.

Seidenberg, Abraham

1983   "The Separation of Sky and Earth at Creation (III)." *Folklore* 94: 192–200.

Seidl, Ursula

1957–71   "Göttersymbole und -attribute. A. Archäologisch. I. Mesopotamien." *Reallexikon der
                Assyriologie* 3: 483–90.

1989   *Die babylonischen Kudurru-reliefs: Symbole mesopotamischer Gottheiten.* Orbis Bi-
                blicus et Orientalis 87. Freiburg: Academic Press; Göttingen: Vandenhoeck & Rupre-
                cht.

1994   "Achaimenidische Entlehnungen aus der Urartäischen Kultur." In *Achaemenid His-
                tory,* Volume 8: *Continuity and Change* (Proceedings of the last Achaemenid History
                Workshop in Ann Arbor, 6–8 April 1990), edited by Heleen Sancisi-Weerdenburg,
                Amélie Kuhrt, and Margaret C. Root, pp. 107–29. Achaemenid History 8. Leiden:
                Nederlands Instituut voor het Nabije Oosten.

Shahbazi, Alireza Sh.

1974   "An Achaemenid Symbol I: A Farewell to 'Fravahr' and 'Ahuramazda.'" *Archäolo-
                gische Mitteilungen aus Iran,* n.F., 7: 135–44.

1980   "An Achaemenid Symbol II: Farnah '(God Given) Fortune' Symbolized." *Archäolo-
                gische Mitteilungen aus Iran,* n.F., 13: 119–47.

Slanski, Kathryn E.

2007   "The Mesopotamian 'Rod and Ring': Icon of Righteous Kingship and Balance of
                Power between Palace and Temple." In *Regime Change in the Ancient Near East and
                Egypt: From Sargon of Agade to Saddam Hussein,* edited by Harriet E. W. Craw-
                ford, pp. 37–59. Proceedings of the British Academy 136. Oxford: Oxford University
                Press.

Soudavar, Abolala

2003   *The Aura of Kings: Legitimacy and Divine Sanction in Iranian Kingship.* Bibliotheca
                Iranica, Intellectual Traditions 10. Costa Mesa: Mazda Publishers.

2006   "The Significance of Av. čiθra, OP. çiça, MP. čihr, and NP. čehr, for the Iranian Cos-
                mogony of Light." *Iranica Antiqua* 41: 151–85.

2010   "The Formation of Achaemenid Imperial Ideology and Its Impact on the Avesta." In
                *The World of Achaemenid Persia: History, Art and Society in Iran and the Ancient
                Near East* (proceedings of a conference at the British Museum 29th September–1st
                October 2005), edited by John Curtis and St. John Simpson, pp. 11–38. http://www.
                soudavar.com/ACHAEMENID%20IMPERIAL%20ideology-5.pdf.

Spycket, Agnes
2000   "La baguette et l'anneau: Un symbole d'Iran et de Mésopotamie." In *Variatio Delec-
                tat: Iran und der Westen, Gedenkschrift für Peter Calmeyer,* edited by Reinhard Dit-
                tmann, pp. 651–66. Alter Orient und Altes Testament 272. Münster: Ugarit.

Stolper, Matthew W.
1989   "The Governor of Babylon and Across-the-River in 486 B.C." *Journal of Near East-
                ern Studies* 48: 283–305.
1990   "Late Achaemenid Legal Texts from Uruk and Larsa." *Baghdader Mitteilungen* 21:
                559–624.

Unger, Eckhard
1965   "Die Symbole des Gottes Assur." *Belletin Türk Tarih Kurumu* 29: 423–83.

van Buren, Elizabeth D.
1949   "The Rod and Ring." *Archiv Orientální* 17: 434–50.

Van De Mieroop, Marc
2003   "Reading Babylon." *American Journal of Archaeology* 107: 257–75.

Vanderhooft, David Stephen
1999   *The Neo-Babylonian Empire and Babylon in the Latter Prophets.* Harvard Semitic
                Museum Monographs 59. Atlanta: Scholars Press.

Waters, Matt
2004   "Cyrus and the Achaemenids." *Iran* 42: 91–102.

Weissbach, Franz H.
1906   *Die Inschriften Nebukadnezars II im Wâdi Brîsa und am Nahr el-Kelb.* Wissenschaft-
                liche Veröffentlichungen der Deutschen Orient-Gesellschaft 5. Leipzig: J. C. Hin-
                richs.

Westenholz, Joan Goodnick
2000   "The King, the Emperor, and the Empire: Continuity and Discontinuity of Royal Rep-
                resentation in Text and Image." In *The Heirs of Assyria* (Proceedings of the Opening
                Symposium of the Assyrian and Babylonian Intellectual Heritage Project in Tvär-
                minne, Finland, 8–11 October 1998), edited by Sanno Aro and Robert M. Whiting,
                pp. 99–125. Melammu Symposia 1. Helsinki: Neo-Assyrian Text Corpus Project.

Winter, Irene J.
1986   "The King and the Cup: Iconography of the Royal Presentation Scene on Ur III
                Seals." In *Insight through Images: Studies in Honor of Edith Porada*, edited by Mari-
                lyn Kelly-Buccellati, pp. 253–68. Bibliotheca Mesopotamica 21. Malibu: Undena.
1992   "'Idols of the King': Royal Images as Recipients of Ritual Action in Ancient Mesopo-
                tamia." *Journal of Ritual Studies* 6: 13–42.
1994   "Radiance as an Aesthetic Value in the Art of Mesopotamia (with Some Indian Par-
                allels)." In *Art, the Integral Vision: A Volume of Essays in Felicitation of Kapila
                Vatsyayan,* edited by Baidyanath N. Saraswati, S. C. Malik, and Madhu Khanna, pp.
                123–32. New Delhi: D. K. Printworld.

1997   "Art *in* Empire: The Royal Image and the Visual Dimensions of Assyrian Ideology." In *Assyria 1995* (Proceedings of the 10th Anniversary Symposium of the
Neo-Assyrian Text Corpus Project, 7–11 September 1995), edited by Simo Parpola
and Robert M. Whiting, pp. 359–81. Helsinki: Neo-Assyrian Text Corpus Project.

7

THE KING IS DEAD, LONG LIVE THE KING: THE LAST DAYS OF THE ŠU-SÎN CULT AT EŠNUNNA AND ITS AFTERMATH

CLEMENS REICHEL, UNIVERSITY OF TORONTO

Numerous studies have been devoted to the origin, ideological basis, and legitimization of divine kingship and its cultic manifestations in the world of the ancient Near East. By comparison, little attention has been paid to the decline or termination of such cults following political crises or collapses.[1] This is unfortunate since numerous examples in both ancient and modern times have shown that it is the demise of a political system that forces its key protagonists to unmask and show their real faces and motivations hidden behind their institutional roles. For a volume dedicated to the ideology and empirical manifestations of divine kingship it seems appropriate, therefore, to address this topic with a case study.

One of the best examples for the rise, manifestation, and demise of this phenomenon is the period of the Third Dynasty of Ur (often simplified to "Ur III period"), which ruled southern Mesopotamia from 2118 to 2004 B.C.[2] Following the Akkadian period (ca. 2350–2150 B.C.), which had seen the first deified kings with Naramsin (2254–2218 B.C.) and Šarkališarri (2217–2193 B.C.),[3] and preceding the Isin-Larsa period (ca. 2000–1800 B.C.), which saw the demise of this phenomenon, this period, which covered a little more than a century, truly represents the apex for divine kingship in ancient Mesopotamia. Šulgi (2094–2048 B.C.), the second ruler of this dynasty, was the first of its rulers to assume divine status, a position retained by his successors Amar-Su'en (2047–2038 B.C.), Šu-Sîn (2037–2029 B.C.), and Ibbi-Sîn (2028–2004 B.C.) (fig. 7.1). Numerous royal inscriptions, hymns, and ritual practices bear ample witness to the ideological significance of divine kingship during this time period. The cult to the king was visually manifested by the fashioning of artwork, including royal statues and steles, and by temples or chapels to these divine kings. Numerous economic texts mention the building of or provisions for É's, the Sumerian term for "temple," dedicated to Ur III kings.[4] The spread of these É's within the Ur III state was impressive. As figure 7.2 shows, four of them (in Umma, KI.AN, Gu'abba, and Girsu) were dedicated to Šulgi, two (in Umma and Girsu) to

---

[1] See Yoffee and Cowhill 1988 and Tainter 1988 for recent discussions of collapse models suggested for the ancient Near East and for Mesoamerica.

[2] All dates given in this paper follow the Middle Chronology. In rendering personal or geographic names I have used diacritics (e.g., š, ḫ) but generally retained commonly used transliterations (e.g., Naramsin instead of Naram-Sîn) without attempting ultimate consistency.

[3] Materials for the rise and fall of the Akkadian dynasty have been summarized recently by Westenholz (1999). Historical, historiographic, and literary sources concerning the demise of the Akkadian empire have been studied by Glassner (1986).

[4] In his study of the Ur III kingship, Claus Wilcke (1974: 190–91 n. 51) cautioned against a universal translation in this context of "É dRN" as "temple of (divine) RN," pointing out that É also can translated as "house" or "household." Though caution in the use of modern-day translations for Sumerian terms is generally justified in light of possible misinterpretations, I doubt that a translation "temple" for É can really be kept separate from a meaning "house" or "household." In addition to serving as a place of worship, a temple also embodies the household of the deity with its personnel, land or livestock holdings, and attached manufactures. Even the palace (Sumerian É-gal, literally "big house") of the Royal Dynasty at Ur was referred to as an É: brick inscriptions

Amar-Sîn, and no less than five (in Umma, Ur, Adab, Girsu, and Ešnunna) to Šu-Sîn.[5] This paper addresses the end of the cult to Šu-Sîn, the fourth king of the Ur III Dynasty in southern Mesopotamia. The dataset used in this study does not originate from the capital but from a city in a somewhat "peripheral" location within this state. As this study shows, however, the "peripheral" nature of this dataset provides us with an angle on the collapse of this system that is different from any information retrieved from the royal capital itself.

In his summary of the Ur III period, Sallaberger (1999: 170–71) already pointed out the great difference in the nature of temple building projects during the reign of Šu-Sîn compared to those undertaken during the reign of his predecessor Amar-Su'en.[6] Textual evidence indicates that Šu-Sîn did not continue his predecessor's ambitious work on building and refurbishing city temples — only the temple of the city god Šara at Umma was completed during his reign.[7] Instead, numerous temples to Šu-Sîn himself were built by governors in several cities of the Ur III state.[8] We are fortunate that one of these temples was actually discovered during excavations. It was found to the northeast of Baghdad at the site of Tell Asmar, the ancient city of Ešnunna, in 1930 during the Oriental Institute's Diyala Expedition (Frankfort, Lloyd, and Jacobsen 1940). The map shown in figure 7.3 shows that Ešnunna expanded greatly during the Ur III period. It is at once noticeable that the Šu-Sîn Temple was not built on the ancient city mound in the northwestern part of the site that constituted Ešnunna during the third millen-

---

found in the building's central courtyard identify it as é-ḫur-sag, literally "mountain house" or "mountain temple" built by king Šulgi (see Woolley 1974: 38 for the find context of the bricks; Frayne 1997: 112–14 [3], for a recent edition of the inscription), indicating that É as "temple household" could also include the royal household. A functional syncretism of "palace" and "temple" is also suggested in this building's architecture while following a standard layout of a palace, its facade shows the niched decoration usually associated with religious architecture (Woolley 1974: pl. 56).

[5] The textual references used to compile figure 7.2 were collected by Wilcke 1974: 190–91 n. 51 (é ᵈšul-gi) and by Sallaberger 1999: 166, 170 (É ᵈamar-ᵈsîn, é ᵈšu-ᵈsîn). To these references text Erlenmeyer 94 (Englund 1992: 87–88), which dates the reign of Šu-Sîn and lists fishing troops for É's of Šulgi, Amar-Su'en, and Šu-Sîn in reverse lines 3, 6, 9, can be added. For a suggested identification of KI.AN with Tell Šamit, see Edzard and Farber 1974: 97–98; for the location of Gu'abba southeast of Lagash, see ibid., 63–65.

[6] The scope of this paper does not allow a comprehensive review of the relationship between Amar-Su'en and Šu-Sîn. In this paper I have followed Sallaberger (1999: 167–88) in identifying Šu-Sîn as Amar-Su'en's son, based on the legend of the seal of Babati, which identifies Šu-Sîn as son of Abī-Simtī, Amar-su'en's wife (Whiting 1977b). References to dissenting viewpoints, which identified Amar-Su'en as brother of Šu-Sîn, have been collected by Frayne (1997: 285–86). Texts with Amar-Su'en year dates (Amar-Su'en years 6–8) that bear seal impressions naming Šu-Sîn as "king of Ur" have raised the possibility of a co-regency, though this interpretation remains much debated (cf. Lafont 1994;

Sallaberger 1999: 166). Attempt to suppress the Amar-Su'en's memory by eliminating him from the list of royal recipients of offerings at Nippur, ending the Amar-Su'en festival at Umma, and by renaming the Amar-Su'en Temple at Girsu (see Sallaberger 1999: 167) indicate a tense relationship between Šu-Sîn and his predecessor.

[7] The completion of this temple is commemorated in numerous building inscriptions on door sockets and stone blocks presumably from Umma (Frayne 1997: 326–29 [16–18]). Remains of a monumental temple with a niched entranceway facade were uncovered from the late 1990s onwards at the site of Tell Jokha (ancient Umma) by an archaeological team from the Iraqi Department of Antiquities under the direction of Nawala al-Mutawali. The results of these excavations so far have not been published. Photographs of this temple's facade taken by site visitors during excavation, however, show that the lower courses of the temple's brickwork were executed in baked brick, of which at least some were stamped with inscriptions naming Šu-Sîn as the builder of the temple (McGuire Gibson, pers. comm.), making it likely that these are the remains of the Šu-Sîn's Šara Temple at Umma.

[8] Aside from the temple discussed in this paper, building inscriptions record the construction of Šu-Sîn Temples by Ḫa-ba-lu₅-gé, governor (ensí) at Adab; by Irₗₗ-ᵈNanna, grand vizier (sukkal-maḫ) and governor at Girsu, and by Lugal-má-gurₓ-re, governor or Ur (Frayne 1997: 321–26 [11, 13, 15]). A door socket from Ur, found in secondary context in the Gipar of the goddess Ningal, records the construction of a temple for Šu-Sîn by an individual named [ ]-kal-la (ibid., 324–25 [14]). Since [ ]-kal-la's title "general" (šagina) does not state an affiliation with a particular city, however, it is uncertain whether this temple was built at Ur or elsewhere.

nium B.C., but on new ground in the middle of a new lower town.[9] It was not an isolated structure; but, in fact, located roughly in the center of an agglomeration of buildings that clearly
betray "palatial" character. Along its western side it abutted and was joined through a doorway
to the "Palace of the Rulers" that was home to Ešnunna's governors from about 2050 to 1800
B.C. and the center of this city's administration (fig. 7.4). The temple had a square layout; each
side measured approximately 28 m with outside walls up to 3 m wide. The center part of the
temple contained a square paved courtyard, to which most of the surrounding rooms opened.
The room arrangement of the temple was largely symmetrical. Its entrance in the northwest,
accordingly, was in direct line with the temple's broadroom cella, allowing — at least theo-
retically — a direct view into the cella from the outside. The middle of the cella's back wall,
which was in direct line with its doorway toward the courtyard, contained a stepped podium
that likely accommodated a cult image. A doorway on the western side of the cella opened into
a small room that may have been a repository for cultic paraphernalia. This building represents
one of the earliest surviving examples of the "Babylonian" temple with a rectangular cella
("Breitraumcella") opening to a central courtyard, a layout that was to become the standard
temple type in Babylonia for the next two millennia.[10] What makes its plan somewhat unusual
is a doorway that connects the temple with the throne-room suite of the adjacent Palace of the
Rulers, indicating a strong connection between the city's administration and the cult performed
at the temple.

An inscribed door socket found inside the cella on the western side of the doorway con-
firms that the governor of Ešnunna was the builder of this temple as well as the recipient of
this cult (figs. 7.5–6):[11]

Transliteration:	Translation:
1. ^{d}šu-^{d}EN.ZU	"(For the deified) Šu-Sîn,
2. mu pà-da	whose name had been called
3. an-na	by (the god) Anu,
4. ki-ág ^{d}en-líl-la	beloved one of (the god) Enlil,
5. lugal ^{d}en-líl-le	the king whom Enlil
6. šà-kù-ge pà-da	had chosen into his pure heart

[9] My dating of Ešnunna's expansion differs from that
of the excavators, who assigned it to the Isin-Larsa period (ca. 2000–1800 B.C.). The location of the Šu-Sîn
Temple and the adjacent Palace of the Rulers (see discussion for the date of this complex) in the center of the
lower town make a post-Ur III date for the city's expansion impossible to maintain — a palace and major cult
center would not have been built outside of the city. The
evidence given by the excavators for their own dating is
thin. The city wall was dated to the "Larsa" period (ca.
1900–1800 B.C.) based on brick measurements (Delougaz, Hill, and Jacobsen 1967: 199), but no measurements
are given in support of this argument, and the possibility
of a multi-phase construction, in which the latest refur-
bishment dates to the Larsa period, is not even raised.
Test trenches across the lower town revealed architectural remains that largely dated to the Isin-Larsa period
(ibid., 203–09), but in most cases those trenches only
reached the latest preserved level of occupation. Tablets
dating to the immediate post-Ur III period at Ešnunna
were found in the southern part of the site (square K43;

ibid., 206). A building discovered in Trench B (squares
G38–39) was dated to the Akkadian period "owing to
the character of the finds in it" (ibid., 207). The object
registers do not list any finds from these squares, but if
the dating suggested by the excavators was based on pottery types, it should probably be adjusted to Ur III (cf.
Gibson 1982: 537–38).

[10] See Heinrich (1982: 18–21) for the origins and characteristics of this temple type and for a definition of the
"Breitraumcella." Its earliest attested occurrence is found
in a temple within the Gipar of the goddess Ningal at
Ur (Woolley 1974: 43–44, pl. 57), originally built by
Urnammu and subsequently rebuilt by Amar-Su'en. This
temple shows a slightly more elaborate layout, however,
since the cella was preceded by an antecella of about the
same size toward the courtyard.

[11] Published by Jacobsen (1940): 134–35 (translation
and transliteration), pl. 13 (copy). For a recent edition
with additional literature, see Frayne 1997: 322–23 [12].
One of these door sockets (find number As. 31:792) is
on display at the Oriental Institute Museum (museum

7.	nam-sipa kalam-ma	to shepherd the land
8.	ù an-ub-da-limmu-ba-šè	and the four world quarters,
9.	lugal kal-ga	mighty king,
10.	lugal uríki-ma	king of Ur,
11.	lugal an-ub-da-limmu-ba	king of the four world quarters,
12.	dingir-ra-ni-ir	his (i.e., Ituria's) god:
13.	*i-tu-ria*	Ituria,
14.	ensí	governor
15.	áš-nun-naki-ka	of Ešnunna,
16.	ìr-da-né-e	his (i.e., Šu-Sîn's) servant,
17.	é-a-ni	(has built) his (i.e., Šu-Sîn's) temple
18.	mu-na-an-dù	for him."

The inscription on this door socket introduces the dynasty of Ešnunna's governors to this story. Little more that his name is known about governor Ituria — most notably, no inscription provides his patronym. Following Šu-Sîn's death in 2029 B.C., Ituria continued to hold the office into the reign of Ibbi-Sîn, Šu-Sîn's son and successor,[12] but soon afterward was followed by his son Šuiliya.[13] We do not know if Šuiliya's ascent to Ešnunna's throne coincided with the end of Ur's control over Ešnunna; by 2026 B.C., however, Ešnunna's Ur III calendar had been replaced by a local one, and year formulae in texts now reflected actions taken by Šuiliya. By assuming the title "king" (lugal) instead of "governor" (ensí), this new ruler made it clear that he was no copycat of his father. His seal, preserved on a clay sealing (fig. 7.7), shows him facing Tišpak, Ešnunna's city god, in a proud, defiant way recalling earlier Akkadian royal depictions such as one found on the Naramsin Stele and "king of the four world quarters" (*šar kibrat arba'im*), he also claimed divine status, following the example set by previous rulers of the Akkadian and Ur III dynasties.

---

number OI A8164). The find number of the other one is As. 31:793a (not As. 31:246, as erroneously reported by Jacobsen) and is now in the Iraq Museum.

[12] The fact that Ituria was still governor of Ešnunna after Ibbi-Sîn's ascent to the throne is apparent from the legend of a seal belonging to Ituria's son Šuiliya, in which Šuiliya is identified as "son of Ituria, the governor" while acknowledging Ibbi-Sîn's overlordship in the inscription (Frankfort, Lloyd, and Jacobsen 1940: 143 [5]):

1.	di-bí-dEN.ZU	"Ibbi-Sîn,
2.	[lu]gal kal-ga	mighty king,
3.	lugal uriki-ma	king of Ur
4.	lugal an-ub-da-limmu-ba	king of the four world quarters:
5.	dšu-i-lí-a	Šuiliya,
6.	dub-[sar]	the scribe,
7.	dumu *i-tu-[ri-a]*	son of Ituria,
8.	ens[í]	the governor,
9.	ÌR-sú	(is) his servant."

The issue of Šuiliya's divine status as a prince in this inscription is addressed in footnote 13 below.

[13] The reasons for reading DINGIR-*šu-i-lí-a* as dŠuiliya as opposed to Ilušuliliya (as used by Jacobsen) have been discussed by Whiting (1977b), and not much can be added to that. Jacobsen based his reading of the name on a legend of a seal that Šuiliya held as a prince (see n. 12 above), in which he acknowledged Ibbi-Sîn as overlord and in which he is identified as "DINGIR-šuiliya, scribe, son of Ituria, the governor." Since "... it would clearly be impossible to assume that the owner of the seal was already deified at a time when he merely was a young scribe in the service of Ibisin" Jacobsen concluded that the name had to be read Ilušuliliya, not dŠuiliya (1940: 143). As Whiting had already noted, the sealing with this inscription unfortunately is missing and therefore cannot be collated. The deification of a crown prince during that time period is not unheard of. As Wu Yhong (1992) pointed out, a roughly contemporary inscription by king Iddi-Sîn of Simurrum, a political entity in the lower Zab area, shows both the names of Iddi-Sîn (1.1: di-di-dSîn) and of his son Zabazuna (1.4: dza-ba-zu-na) written with a divine determinative (Al-Fouadi 1978: 123 [A.3, A.4]). Unlike Ituria and Šuiliya, however, both father and son are deified here.

Unlike the Šu-Sîn Temple, the adjacent Palace of the Rulers provided no building inscription that would have identified its builder. The excavators noted that the palace walls bonded with the brickwork of the temple's *kisû*, an outer revetment of the temple. Since this *kisû* was a secondary construction, they concluded that the building of the palace had to postdate that of the temple.[14] By calling it "Palace of the Rulers," they interpreted it as the residence of Ešnunna's rulers, built during Šuiliya's reign after the end of the Ur III rule over the city (Lloyd 1940: 27). This interpretation, however, makes little sense — why would Ešnunna's first independent ruler have built his new palace as a mere add-on to a temple in which a foreign overlord, who now presumably was vilified, had been worshipped as a god?

A closer look at the evidence casts serious doubts on the construction sequence suggested by the excavators. Figure 7.8 shows the date ranges of over 140 Ur III texts and sealings from the palace and the temple organized by findspots. The fact that the overwhelming majority of these texts were found in the *palace*, not in the temple, suggests that the palace was built *during*, not *after* the Ur III period. Several texts date back to the middle of Šulgi's reign (Šulgi 25 = 2070 B.C.), some forty-five years before Šuiliya's ascent to Ešnunna's throne. It seems sensible to suggest, therefore, that the Palace of the Rulers was built at about the same time as the seat of the Ur III governor of Ešnunna. Instead of postdating the Šu-Sîn Temple, the palace's construction would therefore predate the temple by about forty years.

This re-dating might explain another oddity in the layout of these buildings — the difference in orientation between palace and temple, shown in figure 7.9 (the orientation of the palace is indicated by a line running from the niche of the cella in the so-called "Palace Chapel," a sanctuary along the western side of the palace, through its entranceway). At an orientation of 320° 18′ to true north, the line through the Palace Chapel — and the palace as a whole — is tilted 14° 36′ farther to the northwest than the line running through the Šu-Sîn Temple, which runs at an orientation of 334° 54′. There are no obvious spatial constrains from other buildings that would have had to be taken into account for either temple or palace. The revised construction sequence proposed above now offers a possible explanation for this awkward deviation. In a largely overlooked study added to the original publication of the palace complex, Günter Martiny pointed out that the axis running through the Šu-Sîn Temple points toward the city of Ur, the capital of the Ur III state, located some 300 km to the southeast of Tell Asmar (Martiny 1940). It is not hard to imagine cultic reasons that necessitated a proper alignment of the king's temple and statue with the royal palace at Ur, even if this resulted in a misalignment between the temple and palace.

In light of this reinterpretation, the bonding brickwork between temple *kisû* and palace needs to be explained differently. Ironically, the excavators' own field notes provide a much more plausible interpretation. A note and sketch in the field notebook of Seton Lloyd, who worked as excavator and architect during the palace's excavation, indicates that the northwestern and northeastern walls of the room due north of the throne room (marked in fig. 7.9), which were built at an oblique angle to each other and to the rest of the palace, were secondary constructions.[15] Most likely they were rebuilt during the construction of the Šu-Sîn Temple, presumably to catch the difference in orientation between the palace and the temple.

---

[14] "... the fact that the *kisû* terminates abruptly on a line with the northwest corner of the temple and that the outer wall faces are everywhere traceable behind it suggests that the retaining wall was a later addition to the original building, probably constructed at the same time as the adjoining palace and by the same builder" (Lloyd 1940: 12–13).

[15] Seton Lloyd's field notebook from the 1931/32 season, entry dating to January 10, 1932 (Oriental Institute Museum Archives).

To the present day, the Šu-Sîn Temple of Ešnunna remains the only archaeologically identified temple of an Ur III king. This may be more than a coincidence. Textual evidence from
elsewhere suggests that temples to Ur III kings were generally relatively small. Erlenmayer 94,
for example, a text from Umma dated to the reign of Šu-Sîn, lists fishermen assigned to several temples at Umma. Following sixteen fishermen for the temple of Šara, Umma's city god,
four for the temple of Nin-ur-ra, and two for the É-mah, two fishermen each are assigned to
the temples of kings Šulgi, Amar-Su'en, and Šu-Sîn, indicating that much smaller households
had to be provided for compared to the temples of the city's major deities.[16] The monumental appearance of the Šu-Sîn Temple at Ešnunna is therefore noticeable — its wall thickness
actually surpasses that of the Palace of the Rulers. This may be less a coincidence than a
visual manifestation of Ešnunna's peculiar position within the Ur III state. Despite its geographically peripheral location within the Ur III state, Ešnunna enjoyed the same withdrawal
privileges from the central redistribution center at Drehem (ancient Puzriš-Dagan) in the Ur
III economic system as the "core" provinces in the central Mesopotamian plain.[17] The reason
for that might be sought in Ešnunna's close relationship with the Ur III royal dynasty. In her
offerings at Drehem, Šulgi-Simtum, the wife of King Šulgi (2094–2048 B.C.), showed special
devotion to two goddesses named Bēlat-teraban and Bēlat-šuḫnir, who were closely connected
to the governor's dynasty at Ešnunna but who otherwise played next to no role in the Ur III
pantheon.[18] The queen's focus on these goddesses indicates that she had close ties to Ešnunna
and possibly came from there.[19] The title "Sanga-Priest of Bēlat-teraban and of Bēlat-šuḫnir"
was subsequently held by Bābātī, brother of Amar-Su'en's wife Abī-simtī and hence uncle of
Šu-Sîn, who around 2035 B.C. at least temporarily resided at Ešnunna.[20] During Šu-Sîn's reign
a special bond existed between the king and Ešnunna's governor. As pointed out above, no inscription ever mentions Ituria's patronymic, suggesting that he was not a direct descendant of

[16] This text was published by Englund (1992: 87–88).
The passage under discussion is:
rev.

1. dingir-ra-àm	"Dingir-ra-am
2. 2 du[mu] ʿur-ᵍⁱˢgigirˈ	(and) two sons of Ur-Gigir
3. é ᵈʿšul-gi-raˈ	(are fishermen assigned to) the Šulgi Temple.
4. lú-ᵈšara	Lú-Šara
5. ʿziˈ-zi-ga	(and) Zi-zi-ga
6. é ᵈʿamar-ᵈEN.ZUˈ	(are fishermen assigned to) the Amar-Sîn Temple.
7. X [ ]-nun	X [ ]-nun
8. X X [ ]	(and) X X [ ]
9. é ᵈšu-ʿᵈEN.ZUˈ	(are fishermen assigned to) the Šu-Sîn Temple."

[17] See Steinkeller 1991 for a comprehensive overview
of the administrative organization of the Ur III state; see
ibid., 19 n. 12, for Ešnunna's special position within the
Ur III provincial system. While being part of the "bala"
system, which characterized the "core provinces" of the
Ur III state, Ešnunna also paid the gun ma-da tax that
was rendered by the military personnel in the "peripheral" provinces of this state.

[18] The close relationship between Ešnunna's ruling family and these goddesses is particularly noticeable during the reign of Šuiliya, whose seal qualifies him as the
"beloved one of Bēlat-Teraban (and of) Bēlat-[šuḫnir]

(na-ra-a[m] ᵈbe-la-at-te-ra-ba-an ᵈbe-la-at-[suḫ-nir];
As. 31:T.670 lines 8–10 [Frankfort, Lloyd, and Jacobsen 1940: 143 no. 6]). A similar epithet for Šuiliya is
found in the legend of the seal of his servant At-ta-a-a, in
which the two goddesses are preceded by Ešnunna's city
god Tišpak (na-ra-am ᵈtišpak ᵈbēlat(NIN)-te-ra-ba-an ù
ᵈbēlat(NIN)-šuk-nir; As. 31:T.663 lines 2–4 [Frankfort,
lloyd, and Jacobsen 1940: 144 no. 8, collated]).

[19] See Sallaberger (1993: 18–20) for a summary on
Šulgi-Simtum and evidence in support of this theory.
Based on several occurrences of ti-ra-ba-anᵏⁱ in Old Akkadian texts from Gasur (Nuzi) (see Edzard, Farber, and
Sollberger 1977: 159 for references), Jacobsen (1940:
143–44) suggested that the home cities of these two goddesses were located in northern Mesopotamia, probably
in the area of Subartu.

[20] Bābātī's presence at Ešnunna is ascertained from several texts from the Palace of the Rulers. The great historical significance of As. 31:T.615, which had been found
in the Palace Chapel (locus L32:3) and which mentions
the distribution of linseed flour (zíd-gu) and flour (zíd)
by the governor of Ešnunna to Tiš-atal, king of Nineveh,
and to his accompanying men, has already been discussed by Whiting (1977b). The tablet is sealed with the
seal of Bābātī, which identifies him as "Sanga-Priest of
Bēlat-šuḫnir and of Bēlat-teraban" ([sanga] ᵈbe[-la-at-
šuḫ-nir] ù ᵈ[be-la-at]-te-ra-ba-ʿanˈ [lines 15–17]). Addi-

the previous governor. We only know one previous Ur III governor at Ešnunna, an individual named Urgu'edinna, whose name is attested in texts dating between 2064 and 2038 B.C. (Šulgi 31–Amar-Su'en 8).[21] The latter year date is notable since it was the penultimate year of Amar-Su'en's reign, when internal trouble shook up the Ur III state and conflicts between the king and his soon-to-be-successor Šu-Sîn likely began to culminate. With Ešnunna's in a somewhat peripheral location from Ur, potentially prone to secession or attacks from the east, it is possible that Šu-Sîn replaced Urgu'edinna with a loyal follower of the new king. Ituria's construction of a monumental Šu-Sîn Temple right next to Ešnunna's governor's palace might not only have been a physically expressed endorsement of Ur III's overlordship over Ešnunna but also an expression of personal loyalty to a king who instated him as governor of the city and on whose support he therefore depended quite heavily.

The cult to Šu-Sîn at Ešnunna, however, was to be short-lived. While we have no direct, unambiguous information on how the cult at his temple was terminated we have some indirect evidence from a group of seven texts from the temple's cella. These texts recorded issues of food and garments by an administrator named Abilulu, their common element being the summary phrase "deductions from the holdings under the control of Abilulu" (zi-ga ki *A-bi-lu-lu-ta*), following a list of items provided (table 7.1). Commodities listed in these texts include provisions such as oil (ì-giš, še-giš-ì), beer, and beer bread but also garments and cloth. Most recipients are individuals with no further specification regarding their title or function — it seems likely, though, that they are part of the temple's personnel. Two texts, however, mention deities as recipients — Enlil, Bēlat-teraban, and Bēlat-šuḫnir — and Šu-Sîn himself. None of the texts have a year date, and with one exception all of them date to month 8 of the Ur III calendar — the month "Feast of Šulgi" (ezen [d]šul-gi).

---

tional support for Bābātī's presence in Ešnunna is found on another tablet fragment (As. 30:T.284, unpublished) from the Palace Chapel (locus L31:5), which lists him as the receiver of items and bears a seal impression mentioning Ituria as Bābātī's overlord:

obv.
  1'. ki ⌜x⌝-[   ]
  2'. *ba*-[*ba-ti*]
rev.
  3'. šu ba-ti
  (rest lost)

The seal legend (published by Jacobsen 1940: 142 no. 3; collated) reads:
  1. *i-tu-ri-a*
  2. ensí
  3. *ba-ba-ti*
  [   ]

[21] These texts, which are as yet unpublished, are As. 31:T.333, As. 31:T.348 (Šulgi 31), and As. 31:T.340 (Amar-Su'en 8).

Table 7.1. Texts of Abilulu from Temple Cella (O30:18) Dating to the Ur III Period

Find Number	Locus	Topic	Issuing Party	Receiving Party	Month	Other Points
As. 31:T.212	O30:18	cloth	zi-ga ki A-bi-lu-lu-ta	Aḫum-il Lū-šalim Lú-*šu*-den-líl	8	gaba-ri Ša-kuš-ḫé-du$_{10}$
As. 31:T.214	O30:18	cloth	zi-ga ki A-bi-lu-lu-ta	dumu *Ahu-ṭāb* Ur-Sîn	8	gaba-ri Ša-kuš-ḫé-du$_{10}$
As. 31:T.238	O30:18	cloth	zi-ga A-bi-lu-lu-ta	Elkānum MAR.TU	8	gaba-ri Ša-kuš-ḫé-du$_{10}$
As. 31:T.213	O30:18	oil (še giš-ì)	ki A-bi-lu-lu-ta šuba-an-ti	*Šū-Kūbum*	8	gaba-ri šà Áš-nun-na^{ki}
As. 31:T.236	O30:18	oil (ì-giš) for bread (ninda-ì-dé-a)	zi-ga ki A-bi-lu-lu-ta	Workmen, Enlil, Bēlat-teraban, Bēlat-šuḫnir, Temple Cella (šà é-a)	8	—
As. 31:T.243	O30:18	oil (ì-giš)	zi-ga ki A-bi-lu-lu-ta	Ibbī-Enum Šū-Sîn Ilšu-bani [ ]	8	—
As. 31:T.219	O30:18	beer bread (^{kaš}bappir-DU)	zi-ga ki A-bi-lu-lu-ta	Nasi'um-rēšu ^{lú}lungà	6	šà Áš-nun-na

This is no unknown phenomenon — transactions recorded day by day during a month usually were transferred into a monthly account by the end of that month, making a specification of the year date on these temporary records superfluous. Once the information had been transferred, however, such tablets generally were recycled. The question, therefore, arises as to why the Abilulu tablets had survived. It is notable that the latest text from Ešnunna using the Ur III calendar — a fairly reliable indicator of Ur III control — dates to Ibbi-Sîn's year 3 (2026 B.C.) month 9 (ezen ^{d}Šu-Sîn "Feast of Šu-Sîn"), the month following month, "Feast of Šulgi" to which most of the Abilulu tablets from the Šu-Sîn Temple date.[22] This seems to be more than a coincidence. With Ešnunna's independence from Ur the days of the Šu-Sîn cult would have been over almost immediately, making the management of its accounts obsolete. Abilulu's accounts for month 8 — by month 9 a compilation of useless data — were discarded in the temple cella. Their discovery, however, helps to narrow down the date of Ešnunna's independence significantly: year 2026 B.C. month 9 itself only provides a *terminus post quem*, that is, Ešnunna's independence from Ur could date to this month or anytime thereafter. The fact that Abilulu's accounts from the previous month had not yet been transferred, however, suggests that it happened early in month 9. Consequently, the early days of month 9 in 2026 B.C. most likely also represent the last days of the Šu-Sîn cult at Ešnunna.

The layout the Šu-Sîn Temple (fig. 7.11) indeed shows a significant secondary change following a fire destruction of its northwestern part. The main entrance between its central courtyard (O30:17) and its cella (O30:18) was blocked. Access to the (now former) cella was

[22] As. 30:T.290 (see already Whiting 1987b: 33 n. 3). The year formula year: "Simurrum was destroyed" (mu si-mu-ru-um^{ki} ba-ḫul) in this text, which is used for Šulgi year 25 or Ibbi-Sîn year 3 (Sigrist 1992: 370–71), can confidently be assigned to the latter one since the text dates to month "feast of Šu-Sîn" (ezen-^{d}Šu-Sîn), which obviously would not have been around during Šulgi's reign.

provided instead through a new doorway in the temple's northwestern corner that connected the throne-room suite and the cella through the temple's "sacristy" (O30:8). The excavators dated these changes to the immediate post-Ur III period. It seems reasonable to assume that the end of the Ur III period went hand in hand with some turmoil that resulted in a fire within the temple and a subsequent desecration of the temple. Walling up the cella's doorway from the courtyard would have been an unmistakable sign to any doubting soul that the cult of king Šu-Sîn at Ešnunna was out of business. Connecting the cella to the throne-room suite also made it clear whose purpose it now served. Based on the summary of the historical events given above it seems sensible to assume that these changes date to or shortly after month 9 of 2026 B.C., that is, into the early part of Šuiliya's reign. Surprisingly, this is where excavators' final report on the excavation becomes vague. The fire, desecration, and changes in the layout of the temple are described in a chapter that summarizes the building activities of Šuiliya's successor Nūraḫum (ca. 2010–2005 B.C.; Lloyd 1940: 42). Nūraḫum's ascent to Ešnunna's throne appears to have been much less glamorous than Šuiliya's. Sometime before 2010 B.C. troops from Subartu, a political entity in northern Mesopotamia, invaded Ešnunna. It was only with the help of Išbi-Erra of Isin, a powerful city-state that had emerged in southern Mesopotamia as a powerful competitor to and coffin nail for the ailing Ur III state, that Ešnunna regained its independence in 2010 B.C. (Išbi-Erra year 9) and Nūraḫum was instated as ruler of Ešnunna.[23] But Nūraḫum's wings had been clipped: unlike Šuiliya he did not claim divine status, and instead of the title "king" he modestly referred to himself as ensí, "city ruler" or "governor" — the same title that Ituria held before Ešnunna's independence from Ur. All this indicates that Nūraḫum's ascent to the throne of Ešnunna clearly did not happen on his own terms. Evidence for widespread rebuilding measures under Nūraḫum is found all over the palace in numerous stamped bricks that bear Nūraḫum's name, most notably in the area of the Palace Chapel, which Nūraḫum razed and replaced with a large courtyard in a clear attempt to obliterate it (marked fig. 7.10). But as far as I can tell, no Nūraḫum bricks have been found in the area of the Šu-Sîn Temple.

A re-analysis of the cella's archaeological sequence and of the findspots of datable material, especially of clay sealings with seal impressions, suggests a somewhat different scenario.[24] Figure 7.12 shows a photograph of the cella during excavation, taken from is northwest side and facing its entrance.[25] In this photograph two patches of a secondary, higher floor (marked

---

[23] In the dating of Nūraḫum's ascent to the throne to 2010 B.C., I have followed Whiting's reconstruction of events (Whiting 1987a: 25–26). The main source for the events surrounding it is a letter written by Puzur-Numušda of Kazallu to king Ibbi-Sîn of Ur (Ali 1970: 161–62). Whether Šuiliya or Nūraḫum was deposed by Subartu is ultimately not certain. Whiting (1987b: 26) opts for Šuiliya but offers no conclusive argument to support his decision. The crucial lines (lines 37–40) in the Puzur-Numušda letter, however, state that Nūraḫum was *returned* to his place (ki-ni-še gur), suggesting that he already had a claim to it before the Subarean invasion: ᵐnu-ur-a-ḫi ensí èš-nunki-na ... ki-ni-še ba-an-gur-ru-uš "He (Išbi-Erra) returned Nūraḫum, governor of Eš-nunna (... and other rulers deposed by the Subareans ...) to their places." The repeal of the invasion is also commemorated in two of Nūraḫum's date formulae, where

the agency leading to victory is assigned to the city god Tišpak instead of Išbi-Erra:

mu ᵈTišpak lugal-e sagdu(SAG×DU) su-bir₄-a-ke₄ tibír-ra bí-in-ra-a

"Year: Tišpak struck the head of Subartu with a fist"

mu ús-sa ᵈTišpak lugal-e sagdu(SAG×DU) su-bir₄-a-ke₄ tibír-ra bí-in-ra-a

"Year after: Tišpak struck the head of Subartu with a fist"

(Jacobsen 1940: 170–71, nos. 42–43).

[24] A detailed re-analysis of the Šu-Sîn Temple sequence was given elsewhere (Reichel 2003). In this discussion I only repeat those elements that are relevant to the argument presented here.

[25] Negative as325; taken on December 13, 1931; previously published in Frankfort, Lloyd, and Jacobsen 1940: fig. 12; Reichel 2003: fig. 11.

"a" and "burnt floor") are visible some 30 to 40 cm above the cella's earliest floor (marked "b" and "earlier floor"). According to the excavators, the secondary floor was easy to follow, for it had been hardened by fire. Embedded into this floor right in front of the cella's niche were two drains — quite clearly installations for libations that were poured out before the cult image in the cella. In the backfill, right up against the neck of the larger drain and therefore clearly associated with the deposition of these drains, the excavators found a clay sealing with the seal of Uṣi-dannum, a "cupbearer" (sagi) of Nūraḫum (fig. 7.13).[26] The sealing provides an important *terminus post quem* for these drains: their installation cannot predate the reign of Nūraḫum, hence not earlier than 2010 B.C. As stated before, there is no obvious reason or rationale for a continued Šu-Sîn cult in this temple after 2026 B.C., the year of Ešnunna's independence from Ur. If cultic installations were installed more than fifteen years later, however, then the question arises who was worshipped in it.

A tablet (As. 31:T.203) found in temple's courtyard (locus O30:17) close to the cella's entrance may provide a clue. It is part of a long list recording oil rations (ì-giš) given to various people. While the first three lines of column I list oil rations for the king (ì-ba lugal), column II, as far as preserved, lists rations of 1/2 sìla of oil to personnel whose names all have Šuiliya's name as a theophoric compound.[27] Though the name of the king himself is not preserved, the year date on the text is unambiguously post-Ur III and almost certainly to be assigned to Šuiliya.[28] It is possible that following the end of the Ur III overlordship over Ešnunna instead of destroying the temple Šuiliya simply took it over and adapted it for his own cult. The rationale behind this step could have been as much ideological as it was economical. As elaborated above, Ešnunna enjoyed close ties to the Ur III dynasty under Ituria. Modern eyes tend to associate foreign overlordship with oppression, but such a view may be misguided. With its monumental appearance, the Šu-Sîn Temple may well have served as a visual guarantee for and manifestation of divine overlordship at Ešnunna, hence promising stability and continuity. A desecration or destruction of the temple after the end of the Ur III overlordship could well have resulted in confusion or uproar. Šuiliya may well have been advised to simply perpetuate the notion of divine kingship by assuming it himself with all its titles and epithets and by seizing control of the one place that epitomized divine kingship better than anything else. Taking over the Šu-Sîn Temple for his own cult may not only have smoothed the transition from Ur III control to post-Ur III independence — it may also have propagated the con-

---

[26] Jacobsen's field catalog of datable tablets and sealings record the provenience of As. 31:T.244 as "… up against the neck of 'pottery drain' in front of niche ca. 5 cm below burnt floor" (Jacobsen Tell Asmar field notes 1930/31; Oriental Institute Museum Archives). The seal legend (originally published by Jacobsen 1940: 145 no. 11; collated) reads:

1. nu-úr-a-ḫu-um   "Nūraḫum,
2. na-ra-am ᵈtišpak   beloved one of Tišpak:
3. ú-ṣi-da-num   Uṣi-dannum,
4. sagi* ÌR-sú   the cupbearer, (is) his servant."

[27] This text was discussed with partial transliteration by Whiting (1977a: 175). The list of compound names of Šuiliya in As. 31:T.203 col. II is:

1. [   ]
2. 1/2 sìla ᵈŠu-ì-lí-a/-i-šar-lu-ba-lí-iṭ
3. 1/2 sìla ᵈŠu-ì-lí-a/-i-šar-ra-ma-aš

4. 1/2 sìla ᵈŠu-ì-lí-a/-i-šar-ki-ᵈutu
5. 1/2 sìla ᵈŠu-ì-lí-a/-i-šar-ki-in
6. 1/2 sìla ᵈŠu-ì-lí-a/-sa-tu-ni,
7. 1/2 sìla lugal-me-ne
8. 1/2 sìla ᵈŠu-ì-lí-a/-šar-gul-li-SI-i[n],
9. 1/2 sìla ᵈŠu-ì-l[í-a]/-dan-[   ]
(rest missing)

[28] The date formula on As. 31:T.203 is mu ⌈ús-sa⌉ ibi[la] lugal máš-e [ì-pà] mu ús-sa-⌈bi⌉ "Second year after (the year when) the son of the king was chosen by an omen." For the date formula, see Jacobsen 1940: 174 no. 48 (text not listed there). The assignment of this date formula to Šuiliya as opposed to Nūraḫum is supported by the fact that both text and year date refer to the ruler as "king" (lugal) as opposed to "city ruler" (ensí) (see already Whiting 1977a: 174 n. 10).

tinued legitimacy of kingship at Ešnunna before the great gods. The fact that Nūraḫum later on refurbished the temple cella with new libation drains suggests that he maintained the cult to his divine predecessor despite his own inability to follow Šuiliya's footsteps toward deification.

Table 7.2. Texts of Abilulu Dating to the Reigns of Šuiliya and Nūraḫum. Date Formulae Are Numbered as Listed by Jacobsen (1940: 171–74). Fractions in these Numbers Indicate Variants of the Same Year Formula; the Assignment of these Years to Šuiliya and Nūraḫum Follows Whiting (1977a: 174 n. 10)

ŠUILIYA							
Find Number	Locus	Topic	Issuing Party	Receiving Party	Date Formula	Month	Other Points
As. 31:T.591	M32:12	copper items	ki A-bi-lu-lu-ta ba-zi	—	48.0	5	GÌR Níg-^{d}ba-ú
NŪRAḪUM							
Find Number	Locus	Topic	Issuing Party	Receiving Party	Date Formula	Month	Other Points
As. 31:T.460	M32:12	confiscated property	é-du$_6$-la-didli-ta mu-DU	A-bi-lu-lu šu ba-ti	42.1	1–12[2]	—
As. 31:T.480	L32:2	cloth, oil, honey	ki A-bi-lu-lu-ta ba-zi	—	43.0	4	GÌR Lú-KA-[ ]
As. 31:T.541	M32:12	cloth (túg-ba gemé àr-àr)	ki A-bi-lu-lu-ta šu ba-ti	Ur-tummal	43.3	9	(seal of Ur-tummal)
As. 31:T.423	M32:12	reed mats (sa-gu gada nu-e-ra)	ki A-bi-lu-lu-ta šu ba-ti	WA-ṢI-ṢI	43.3	12	—
As. 31:T.454	O30:19	wool (síg-DU)	ki A-bi-lu-lu-ta šu ba-ti	Nūrum	44.0	3	—
As. 31:T.474	L32:2	cloth	—	A-bi-lu-lu ì-dab$_5$	44.0	10	—

For those who had less influence on ideological considerations than on the logistics of running a business the story had a happy ending. Though Abilulu, the administrator who worked at the Šu-Sîn Temple, did not retain his position in the redefined Šu-Sîn Temple, a number of texts from the western part of the palace show that after the end of the Ur III overlordship over Ešnunna he worked in the so-called "Palace Chapel" on the west side of the palace — probably the sanctuary of Bēlat-teraban and Bēlat-šuḫnir, the personal gods of the Ešnunna dynasty — doing exactly the same work as he did in the Šu-Sîn Temple: issuing provisions to temple personnel (zi-ga ki *A-bi-lu-lu-ta*; see table 7.2 and fig. 7.14). These texts date to both the reigns of Šuiliya and Nūraḫum, indicating that he continued his work for at least another fifteen years. Maybe Abilulu was considered too loyal to the Šu-Sîn cult to give him security clearance for the newly instated cult in the temple, but apparently this was no reason to get rid of a good administrator.

As indicated before, the northwestern corner of the temple was subsequently destroyed by fire; the burnt debris covered the floor that contained Nūraḫum's libation drains. The subsequent alterations in the layout of the cella, including the blockage of its doorway, were associated with yet another, higher floor, which also covered the niche now formed by the blocked doorway (fig. 7.12). In the middle of this niche a rectangular clay "slab" was found, which the excavators misunderstood as an empty foundation deposit associated with the temple's doorway (fig. 7.15). The recovery of a clay sealing (As. 31:T.256) from it, however, makes it clear that this is a recycling pit for clay sealings and possibly tablets. The sealing itself shows an impression of the seal of Bilalama, son of the ruler Kirikiri (fig. 7.16), who succeeded Nūraḫum around 2005 B.C. The date of this sealing suggests that the temple's desecration and the alteration should be dated to Kirikiri, which makes perfect sense. As I argue elsewhere, the transition between Nūraḫum and Kirikiri, whose name denotes a foreign (Elamite?) origin, appears to have been less than peaceful — probably epitomized best by the fact that Kirikiri had Nūraḫum's seal recut for his own son Bilalama (Reichel 2003). With Kirikiri's seizure of power, any reason to maintain the cult to Šu-Sîn, Šuiliya, or any other previous ruler of Ešnunna would have ceased to exist. The discovery of a door sealing with the seal of Bilalama (As. 30:T.650; see fig. 7.16) in O30:18, the former "sacristy" west of the cella but now its entrance room, suggests that the former temple cella had been turned into an office under the control of the crown prince, which may explain its enigmatic realignment as an extension of the throneroom suite (marked in fig. 7.11). During the reign of Bilalama two kilns were added in the cella, including one in the former cult niche.[29] The retrieval of a tablet (As. 31:T.9, a partial draft for a seal legend) in the larger kiln (visible in fig. 7.12) suggests that they were used to bake tablets. Whether the conversion of the cult place to a divine king into a chancellery had the same ideological aftertaste to contemporary people as it has for us is difficult to say, but with this action any evidence for a cult to a divine ruler had been rooted out here for sure.

With Šuiliya's demise, not only divine kingship, but also kingship itself disappeared altogether from Ešnunna for a good 150 years. While in the rest of Mesopotamia divine kingship ended during the Isin-Larsa period, ironically it returned to Ešnunna during its resurgence as a major power player in the late nineteenth and early eighteenth century.[30]

It may be somewhat peculiar that Ešnunna, which on the scale of Mesopotamian cities really represents somewhat of a "backwater," provides the one surviving architectural manifestation of a cultic concept that actually originated from the heartland of Mesopotamia. Given the setting and circumstances described in this study, however, we may consider this yet another case in which a "view from the periphery" enhances our understanding of a phenomenon that remains physically elusive in central Mesopotamia.

[29] Shown in plan in Frankfort, Lloyd, and Jacobsen 1940: pl. 3.

[30] The presence and absence of divine kingship in Mesopotamia during the Isin-Larsa period deserves a separate discussion. All rulers of the Isin dynasty from Išbi-Erra (2017–1985 B.C.) to Damiq-ilišu (1816–1794 B.C.) were deified. Deification in the Larsa dynasty first occurred under Sūmû-El (1894–1866 B.C.) and his successor Nūr-Adad (1865–1850 B.C.) but did not recur until the reigns of Rīm-Sîn I (1822–1763 B.C.) and Rīm-Sîn II (1740–1736 B.C.), the dynasty's final rulers. At Ešnunna the first ruler after Šuiliya to claim divine descendance was Ipiqadad II (ca. 1800 B.C.). An "Audience Hall" built by his son Naramsin at the northeastern edge of the palace may echo some aspects of the former Šu-Sîn Temple, though its function seems to have been tied to public appearances of the Naramsin himself (Jacobsen in Frankfort, Lloyd, and Jacobsen 1940: 97–115; figs. 87–88). Divine status continues under Daduša, Naramsin's brother and successor, but disappears in the course of his reign. It is noticeable that at Ešnunna every holder of the title "king" (lugal) also claims divine status. A more detailed discussion of this phenomenon will be offered in the revised version of Reichel 2001.

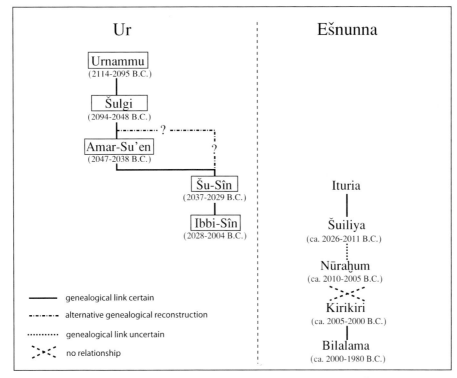

Figure 7.1. Genealogy of Ur III Kings and of Governors of Ešnunna

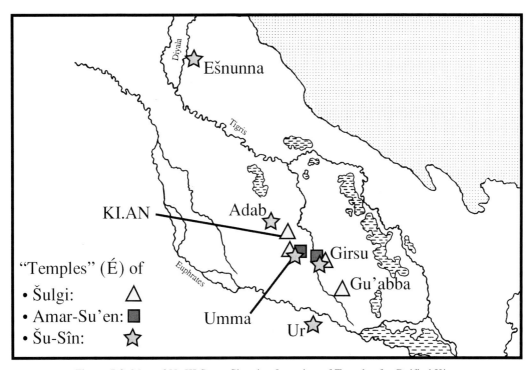

Figure 7.2. Map of Ur III State, Showing Location of Temples for Deified Kings
(map based on Steinkeller 1991, fig. 1)

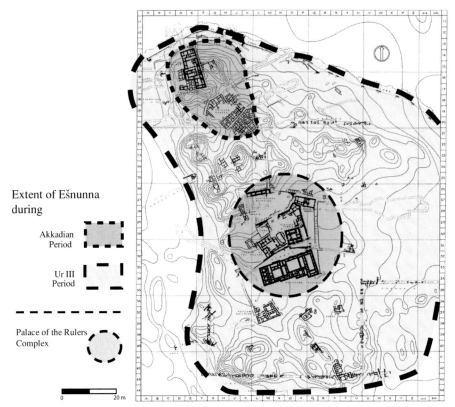

Figure 7.3. Site Map of Tell Asmar (ancient Ešnunna) Showing Approximate Extent of the City during the Akkadian and Ur III Periods (adapted from Delougaz, Hill, and Lloyd 1967, pl. 23)

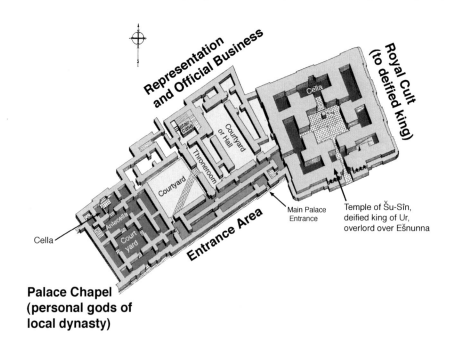

Figure 7.4. Isometric View of the Šu-Sîn Temple and Palace of the Rulers (original state), Showing Principal Functional Units (adapted from Frankfort, Lloyd, and Jacobsen 1940, pl. 1)

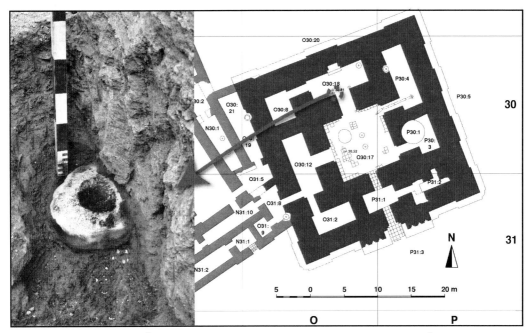

Figure 7.5. Plan of the Šu-Sîn Temple and Close-up Photograph of Entrance into Šu-Sîn Temple,
Showing Western Door Socket (As. 31:793a) with Inscription of Ituria Partially Exposed
(Diyala Expedition negative as/310; Oriental Institute)

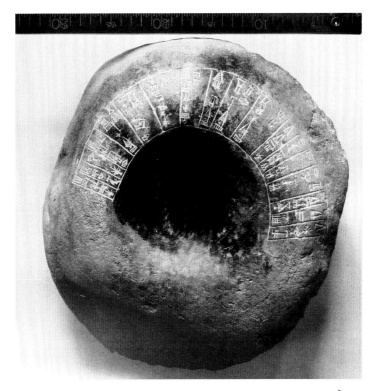

Figure 7.6. Western Door Socket (As. 31:793a; Iraq Museum) from Doorway into Šu-Sîn Temple Cella.
The Inscription Identifies Governor Ituria as the Builder of the Šu-Sîn Temple
(Diyala Expedition negative as/332; Oriental Institute)

Figure 7.7. Seal of Šuiliya Showing the King Facing Tišpak in a "Warrior-king"-like Posture. Drawing Based on Impressions on Sealing As. 31:T.670 (Frankfort, Lloyd, and Jacobsen 1940, fig. 100B)

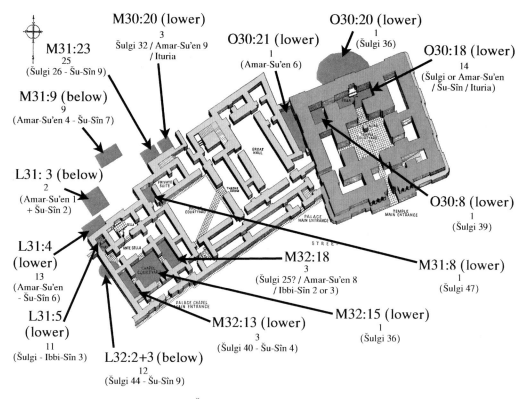

Figure 7.8. Isometric View of Šu-Sîn Temple and Palace of the Rulers, Showing Range of Dates Found on Tablets Dating to the Ur III Period by Findspots (adapted from Frankfort, Lloyd, and Jacobsen 1940, pl. 1)

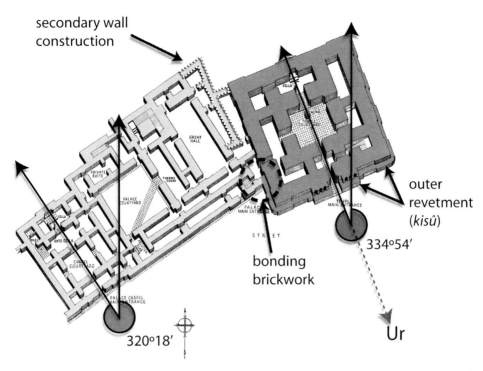

Figure 7.9. Isometric View Showing Difference in Orientation between Palace of the Rulers and Šu-Sîn Temple; Zones of Bonding Brickwork between Temple *kisû* and Palace as Well as Secondary Walls Are Marked (adapted from Frankfort, Lloyd, and Jacobsen 1940, pl. 1)

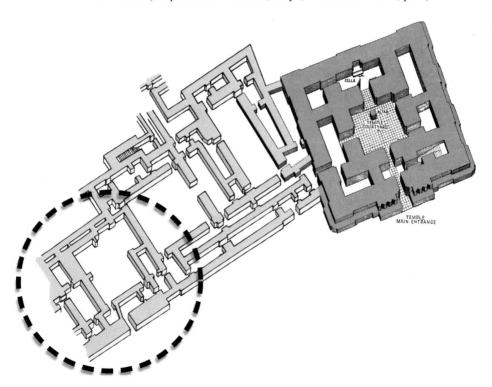

Figure 7.10. Plan of Palace and Temple during Reign of Nūraḫum (after 2010 B.C.)

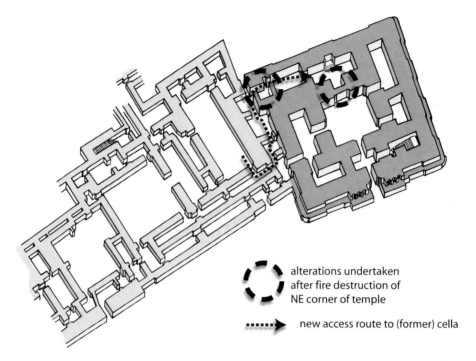

Figure 7.11. Isometric View of Palace and Temple after Rebuilding of Northwest Corner of Šu-Sîn
Temple Following Fire Destruction. Alterations in Layout and New Access Route to (former)
Temple Cella Are Marked

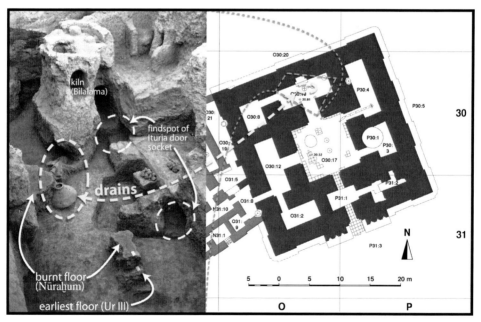

Figure 7.12. Cella of Šu-Sîn Temple Seen from Northwest, Facing East. The Photo, Taken in December
1931, Shows Remains of the Later Burnt Floor above the Cella's Original Floor with Libation Installations (drains) in Front of the Cult Niche (not visible) Embedded in It. The Findspot of the Door Socket
with Ituria's (see figs. 7.5–6) Inscription is Still Visible. The Kiln Visible in the Background Was Added
Later on during the Reign of Bilalama (Diyala Expedition negative as/325; Oriental Institute)

Figure 7.13. Cella of Šu-Sîn Temple: Close-up of Larger Drain (see fig. 12) with Findspot of Clay
Sealing (As. 31:T.244) Showing Seal of Uṣi-dannum, Cupbearer (sagi) of Nūraḫum
(Diyala Expedition negative as/319; Oriental Institute Diyala Project)

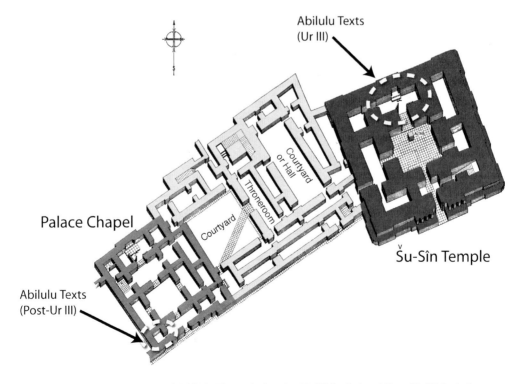

Figure 7.14. Findspots of Abilulu Texts during the Ur III Period and Post-Ur III Period
(adapted from Frankfort, Lloyd, and Jacobsen 1940, pl. 1)

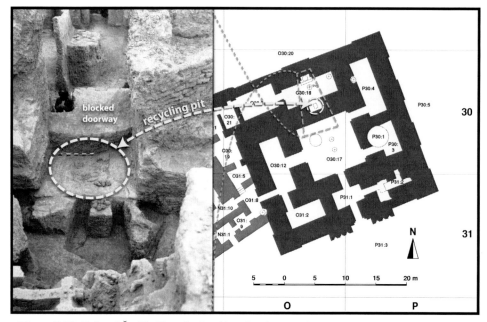

Figure 7.15. Cella of Šu-Sîn Temple, Looking South toward Entrance; Blocked Doorway and
Recycling Pit (findspot of sealing As. 31:T.256) Are Clearly Visible
(Diyala Expedition negative as/326; Oriental Institute)

Figure 7.16. Clay Sealings with Impressions of Bilalama Seal

BIBLIOGRAPHY

Al-Fouadi, Abdul-Hadi
> 1978   "Inscriptions and Reliefs from Bitwata." *Sumer* 34: 122–29.

Ali, Fadhil A.
> 1970   "Three Sumerian Letters." *Sumer* 26: 145–78.

Boese, Johannes, and Walther Sallaberger
> 1996   "Apil-kīn von Mari und die Könige der III. Dynastie von Ur." *Altorientalische Forschungen* 23.1: 24–39.

Cooper, Jerrold S.
> 1999   "Sumerian and Semitic Writing in Most Ancient Mesopotamia." In *Languages and Cultures in Contact: At the Crossroads of Civilizations in the Syro-Mesopotamian Realm* (42nd Rencontre Assyriologique Internationale), edited by Karl van Lerberghe, pp. 61–77. Orientalia Lovaniensia Analecta 96. Leuven: Peeters.

Delougaz, Pinhas; Harold D. Hill; and Seton Lloyd
> 1967   *Private Houses and Graves in the Diyala Region*. Oriental Institute Publications 88. Chicago: University of Chicago Press.

Edzard, Dietz Otto, and Gertrud Farber
> 1974   *Die Orts- und Gewässernamen der Zeit der 3. Dynastie von Ur*. Répertoire géographique des textes cunéiformes 2; Beihefte zum Tübinger Atlas des Vorderen Orients, Reihe B 7. Wiesbaden: Reichert Verlag.

Edzard, Dietz Otto; Gertrud Farber; and Edmond Sollberger
> 1977   *Die Orts- und Gewässernamen der präsargonischen und sargonischen Zeit*. Répertoire géographique des textes cunéiformes 1; Beihefte zum Tübinger Atlas des Vorderen Orients, Reihe B 7. Wiesbaden: Reichert Verlag.

Englund, Robert
> 1992   "Ur III Sundries." *Acta Sumerologica* 14: 77–102.

Frankfort, Henri; Seton Lloyd; and Thorkild Jacobsen
> 1940   *The Gimilsin Temple and the Palace of the Rulers at Tell Asmar*. Oriental Institute Publications 43. Chicago: University of Chicago Press.

Frayne, Douglas
> 1997   *Ur III Period, 2112–2004 B.C.* Royal Inscriptions of Mesopotamia, Early Periods 3/2. Toronto: University of Toronto Press.

Gibson, McGuire
> 1982   "A Re-evaluation of the Akkad Period in the Diyala Region on the Basis of Recent Excavations at Nippur and the Hamrin." *American Journal of Archaeology* 86: 531–38.

Glassner, Jean-Jaques
> 1986   *La Chute d'Akkadé: L'avénement et sa mémoire*. Berliner Beiträge zum Vorderen Orient 5. Berlin: Dietrich Reimer Verlag.

Heinrich, Ernst
> 1982   *Die Tempel und Heiligtümer im alten Mesopotamien: Typologie, Morphologie und Geschichte*. 2 volumes. Denkmäler Antiker Architektur 14. Berlin: Walter de Gruyter.

Jacobsen, Thorkild

1940   "Historical Data." In *The Gimilsin Temple and the Palace of the Rulers at Tell Asmar*, edited by Henri Frankfort, Seton Lloyd, and Thorkild Jacobsen, pp. 116–200. Oriental Institute Publications 43. Chicago: University of Chicago Press.

Lafont, Bertrand

1994   "L'avènement de Šu-Sîn." *Revue d'Assyriologie et d'Archéologie Orientale* 28/2: 97–119.

Lloyd, Seton

1940   "The Main Complex." In *The Gimilsin Temple and the Palace of the Rulers at Tell Asmar*, edited by Henri Frankfort, Seton Lloyd, and Thorkild Jacobsen, pp. 7–91. Oriental Institute Publications 43. Chicago: University of Chicago Press.

Martiny, Günter

1940   "The Orientation of the Gimilsin Temple and the Palace Chapel." In *The Gimilsin Temple and the Palace of the Rulers at Tell Asmar*, edited by Henri Frankfort, Seton Lloyd, and Thorkild Jacobsen, pp. 92–96. Oriental Institute Publications 43. Chicago: University of Chicago Press.

Reichel, Clemens

2001   Political Changes and Cultural Continuity at the Palace of the Rulers in Eshnunna (Tell Asmar) from the Ur III Period to the Isin-Larsa Period (ca. 2070–1850 B.C.). Ph.D. Dissertation, University of Chicago.

2003   "A Modern Crime and an Ancient Mystery: The Seal of Bilalama." In *Festschrift für Burkhart Kienast: Zu seinem 70. Geburtstage dargebracht von Freunden, Schülern und Kollegen*, edited by Gebhard J. Selz, pp. 355–89. Alter Orient und Altes Testament 274. Münster: Ugarit-Verlag.

Sallaberger, Walther

1993   *Der kultische Kalender der Ur III-Zeit*. 2 volumes. Untersuchungen zur Assyriologie und vorderasiatischen Archäologie 7. Berlin: Walter de Gruyter.

1999   "Ur III Zeit." In *Mesopotamien: Akkade-Zeit und Ur III-Zeit*, edited by Walther Sallaberger and Åge Westenholz, pp. 121–414. Orbis Biblicus et Orientalis 160/3. Freiburg: Universitätsverlag; Göttingen: Vandenhoeck & Ruprecht.

Selz, Gebhard

2001   "'Guter Hirte, Weiser Fürst' – Zur Vorstellung von Macht und zur Macht in der Vorstellung im altmesopotamischen Herrschaftsparadigma." *Altorientalische Forschungen* 28/1: 8–39.

Sigrist, Marcel

1992   *Drehem*. Bethesda: CDL Press.

1999   "Livraisons et dépenses royales durant la Troisième Dynastie d'Ur." In *Ki Baruch Hu: Ancient Near Eastern, Biblical, and Judaic Studies in Honor of Baruch A. Levine*, edited by Robert Chazan, William W. Hallo, and Lawrence H. Schiffman, pp. 111–49. Winona Lake: Eisenbrauns

Steinkeller, Piotr

1991   "The Administration and Economic Organization of the Ur III State: The Core and the Periphery." In *The Organization of Power: Aspects of Bureaucracy in the Ancient Near East*, edited by McGuire Gibson and Robert D. Biggs, pp. 15–33. Studies in Ancient Oriental Civilization 46. Second edition. Chicago: The Oriental Institute.

Westenholz, Åge

1999   "The Old Akkadian Period: History and Culture." In *Mesopotamien: Akkade-Zeit und Ur III-Zeit*, edited by Walther Sallaberger and Åge Westenholz, pp. 17–117. Orbis Biblicus et Orientalis 160/3. Freiburg: Universitätsverlag; Göttingen: Vandenhoeck & Ruprecht.

Woolley, C. Leonard

1974   *The Buildings of the Third Dynasty.* Ur Excavations 6. London: British Museum; Philadelphia: University Museum, University of Pennsylvania.

Whiting, Robert M.

1977a   "The Reading of the Name DINGIR-šu-ì-lí-a." *Journal of the American Oriental Society* 97: 171–77.

1977b   "Tiš-atal of Nineveh and Babati, Uncle of Šu-Sîn." *Journal of Cuneiform Studies* 28: 173–82.

1987a   *Old Babylonian Letters from Tell Asmar.* Assyriological Studies 22. Chicago: The Oriental Institute.

1987b   "Four Seal Impressions from Tell Asmar." *Archiv für Orientforschung* 34: 30–35.

Wilcke, Claus

1974   "Zum Königtum in der Ur III-Zeit." In *Le Palais et la royauté, archéologie et civilisation: Compte Rendu* (19th Rencontre Assyriologique Internationale), edited by Paul Garelli, pp. 177–232. Paris: Paul Geuthner

Wu, Yhong

1992   "The Deification of Šu-iliya of Eshnunna while Being a 'Scribe.'" *Nouvelles Assyriologiques Brèves et Utilitaires* 1992/4: 78.

8

ROYAL DEIFICATION: AN AMBIGUATION MECHANISM FOR THE CREATION OF COURTIER SUBJECTIVITIES

REINHARD BERNBECK, BINGHAMTON UNIVERSITY

INTRODUCTION

In this paper, I discuss two theses on divine kingship. First, I claim that an understanding of divine kingship needs to look beyond the often mentioned legitimacy of a royal office holder or the legitimacy of that office itself. A close inspection of *practices* of governing is necessary. Second, and related to the first thesis, the divine aspect of rule focuses on the conduct of governmental elites themselves, rather than on steering the conduct of commoners.

I limit my discussion to a series of reflections on problems of *deification* of kings, rather than an institutionalized divine kingship, since I refer mainly to a case from the ancient Near East, where kings were never divine as a matter of routine. I preface my discussions of the case of the Old Akkadian king Naram-Sin, with some theoretical observations on the deification of kings, the types of contexts which are amenable to such a process, and the consequences they entail. I focus on the nexus of legitimating aspects of power and governmental practices. The process of deification, as a rare practice *within* governmental structures, should lead us to pay close attention to two different kinds of practices: those that help in the establishment of a new governmental regime and those that result from such a regime. Likely, government under divine kingship "works" in different ways than more secular kinds of royal rule.

Divine kingship manifests itself in many different ways, in royal *rites de passage*, in regicidal tendencies, etc. (Feeley-Harnick 1985). Ancient Mesopotamia, the field with which I am concerned, did not know long-term, institutionalized divine kingship, as was the case in ancient Egypt or in the Aztec kingdom.[1] On the level of practices of power, we can therefore expect differences between these regions. In Egypt, rituals associated with a divine ruler were highly routinized and relegated to a doxic realm (see Weber 1972: 142–48). Deification in ancient Mesopotamia was more open to problematizing and questioning because it was a recurrent process of establishing (and re-establishing) such a type of power. Instances of the installation of divine royal status in Mesopotamia were likely accompanied by what Hobsbawm and Ranger (1983) so aptly called "inventions of tradition."

The terminology of divine kingship suggests a categorical distinction between this and secular types of rule. However, I argue for more gradual distinctions. Is the problem to be treated the deified nature of a ruler, or is it the degree to which rulership was sacred? Is sacredness limited to kings, or are not presidents and other kinds of modern rulers also (and always) to some extent sacralized? In my elaborations, I follow Kertzer (1988) who has opted strongly for the latter from a cultural-comparative position and has gathered enormous amounts of material to underscore his contention that all political rule has sacred and ritual elements.

---

[1] For the latter, see the insightful comparative account of Eric Wolf (1999: 147–55) on the deification of the *tlatoani* under Moctezuma.

DIVINE KINGSHIP AS A FORM OF GOVERNMENTALITY

The analysis of the practices of divine kingship is best done in terms of governmentality. Originally, Foucault (1991, 2004) applied this notion to the relationship of the ruling institutions to the ruled in a bureaucratic state. The literature (e.g., Dean 1999; Rose 1996, 2007) that has sprung from this idea includes at least three major elements which are relevant to a discussion of divine kingship. First, govern-"mentality" is a general way of conceptualizing governing on the part of the ruling classes, of imagining relations to subordinates. Second, such a concept of steering subordinates always includes an idea of how to shape them into more or less obedient subjects. Third, the mentality of governance and the imagined goals must be connected to specific technologies of power.

MENTALITIES OF GOVERNING

The examination of mentalities of governing should not only include concepts about the managing of subject people, but also ideas about self-subjection under transcendent realms. To some extent, one may find a mirroring of the relationship of rulers to god(s) in the rulers' behavior toward their subalterns. In the concrete case of the deification of a king, we need to clarify what the relationship between gods and kings was, since a king who turns into a god changes his role significantly, from an eminent participant in cults directed toward others (deities) to being themselves the object of a cult. In the words of the theologian Mowinckel, if a king was hitherto preoccupied with sacrificial practices, that is, actions on behalf of a community toward the gods, he is suddenly located at the opposite end, the sacramental one. Priests now conduct acts on his behalf toward a community.

Such a stark reversal of roles cannot occur at all times and places. Favorable circumstances depend in part on the nature of gods. If the transcendent realm is imagined as utterly different from the human one, a king's role reversal becomes almost impossible. For example, in the case of the Old Testament, Yahwist theologies do not allow any equation of a human with a god without running the risk of being considered sacrilegious. On the other hand, gods such as the ancient Mesopotamian ones had subjectivities that were not so different from those of Mesopotamian people. Gods had aspirations, they were competitive, felt jealousy, fought each other, and were emotional. They had divided up their divine tasks just as humans had done with theirs and had powerful rulers such as Enlil or Marduk. This close analogy to the human realm gives a first hint why deification of kings could occur several times in ancient Mesopotamia. However, even in ancient Mesopotamia, the godly and human worlds were kept separate, with a few exceptions. One such example is the figure of Gilgamesh, partly human, partly god, a typical tale from an era "before difference," before the appearance of distinctions in the world.

In view of the Gilgamesh epic, deifying a king is a move "back" to a heroic, mythical age, or what we may call a golden age. The political strategy to achieve this effect is *ambiguation*,[2] a uniting of worlds that had originally been one and the same, but have since been separated (Selz 1998: 283–84 n. 5). However, this politically driven move of ambiguation does not include all of society but just its uppermost political representative, the king. As the king

---

[2] I adapt this term from Battaglia's (1997) brief ethnographic account. In her view, ambiguation plays out as either a concealment or a revelation of agency. Both cases lead to speculative thinking because of the creation of an ambiguous space in human relations. But while Battaglia focuses on the concealing mechanisms of ambiguation, the deification of a ruler is the effect of a revelation of agency.

mingles with the gods, social distance increases first and foremost between him and those who directly surround him.

Under which historical conditions can such extreme distancing between a ruler and his entourage occur? In a search for generalities, I widen the field to include general tendencies toward sacralization of rulership. Deification of kings is only an extreme case of the sacralization of powerful political figures. Rulers who became sacralized are often — and this may not be astonishing — at the origin of new forms of government. King David, George Washington, Augustus, but also modern political figures such as Lenin and Khomeini, may be counted among them. What characterizes those for whom we have sufficient historical detail is a combination of three elements: a charismatic personality (see Berger 1963: 949), political success, and a rise to power during a historical crisis (see also Balander 1967: 117–29). I assume that a combination of these conditions is sufficient for what I call the *primary* deification of rulers, that is, for a process where extra-worldly qualities of political rule do not come with the position into which a powerholder enters. Rather, they are acquired by this specific powerholder himself (very rarely herself).[3]

Primary deification is a highly problematic process, as it implies that a ruler is successful in elevating him- or herself to a hitherto undefined or only mythically known status.[4] The attempt at a radical distancing from courtiers through deification can only mean that such a person must be able to exert charisma. It also implies a high dose of self-esteem and a narcissistic personality. In combination with contingencies such as a crisis in the political, military, or economic sphere, and a successful solution to the crisis, such a ruler can show practical skills in addition to his personal capabilities of influencing the actions and thoughts of others.

Once installed, a divine king may try to make the new regime hereditary. However, if I am right in my assumption that primary deification depends on a combination of charisma, self-esteem, and a favorable historical context, transferability is an equally difficult process. This is so because charisma is not a characteristic that can be passed on like a function from one ruler to the next. Rather, to sustain deification it needs to be transferred into a firm tradition of entrenched divine kingship, a process that was either not attempted in the ancient Near East or was unsuccessful.

DIVINE RULE AND THE SHAPING OF SUBJECTS

People who are most directly concerned by the deification of a king are the inner circles of power. How are they going to conduct themselves toward a being that has metamorphosed into a god? Since all governing implies a certain degree of ritual, it is most likely that such ritual increases drastically in elaboration to show the king's new self and to reinforce the idea of distance of the elite to him. Ceremonialization freezes interactions between a ruler and courtiers into rigid forms. Norbert Elias (1976) has interpreted such processes at the French court as civilizing the aristocracy, a reigning in of acting out emotions.[5] While Elias takes the long-term view to show how peasants and others may have been increasingly shielded from the caprices

---

[3] It would be wrong to couch this process in Bourdieu's (1999: 62–67) term of "symbolic capital," a notion that suggests convertibilities where there are none.

[4] There is an underinvestigated parallel in this process to the theory of "royal absolutism" and sovereignty, according to which kings had to be above the law in order to make laws (Burgess 1992). This leads us further into

modern exceptionalist theories of the sovereignty such as C. Schmitt's (see Agamben 2003).

[5] In an excellent paper with vivid descriptions, de Baecque (1994) shows the reverse process of the French national assembly using changes in ritual and protocol to produce increasing nearness to the king in the years of the French revolution.

of the nobility, Mario Erdheim (1982: 368–437) analyzes the etiquette of French absolutism as an almost pathological mechanism of suppressing inequities of power *within* the governmental apparatus into the subconscious, a highly original further elaboration of Elias' work.[6]

In a historically and culturally different context, Clifford Geertz (1980) interprets the restraining powers of protocol toward the king in the Balinese *Negara* states as part of a symbolism of a larger order. He argues against the functionalism of disciplined elite subjects as enviisaged by both Elias and Erdheim and claims that etiquette ensures order of the world in the symbolic realm. Such protocol implies high stress for courtiers because failure, that is, inappropriate action, might have cosmological implications beyond the foreseeable state of affairs. In his view, the "dramas of the theatre state ... were, in the end, neither illusions nor lies, neither sleight of hand nor make-believe" (Geertz 1980: 136).

These two interpretations of a closely similar phenomenon of etiquette in elite circles of power are incompatible. Elias and Erdheim assert implicitly the relative autonomy of secular rule as a realm of planned submission of others, while Geertz understands courtly practices as a form of ritual that is close if not identical to religious ritual, especially in its integrative, solidarity-evoking functions (similarly Kertzer 1991: 87). The difference hinges on the understanding of etiquette itself. For Elias and Erdheim, the phenomenon works as a means of reducing potential resistance toward a situation where a king has exalted himself beyond all reach. Deification of kings in ancient Mesopotamia may then be conceptualized as a means toward an end, the maintenance of extreme distance by a ruler to his immediate subjects, a shielding off for the protection of individual power. It is not so much the king's transcendent status as god, but rather the ritualization of governmental practices that guarantees the stability of political power relations within the institutional apparatuses of government through constant interpellation of those who deal with the king on a daily basis. Etiquette and courtly ritual are a social means of political domination within the ranks of power, a means that works mainly on the psyche of the elites by rendering subconscious their own status as subjected to the ultimate ruler.

For Geertz, such a means-ends relation of dominance is too simple. He suggests that courtly etiquette is an important component of sustaining a world order. In this, he follows the basic Durkheimian idea that ritual produces solidarity and stability, even when discussing instances of rupture (e.g., Geertz 1959). The establishment of protocols is part of a symbolic representation of the cosmos. However, such order is established only under the threat of the revelation of what we as outsiders see as its arbitrariness. What is at stake in royal etiquette are not power relations between people, but a much wider fear of a breakdown of the universe. In a Geertzian sense, the ambiguous figure of a deified king needs to be treated with the greatest caution, as a wrong move potentially exposes the king as a human being; such admission is not allowed. The king is part of a metonymical order whose crisis would trouble the whole ritual setup and doxa of political practices and worldview alike, for both the king and his followers. To avoid potential disclosure of this state of affairs, all sides have an interest in adhering to a rigid set of practices whose mannerisms minimize the potential for a revelation of real relations.[7] Thus, a lot of energy is spent by the governing bodies on the ritualizing of interactions, driven by an anxiety that leads to establishing procedures that symbolize the "right" relations of respect and distance. Under such circumstances, the practices of governing turn on themselves, that is, the

---

[6] A substantial critique of Elias' work appeared in Hans Peter Duerr's four-volume discussion, of which the first one is most relevant for this discussion (Duerr 1988). On the Duerr-Elias dispute, see, for example, Krieken 2005.

[7] Accounts of African kingship tend to follow similar argumentative lines (e.g., Mair 1974: 162–65).

ruling class has first and foremost to rule itself in the strictest way possible in order to reproduce social order as a whole.

We may find an echo of the two positions outlined above in Sahlins' *Islands of History*
(1985). Sahlins claims that history is not made in all societies in the same way. "Praxiologi-
cal" societies make history from the bottom up, whereas in societies with divine kings, history
is produced by ritual practices of a king. This latter idea is in many ways similar to Geertz's
focus on cosmology with the king at the center (see also Kelly and Kaplan 1990). However,
it is problematic to dichotomize the making of history according to the apex of political structures alone. The Akkadian example, discussed below, is a good case for investigating the relationship between royal status and historical action.

TECHNIQUES OF GOVERNING

A third element of governmentality is techniques of power. In the case of royal deification, such techniques are to be found in the practices that produce and sustain a distanciation
and formalization of interactions between a divine king and his courtiers. I submit that such
processes can best be understood through a reference to the theoretical concept of *Handlungsräume*, a notion that is directly related to practices of governmentality. This German term,
used often by historians, differs in a subtle but substantial way from "agency" in the social
science discussions in Anglophone anthropology. *Handlungsraum* implies not only a potential
to act, but also a potential to not act. It is the latter that is of crucial importance in a discussion
of protocols of divine kingship. The more regulated interactions between king and entourage
become, the more sharply the *Handlungsraum* of elite personnel decreases while the deified
king's ability to act (or not) is vastly amplified. In this context, the development of etiquette,
described by Bell (1992: 218–23) as "ritualization," is a negative technique of power, imping-
ing on the conditions of possibilities of action.[8]

Such restricting innovations in hierarchical interactions with the highest political office
turn into prescribed performances for those of lower rank in such a relation. The co-presence
of the king and others takes on an atmosphere of tension, created by the threat of a transgression of the ritual. Political protocol has the status of a ritual performance with a high risk of
failure. Anthropologists have mostly neglected this aspect of courtly and other rituals "because
much ritual action is rule-governed, thus appearing to render ritual free of risk" (Howe 2000:
69). However, Howe points out that the enactment is always open to incorrectness. And when
the *Handlungsraum* of a participant is highly restricted to begin with, such risks are all the
higher.

Furthermore, a reduced *Handlungsraum* and anxieties during face-to-face meetings with
a divine king will lead to frustrations and internal repression, as well as a search for an outlet
for increasing tension. Rumors and gossip likely mushroom within the elite, discourses also
characterized as "hidden transcripts" (Scott 1990) that are all the more prevalent as battles
over etiquette replace other forms of political practice. I suspect that the structures of such
discursive, metaphorical "resistance" were aimed principally at the king, but that there were
also numerous denunciations of courtiers' relations to the king. Thus, faced with a diminishing
Handlungsraum, the elite seeks for itself a substitute in veiled, vain discourses. Governmental-

---

[8] I am reminded of Durkheim's (1968) distinction between "positive" and "negative" cults, the latter consisting of tabus and strictly imposed avoidances. Processes
of royal deification are likely to engender especially
"negative cults."

ity becomes largely an exercise in self-deprecating introspection. In the following section, I analyze a historically specific set of technologies of governing.

THE CASE OF NARAM-SIN

I take the best-known case of a divine king of ancient Mesopotamia, Naram-Sin (see Farber 1983). His reign can be dated to the twenty-third century B.C. He was the fourth king of the so-called Old Akkadian dynasty, and the grandson of its founder, Sargon. We have at least three different types of written documents about this king. Some come from his own lifetime, such as the now famous Bassetki statue, a bronze base of a statue that was stolen from the Iraq Museum in the course of the American invasion in 2003 and was recovered in November of the same year. The disk-shaped base contains an inscription about Naram-Sin's nine battles in one year and his deification (Gelb and Kienast 1990: 81–83). Secondly, there are Old Babylonian or later copies of Old Akkadian inscriptions of Naram-Sin, inscriptions that had been chiseled into statues or other items that were exhibited in temples. The copies may have been slightly changed through mistakes or other processes of tradition, but we have only a few indications of potentially intentional manipulations of such texts (Cooper 1990). Finally, there is a number of post-Akkadian texts whose historical reliability is highly questionable (Westenholz 1997). The Curse of Akkad (Cooper 1983) places Naram-Sin in a highly unfavorable light, as a ruler who did not obey the gods and destroyed Enlil's main temple in Nippur, the Ekur, an act for which the whole city of Akkad was razed to the ground. However, we know from brick and other inscriptions from Nippur that Naram-Sin actually repaired the temple.

Almost fifteen years ago, Mario Liverani (1993) conveniently summarized our biased knowledge of the Old Akkadian period, pointing out essentialized dichotomies such as Sumerian versus Akkadian, desert versus sown, etc., as underlying our interpretations of the Akkadian empire. He suggested that we pay more attention to the role of ancient propaganda and interests in transmitting specific knowledge while silencing others in our attempts to understand the history of the Akkadian dynasty. I aim to extend this concern and include practices of power.

As already mentioned, deification requires massive self-esteem on the part of the king concerned. However, ancient Near Eastern potentates have left us only scant elements of their "personality." The reason for the disinterest in such traits is that, unlike in our culture, the essentials of a self may not have been conceptualized as psychological at core, but rather as public. Contrary to expectations, Naram-Sin is *post hoc* depicted as contradictory in his decisions, sometimes overconfident and acting against the gods' will. Then again, he is being brought to reason — or not, depending on the tale. We may therefore conclude that in hindsight, an incoherent personality was not so much a problem. Agreement in the assessment of past figures and their character was of no concern.

One of the more obvious elements of kingship that change with Naram-Sin is his titulature ,which takes on the determinative of a god. The title of Sargon and his sons and successors Rimush and Manishtusu was *sar kissati* or "king of the universe." (This claim to power surely went beyond a city-state and may have had a double meaning, as it was likely derived from the city of Kish.) Naram-Sin, however, declared himself *sar kibratim arba'im* "king of the four world regions" (Westenholz 1999: 47). Both titles were still used, often in combination, more than 1,500 years later in Neo-Assyrian times, but it is clear that Naram-Sin tried to set himself apart from his predecessors. Furthermore, the title "king of the four regions" suggests a geometry of power where the king is centrally located, with the four regions under his command. This notion is absent from the more vague *sar kissati* which, even if indirectly, refers to a specific city in northern Babylonia.[9]

NARAM-SIN'S IMAGERY AND ITS RELATION TO TECHNIQUES OF POWER

The king Naram-Sin is also iconographically represented in entirely new ways. In accord with his divine status he has the horns of a god, albeit a lower status one with only two instead of the six horns, the latter being reserved for major gods. A lot has been said about the Naram-Sin stele, which fascinates both because it is such an exceptional piece of art in the Mesopotamian canon, and because it is so much closer than almost any other ancient Mesopotamian representation to our own ideas of naturalistic art. I add a few observations about this monument that are pertinent to visual hints at a new governmentality. The monument has a triple vertical structure, with abstract symbols at the top, the stars, standing for major gods, in the middle Naram-Sin and a plain mountain, likely Mount Sidur; and below to the right Lullubeans, the enemies, and Akkadian soldiers to the left. The distance between the lower and middle parts of the stele is much smaller than that to the abstract symbols at the top. For a battle, the scene is strange, as one might expect Naram-Sin's own soldiers to look toward the enemies rather than upward. Also, if in battle, one would expect defensive weaponry such as shields, prominent on earlier steles depicting war and battle, rather than emblems. Naram-Sin's soldiers do not give the impression of a fighting force. Instead, with their gaze oriented upward, they are an admiring force, an effect that is all the more striking as the king is left in a largely empty decoration field in front of the mountain. Westenholz's observation (1999: 68) that the army depicted on the stele does not consist of soldiers but of high level captains would fit quite well with this interpretation.

The soldiers and enemies in the relief are set more or less syntactically, with gazes of almost all of them converging at an empty spot on the mountain (fig. 8.1). That imaginary spot is at the same height as the king's eyes. Why this arrangement? The usual spatial setting for such a scene is registers, with soldiers following the king in a row into battle.[10] Since there are no registers here, all represented people are united in one representational field. However, what really links them is not a bodily relationship with each other, as in so many earlier steles or on contemporary cylinder seals, but the point at which their gaze meets.

I suggest that this focus on seeing is due to an analogy between the mountain on the stele and the stele itself. Jutta Börker-Klähn (1982) and others have argued that the Naram-Sin stele's original shape might have been quite similar to the mountain on the representation. If so, the point of converging gazes on that mountain would correspond with the location of Naram-Sin's eye on the actual stele. That is, gazes of Akkadian soldiers and Lullubean enemies meet in a point in space that coincides with the eye of the deified ruler. This is a complex and hidden geometry of power that implies both seeing the king in spots where he may not be immediately seen, that is, on the mountain, and being seen from there by him. The implication is that Naram-Sin's gaze captures his subjects even when they are not aware of it. If my reading of the stele has value, it implies strong visual processes of subjectification. As Foucault

---

[9] Westenholz (1999: 47) suggests that the DINGER sign in connection with Naram-Sin's name should be read as an adjective, i.e., "divine Naram-Sin," implying that deification was not intended. Two arguments speak against such an interpretation. First, the iconographic documentation shows him clearly with a horned crown, an attri-

bute of a god. Second, in ancient Mesopotamia, the titulary of kings was important enough not to be relegated to a determinative.

[10] The earlier Sargon stele is a good example of such a constellation.

(1977) explained so well by way of the example of the panopticon, the potential of being seen is a powerful means to create submission of individuals under a larger state machine. Another important aspect of Naram-Sin's stele representation is the orientation of lines of sight. They do not meet each other, but establish dyadic relations with the king. Direct relations between humans below the level of the divine king are explicitly left out.[11]

It is perhaps unnecessary to point out that in Naram-Sin's stele, the various Akkadian soldiers closely imitate the king's gestures, with the left arm bent in a right angle toward the chest, no matter whether they hold composite bows, war axes, or standards, whereas the enemies are shown in various poses that we consider much more "lively," but which are clearly a sign of weakness. This leads me back to the power of etiquette and discipline: even in war, it was important to conform to strictly prescribed movements of the body and to concerted movements in harmony with the king in order to be successful. Imitation of a godly ruler was required, however, a fundamental difference in similarity needed to be maintained. The stele, read this way, conforms to a political system of (elite) warriors forming dyadic relations with a superhuman king.

Naram-Sin's deification should be seen in the context of a longer-term development. This becomes especially clear when considering the seals and sealings from the Akkadian period. We find many more contest scenes between gods than in preceding Early Dynastic times, suggesting a new understanding of the lives of gods. Local panthea in Early Dynastic times may have been more analogous to extended families and their households, followed by a definitive shift toward more competitive gods in the Akkadian period. One could even conclude from the evidence of seal depictions that it befits a king who is successful in wars, the ultimate "contest," to be deified. Furthermore, the appearance of presentation scenes with the popularity of an unspecific tutelary god on seals, mirrors the tripartite hierarchy of the Naram-Sin stele of major god(s), minor god(s) — including Naram-Sin — and humans. Interestingly, according to their inscriptions, seals with this scene belonged exclusively to political officials and priests (table 8.1), pointing to the fact that the Akkadian elite had fully accepted the process of ambiguation (Nissen 1993).

Table 8.1. Akkadian Cylinder Seals: Scenes and Inscriptions, Classified by Types of Profession; Data from Boehmer 1965 and Edzard 1968/69

	Man Fighting Animals	Fighting Gods	Sun-god	Water-god Ea	Vegetation Deity	Serpent God	Presentation Scene	Drinking Scene
Priests	5				1		1	1
Political Officials	14	1		1	1		3	
Scribes	32		1	2	3	3		
Judges, Police	6				2			
Merchants	5					1		
Service	6			1				
Manufacture, Inspectors	4							
Manufacture, Producers	11	3	1					

[11] In Grosrichard's opinion, such a reading has an orientalist bent. He remarks that European ideas conceptualize oriental despotism as "the empire of the gaze which is simultaneously everywhere and nowhere, unique and without number" (Grosrichard 1998: 57).

CONCLUSION

By way of a conclusion, I want to come back to Liverani's contention (1993) that texts about Naram-Sin as an "evil king" have no historical kernel. The most damning of these is the Curse of Akkad, which puts the blame for the city's destruction on Naram-Sin's wanton demolition of the Ekur Temple after unfavorable omens from Enlil. An intriguing argument is that the text does not refer to the physical damage of the Ekur, but rather to the destruction of its economic independence, combined with a refurbishing of its architecture.

It was not the move of ambiguation of the king's person into the divine realm that constituted a problem. Rather, it was the ulterior motives that drove this change and the "repairs" at Ekur, as well as the wars and artistic representations: the main subjects of all these exploits were the elites of the Akkadian state, whose *Handlungsräume* were severely curtailed in the process. The king's deification insured a new inequality in relation to his entourage, requiring utmost care from their side in interactions with him and allowing increased unpredictability from his. Such inequality could encroach all the more effectively on the elite as relations among them became more and more partitioned. The king deals with his direct subordinates in dyadic relations, singling out elite individuals, preferring familial subordinates and installing them in key positions. The latter strategy is already known from the founder of the dynasty, Sargon, who put his daughter in charge of the Nanna Temple in Ur. However, Naram-Sin widened the influence of direct family members and installed not only his daughter Enmenanna as high priestess of the moon-god in Ur, but also made another daughter, Shumshani, the priestess of the sun-god at Mari; two of his sons were governors in Marad and Tutum, and another daughter was (likely) the queen of Urkesh (Buccellati and Buccellati 2003).

It may be these particular aspects of Akkadian governmentality, the establishment of family members and a focus on dyadic relations with different kinds of courtiers, that led to a perceived "individuality" in Akkadian art. However, the focus on the single person in bodily representations should not lead us to conclude that Akkadians had some sort of individualistic mentality that could be contrasted to the Sumerian collective spirit. Rather, such depictions both sought to instill and reproduce concrete practices of ruling, practices that were highly regularized and ceremonialized. Overall, in the Akkadian period, attention to visual observation manifests itself in detailed renderings of landscapes, human bodies, and animals. Powers of the gaze are none other than the gaze of power.

In the final analysis, Naram-Sin's deification appears perhaps as an apogee of a new governmentality, but one we find again in Ur III times. Deification was a decisive step beyond what had been achieved so far by Akkadian kings. The move may be thought of as parallel to the absolutism of Louis XIV. If we take all the pictorial and textual evidence into account, it seems quite likely that Naram-Sin did not just succumb to his own narcissism, but rather had a more distanced relation to the technologies of power he introduced. He was a shrewd manipulator of religious and political aspects of power, someone who enveloped the political elites into a state of projecting their own phantasms of power onto this king (see also Westenholz 1999: 46–52). Thus, Geertz's explanation of a king who believes just as much as his elites in an overarching cosmology is an unlikely scenario for this ruler. I rather favor the Elias-Erdheim thesis of a conscious attempt by the highest state official of taming and humiliating courtiers into positions that were less elevated than before.[12] This situation also explains the

---

[12]A similar view on the Aztecs can be found in Kurtz
1991, especially pp. 152–54.

awkward and contradictory memorialization of Naram-Sin. Deified and worshipped for a long time, he was also remembered already less than one hundred years after his death as the proto-typical evil ruler. I assume that the elites felt a need for *post hoc* self-redemption from a humil-iating situation of having been turned into puppets of a divine regime. Interestingly, when read this way, rather than as an "antidote against the bombastic claims of the rulers" (Michalowski 1987: 64), the personality of Naram-Sin as depicted in the Curse of Akkad resembles the elites more than the king himself. In this and other tales, the king is a frustrated leader, intent on acting but held down by a humiliating divine power that sets him insurmountable limits. If we substitute the elite for the king, could there be a better analogy to the relation of the divine king with his entourage than such a tale? The traditions of the evil king may therefore just be an ancient kind of *Vergangenheitsbewältigung* through sublimation.

****

    I thank Nicole Brisch for her invitation to Chicago. She piqued my interest in the subject of divine kings and thus widened my intellectual horizon. Susan Pollock gave valuable advice on drafts of this paper, and discussions in Chicago provided me with good critique.

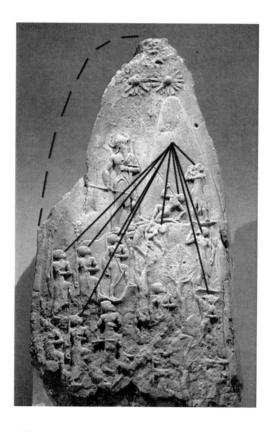

Figure 8.1. Victory Stele of Naram-Sin against
the Lullubeans, Found at Susa.
After Orthmann 1975: pl. 104

BIBLIOGRAPHY

Agamben, Giorgio

  2003   *Stato di eccezione*. Turin: Bollati Boringhieri.

Balandier, Georges

  1997   *Anthropologie politique*. Paris: Presses Universitaires de France.

Battaglia, Deborah

  1995   "Problematizing the Self: A Thematic Introduction." In *Rhetorics of Self-Making*, edited by Deborah Battaglia. Berkeley: University of California Press.

  1997   "Ambiguating Agency: The Case of Malinowski's Ghost." *American Anthropologist* 99: 505–10.

Bell, Catherine

  1992   *Ritual Theory, Ritual Practice*. Oxford: Oxford University Press.

Berger, Peter L.

  1963   "Charisma and Religious Innovation: The Social Location of Israelite Prophecy." *American Sociological Review* 28 (6): 940–50.

Boehmer, Rainer M.

  1965   *Die Entwicklung der Glyptik während der Akkad-Zeit*. Berlin: Walter de Gruyter.

Börker-Klähn, Jutta

  1982   *Altvorderasiatische Bildstelen und vergleichbare Felsreliefs.* 2 volumes. Baghdader Forschungen 4. Mainz am Rhein: Philipp von Zabern.

Bourdieu, Pierre

  1999   "Rethinking the State: Genesis and Structure of the Bureaucratic Field." In *State/Culture. State Formation after the Cultural Turn*, edited by George Steinmetz, pp. 53–75. Ithaca: Cornell University Press.

Buccellati, Giorgio, and Marilyn Buccellati

  2003   "Tar'am Agade, Daughter of Naram-Sin, at Urkesh." In *Of Pots and Plans: Papers on the Archaeology and History of Mesopotamia and Syria Presented to David Oates in Honour of his 75th Birthday,* edited by Lamia al-Gailani Werr, John Curtis, Augusta McMahon, Joan Oates, and Julien Reade, pp. 11–31. London: NABU.

Burgess, Glenn

  1992   "The Divine Right of Kings Reconsidered." *The English Historical Review* 425: 837–61.

Cooper, Jerrold S.

  1983   *The Curse of Agade*. Johns Hopkins Near Eastern Studies. Baltimore: Johns Hopkins University Press.

  1990   "Mesopotamian Historical Consciousness and the Production of Monumental Art in the Third Millennium B.C." In *Investigating Artistic Environments in the Ancient Near East*, edited by Ann C. Gunter, pp. 39–52. Washington, D.C.: Smithsonian Institution Press.

Dean, Mitchell

  1999   *Governmentality: Power and Rule in Modern Society*. London: Sage.

De Baecque, Antoine

  1994   "From Royal Dignity to Republican Austerity: The Ritual for the Reception of Louis XVI in the French National Assembly (1789–1792)." *Journal of Modern History* 66: 671–96.

Duerr, Hans Peter
    1988   *Nacktheit und Scham.* Der Mythos vom Zivilisationsprozess 1. Frankfurt: Suhrkamp.
Durkheim, Emile
    1968   *Les formes élémentaires de la vie religieuse.* Paris: Presses Universitaires de France.
Edzard, Dietz O.
    1968/69   "Die Inschriften der altakkadischen Rollsiegel." *Archiv für Orientforschung* 22:
                18–20.

Elias, Norbert
    1976   *Über den Prozeß der Zivilisation: Soziogenetische und psychogenetische Untersu-
                chungen.* 2 volumes. Suhrkamp Taschenbuch Wissenschaft 158–59. Frankfurt: Suhr-
                kamp.

Erdheim, Mario
    1982   *Die gesellschaftliche Produktion von Unbewußtheit: Eine Einführung in den ethno-
                psychoanalytischen Prozeß.* Frankfurt: Suhrkamp.

Farber, Walter
    1983   "Die Vergöttlichung Naram-Sins." *Orientalia,* n.s., 52: 67–72.

Feeley-Harnik, G.
    1985   "Issues of Divine Kingship." *Annual Review of Anthropology* 14: 273–313.

Foucault, Michel
    1977   *Discipline and Punish: The Birth of the Prison.* New York: Pantheon Books.
    1991   "Governmentality." In *The Foucault Effect: Studies in Governmentality,* edited by
                Graham Burchell, Colin Gordon, and Peter Miller, pp. 87–104. Chicago: University of
                Chicago Press.
    2004   *Naissance de la biopolitique: Cours au Collège de France (1978–1979).* Hautes
                études. Paris: Gallimard.

Geertz, Clifford
    1959   "Ritual and Social Change: A Javanese Example." *American Anthropologist* 61:
                991–1012.
    1980   *Negara: The Theatre State in Nineteenth-Century Bali.* Princeton: Princeton Univer-
                sity Press.

Gelb, Ignace J., and Burkhart Kienast
    1990   *Die altakkadischen Königsinschriften des Dritten Jahrtausends v. Chr.* Freiburger
                altorientalische Studien 7. Stuttgart: Franz Steiner.

Grosrichard, Alain
    1998   *The Sultan's Court: European Fantasies of the East.* Translated by Liz Heron. Lon-
                don: Verso.

Hobsbawm, Eric, and Terence Ranger, editors
    1983   *The Invention of Tradition.* Cambridge: Cambridge University Press.
Howe, Leo
    2000   "Risk, Ritual and Performance." *Journal of the Royal Anthropological Institute* N.S.
                6: 63–79.

Kelly, John D., and Martha Kaplan
    1990   "History, Structure, and Ritual." *Annual Review of Anthropology* 19: 119–50.
Kertzer, David I.
    1988   *Ritual, Politics, and Power.* New Haven: Yale University Press.

1991   "The Role of Ritual in State Formation." In *Religious Regimes and State Formation: Perspectives from European Ethnology*, edited by Eric R. Wolf, pp. 85–104. Albany: State University of New York Press.

Krieken, Robert van

2005   "Occidental Self-Understanding and the Elias-Duerr Dispute: 'Thick' versus 'Thin' Conceptions of Human Subjectivity and Civilization." *Modern Greek Studies* 13: 273–81.

Kurtz, Donald V.

1991   "Strategies of Legitimation and the Aztec State." In *Anthropological Approaches to Political Behavior*, edited by Frank McGlynn and Arthur Tuden, pp. 146–65. Pittsburgh: University of Pittsburgh Press.

Liverani, Mario

1993   "Model and Actualization: The Kings of Akkad in the Historical Tradition." In *Akkad: The First World Empire. Structure, Ideology, Traditions*, edited by Mario Liverani, pp. 41–68. Padua: Sargon srl.

Mair, Lucy

1974   *African Societies*. Cambridge: Cambridge University Press.

Michalowski, Piotr

1987   "Charisma and Control: On Continuity and Change in Early Mesopotamian Bureaucratic Systems." In *The Organization of Power: Aspects of Bureaucracy in the Ancient Near East*, edited by McGuire Gibson and Robert Biggs, pp. 55–68. Studies in Ancient Oriental Civilization 46. Chicago: The Oriental Institute.

Nissen, Hans-Jörg

1993   "Settlement Patterns and Material Culture of the Akkadian Period: Continuity and Discontinuity." In *Akkad. The First World Empire. Structure, Ideology, Traditions*, edited by Mario Liverani, pp. 91–106. Padua: Sargon srl.

Orthmann, Winfried, editor

1975   *Der alte Orient*. Propyläen-Kunstgeschichte 14. Frankfurt: Ullstein.

Rose, Nikolas

1996   *Inventing Our Selves*. Cambridge: Cambridge University Press.

2007   *The Politics of Life Itself: Biomedicine, Power, and Subjectivity in the Twenty-First Century*. New Jersey: Princeton University Press.

Sahlins, Marshall

1985   *Islands of History*. Chicago: University of Chicago Press.

Scott, James

1990   *Domination and the Arts of Resistance*. New Haven: Yale University Press.

Selz, Gebhard

1998   "Über mesopotamische Herrschaftskonzepte. Zu den Ursprüngen mesopotamischer Herrscherideologie im 3. Jahrtausend." In dubsar anta-men: *Studien zur Altorientalistik; Festschrift für Willem H. Ph. Römer zur Vollendung seines 70. Lebensjahres mit Beiträgen von Freunden, Schülern und Kollegen*, edited by Manfred Dietrich, Oswald Loretz, and Thomas E. Balke, pp. 281–344. Münster: Ugarit-Verlag.

Weber, Max

1972   *Wirtschaft und Gesellschaft*. Tübingen: J. C. B. Mohr.

Westenholz, Åge
    1999   "The Old Akkadian Period: History and Culture." In *Mesopotamien: Akkade-Zeit und Ur III-Zeit*, edited by Pascal Attinger and Markus Wäfler, pp. 17–120. Orbis Biblicus et Orientalis 160. Freiburg: Universitätsverlag; Göttingen: Vandenhoeck & Ruprecht.

Westenholz, Joan Goodnick
    1997   *The Legends of the Kings of Akkade: The Texts.* Mesopotamian Civilizations 7. Winona Lake: Eisenbrauns.

Wolf, Eric
    1999   *Envisioning Power: Ideologies of Dominance and Crisis.* Berkeley: University of California Press.

9

THE SACRALIZED BODY OF THE AKWAPIM KING

MICHELLE GILBERT, TRINITY COLLEGE

"Through a special ritual of enthronement, a particular person ... is transformed into a 'fetish-body.'" (de Heusch 1997: 213)

"[The] king is symbolically killed at the moment he is installed, making him into a 'living dead man.'" (de Heusch 1997: 218)

THE TRANSFORMATIVE POWER OF AKWAPIM ROYAL RITES AND A BRIEF DISCLAIMER

Luc de Heusch suggests (1997: 213–14, 2005a) that in many African societies kings are "ancestralized" and turned by the enthronement rites into a "body fetish" with magical/mystical/religious power; that the rites transform him into a "sacred monster" (1997: 217) who articulates the natural and cultural orders.[1] He builds on the ideas of Sir James Frazer in *The Golden Bough* that emphasize the ritual function of kingship, and that contain two different theories of kingship.[2] First, that the kingship is identified with fertility, and the well-being of the kingdom is identified with that of the king's body, and therefore the king must be removed (or put to death) before any illness or physical decay endangers the society and threatens "nature's life-force." Second, the king absorbs the "sins"/deaths of his subjects, and therefore in order to avoid endangering himself and the kingdom, he must continually be repurified or sacrificed as a scapegoat to thus carry away the evil. As Quigley notes, "for this reason royal ritual is never-ending" (2005: 10).

Rene Girard, in *Violence and the Sacred* (1977), follows Frazer's hypotheses and focuses on the idea that the key to interpreting kingship is to see the king as scapegoat. He argues that "violence is the heart ... of the sacred" (Girard 1977: 31), that interpersonal violence is deflected into violence toward ritually slain sacrificial creatures, that ritual serves cathartic purposes, and that sacrifice is an act of violence without the risk of vengeance (1977: 13). Girard then opines that a surrogate victim provides the key to kingship and culture more generally, and that regicide is explicable solely by reference to its scapegoat function.[3] De Heusch (1997) describes surrogate victims among the Jukun, Rukuba, and Mossi. He notes that the Jukun king, who is identified with the plants the Jukun cultivate, is treated, when necessary, as a scapegoat; that he is secretly killed after a bad harvest or drought, as these natural catastrophes are thought to be due to the king's weakened mystical force. He also observes that the Rukuba king of Nigeria must continually be re-purified, or sacrificed as a scapegoat.

---

[1] Many examples exist. For an extraordinarily vivid case, see Filip de Boeck's (1994) description of how the Aluund king is set apart from his kin and others in installation rites, hemmed in by rigorous taboos, and secluded thereafter mostly in his house; see also Fortes' seminal essay on Asante installation rites (1968).

[2] See also Quigley's useful introduction to *The Character of Kingship* (2005).

[3] Quigley (2005: 12); see also de Heusch (2005b), who is highly critical of Girard's argument.

Among the Mossi in Burkina Faso (see de Heusch 1997: 219–22, who draws on the work of Michel Izard), a stallion (the king's double) is enthroned at the same time as the king and the king rides him during official ceremonies. The horse and the king are the only fully male creatures in the palace — others are women, girls, uncircumcised boys, female and castrated animals. The stallion never couples with mares — it has no descendants. The king, after installation, has no sexual relations with his predecessor's widow though she takes the title "king-wife" (he spends one night with her but is forbidden to make her pregnant). This sexual interdiction is a mark of the sacred quality of the king and separates him from normal kinship behavior/relations. The Mossi kingship, we are told, is a synthesis of two concepts: *naam* or authority that is held hereditarily by royal lineage members, and *panga* or violence which the king acquires on enthronement. When the king dies there is a dissociation between these two aspects of kingship: the king's eldest daughter takes his place as the holder of *naam* (and rules as *napoko*) and his youngest son (given the title *kurita*) takes over *panga* and is expelled from the kingdom, dressed in regal clothes and riding his father's stallion. The stallion, associated with *panga*, is then killed in the same place as the king was installed. In Frazerian terms he is a scapegoat for the king (de Heusch 1997: 221). The king is symbolically killed after his actual demise.

One may well ask whether the idea of "scapegoat" has a Semitic template, whether Frazer, like Robertson-Smith before him, was simply working backward from Semitic templates of sacrifice to a presumed more primitive form.[4] One may similarly question, though Girard (1977: 7) does not, the influence of Christianity on Victor Turner or Godfrey Leinhardt when they argue that sacrifice is a collective act of substitution at the expense of the victim who absorbs the internal dissension in the community. De Heusch (2005b: 63–65) is critical of how Girard places sacrifice at the center of his theory. His own position is that the positive function of kingship is to ensure prosperity and fertility and that regicide is simply the negative aspect of this.

Luc de Heusch's discussion of surrogate human victims and scapegoats among the Jukun, Rukuba, and Mossi have inspired me to re-examine Akwapim royal rites of installation and death and to pay more attention to the reality of regicide and to the idea of royal surrogates. The king of Akwapim, a small Akan kingdom in southeastern Ghana, is set apart by those over whom he will reign and sacralized by a series of installation rites. Being born of a particular lineage is not sufficient; he must be transformed by inauguration rites from an ordinary person into a non-person, transformed into a "fetish," a container of sovereignty who articulates the "natural" and "cultural" orders and whose formally unblemished body is the outward sign of his inner state — a body that is the visual summation of the state of the kingdom (Gilbert 1987). The Akwapim king's bodies, "natural" and "politic,"[5] are conjoined by means of installation rites involving stools (ancestral shrines) that are "blackened" with sacrificial blood, initially that of a lineage member, later that of a slave, and, since the early twentieth century, of a sheep (Gilbert 1987, 1989). The king is identified with his ancestors by the black stools and he is then anointed with the power of particular deities for further protection and strength. A major rite that involves the whole kingdom and includes one week of continuous activity is

[4] I thank Father Mark Gruber for suggesting this and for reading an early draft. De Heusch (2005b: 63–64) similarly points to the influence of Christianity in Girard's *Violence and the Sacred* and in his later work.

[5] See Kantorowicz 1957. Implicit in this is the insoluble problem that the kingship (body politic) never dies and is corporate; but the body natural (the biological individual) is mortal.

performed annually in Akropong, the capital of the kingdom, to maintain the king in his office. This rite, significantly called *Odwira* [purification], cleanses the king and the entire kingdom from the dangerous evil and pollution of the previous year(s).[6] Should the king become ill, Odwira cannot be performed and, were that to occur, the believed consequences would be famine and illness for the whole kingdom. In such circumstances Akwapim people force their king to abdicate or they "destool" him; with cunning diplomacy they change the idiom of the argument from individual to institution and say "we serve the stool, not the person."

The Akwapim king-elect is metaphorically put to death in the installation rite (see below); he is then a "living-dead man," to use de Heusch's term. But there are two other royal officials whose deaths bear close scrutiny because they may be royal surrogates of a sort. The Akwapim king's "soul-child" [ɔkra] is a kind of human surrogate who is killed just after the king's actual death (or if the king is alive, the soul-child is released from his office when he reaches maturity — which amounts to the same thing) (fig. 9.1). I suggest further that the killing of the court crier or "herald" [ɛsɛn] who helps the king-elect to choose the ancestral character of his upcoming reign during the royal installation rite may also be considered a surrogate sacrifice; in that while he represents the non-ancestral power of the "wild," he is also at the same time a metaphor for the king (fig. 9.2). He is a sort of foil for the king — like the royal fool in many European kingdoms, and as Girard points out, "the fool shares his master's status as an outsider ... and is eminently sacrificeable" (1977: 12). Finally, I suggest that the meaning of sacrifice of human blood on the shrines for the king's ancestors to renew his fertility, and the meaning of the anointment of the king with his "ancestral dust" during Odwira and with blood used to anoint the ancestral black stools, needs further examination, as an example of surrogate "alimentary incest" — anthropophagy.

Lastly, a brief disclaimer. Evans-Pritchard, in his Frazer lecture on the Shilluk of the Sudan, delivered in 1948 and eventually republished in *Social Anthropology and Other Essays* (1962), revisited the central issue of regicide and argued that it is the kingship, not the king, that is divine, thereby privileging the underlying political arrangements.[7] Quigley (2005: 2) concurs and says the "divinity of kings is an ethnographic oddity." De Heusch disagrees and says that Frazer was mistaken to call this institution "divine kingship," as the king is "not assimilated with a divinity," but because of the installation rite that sacralizes his body, becomes a "god-thing" (2005a: 25). I suggest further that the distinction between "divine" and "sacred" kings is a hair-line distinction that is Western and Christian, the concern primarily of theology and only relevant to anthropology if the local people make such a distinction. Akwapim people do not. Thus, one may say that Akwapim kings are divine in that their authority is endorsed by the ancestors and deities and their being invested with invisible, eternal, immortal powers that are protective and punishing. Kings are deemed in Akwapim to be "holy" [kronkron].[8] Beyond this, lesser chiefs who "sit on stools" are also similarly empowered with enhanced moral status, though to a lesser extent, and thus may also be considered sacred or divine. There are

---

[6] See Gilbert (1994) for how internal politics affect the performance of this rite. Quigley (2005: 4) notes that "The purpose of all ritual is either to transform a person from one status to another or to maintain him in that status. It amounts to the same thing — the overriding of nature by culture."

[7] For a rejoinder, see Young on the Jukun (1966); see Feeley-Harnik (1985) for an early and perceptive survey of theories concerning divine kingship.

[8] A praise poem on the talking drum makes this point metaphorically (Gilbert 1987: 307); Christaller's dictionary (1933) delineates the range of meanings encompassed by *kronkron*.

degrees of sacredness. Quigley (2005: 2) refers to this idea as "refractions of the monarchy." Thus whether or not the king is sacred or divine is an academic point and it is not the most useful place to begin.

I wish in this essay to look at the transformation of the king's body upon installation and at death, and at the never-ending need for purification of the king and kingship in the Odwira rite. I will show, as well, that there is more than one body to consider and ask whether or how the *ɛsɛn* and *ɔkra* may be considered to be surrogate victims for the king as in the Mossi example.

A BEING SET APART

> "[the] function of the king is to stand apart as a perfect being separated from the contaminating concerns of ordinary people and the political and economic mechanisms which allow these concerns to be carried out" (Quigley 2005: 5).

Just as ritual performance can be dangerous because it brings together domains normally kept apart, so the Akwapim king, who combines attributes of the living as well as of his ancestors, is considered dangerous as well as beneficent. He is separated symbolically from ordinary people, but he also partakes of all human features, rather than the limited few possessed by ordinary people.[9]

The king is distinguished from ordinary people in many ways. One is that symbolically he does not share their limitations of time or space. The king is said to straddle the spheres of the living and the dead and is given symbolic immortality — he does not die. It is recognized that at death the king's body "goes into the earth," but his spirit is thought to be still living. Living persons eat food with salt but the dead do not. Nevertheless, small amounts of salt are placed in offerings to the king's ancestors since they are regarded as still living and not as dead. Akropong people do not say that the king has died. Rather they say "he has gone to his village"; or "something has happened"; or "a big tree has fallen." Ordinary people die and are dead, but not the king. The ambiguity is seen in the way an elder explained this to me: "We do not say the king has died. We say his *okyeame* [spokesman/linguist] is sick. If we say he is dead, it is almost like … a curse, a sacrilege."

In a similar fashion, the king does not occupy ordinary space: He neither steps barefoot on the ground, nor walks without an umbrella over his head, showing that he is neither of the earth nor the sky, the domains of people and deities. The king's freedom of movement is carefully controlled and when he walks, he is supported by attendants, as he must not fall. He must show evidence of sexual activity (formerly kings had many wives)[10] as his health and fertility represents the well-being of the kingdom. The king appears neither to eat nor drink since he does these things only in seclusion in the palace. He is prevented from talking or being addressed in the same way as are ordinary people. Because he speaks with the power of his ancestors, his words are dangerous, and therefore in public an *okyeame* interprets his murmured words to the people and repeats their words to the king. His used bath water is thrown away by reliable attendants: were they themselves to bathe in it afterwards it is said that it would make them too powerful to control. Finally he is distinct from ordinary people even when asleep. He is awakened by a special attendant because his ancestors are more powerful than those of ordinary people:

---

[9] See Gilbert 1987 for some of the following material in a rather different form.

[10] Many wives was not merely a sign of power, as is usually stated.

To wake him up, you knock at his pillow and then you turn away. You cannot make him look at your face. If he is to talk to you it must be while you are turned away. If he looks at you and you see the power in his eyes, it may hurt you, because he has been asleep with his ancestors.

Because of his sacred qualities, the king is hedged about with taboos of many kinds. Some of these prohibitions separate him from the pollution of others — especially menstruating women and the recently dead. Others may reflect the categorical separation of ancestors and deities. In general, the king must keep himself in a state of physical perfection, as an outward sign of his inner moral perfection and of the proper conjunction of his two bodies, the "natural" and the "politic." To aid this, any possible pollution is absorbed or deflected by officials — in particular by his *akrafo* [soul people; s. *ɔkra;* from *kra*: soul, *fo*: people]. Akwapim people believe that a soul (or spirit) dwells inside everyone, but the *kra* may also be separate, something that can protect or hinder in one's various enterprises (and for this reason offerings are made to it). The soul of an important person may reside partly in another person, so a king will chose someone born on the same day of the week as he (who thus shares an affinity) and make him his *ɔkra*.[11] The more powerful a king is, the more soul people [*akrafo*] he will need to have. They "belong to the king" and share their destiny and identity with the king. If something unfortunate happens to one of them (especially if it were an injury involving blood), it would be as if it had happened to the king and pacification or purification in the form of sacrifice would need to be made; similarly, if someone curses the king, a sheep would be sacrificed to reverse it and the *akrafo* would put the blood on their first finger, touch their tongue to it, and spit it out; the meat then belongs to them and they can safely eat it. In the early to mid-twentieth century, whenever the king left the palace, one of his soul people always accompanied him. The king's *akrafo* greet people before they are able to approach the king (to deflect any harm); they are like a spiritual bodyguard. One child *ɔkra* is always seated at the king's feet; he tastes his food (in case it is poisoned), and sleeps at the foot of his bed. When the child *ɔkra* grows too large to be carried seated in front of the king in a palanquin, customarily he is given a wife and some land and released from his duties: he is replaced (fig. 9.4).[12] The child *ɔkra* wears a feather headdress which keeps evil from the king. It is made of male-eagle feathers, leopard skin, small squares of human skull joined by golden wires, gold-covered ram's horns, and cast-gold ornaments. The eagle and leopard are dangerous animals that devour their prey and are considered kings of the sky and forest, respectively; the ram, symbol of strength and purity, is the domestic animal *par excellence*, and the preferred one for oblations. *Akrafo* have no political role; they are sin-eaters and absorb the pollution to which the king is exposed. They also share the destiny of the king; and formerly most were killed when the king died in order to be able to serve him in the land of the ancestors.[13] Note that no sacrificial blood is used for purification of the *akrafo*, though it is an integral part of all other purification rites. I return to the subject of the *ɔkra* as the king's surrogate victim later in this essay.

At the same time as the king is given symbolic attributes that differ from those of ordinary people, he is also the only person with characteristics of all men. The talking drum says:

---

[11] The same structural pattern is repeated for lesser chiefs.

[12] By the late 1990s very few people were willing to serve as *akrafo*. There was also a shortage of land and

no certainty about how the king's *ɔkra* would be recompensed when he was released from office.

[13] The position of *ɔkra* is an ambiguous one; formerly most had slave ancestry (Gilbert 1994: 122 n. 42).

King, part of you is *odum* [a hard tree, *Chlorophora excelsa*]
part of you is *onyaa* [a soft tree, *Ceiba pentandra*]
part of you is *fɛtɛfrɛ* [a strong tree, *Bussea occidentalia*]
part of you is *kakapempe* [a brittle tree, *Voacanaa Africana*]

That is to say that part of him is angry, part forgiving, part tactful, part aggressive.

The king, finally, is said to be able to do the impossible: "he can remove a ring through his shoulder." But however great his power, the king is surrounded by ritual prohibitions that he cannot break, and he cannot rule alone. No matter how respected and feared, the king should continually consult his elders. If he reigns arrogantly and dictatorially, he will lose support and there may be plots to destool him. It is never forgotten that it is because of the state that the king is powerful; without the state he is nothing. The talking drum says "It is the river that makes the fish proud."

ENSTOOLMENT AND THE BODY/FETISH

There are eleven electors of the Akwapim king: all are of the Asona[14] clan. They include eight from inside Akropong: the chiefs of the original seven non-royal Asona lineages in Akropong called the *ɔkoman* [lit., "they came to fight"]; and the Queen Mother (a senior woman in the royal lineage, not literally the king's mother); and three town chiefs from outside Akropong, chosen for various historical reasons.[15] Selection of a new king is made without delay, as it is inconceivable for the state to exist without a king.[16] The basis for selection is two-fold: physical or "blood" (i.e., membership in the royal "house," determined matrilineally), and moral or "character" (which derives from the patriline). The new king must be legitimate, his physical body must be complete or whole, and his moral character good. Formerly, a member of the royal family, the *Asonkohene*, was heir-apparent and leader of the young men — this hereditary position was abolished in 1948 in an attempt to contain continuous succession intrigues.

When the king's stool is vacant, the *ankobea* [lit., "they do not go anywhere"], who are trusted advisors and powerful ritual specialists and sons and grandsons of former kings, tell the *Kurontihene* (chief of Akropong, the capital, and head of the Divisional or Wing Chiefs of Akwapim, and not an Asona)[17] to ask the Queen Mother whom she will present as candidate for king. The Queen Mother privately asks the advice of the *ankobea* and then formally meets with the elder women of the seven non-royal Asona lineages (*ɔkoman*), as women are believed to possess specialized knowledge about succession and inheritance. At this meeting of women, the chief of Kodumase is included as the only man in the group. In the early days of the Akwapim kingdom his lineage provided three of the first Akwapim kings, but at one point they could not provide a candidate and were left out of the succession. Nevertheless, they were one of the original royal Asona and were not distrusted; thus the *Kodomasehene* advises them as they decide who should be the next king and acts as Asona spokesman.

---

[14] The royal clan and most of the important early clans in Akropong are Asona.

[15] The Akwapim kingdom was established in the 1730s by warriors from the neighboring kingdom of Akyem. It is ethnically diverse with both Akan and Guan. In 1994, after a violent conflict, the Wings or Divisions of the kingdom seceded along ethnic lines and set themselves up as independent kingdoms (Gilbert 1997). The secession has never been officially recognized. Here I describe Akwapim pre-1994.

[16] Today final authorization of the king's enstoolment is by notice in the official government gazette. The papers are sent to the House of Chiefs and the Eastern Regional Commission has the final authority to accept or reject the candidate.

[17] The *Kurontihene* acts as regent in the king's absence and represents the ordinary people of the state. He is of Akwamu ancestry.

The Queen Mother and *Asonahene* now meet. The *Asonahene* is chief of the most senior branch of all the ruling Asona families; his line once provided a number of early Akwapim kings but they were later struck from the line of succession.[18] The kingmakers then plan to meet in the palace (together with the *ankobea*): The Queen Mother will be the only woman present. She is asked for her nominee and may nominate three candidates. If they are all rejected, the *ankobea* could propose their own candidate.

When agreement is reached, the chief of the *ankobea* summons the candidate. The king-elect "hides" and then is "captured": he must claim not to desire this onerous office; he must seek neither political nor ritual power. In other words, it must "come down upon him" not rise up from human intentions; he is discovered as the sacred-elect, not made by human politics. The nominee is brought by the Kodumase chief and he is examined by the *ankobea* and *ɔkoman* to see that he is "whole" and "unblemished."[19] His physical body must be "complete" and without bodily defect, for as king the well-being of his body is a symbol of that of the state. The purity of his moral character is the essential factor, but purity not being visible, the body stands for his inner quality.

The *Kodumasehene* takes the nominee to the *Kurontihene* and swears the Asona electors have selected this man and that the nominee is "perfect." The *Kurontihene* inspects him on behalf of the people in order to confirm what they say is correct and hands him back to the *ankobea* for a period of seclusion. The following morning, at Santewase [under the Santew tree: *Milletia thonningii*], a public place near the palace that is the recognized meeting place for ordinary citizens, the nominee is brought and a sheep is sacrificed and its blood poured over the nominee's feet to cleanse him. This is the first sign of separation from his former status as an ordinary person. The bloody feet are a sign of the violent wrenching of his old form from the past into a new sacred order. The bloody feet prefigure his capacity to be sacrificed. He is then handed over to the *ankobea* and confined by them. During this period of seclusion he is seated on the skin of a white sheep and his face and arms are covered with pure white clay.[20] The Divisional Chiefs, who represent the state as a polity, now visit to settle any previous disputes they may have had with him in his former role; they visit at night, "hidden," and outside ordinary secular time. By this they extinguish the social and political characteristics he had as an ordinary man.

Soon after, the king-elect is taken at night to the stool house in the palace. His cloth that he wore as an ordinary man is removed and handed to the *Asonahene*, and his sandals are given to *Kodumasehene*; they will keep these things so long as he is king. The king-elect is now without clothes, without signs of his former social person. He is outside all social life; his previous jural *persona* as an ordinary man has been removed and he is symbolically and politically in the state of being newly born (and morally innocent).

---

[18] The *Asonahene*'s ancestor, Ofei Boa, was the first king of Akwapim, but after he allegedly murdered his servant, his black stool was taken from him and he was exiled and his descendants were struck from the line of succession (direct violence by a king is neither expected nor accepted as a sign of his power). They seem to have been brought back around 1850 and the title was created for them in 1918 or 1920 (GNA 11/1101 Akwapim Enquiry, 1922 and 1919). The title, *Asonahene*, brings the Akwapim model of government into greater accord with the general Akan pattern. His role is like *abusua panyin*

[clan elder] for all the Asona clans in Akwapim. See Gilbert 2006 for more on the *Asonahene, Kodomasehene*, and the history of these early Akwapim kings.

[19] That is, he must not be circumcised, nor missing any toes, etc.

[20] This is a sign of liminality. Mediums wear white cloth and their skin is covered in white clay. Kaolin comes from the bottom of rivers and rivers are considered to be *abosom* [deities]. White clay has multiple meanings — when one's right arm is smeared with kaolin this is a sign of success, as in a law case.

The king-elect is then blindfolded and led by the *Kodumasehene* to the stool room. A libation is poured to inform the ancestors of the coming events. The blindfolded king-elect is told
to choose a stool.[21] In the darkened room are only the six black stools,[22] ancestral shrines that
are said variously to represent reigns of peace, or war, disputes, or disorder in the state. Some
say if the new king touches that of a warrior, then his own reign will have wars; if that of a
peaceful king, his will be a peaceful reign. The choice of the stool gives him a new identity
and it is supposed to be guided by a power beyond the control of the king, or perhaps even his
ancestors; but in fact the *ɛsɛn*, or "herald," who keeps order in the palace (and who is generally a dwarf or hunchback whose deformed body is the antithesis of that of the king), has been
hidden in the stool room and calls out to guide the king to the stool considered by the palace
elders to be good for the state and the particular royal line. Having chosen a stool, the king is
instructed to pour libation on the stool, and the assembled *ankobea* are informed and sing war
songs. It is said that in the past the *ɛsɛn* was now beheaded. The *ɛsɛn* forms a symbolic bridge
between society and the wild and uncontrolled powers of nature. He wears a hat made from
colobus monkey fur and a large gold Islamic amulet; the colobus monkey is said to supervise
the animals in the animal kingdom and his fur is deemed the most beautiful of all in the animal kingdom. The *ɛsɛn* sits on an elephant neck bone rather than a stool, and elephants are the
most powerful of animals. The *ɛsɛn* thus is like the king, though in his body he is the king's
opposite. The *ɛsɛn* is the king's extra-societal analogue; he represents the wilderness. The *ɛsɛn*
with provocative and insulting language creates order in the palace, just as the colobus monkey
creates order in the animal world. The *ɛsɛn* represents in body and costume the non-ancestral
powers of forest and savanna and thus is a foil for the king. So, is killing the *ɛsɛn* during the
royal installation rite a surrogate sacrifice of the king? I think not, though certainly the king
articulates the social order and natural order — and as we have seen, royal death is routinely
likened to a natural calamity, namely, a big tree falling. Note that Akwapim people make a
strong distinction between the town [*akurow*] or house [*fie*] and the forest or bush [*nwura mu*];
the categories of culture and nature in everyday life must not be blurred.[23] I return to the question of the death of the *ɛsɛn* below.

Another libation is poured and the stool chosen by the new king is anointed with the blood
of a slave sacrificed for that purpose (today a sheep is substituted).[24] The head of the animal
and other parts are cut in small pieces and scattered in the courtyard for the "ancestors who

---

[21] The description of the *ɛsɛn* aiding the king-elect to
choose a stool is the "ideal," narrarated to me by several palace elders in the 1970s, and possibly influenced
by B. S. Akuffo's *Ahenfi Adesua*. I cannot here describe
the contradictions in actual practice, but the current stool
room is so small that there would scarcely be room for
the *ɛsɛn* to hide.

[22] There are unaccountable contradictions regarding time
and which kings are represented by these stools.

[23] The bush is dangerous and full of wild animals, giants
[*sasabonsam*], and dwarves [*mmoatia*], as well as powerful rivers and trees that are useful for healing, etc. The
town, in contrast, centered under a shady tree, is peaceful; it is the place for human activity including death and
legitimate copulation. When pestilence or other disasters
threaten, Akwapim women cast away danger in a night-
time rite by blocking the road at the edge of the town

[*kurotia*] with their old *fufuu* pounding sticks. In between
these spatial extremes were places for decaying and pol-
luting things: women's menstrual huts, rubbish heaps for
depositing "bad deaths" [*atofo*], and shrines for lesser deities. The king, who lives in town, is empowered by the
deities of the forest and by his ancestors whose graves
are outside the town. The king comes from outside the
town, and if destooled, returns to the forest outside. See
also McLeod's insightful essay (1978) on Akan gold
weights, in which he argues that the system of exchang-
ing different goods or creatures through gold-dust blurs
the basic categorical distinctions on which the Asante
build their world, and therefore certain creatures were
never portrayed on gold weights.

[24] In the past there was certainly more human sacrifice
than I have described here.

are gathered there" to have a share. Some of the blood is used to anoint the stool chosen by the king-elect and to mark his head, thus identifying him with his ancestors and allowing their power to come into him. It is said that on this day "He is now a king."

The acquisition of ancestral identity (when the king-elect selects a black stool associated with a particular ancestor) is clearly analogous to the transformation of an infant. A newly born baby is not a social being until the eighth day after his birth, when he is "out-doored," given a name, clothed, and decorated with beads. The king-elect is at first nude and temporarily without social status; when he touches the royal stool he thereby receives a name and ancestral identity, though he does not yet have the full accoutrements of a kingly person, nor full kingly authority. Note too that while black stools are repeatedly anointed with the sacrificial blood of slaves (now sheep), the victim whose blood, head, heart, and sex organs were used to create and empower the stool originally was a member of the king's own lineage.[25] The new king is thus involved in a transgression bordering on cannibalism (the opposite of all humanity): he is being anointed with the blood of his ancestors and may even wash or drink a little of this blood mixed with water for protection or empowerment.[26]

The black stool chosen by the new king is now carried to the *banmu* ["inside the fence"], a fearful place opposite the palace, shrouded in secrecy. The stool is placed on top of a stone [*ɔserebo*] formerly used apparently for sharpening knives for the execution of sacrificial slaves; beneath the stool is an elephant hide (elephants, considered to be the most powerful animals of the bush, are identified with the king; the stool, being so sacred, cannot touch the earth). The new king, carried on the back of a palace attendant as though a baby, is brought to the *banmu* through a small side door in the palace. The *ankobea* elders who are responsible for a king's funeral surround the stool and the new king is lowered onto it three times. The central act of the installation rite is when his buttocks lightly touch the stool: the king has now been given the power and sacredness of his ancestors. Those who are assembled sing war songs that are appropriate for funerals of stool elders. Akropong elders say "If someone is dead, it is from war. Death is a serious matter. Therefore we sing songs indicating a serious thing has happened in the 'house.'" The place, identity of the ritual officials, and the songs affirm that the former "person" is now dead, and the nudity of the king-elect and identification with the new stool suggest his rebirth. A sheep is sacrificed and libation is poured. The king is then carried back to the palace, again on an attendant's back — he is still like a baby. This time, however, they pass through the main entrance of the palace and libation is poured to inform the ancestors. They all return to the stool house where they remain awake all night. This is similar to the wake keeping of a funeral and signals that the king's former status is extinguished. Symbolically, it suggests the king himself is dead and has joined the ancestors. He is now part of the

---

[25] Black stools are created with gun powder, spider's web, and blood drawn from the neck of a lineage member. The heart, head, and sex organs are put on the stool for a while and then "power has come into the stool" (Gilbert 1989). Later on, sacrificial victims were rarely, if ever, lineage members but were slaves or war captives. The first victim thus came originally from the lineage ancestor: he was an insider who represented the whole group; later victims came from outside society (slaves and war captives, especially those kept in a special farming village belonging to the king). They were passive mediators (or scapegoats) between the living and the royal ancestors. In the twentieth century, castrated

rams considered to be symbolically clean and peaceful were used for sacrifice instead. Girard contrasts "surrogate victims," who come from inside the community, to "ritual victims," who come from outside; he notes there is a double substitution in "ritual sacrifice" (1977: 102).

[26] The revenging power of these sacrificial victims (and of others sacrificed or killed for other reasons), which may continue for decades to threaten the king and kingdom, is pacified during Odwira by means of rites devoted to a deity [*suman*] called Odosu. It is a brass pan shrine surrounded by human skulls. Rites for Odosu still include drinking (of schnapps, perhaps once of blood) from the skulls of former severed victims' heads.

"living dead," identified with the royal ancestors in general and with the previous ruler whose stool he touched specifically. Akropong elders describe this moral and physical transformation by saying "the king has been made complete [wabɛyɛ, lit. "he has become"]." Elders in the 1970s explained that abɛyɛ is analogous to the process of making oil from palm nuts [abɛ: palm tree, *Elaeis Guineensis*], in which palm nuts are transformed from a wild plant into a domestically consumable one. Palm oil, significantly, is red, a color associated with danger and death.

The king enters the palace through the main door as a king now for the first time. He has everything except the public recognition of his new status. He has the internal body of the king, but he has not yet been clothed as one. One other rite occurs to strengthen him before he is publicly installed. There is a small room in the palace reserved for *asuman* [deities and talismans] that have been brought from many places, and that are used to protect the king. The palace elders, having sworn to show the new king all the "secrets" in the palace, take him to the *asuman* to make him strong. The verb used to express this is kɔben no; it literally means go cook it [*ben* "cook"], though there is the implication of becoming clever and knowledgeable. This king is protected by the *asuman* and strengthened by knowledge. He is symbolically "cooked," and so made "perfect."

The final phase of the enstoolment process occurs later, when all the Divisional and town chiefs of Akwapim are assembled with the Akropong chiefs and elders in the large courtyard of the palace in order to recognize the new king as head of state. In silence, a special sword, used in war, is handed to each Divisional Chief in turn. Then the *Kurontihene* tells the king he is handing over the power of Akwapim to him. He also advises him not to ignore the advice of his people or abuse them by calling them "fools" or "slaves." (The king must now belong to all the people.) The king is then carried, hidden, to the boundary of the town. At the end of the town, he is raised high in a palanquin and dressed in the finest cloth and most beautiful regalia, he is carried beneath a state umbrella through the main street of Akropong for all the people to see. Drums beat, horns blow, and guns are fired. The period of seclusion is finally ended. The people see him now as a king for the first time and praise his beauty and majesty. Then in front of the palace, under the shady Mpeni tree (whose coolness represents the peace of the kingdom), the king swears an oath to the Queen Mother saying he will serve her and accept her advice and swears his loyalty to all the chiefs in turn. They also swear to him. Money and drink are distributed. The money is called the "head pad for service" [ɔsom "to serve"; *kahyire* "head pad"] for these people will serve the new king and support him as they would a load for which they are responsible. They will serve him, but he will always remain dependent on them for support. From this time onward, he is king of Akwapim [*Okuapemhene*].

ODWIRA MEANS PURIFICATION

Frazer argues that as the king absorbs the sins of his subjects, he must rid himself of the contagion lest he imperil himself and the kingdom. The king thus must continually be re-purified; and royal ritual is never-ending, for as soon as the purification rite has been completed, the king re-enters the world of compromising relations (Quigley 2005: 6–10). Odwira is an annual rite performed in Akropong, capital of the Akwapim kingdom.[27] Odwira means "purification" and, just as the enstoolment rite of the king is performed by functionaries who may not

---

[27] Akwapim is the only Akan kingdom other than Asante where odwira is celebrated. See McCaskie 1995 for a brilliant and detailed historical reconstruction of odwira in nineteenth-century Asante.

hold the office themselves and who represent both the people and some divine force, so too the purification of the kingdom and king is performed by priests and functionaries who are separate from the king (cf. Quigley 2005: 19).

Odwira centers on the person of the king: it is a ritual that renews him and thus the kingship. It lasts for over two months with a central week of heightened and continuous activity. In Odwira, history is dramatically deconstructed into its constituent parts, cleansed, and then reconstructed. The king symbolically dies and is given renewed life, and history and the sacred topography of the town are conjoined. The performance of Odwira is deemed to be essential for the kingdom: if it is not performed, it is believed that disaster, famine, and pestilence will follow. Were the king to fall ill or should local disputes and intrigues escalate, the performance of Odwira would be canceled or curtailed. While Akropong people desire and proclaim Odwira to have an unalterable script (symbolic of the continuity of the kingdom), in actuality the performance varies subtly each year, demonstrating the incumbent king's possession or lack of power. This variation is read as political commentary. Akwapim people look to ritual to understand politics. I have described the dramatic pull between innovation and repetition and the political manipulations in three different performances of Odwira elsewhere (Gilbert 1994). Here I will briefly summarize the structure of the rite and remark on a few events that renew the power of the king and purify him.

Odwira was called a yam festival by the early Europeans because, among other things, it is a harvest festival for the first yam, the staple crop. The word *Odwira* comes from the root "to cleanse" [*dwira*] and addresses a different aspect of the same rite: namely, that the town must be purified from the pollution of the previous year so that all may eat. Akropong people say, "we wash before we eat." The main focus of Odwira, however, is on the king, whose individual well-being represents that of the kingship.

Six weeks before Odwira week begins, funerals, drumming, and yam-eating are banned. Death and communication between the living and ancestors cease. The orderly passage of time stops.[28] This frames the total cycle. On Monday of Odwira week, ritual officials clear the path to Amanprobi, the royal mausoleum and first state capital five miles away, so that all the ancestors can visit the town. The following day the new yam is publicly displayed by the first non-royal Asona lineage. Now everyone may eat yam: social order is reborn. Early the same morning, the king's stools used for sitting are washed (again the reference is to washing before one eats; the king's black stools will be "fed" later in the week). The ritual officials leave for Amanprobi. When later in the day they return to the palace, the ban on sound is lifted to show "Odwira has arrived." At the palace they are welcomed by the king and townspeople. The chief of the royal mausoleum wears spectacular black-and-red mourning cloth; the executioners wear blood-stained smocks made of cloth from the north (associated with power). The king, dressed in deep mourning, is then hidden by cloth and anointed in silence with the grave-dust of his ancestors that is brought back from Amanprobi by the chief of the royal mausoleum and the executioners. Thus he is given the renewed power to rule. The ancestors have arrived in town, the palace officials are agitated, the king is represented in a liminal state between life and death, and there is an inversion of the proper spatial and moral order. Death has been brought to the town, and it was absorbed by the king.[29] Wednesday, the beginning of the new year, is a day of mourning and fasting. The Queen Mother comes to the palace at dawn to weep

---

[28] This is called *adae butuw* [*adae* "sleeping"; *butuw* "turn"]. The ancestors and the chiefs sleep — it is as if they enclose themselves in a cocoon [*abu*].

[29] One might state this in a different way, perhaps with a more theological inflection, and say that death in the form of ancestral dust renews life.

for the dead; the townspeople, who grieve because the dead have been brought home, drink but do not eat; women sing bawdy songs and adultery is condoned. The day is marked with inversion, typical of funerals. Later the king, dressed for war, is displayed as one whose ancestors defended the state. Death in the bush leads to peace in the town. After midnight, the royal black stools are taken to a river to be cleansed of the year's pollution. Thursday is a day of feasting and life: the townspeople eat and the royal black stools are fed. In the afternoon there is a procession from the palace to Nsorem, a former royal burial ground and site of the second capital. Food is carried by young women for the ancestors of the Asona lineages. The last of the carriers is the *ohene yere* ["king's wife"] who carries mashed yam for the king's ancestors in a silver pan (representing purity). Having fed the royal ancestors, she returns to the palace and the pan is placed three times in the king's lap and then she herself is seated in his lap three times. Feeding the royal ancestors shows she is their wife; now she is shown to be the wife of their descendants, the living king whose implied fertility ensures that of the kingdom. This signals the public recognition of the renewal of the king's "body natural." On Thursday night the town is closed off and "secret" rites are performed by the royal executioners to contain the revenging spirit of sacrificial victims. These rites protect the king and townspeople from their vengeance, even though human sacrifice ceased long ago, and show the continuity of ideas about pollution and kingship and the control of power at the heart of political legitimacy.

Friday is a day of celebration and the town is ritually cleansed by the priest of the main town deity, Ntoa, who sprinkles water with a broom on all those gathered to see the procession of chiefs. Guns are fired, drums beat, and women dance, calling out the king's praises. The king is displayed in his palanquin with his child *ɔkra* seated before him and then all gather in front of the palace under the Mpeni tree (whose roots are said to spread to every house in Akropong) to view the king, in full majesty. His "body politic" has been renewed; the splendor of the kingship is displayed with all his chiefs. Libation is poured and the chiefs wish the king a happy new year, their presence recalling their oath that if called they would come to him, rain or shine. Lastly, the executioners, holding swords in their right hands and covering their mouths with their left, speak in verse of former kings' bravery and valiant deeds. They may even touch the king's jaw with their hands, thus reminding him of the precariousness of his power and his dependence on them. The king must be accountable; he is not alone with power. This is a public display of the relationship between coercion and consent in the articulation of society. The king then addresses the crowd. He is presented as a living ruler as well as an ancestor, holding together the diversities of the kingdom. Odwira continues for another three weeks of less public rites. Purification of the town complete, what remains is to purify the king.

On the following Friday, called Fida Fofie,[30] in secrecy, the king's *akrafo* go to the river and wash; they then return with water to cleanse the king in a small private rite conducted mostly in silence, in which they encircle the head of an *ɔkra* with an egg[31] to absorb the evil and then smash it to the ground; they then bless the king and (now that they are clean) eat a meal together. This is the first time the king eats yam [*ɔde*], the only "real" food. This fast-

---

[30] For an explanation of the Akan calendar, see McCaskie 1995: 151–57, 180; and Bartle 1978.

[31] Eggs are also used to feed the "soul" [*kra*]. When a girl first menstruates, she eats an egg with another girl born on the same day as she; if someone escapes an accident, or if a chief attends a funeral, he will eat an egg as an offering to his "soul." Eggs are like life; and they are complete — "white" and "red" (the same as offerings of mashed yam [*ɔtɔ*]: plain white and "red" with palm oil). Red and white (with black) are the only "real" colors, and in some contexts may refer to blood and semen, or to the matrilineage and group of patrifiliation (Gilbert 1989: 81–82).

breaker signals the resumption of the ordinary passage of time for the king. The king then offers food publicly to the townspeople and in the afternoon the elders (*ankobea* and *ɔkoman*) meet to bless the king. Finally, on the following Sunday, the feather headdress worn by the king's child *ɔkra* is purified and fed — without any blood sacrifice. This marks the end of Odwira. The ancestors return to the land of the dead and the proper order of society is finally reconstructed. This rite is repeated annually.

DEATH AND REGICIDE: THE BODY OF THE KING AND HIS ƆKRA

Regicide, while institutionalized in a number of sacred kingships in Africa (e.g., Jukun and others), is not characteristic of any Akan society, although informal accusations of suspicious deaths due to poisoning are frequently heard in Asante and several Akwapim kings are reputed to have died under suspicious circumstances: Asa Kurofa, for example, seems to have been assassinated in 1875, Kwame Tawia was possibly poisoned in 1879; Owusu Ansa is said to have taken poison in 1914 and the same is said of FWK Akuffo in 1927 (see Samson 1908). I do not consider these or the early terrible war-time custom of beheading one's own king in order to prevent the enemy from so doing to be institutionalized regicide.

Destoolment functions in Akwapim symbolically as regicide does elsewhere: it is a social and symbolic death. Akan kingdoms, as a whole, are plagued by litigation and destoolment procedures (Robertson 1976). Formal causes for destoolment comprise defects in the person of the king and his abuse of power. They include drinking in the streets, seducing other men's wives, offending ones elders or alluding to their slave ancestry, bringing a priest into the palace without the elders' knowledge, walking alone at night without an attendant, asking for loans of money, driving the children of former kings away from the palace without cause, going alone to the stool room to pour libation to the ancestors, failing to abdicate if he has a contagious disease or has not begotten a child after three years, incest. While any of these factors may be used as grounds for destoolment, they may be ignored until such time as there is enough general political support to pursue these highly disruptive procedures. Government interests prevailed during the period of the Convention People's Party to ensure that destoolments were common; destoolments have been actively discouraged by recent governments for fear that they would be destabilizing.

Rites of destoolment are the mirror image of inauguration rites (cf. Fortes 1968: 6): one desacralizes and the other sacralizes. Both are performed by the same officials. Destoolment (getting rid of an undesirable king) is related to abdication (getting rid of a sick king): both imply an element of compulsion and both are related to problems of litigation. Destoolment is generally brought about by the lesser attendants in the palace who know the king's behavior well; they inform the elders who in turn bring charges. An Akan proverb asserts "When an insect bites you it is from your own cloth." First, the *ankobea* report to the Queen Mother, who in turn invites the kingmakers to examine the charges. If the king denies the charges in private, he will be invited to answer in public. The place of assembly is in front of the palace under the Mpeni tree. The king goes to the assembly with only a few attendants. If he can answer the charges, he does so; if he is guilty they hoot at him three times, thereby insulting him as an ordinary man — an act inconceivable toward a king. Note that while the king may be personally abused, no one may curse his ancestors, for it is the king, not the kingship, that is in question. The king is then informed that he is no longer king and should he call himself one, he will break the great state oath and be killed by the powerful Akwapim deities. Two shots are fired from a gun and the former king is given an ordinary stool made of wood to sit on; his sandals and cloth are removed (desacralized) and the clothing he wore before his enstoolment are returned to him by the *Asonahene* and *Kodumasehene* who had kept them safely throughout his reign. His head is hit three times with the sandals and he is told that he should go as an ordinary person with one wife and one attendant to the village to tap palm wine and drink. He is not permitted to remain in Akropong. Palm-wine tapping implies an isolated life in the bush outside the town. (Note that they do not suggest he become a hunter. A common myth suggests that it is hunters who acquire land and found towns as others join round them, thus becoming chiefs. Hunters, of course, are associated with killing; thus through violence power comes from the outside, and the hunters become stranger-kings.)[32] Finally, the priest of the major Akropong deity swears an oath against the ex-king and calls on the deities to kill the destooled king if he ever acts like a king again. Note that it is the deities that are called upon to kill, not the ancestors. There is a change from ancestral protection to the destructive force of the deities who can punish without mercy.

As the well-being of the king symbolizes that of the state, if the king becomes ill, Odwira cannot be performed and it is believed that grave misfortune will follow. Should the illness persist, something must be done. While the Shilluk would ritually strangle their sick or impotent king to save the kingship, in Akropong the solution was "voluntary" abdication — two cases are known in the twentieth century of abdication due to illness. Should he become ill but then recover, it is thought comparable to a king who has been to war and succeeded: for example, Nana Kwame Fori I (r. 1880–94) who recovered from smallpox (Akuffo 1950: 147).

I turn finally to an abbreviated discussion of a funeral for a king. A royal funeral is an exceedingly serious event — both fearsome and terrible.[33] People do not say a king has died, they say euphemistically "something has happened" or that he is "sick and has been taken to a herbalist," or "gone to his village." In the past many people were killed at this time. Those who were the king's close personal attendants would be killed to attend him in the land of the ancestors. People dared not go near the compounds of the executioners. The king's wives were placed in the grave in the belief that the ancestors are married and life in the land of the ancestors is just as in the land of the living; some said it was just the head, but for the favorite wife, it was the whole body. Other people, strangers and slaves, were killed so their spirits could go to support the king, but also to show the disorder that had come to town. I was told "they are like fowl and goats met in the street ... so when in sorrow, or when a crisis has come, we slaughter them and just leave them anywhere, in the streets and the outskirts of the town."[34] They also take palace attendants — one or two *akrafo*, an *ɛsɛn*, and horn-blowers — so when the king goes to the land of the ancestors, he would still be a king and their spirits will go with him. It is said that formerly if you had a bad slave in the house, you could exchange him for someone who had been caught to die; and that in the old days, each of the senior Divisional Chiefs came at night bringing the head of someone they had killed — no one came empty-handed. I was told that "in the old days, you do not go to the place where the dead body is with dust under your feet — you must walk in blood to the place."

---

[32] For more on the logic of archaic kingship and the origin of force and violence outside of the moral constraints of kinship society, see Rowlands' (1993) analysis of changing meanings of Benin human sacrifice as tied to the history of Benin kingship, the ambivalence of forces for creation and destruction for legitimizing royal power, and his critique of de Heusch, Sahlins, and others.

[33] It is difficult to gather material on royal funerals because people do not like to speak about such matters and also because when I was in Akwapim a king had not "died" on the stool for many years.

[34] There is a repetition of this in miniature on Odwira Tuesday when the executioners return from Amanprobi bringing the ancestral spirits. This is called *wirempe*.

A royal death is officially announced at night. War songs are sung near the dead body by the executioners. When those in town hear the songs, they know "trouble has come." Royal children and kin smear their faces with gunpowder; elders place red ochre on their face and arms, indicating their "eyes are red," that is, they are sad and angry. The whole town mourns. Men and women wear black or reddish ochre-colored cloth; all go barefoot and formerly women cut off their hair. The deceased king is laid in state, covered with precious cloths, and mourners come to view him and then sit together singing. The *akrafo* (regarded as widows of the deceased) sit near the dead body when it is laid in state. The corpse is taken for burial at night, laid in state again at Amanprobi village, and buried in daylight in a sacred nearby grove. The grave is deep because the coffin is put on top of the dead bodies. I was told that "blood is of no use there: they want the person to accompany the dead."

When a king dies, it is especially serious for his *ɔkra,* as their two identities are linked. One former *ɔkra* told me that "there are only two kings: the Omanhene and the boy who wears the feather headdress" (fig. 9.3). So the living body of the king is divided: the good/pure king reigns and the soul-child absorbs the dirt and impurity; and when the living king "dies," the child *ɔkra* must be put to death to remain with him. I suggest that he is not killed as a scape-goat, but rather their two fates or destinies are joined, so he must be sacrificed. What occurs is a surrogate regicide during the funeral of the king. How precisely this was done in the old days is no longer remembered, as under the British this practice could not be carried out openly for fear of severe punishment. A palace elder in the 1970s told me what he said occurred thirty years before:

> The child *ɔkra* was put in a big brass bowl [*ayowa*]. He sat on a stool in a brass bowl and the deceased Omanhene was placed on him and was bathed there. The last one that was done like this was for Nana Kwadade. The small *ɔkra* died two weeks lat-er...."

This is surely not what he himself had seen. "Thirty years" is a metaphor and should not be interpreted literally. The large funeral for Kwadade I, in 1866, was for many years a com-mon topic of conversation for the elders; reputedly there was a great deal of human sacrifice. Akwapim men do discuss human sacrifice, but they do so very indirectly — evidence of their discomfort and recognition of the fearful past.

We are fortunate to have an earlier (and certainly more accurate) report that corroborates the sacrifice of the *ɔkra*. An elderly indigenous Basel Mission pastor called Theophilus Opoku, who was born in Akropong in 1842 and was the son of Omanhene Nana Addo Dankwa I, wrote in an annual report to the Basel Mission in 1907 that when a king died, the *ɔkra* was "strangled or broken by the neck between two clubs or poles," as he was not permitted to be touched with a knife for any blood to flow out. The "naked body [of the *ɔkra* was then] dragged into the grave and the coffin bearing the royal corpse lowered to sit upon the body of this unfortunate man."[35] In these Mission archives, there is also confirmation of the fact that when the king "died," the other *akrafo* were also killed to serve the king in the land of the ancestors.[36]

---

[35] Opoku (1907, Mission 21 archive, D-1.86.31). This information also explains present-day rites in which the feather headdress (Oboaman) worn by the *ɔkra* is cleansed without the use of sacrificial blood.

[36] The German-Ghanaian Basel missionary Wilhelm Rottmann reported that "In the old days — and in Asante until recently — the soul people, with few exceptions, were slaughtered when a king died in order to be at his disposal on the other side" (1907, Mission 21 archive, D-1.93.29).

The funeral described above is the "earth funeral" [dɔte yi]. The main funeral [ayi kɛse] occurs a year or more later. At the second, very elaborate celebration, an effigy of the king is displayed in an open room and a bull is placed in the town street for townspeople to fire guns into: this is called akyere ["to catch"]; it is a substitute for a human being destined to be killed.

CONCLUSION: ENABLERS AND BOUNDARY CROSSERS

The tensions between the king as a sacred being and as a man and the tensions between the bodies and the things that I have been describing are very complex. The contradictions are not resolvable: the kingship exists in perpetuity, but it is also historic; the sacred king does not die, but he is mortal. The ɛsɛn chooses the character of the king's reign, he guides the king-elect to the ancestral stool that determines the character of his reign, and the ɔkra maintains the reign by absorbing pollution. The ɛsɛn is killed at the beginning of the king's reign, and the ɔkra at the end of his reign. Their parallel deaths frame the king's reign. To get rid of them is to kill the historic time of a particular man. When the ɛsɛn is killed it is a "cover-up"; and it allows the kingship to exist in ahistoric time. The ɛsɛn, who makes order, makes the ordinary person into a sacred king. The ɛsɛn deals with unruly power and chooses the character of a reign for the king-elect (thus manipulating time); then he is finished with his job and so as he is no longer needed, he is killed. His death conceals his role in deciding the character of the reign, his role as guarantor of the king's divine appointment. It is a sacrifice to affect a desirable goal. The ɔkra dies when the king dies: he has fulfilled his role of keeping pollution away from the king; they share a fate. Perhaps a better way to view these ambiguous officials is as enablers,[37] rather than surrogates, although this may be too literal an interpretation.

The deaths of the ɛsɛn and the ɔkra have to do with the structure of the kingship. Another way to think about these officials is to look at the spatial order in the palace, at who sits where. When the king sits in state, his ankobea (trusted ritual officials who are related to him by means of patrifiliation) are seated to his left, along with his Queen Mother. To his right are seated the ɔkoman chiefs (who represent the major matrilineages of the town and are concerned with "politics"). The contrast between the religious and political realms, the dead and the living, is thus shown spatially. The ɛsɛn, the ɔkra, and akrafo, and the akyeame (who mediate and interpret the king's words and the people's words to the king) and the drummers all sit in front of the king, in the middle of the courtyard. So too do the executioners [abrafo]. And all these officials are boundary crossers.[38] The ɔkra (whose "beauty" represents that of the king, whose power comes from outside, and whose headdress shows he is metaphorically identified with the king) is an imperfect surrogate. The ɛsɛn (whose deformity is opposite to the body of the king, and whose power is associated with the forest; who is metaphorically identified with the king in so far as he sits on an elephant bone and creates order in the bush and palace, in nature and culture) is not a surrogate. The akyeame (who sweeten the words of the king, pour libation to the ancestors, and are counselors for the king) function as mediators between the

---

[37] I am grateful to Barbara Bianco for this suggestion, and for her careful reading of an earlier draft.

[38] During Odwira, the Nkonguasoafohene, Adumhene, and Banmuhene (chiefs in charge respectively of the ancestral stools, killing, and the banmu) sit in the center facing the king; on other occasions they are seated to his left with the ankobea. The Banmuhene is perhaps the ultimate enabler: he is in charge of the Banmu — a place of mystery and terror, the place where the king is enstooled and the first place where a king is brought when dead. His assistants supervise those who are killed for a king's burial, and he has the power to pardon anyone about to be killed.

king and the living, king and his ancestors, and living and ancestors and are not put to death, nor are the drummers, who on the talking drums are able to communicate directly with both the ancestors and the king. The executioners, the ultimate boundary crossers, create death and are responsible for controlling and pacifying the revenging spirits of those sacrificed for the king throughout the year. Only the drummers and executioners are privileged openly to trace the ancestry of the king.

Ruel (1990) argues that there is a difference between ritual offerings that take the form of killings and those that do not, and a difference between ritual killings that take the form of a sacrifice (offering to a god or deity) and those that do not. Sacrifices in the sense of slaughtering an animal to be given as a gift to a deity or ancestor [*abɔ ade*] occurred regularly in Akropong: sheep, fowl, and, formerly, humans (slaves) were offered as gifts to the black stools, especially during Odwira, but also at the periodic rites performed every forty-two days at *adae*. But other kinds of killings also occurred on ritual occasions. Akropong people make a distinction between animals that are killed for purification [*dwira*] and those killed for pacification [*pata*]. Not all animals sacrificed are scapegoats in Akropong, and (contrary to Girard) the possible vengeance of the sacrificial victim requires repeated and vigilant attention. Luc de Heusch invites us to broaden our focus on regicide and kingship and to consider the complicated roles of other players who may be surrogates for the king. In this essay I have looked at the sacrifice of two crucial palace attendants and tried to understand this in the light of the character of their relationship to the king, who I have shown to be a "sacred monster" who articulates the natural and cultural orders.

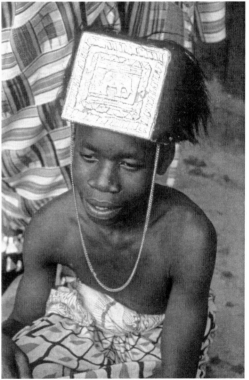

Figure 9.1. The *ɔkra* (soul-child) of Omanhene Nana Addo Dankwa III (Photographer: M. Gilbert)

Figure 9.2. The *ɛsɛn* (court crier) of Kurontihene Nana Boafo Ansa II (Photographer: M. Gilbert)

Figure 9.3. The *Omanhene* (King of Akwapim), Nana Addo Dankwa III (Photographer: M. Gilbert)

Figure 9.4. The King and His *ɔkra* Being Carried in Palanquin (Photographer: M. Gilbert)

BIBLIOGRAPHY

Akuffo, Bennett S.

    1950   *Ahemfi adesua (Akanfo amammere) Okyerewfo.* 2 volumes. Palace Teachings. Akuapem: Akuropen Ahemfi.

Bartle, P. F. W.

    1978   "Forty Days: The Akan Calendar." *Africa* 48/1: 80–84.

Christaller, J. G.

    1933   *Dictionary of the Asante and Fante Language called Tshi (Twi).* Second, revised edition. Basel: Basel Evangelical Missionary Society.

de Boeck, F.

    1994   "Of Trees and Kings: Politics and Metaphor among the Aluund of Southwestern Zaire." *American Ethnologist* 21: 451–73.

de Heusch, Luc

    1985   *Sacrifice in Africa: A Structuralist Approach.* Bloomington: Indiana University Press.

    1997   "The Symbolic Mechanisms of Sacred Kingship: Rediscovering Frazer." *Journal of the Royal Anthropological Institute,* n.s., 3: 213–32.

    2005a   "Forms of Sacralized Power in Africa." In *The Character of Kingship,* edited by Declan Quigley, pp. 25–38. Oxford: Berg.

    2005b   "A Reply to Lucien Scubla." In *The Character of Kingship,* edited by Declan Quigley, pp. 63–66. Oxford: Berg.

Evans Pritchard, E. E.

    1948   *The Divine Kingship of the Shilluk of the Nilotic Sudan.* The Frazer Lecture 1948. Cambridge: University Press. Reprinted 1962 in *Social Anthropology and Other Essays: Combining Social Anthropology and Essays in Social Anthropology,* by E. E. Evans Pritchard, pp. 192–212. Free Press Paperbacks. Glencoe: Free Press, 1962.

Feeley-Harnik, G.

    1985   "Issues in Divine Kingship." *Annual Review of Anthropology* 14: 273–313.

Fortes, M.

    1968   "Of Installation Ceremonies." *Proceedings of the Royal Anthropological Institute of Great Britain and Ireland for 1967*: 5–20.

Frazer, James George

    1890   *The Golden Bough: A Study in Magic and Religion.* 2 volumes. London: Macmillan.

Gilbert, Michelle

    1987   "The Person of the King: Ritual and Power in a Ghanaian State." In *Rituals of Royalty: Power and Ceremonial in Traditional Societies,* edited by David Cannadine and Simon R. F. Price, pp. 298–331. Past and Present Publications. Cambridge: Cambridge University Press.

    1989   "Sources of Power in Akuropon-Akuapem: Ambiguity in Classification." In *The Creativity of Power: Cosmology and Action in African Societies,* edited by W. Arens and Ivan Karp, pp. 59–90. Washington, D.C.: Smithsonian Institution Press.

    1993   "The Leopard Who Sleeps in a Basket: Akuapem Secrecy in Everyday Life and Royal Metaphor." In *Secrecy: African Art that Conceals and Reveals,* edited by Mary H. Nooter, pp. 123–39. New York: Museum for African Art.

    1994   "Aesthetic Strategies: The Politics of a Royal Ritual." *Africa* 64/1: 99–125.

1997   "'No Condition Is Permanent': Ethnic Construction and the Use of History in Akua-pem." *Africa* 67: 501–33.

2006   "Unfinished Narratives: Dangerous Memories." Manuscript. Harvard Conference on Sites of Memory. Republished in 2010 as "Disguising the Pain of Remembering in Akwapim." *Africa* 80/3: 426–52.

Girard, René
1977   *Violence and the Sacred.* Translated by Patrick Gregory. Baltimore: John Hopkins University Press.

Kantorowicz, Ernst H.
1957   *The King's Two Bodies: A Study in Mediaeval Political Theology.* Princeton: Princeton University Press.

McCaskie, T. C.
1980   "Time and the Calendar in the Nineteenth-Century Asante: An Exploratory Essay." *History of Africa* 7: 179–200.

1995   *State and Society in Pre-Colonial Asante.* Cambridge: Cambridge University Press.

McLeod, Malcolm D.
1978   "Aspects of Asante Images." In *Art in Society: Studies in Style, Culture, and Aesthetics,* edited by Michael Greenhalgh and J. V. S. Megaw, pp. 305–16. New York: St. Martin's Press.

Quigley, D.
2005   "Introduction." In *The Character of Kingship,* edited by Declan Quigley, pp. 1–23. Oxford: Berg.

Robertson, A. F.
1976   "Ousting the Chief: Deposition Charges in Ashanti." *Man,* n.s., 2: 410–27.

Rowlands, M.
1993   "The Good and Bad Death: Ritual Killing and Historical Transformation in a West African Kingdom." *Paideuma* 39: 291–302.

Ruel, M.
1990   "Non-sacrificial Ritual Killing." *Man* 25: 323–35.

Samson, E.
1908   *A Short History of Akuapim and Akropong (Gold Coast): An Autobiography.* Accra: By Author.

Young, M.
1966   "The Divine Kingship of the Jukun: A Re-evaluation of Some Theories." *Africa* 36/2: 35–62.

* * * * * * * * * *

Ghana National Archives 11/1101 Akwapim Enquiry 1922 and 1919
Mission 21 Archive, Basel Mission Holdings
    D-1.86.31 Annual Report by Theophilus Opoku for 1906; March 8, 1907
    D-1.93.29 Voluntary Report by Wilhelm Rottmann; January 18, 1909

10

MAYA DIVINE KINGSHIP

DAVID FREIDEL, SOUTHERN METHODIST UNIVERSITY

A BRIEF HISTORY OF THE IDEA

The Classic Maya of the southern lowlands sustained a tradition of displaying public inscriptions, particularly on carved stone steles, between the third and ninth centuries of the present era. It is this area, between the sites of Comacalco in Tabasco on the western side and Copan, Honduras, on the eastern side, Calakmul in Campeche on the north and Cancuen in Petén on the south, to put it in crude geographic terms, which witnessed an enduring, epigraphically documented institution of divine kingship. Within this area rulers referred to other kingdoms (Marcus 1973) and consequently contributed to an overall textual history. The greater Maya lowlands including the Yucatan Peninsula covers about 390,000 square kilometers (Sabloff 1990: 14) and the Pre-Columbian peoples of this larger area were literate in glyphic and episodically participated in divine kingship (Freidel and Suhler 1995). Heinrich Berlin (1958) pioneered in his study of what he termed Emblem glyphs, epithets that might have referred to places but turned out to be dynastic titles of kings (Mathews 1991). Joyce Marcus (1973, 1976) deduced through contextual analysis that the mention of Emblem glyphs reflected relationships between polities. Tatiana Proskouriakoff (1960) working with carved monuments at Piedras Negras, and later at Yaxchilan (1963, 1964), determined that glyphic texts referred to historical royal personages and not deities as proposed by earlier scholars. Peter Mathews and Linda Schele (1974), summarizing the efforts of Berlin, Kubler, Kelley, Coe, and others, outlined for the first time a dynastic sequence at Palenque. Christopher Jones did the same at the great capital of Tikal (Jones and Satterthwaite 1982). In this, often colleageal and always dynamic, fashion epigraphers started putting together dynastic sequences of individuals bearing Emblem glyph titles. Robert Sharer (Morley, Brainerd, and Sharer 1983: 93) tentatively suggested that Maya kings may have ruled by divine right, and by the mid-1980s we had the decipherment of the Emblem glyph title as *k'ul ajaw*. Floyd Lounsbury (1973) deciphered the superfix of the Emblem glyph, first as *aj po* and then as *ajaw* in the 1970s as lord or king. Peter Mathews (1991) among others worked with the so-called "water group" prefix and determined the decipherment as *ch'ul* or *k'ul*, with the general connotation of holy or spirit charged. The *k'ul* prefix and affix *ajaw* framed a glyph that referred to both family and polity in Peter Mathews' effective summary of the matter (1991). In the case of the ruined city I am presently investigating in northwestern Petén, for example, the rulers carried the title *k'ul wak ajaw*, which we translate holy centipede lord based on project epigrapher Stanley Guenter's decipherment of *wak* as an archaic and arcane term for that important insect (Guenter n.d.). The notion that the Maya had divine kings in the Classic period gained credence in the 1980s based in part on this royal epithet.

Linda Schele and Mary Miller (1986) in the Blood of Kings catalogue brilliantly outlined key features of the divine kingship in terms not only of the textual record as then understood, but also through the correlation of that record with relevant features of the rich corpus of Classic Maya art. They described the ruler's roles as statesman, religious leader, and warrior. They also introduced the notion that Classic divine kingship could be extended into the

Late Preclassic period based on collaborative work Linda Schele and I were doing during this time. Students of Linda's, notably Virginia Fields (1989; 1991) and F. Kent Reilly III (1991), worked during the 1980s to anchor insignia and practices of the Maya divine kingship into the prior Olmec civilization of the Middle Preclassic period. Linda Schele and I published on Late Preclassic divine kingship in *American Anthropologist* (Freidel and Schele 1988a), and that same year saw publication of our theoretical treatise on the evolution of Maya state ideology and religion as an adaptation to burgeoning social inequality in the lowlands (Freidel and Schele 1988b; see Joyce 2000 for a reprise of that model); I will come back to this matter later on. I published a summary article on Maya divine kingship in which I reiterated the arguments for shamanic practice and symbolism and suggested that "Maya kings were regarded as the instruments, objects and sacrifices of their constituencies" (Freidel 1992). They were the human stuff of power, and like stone, wood, clay fiber, and food, they were the prosaic materials that could be made luminous, crowned, resplendent, and transformed through acts of devotion, skill and courage." I was involved with the production of two books relevant to the ongoing development of Maya divine kingship, *A Forest of Kings* (Schele and Freidel 1990), which we dealt mostly with political history, and *Maya Cosmos* (Freidel, Schele, and Parker 1993), in which we detailed our arguments for the Maya divine kingship as shamanic. While the former book is now thoroughly obsolete as a result of advances in textual decipherment and archaeology (see Martin and Grube 2000), the latter is still actively cited and critiqued for its views on the nature of the kingship (Klein et al. 2002). The last fifteen years have seen numerous valuable advances in the details of Maya divine kingship and its origins through the epigraphic and iconographic scholarship. The work of Nikolai Grube (2001), Julia Guernsey Kappleman (1997), Stephen Houston and David Stuart (1996), William Saturno, Karl Taube, and David Stuart (2005), and Kent Reilly III (2005) stand out in my mind, but there are many others. Virginia Fields and Dorie Reents-Budet's catalogue for the "Lords of Creation" show (2005) and Mary Miller and Simon Martin's "Courtly Maya" show (2004) catalogue are recent excellent contributions to this literature.

THE NATURE OF MAYA DIVINE KINGSHIP

Maya rulers and their families were the objects of royal cults in which they performed as deities (Freidel 1992). They were venerated and worshipped by their courtiers, nobles who functioned much as priests do in some other ancient civilizations. Divine performances documented through texts, images, and archaeological contexts included the ability to be reborn following death (Freidel, Schele, and Parker 1993: chapter 2), the ability to conjure gods into existence (Stuart 1988), the ability to manifest as particular deities (Marc Zender, pers. comm. 2003), the ability to consort with supernatural companions of a lethal character including war deities (Grube and Nahm 1994), the ability to manifest the central axis of the cosmos, and the ability to communicate with the dead. Following definitions of shamanism outlined by Mircea Eliade (1964) and others, Schele and I regarded these activities by Maya royalty to be prima facie evidence of the shamanic nature of the royal cult and Maya state ideology more generally. This is not to say that the Classic Maya lacked gods, for they had them in abundance (Miller and Taube 1997). What they lacked were deity cults as such and organized priesthoods devoted to gods (Freidel and Guenter forthcoming). They worshipped gods through the royal cults, and the intercessors for the gods were always the royalty where they existed. Lesser royalty in vassal polities performed in the same fashion as the representatives of great dynasties. As to religious activities in small towns and remote villages, what evidence we have suggests that public religion focused on the same panoply of gods found in the major centers. The manner in which the roles of royalty were filled by local patriarchs and matriarchs, shaman, midwives, bonesetters, and herbalists remains an open and intriguing area of inquiry. One could accurately assert that the royalty functioned as priests in their intercessory capacities, but the overlapping of priestly responsibilities and shamanic abilities was evidently substantial and enduring.

Some students of the Maya are uncomfortable with the idea of shamanic kingship because they regard shamanism as a developmental stage associated in evolutionary terms with simpler societies and not with states — which they regard as characterized by organized priesthoods (Marcus 2002). One epigrapher, Marc Zender (2003), has recently written a dissertation asserting that documented sub-royal titles are actually priestly. He proposes that Maya kings were priestly, not shamanic, in performance and that courts were peopled by true priests. This argument will not prevail, however, in the face of alternative interpretations of the same titles put fourth by several other epigraphers, including Sarah Jackson and David Stuart (2001) and Stanley Guenter (Freidel and Guenter forthcoming). The most common title reads worshipper or attendant, and the object of the worship is the ruler, not a distinct deity (see also Coe and Kerr 1996, who read this title "keeper of books"). But if Maya rulers were shaman, could they not rule by whim and edict on the authority of their direct connection to the supernatural? The evidence we have for court practices, in iconography, texts, and archaeology, suggests that they were highly formalized and constrained by tradition (Miller and Martin 2004). Bear in mind that the Classic Maya kings and courtiers were literate and lived in the context of explicit records of philosophy, religion, and history. State shamanism in the Maya case then was clearly hedged in by existing practices, policies, and beliefs concerning the powers and responsibilities of the royalty. In evolutionary terms, Arthur Demarest (1992), following earlier efforts by Michael Coe (1961) and Bennett Bronson (1978), has compared the Classic Maya case to Southeast Asian tropical lowland civilizations. Demarest refers to notions of the Rajeev, particularly as articulated in the Galactic Polity model of Stanley Tambiah (1977). I have some political economic reservations about the application of this analogy to the Maya which I will voice below. The point here is that while the Classic Maya organization may be different from some ancient civilizations in the absence of true priesthoods, it nevertheless sustained power with comparable efficiency and stability.

THE POWER OF MAYA DIVINE KINGS

Arthur Demarest in his exploration of the Galactic Polity model for Maya kingship, especially in his 1992 article in *Ideology and Pre-Columbian Civilizations* but also in his recent general text on the Maya (2004), makes the case that Maya rulers governed primarily on the basis of their vital role as intercessors with the supernatural and not through any key role in the administration of the subsistence economy of their constituents. Demarest freely acknowledges the wealth-making and sustaining roles of kings and royalty. He suggests that public interaction, feasting, gift giving, marriage, alliance formation, and captive display between kings and courts operated as a rationale for a significant long-distance and medium-distance trade in precious commodities transformed into beautiful treasure and insignia used by royalty and nobility to assert status and privilege competitively. Insofar as official charisma was the foundation for power, success in such exchange and competition was critical to the maintenance of the faith and support of constituents.

As Demarest relies heavily on my model of the Maya divine kingship as developed with Linda Schele, it is hard for me to find fault with his definitions of official charisma as expressed in royal performance. Nevertheless, I do have a basically different view of how Maya political economy worked during the Preclassic and Classic periods. The central fact of Classic Maya religion was a focus on the maize god. Karl Taube (1985) elucidated this and it was underscored in *Maya Cosmos* (Freidel, Schele, and Parker 1993). William Saturno (Saturno, Taube, and Stuart 2005) recently discovered at San Bartolo in northeastern Petén remarkable Late Preclassic mural paintings that definitively substantiate the connection between the mythology of the maize god and the cult of the divine king already centuries before the advent of the Maya Classic period. Moreover, Karl Taube, Saturno's iconographer, has documented in a recent Dumbarton Oaks monograph that the image of the maize god as depicted on the San Bartolo murals is the Olmec maize god, well represented in the corpus of art from that antecedent Preclassic civilization (Taube 2004). The people of Mesoamerica, certainly by 1500 B.C., had broadly adopted maize as a valuable source of calories. By the Middle Preclassic period, 900–400 B.C., maize in conjunction with beans, squashes, chilies, and other garden foods was a major prestige food and beginning to become the key staple in the diet of a majority of people. The aforementioned scholarship makes it clear that the focus on the maize god expressed in Classic Maya religion was decisively established as a political and ideological foundation for royal power in the context of Mesoamerica's earliest civilization, the Olmec.

As detailed in Maya Cosmos, the cycle of sacrificial death and rebirth of the Maya maize god, whose cobs are the source of human flesh as described in the sixteenth century Quiche Maya creation story, the Popol Vuh, is the pivotal creed of Classic Maya religion. The death and resurrection performances of Maya kings were linked significantly to this creed. While scholars like Demarest are prepared to regard this link as simply a religious assertion of supernatural command by kings over prosperity, I think the connection is also economic and practical (Freidel and Shaw 2000). Maize is a notoriously drought sensitive crop, and crop failure caused serious periodic famine in northern lowland Maya country as described in the ethnohistorical prophetic Books of Chilam Balam. Maize does not store well for more than a few years in humid tropical environments. Lowland Maya farmers generally prefer to store maize on the husk and in the field for a brief period of time, and then on the cob packed tightly into above ground cribs in hopes of fending off vermin. The local races of maize today in Yucatan, for example, exhibit genetic selection for durable husks in light of this tradition. Maya farmers store maize for short periods locally on their homesteads in the lowlands today, and otherwise store it by selling surplus and buying livestock. In drought cycles, they sell the livestock for food and seed. There is no evidence anywhere that the Pre-Columbian lowland Maya civilization or in the lowland Olmec civilization before it ever concentrated storage of maize or other staples in centers for redistribution. While most scholars of the Maya think that local farming populations were generally self-sufficient with regard to food production (Demarest 2004), I think that was impossible over the long term in light of the characteristics of maize in the humid tropical environment (Freidel and Shaw 2000). The evidence for Pre-Columbian drought cycles, while patchy, is sufficient to suggest that periodically significant portions of the farming population would have been experiencing severe depletion of food and seed stocks in some parts of the lowlands (Gill 2000). I think that the adoption of maize as a staple in the tropical lowland parts of Mesoamerica, such as the Maya lowlands, required, at the same time, commitment to a vertically integrated marketing system from local towns to major centers, and short distance to long distance transport, that could ensure the flow of food to areas where it was most needed and demanded.

Along with that kind of administered marketing system — well attested in the northern Maya lowlands and southern highlands incidentally at the time of the Spanish arrival (Freidel and Scarborough 1982) — the Maya and other Mesoamericans needed currencies in which to store surplus crops against such drought cycles. At the time of the Spanish arrival, greenstone beads, red shell beads, miniature ground stone axes, copper axes, and rings were all used as broadly fungible currencies in the Maya area and in the rest of Mesoamerica (Freidel 1986). Additionally, perishables such as cacao beans, measures of salt, and lengths of woven cotton cloth played roles as currencies. We have explicit descriptions from the Spanish of Yucatec Maya farmers taking surplus maize to market and selling it for jade and shell beads as a storage strategy. I would argue that the divine kings of the Classic period, whose cults were closely tied to the maize gods, bore responsibility for maintaining the regional flow of food through such a marketing system, whatever machinations of competition and conflict they may have indulged.

To be sure, epistemologically it is almost impossible to demonstrate the existence of market places in Maya country, when the models we know are of perishable venders' huts and open plaza spaces. And while there are plenty of jade and shell beads in archaeological contexts, demonstrating that they were used for money before the time of the Spanish arrival is equally daunting. There are court scenes on Classic painted vases that depict the presentation of tribute bags of cacao beans to divine kings, and those beans could register such economic command as I imagine and not just a desire for the tasty and prestigious drink. There are also indirect but perhaps productive means of testing the proposition that control of trade routes was the primary goal of hegemonic competition between divine kings. Demarest would argue that such control of routes moving wealth items like jade would also make sense if kings were driven by status competition. In the last analysis, the notion that Maya divine kings sustained their power solely through an appeal to the faith of their followers, backed perhaps by judicious application of force, relies too much on the compelling brilliance of their performances in office and on the abiding gullibility of their constituents. Kings making sure, as symbols of the maize god and his covenant with humanity, that there really was maize to eat and plant is a royal responsibility I can see ordinary people regarding as central in their rulers.

THE ORIGINS OF MAYA DIVINE KINGSHIP

The lowland Maya civilization emerged as a dominant force in southeastern Mesoamerica after 500 B.C. That is about the same time that the earlier Olmec civilization, which flourished in the lowlands of Tabasco and Veracruz by 1200 B.C., began to wane. The Early and Middle Preclassic (1200–500 B.C.) Gulf Coast Olmec and the larger interaction sphere of culturally affiliated groups across the Isthmus of Tehuantepec and along the Pacific coast of northern Central America clearly had divine kings before the Maya. Just as certainly, the Preclassic lowland Maya adopted key features of their cult of kings as maize god impersonators from the Olmec. The primary insignia of kingship for the Maya is a trefoil sprout image that can have a human or deity face. This is usually worn, singly or in multiples (usually three) as a diadem jewel on a headband of cloth. The name of this insignia is *Huunal* and in the Maya writing system it is a semantic determinative for *ajaw*. The term *Huunal* evidently refers to the bark paper that the Maya used for writing their books, and to the simplest royal crown as a headband made of this paper. At Chichen Itza in the north several people are simultaneously depicted wearing this insignia, but William Ringle and his colleagues have reasonably argued that this is an assembly of kings from many places (Ringle, Bey, and Negron 1998). Generally it identifies the divine rulers and their immediate family members. Virginia Fields documented that this insignia was innovated and used by the Olmec divine kings, and she argued persuasively that it likely represented a sprouting maize kernel (Fields 1989).

As mentioned previously, Karl Taube (Saturno, Taube, and Stuart 2004) has advanced a strong case for the existence of a Middle Preclassic Olmec maize god as the template for the Late Preclassic Maya maize god. The Olmec maize god is one expression of the so-called "were jaguar baby" image that is a pervasive leitmotif of Olmec art. The recently discovered San Bartolo murals, dating to the first century B.C. or squarely in the Late Preclassic period, provide an extraordinary view of the role of the maize god in lowland Maya divine kingship. The visage of the San Bartolo maize god is decisively that of the Olmec were jaguar baby and not the purely human and adult maize god of the Maya Classic. Distinctive features include a thick, raised, and snarling upper lip often over a squared mandibular bar or projecting gum bracket, snub nose, rounded chin, and forehead. The Classic Maya maize god has aquiline features, sloping chin and forehead and is generally a purely human expression of adult male beauty. I did find a Late Preclassic maize god pectoral at Cerros in Belize that is transitional between these two idealized types (Freidel 1976), so it is clear that the Maya were taking inspiration from the existing royal cult paraphernalia and then innovating.

Until recently, field research on the Pacific Slopes of Chiapas and Guatemala suggested that the Maya lowlands lagged behind other parts of southeastern Mesoamerica in the adoption of the Olmec divine kingship. However, in the last several years there has been a growing body of evidence in the Maya lowlands showing that the Middle Preclassic people there were also actively incorporating the divine kingship. Francisco Estrada-Belli working at Cival in northeastern Petén reports an elaborate cruciform Middle Preclassic cached offering that includes polished greenstone celts typical of Olmec caches from La Venta. This cache includes evidence of a wooden post in the center, symbolic of the world tree staff as raised by Olmec kings emulating the maize god.

My colleagues on the Selz Foundation Yaxuna project Travis Stanton and Traci Ardren (2005) determined that a pyramid we excavated in the early 1990s at this central Yucatecan site dates to the Middle Preclassic period. At eleven meters high and 40 × 40 m on a side, such a monument resembles the buildings at the Olmec center of La Venta in its use of a peculiar admixture of red earth and slaked lime plaster to create a friable pink adobe. In 1992 Charles Suhler, co-director of the project, discovered a remarkable cache inside of a small and very strange building at Yaxuna. The building is one of two placed closely together and nearly identical in design. They appear to have been performance platforms used to symbolically travel from the underworld, represented by a sub-surface sanctuary, into the heavens, represented by scaffold structures on the summit, by means of trap-door entrances (Suhler 1991; Freidel and Suhler 1999). Michael Coe (1989) had discovered a description of such a performance platform used in a K'ekchi' Maya accession celebration in the sixteenth century, painted vases showing maize god impersonators emerging from such platforms in the Classic period, and many examples of Classic period buildings that likely served such a general performance purposed. The western wall mural at San Bartolo explicitly depicts a dying maize god and a baby maize god framing an effigy turtle structure inside of which an adult maize god is dancing and playing a drum. The design of the chamber inside the turtle structure is the quatrefoil portal of emergence in Olmec and Maya iconography. Flanking this performance scene of the death and rebirth of the maize god are two scaffold thrones. On one a maize god is being crowned by yet another maize god, while on the other, a human divine king is being crowned with an elaborate crown adorned with a trefoil *Huunal* insignia. We have all the architectural elements in the two performance platforms at Yaxuna to fit this scene of royal accession in association with the maize god story.

Until recently, I thought that the Yaxuna platforms dated to the Late Preclassic period. However, several colleagues of mine who are expert in the ceramics of the northern lowlands have now assured me that the cache vessels Charles Suhler discovered underneath the sanctuary floor of one of the platforms decisively date to the Middle Preclassic period (Freidel et al. n.d.). The larger of the two vessels in the cache contained a jade celt and a jade mirror, both Olmec royal insignia. In an article in preparation, my colleagues and I argue that the Yaxuna performance platforms document the presence of an Olmec style royal accession place in the heart of the northern Maya lowlands coeval with La Venta in Tabasco — that is, approximately 600–700 B.C. If we are correct, then we predict that ongoing work in the Maya lowlands will demonstrate an overlap of two centuries or more between the Olmec and lowland Maya cults of divine kingship.

DIVINE KINGSHIP IN TRANSITION: OLMEC TO MAYA

The demise of Olmec civilization and the rise of lowland Maya civilization are coeval in the transition from the Middle Preclassic to the Late Preclassic periods. This may be coincidence, but in light of the geographical juxtaposition of the Gulf Coast heartland of the Olmec and the Maya lowlands it is likely that these dynamics were conditioned by interaction and competition if not outright confrontation as suggested by Richard Hansen in recent publications. I have suggested that the Olmec Middle Preclassic fluorescence was fueled by the ability of the La Venta divine kings to promote and command trade in commodities vital to the maintenance of maize, beans, and squashes, as the primary subsistence base of an increasingly large percentage of subject populations in Mesoamerican kingdoms. Two key commodities in the political economy of the Olmec were mineral salt as a necessary dietary supplement for people living on maize/beans/squashes and greenstone as a material for currency tokens in which to store maize against crop failure in the humid tropics.

The Gulf Coast Olmec could control salt trade by acquiring it in bulk from the western and northern salt beds of the Yucatan peninsula and shipping it by canoe to La Venta for transport into the interior. In this regard, it is notable that recent surveys of sites in northwestern Yucatan by Anthony Andrews, Fernando Robles Castellanos, and their students have discovered a large number of Middle Preclassic settlements with masonry ballcourts in them (Andrews and Robles Castellanos 2004). The Olmec invented the rubber ballgame in the Early Preclassic period and they manufactured the latex balls with which the game was played. It seems likely that this was one commodity they could trade into the salt mining country. The Olmec could promote greenstone as a currency material by elevating it into a form of wealth and treasure sanctified in religion as magical and representative of divine rule. The La Venta Olmec carved greenstone, principally jadeite but also serpentine and other minerals, into images of rulers and gods, and they manufactured quantities of celts, mirrors, and royal insignia from the material, objects they then buried in caches in sacred space. As a remarkable testimony to the Olmec elevation of greenstone to the status of currency/wealth/treasure, the La Venta rulers created enormous multi-ton cached offerings of serpentine blocks in the northernmost precinct of their ceremonial center (Drucker, Heizer, and Squier 1959). Three of these caches are arranged in a triangle to form the "jade hearth," the Creation time place associated with the resurrection of the maize god and with the fashioning of humanity from his cobs/flesh as discussed by me and Linda Schele in Maya Cosmos and by Kent Reilly in his dissertation. Karl Taube (Saturno,

Taube, and Stuart 2004) and collaborators have identified a very large source of sea green jadeite, the preferred Olmec material, in the Sierra de las Minas Mountains of eastern Guatemala. In sum, two of the vital components of Olmec political economy were situated in Maya country, salt directly in the lowlands and jade in the adjacent highlands.

As the Maya adopted divine kingship and fashioned it into their own cult and ideology, they also no doubt participated in the trade networks of the Olmec and other Middle Preclassic peoples. By 500 B.C., lowland Maya ceremonial centers at places like Yaxuna in the north and Nakbé in the Petén were large and effective rivals to La Venta and other Olmec centers. We may never know how precisely this rivalry played out, as the events occurred before any decipherable writing system and associated chronicles. An outcome, however, was a continuation of the maize god cult as a basis for the cult of divine kingship.

As described above, the Olmec maize god persisted as the lowland Maya visual ideal into the Late Preclassic period. However, this transition was also marked by innovation religiously and artistically. Julia Guernsey (2006), building on the work of Karl Taube, Kent Reilly, and others, has documented the advent of a new god image associated with divine kingship in the Late Preclassic period, a bird deity that is primarily the Central American Scarlet Macaw. The Classic Maya called this bird *Itzam Yeh* or *Itzamnaaj Mut*. This bird was spirit companion or co-essence of an old creator god, *Itzamnaaj*. Kent Reilly (pers. comm. 2007) has pointed out to me that in the western wall murals at San Bartolo, the human king on his scaffold throne is being crowned by a distinctive personage who is wearing the mask-headdress of *Itzam Yeh*. He suggests that when the lowland Maya took over as the preeminent divine kings they asserted that while the maize god was perhaps a foreign deity adopted by them, the ultimate power lay in the hands of a local deity, the old creator god and his bird companion. The Scarlet Macaw is native to western Petén and did not range into Olmec country. In Classic Maya mythology, as discussed in *Maya Cosmos* (Freidel, Schele, and Parker 1993), *Itzamnaaj* teaches the twin sons of the sacrificed maize god how to bring their father back to life.

We are only now beginning to glimpse the outlines of the transition from Olmec to Maya divine kingship and there is no reason to think it was conceptually smooth or easy. Mary Helms (1993) in her cogent exegeses on rulership makes a good case for the importance of the king as stranger as one means of delineating rulers from everyone else and short-circuiting existing protocols of power. But while the Maya no doubt capitalized on this in their adoption of the Olmec maize god and other cult components, they also insisted, I suggest, that divine power emanated from their own distinct and local status as the true people of maize, descendants of a deity whose rebirth took place in their own country.

THE KINGDOM OF KAN: LEGENDARY HOMELAND
OF THE MAYA MAIZE GOD

At the geographic center of the Maya lowlands is a peculiar uplifted and circumscribed swampy country called the Mirador Basin — El Mirador is the name of the largest archaeological site in this area. The basin slowly drains to the northwest, but it has no streams or rivers to speak of and it supports innumerable small ponds and large lagoons in the swamplands between the ridges and uplands that define large islands of dry and useable farmland. Maya pioneers entered this territory by 700 B.C. or slightly earlier, as identified by Bruce Dahlin (2002) and subsequent investigators. They invented a form of intensive gardening that involved quarrying out rich bog muck and laying it on upland prepared plots that could be watered by hand from the ponds and swamps. Nakbé had pyramids eighteen meters high by 500 B.C. and the Mirador Basin exploded with centers and construction during the Olmec-Maya transition and into the later centuries of the Late Preclassic. El Mirador, north of Nakbé and linked to it by an artificial causeway, was a center larger than any the Maya would ever subsequently build. Like the Egyptian pyramids of the Giza plateau, the two great Late Preclassic pyramid complexes of El Mirador, El Tigre, and Dante are simply orders of magnitude larger than anything else in the Maya world. Richard Hansen (Hansen and Guenter 2005), who has researched the Basin for two decades, agrees with Simon Martin (1997), Stanley Guenter, and other epigraphers that the Mirador Basin was likely the home of a Preclassic dynasty of divine kings whose Emblem was a snake head, Kaan in Yucatec Maya. El Mirador evidently collapsed as a political capital at the end of the Preclassic, and the holy snake lords moved to other centers during the Early Classic period (ca. 200–500 A.D.). By the Late Classic period (600–800 A.D.) the snake lords were seated at a site northwest of El Mirador some forty kilometers in Campeche, a site called Calakmul by archaeologists.

I have argued (Freidel 2000) that the Classic Maya regarded the Mirador Basin as the birth place of the maize god because the maize god resurrects through a turtle carapace marked *k'an*, meaning precious, yellow. *K'an nab isimte'*, precious pool maize, is, according to David Stuart (2005), the name of the place were the maize plant form of the resurrected maize god grows. This image is found in exemplary expression on the seventh-century panel of the Foliated Cross at Palenque in Chiapas. The *k'an* cross, a cartouched Greek Cross, is already clearly depicted as a symbol of the Flower Mountain, place of resurrection and rebirth (Saturno, Taube, and Stuart 2005) on the northern wall mural of San Bartolo, where it occurs in the eye of the living mountain. A female deity sits within the maw of the mountain handing a basket containing three tamales (*wah*, earth oven bread puddings), the flesh of humanity, up to the maize god. The words *kaan*, snake, and *k'an*, yellow or precious, are not homophonic in Mayan languages. However, snake, sky, and the number four are homophonic (*kaan, ka'an, kan*) as are yellow/precious and cordage/umbilicus (*k'an, k'aan*). The ancient Maya, and other southeastern Mesoamericans, clearly saw a conceptual connection between these sets of words, for umbilicus cords are regularly depicted with snake heads. In the case of the San Bartolo *k'an* marked Flower Mountain, a great feathered snake emerges from the maw as a ground line on which the entire ritual performance transpires (Stanton and Freidel 2005). So the original realm of the holy kaan lords is also the *k'an* place of the maize god's rebirth. If I am right in this reasoning, then the Classic period *kaan*/snake lords regarded themselves as the stewards of the true earthly birth place of the maize god and the place where humanity was fashioned from his flesh.

THE SECTARIAN WARS OF THE CLASSIC PERIOD

I think that other Maya divine kings witnessed or participated in the fall of El Mirador sometime in the second century A.D. and took this disaster as a sign that this assertion of uniqueness was false. Instead, they recalled the Olmec heritage of their religion and believed that there were many creation places and that all the peoples of their civilized world were equally descendent from the gods. At Tikal the original Preclassic ceremonial space was a pair of buildings that included a square pyramid on the west and a long rectangular building on the eastern side. These buildings, oriented to the east–west sun path and designed generally to observe dawn, replicate the primary sacred axis found at Nakbe and El Mirador. Epigrapher Stanley Guenter (pers. comm. 2005) has a cogent argument for identifying the name of this place at Tikal as *k'ante'el*, precious/yellow forest (maize field), a possible allusion to the Mirador Basin. In the Late Preclassic period when El Mirador was faltering, a royal family at Tikal established a new ceremonial precinct northeast of this original group, and the principal Late Preclassic tomb in the North Acropolis, Burial 85, likely contains the remains of King Yax Ehb Xook, the founder of the dynasty that would rule Tikal for thirty-three kings through the ensuing Classic period. I have interpreted William Coe's meticulous excavation report on the North Acropolis, TR 14, as documenting repeated episodes of deliberate desecration and destruction of the North Acropolis from the time of the dynasty founder through the eleventh successor, Siyaj Chan K'awiil I, at the beginning of the third century A.D.

These efforts, by partisans of the snake kings I would suggest, to extinguish the Tikal dynasty ended with the establishment of alliance between the Tikal royal court and foreigners from Mexico, and specifically from Teotihuacan. In the course of a tumultuous third century history, a hybrid family of Tikal-Teotihuacano internationalists took power and pushed back the "Maya firsters" to the north. There is dramatic evidence for a battle between these groups on the slopes of the great El Tigre pyramid at El Mirador, where distinctive throwing-stick javelin tips of green obsidian from the Teotihuacan-controlled mines litter the surface of the already overgrown and abandoned building.

Tikal was not alone in its internationalist stance. Other dynasties sided with the Teotihuacanoes, including the holy wak (centipede) lords of El Perú-Waka' where I currently direct research, Rio Azul in far northeastern Petén investigated by Richard E. W. Adams of the University of Texas, San Antonio (Adams 1999), and Copan in Honduras, subject to long-term research by Harvard, Pennsylvania, Tulane, and Penn State (Canuto, Bell, and Sharer 2004). For more than a century the internationalist alliance of divine kings held sway over the southern lowlands in what Simon Martin and Nikolai Grube term the New Order. By the early sixth century, the snake kings and their allies were moving south again, establishing vassal kingdoms and taking over the vital trade routes sustaining the lowland economy. In the seventh century the snake kings prevailed over most of Petén, but they never succeeded in effectively subordinating Tikal's royal court. By the early eighth century Tikal had once again repelled the enemy and broken the power of the snake kings. But Tikal's divine kings could never effectively command old enemy kingdoms. Centuries of sectarian war had, in my interpretation, inexorably undermined the security of the complex marketing system that had guaranteed maize and other foodstuffs in the local markets throughout the lowlands, irrespective of faith and allegiance. As Robert Sharer (1994) has observed in his *Ancient Maya* text, the cult of the divine kingship was the shared responsibility of all participating dynasts, and when that principal failed, so did the institution. A series of prolonged droughts in the later seventh and early eighth centuries may well have precipitated famine, migration, and rebellion against royal dynasts and their families when the orderly institutional responses to such crises were rendered inoperable. The ensuing death of the divine kingship as an institution was a slow, complex, and violent business spanning a century and a half. In the northern lowlands, as Bruce Dahlin (2002) has cogently argued the driest and most vulnerable part of Maya country not only survived this era of drought but flourished. Why? In part because the principal capital of this area, Chichen Itza, celebrated a new and revitalized religion in which divine kingship as practiced for more than a thousand years was not the principal institution. Rather than worshipping divine people, the Chichen polity celebrated the power of gods, especially *K'ukulcan*, the Feathered Serpent as articulated by William Ringle and his colleagues (Ringle, Bey, and Negron 1998). This god was, among his principal characteristics at the time of the Spanish arrival, the founder of the civilized arts of craft production and trade. Empirically, the Chichen polity was first and foremost a great commercial power, sustainer of the trade routes and the economy of ordinary people. Political imagination, which had failed in the south, prevailed in the north in this critical juncture.

BIBLIOGRAPHY

Adams, Richard E. W.
    1999   *Río Azul: An Ancient Maya City*. Norman: University of Oklahoma Press.

Andrews, Anthony P., and Fernando Robles Castellanos
    2004   "An Archaeological Survey of Northwest Yucatan, Mexico." *Mexicon* 25: 7–14.

Bell, Ellen E.; Marcello A. Canuto; and Robert J. Sharer
    2004   *Understanding Early Classic Copan*. Philadelphia: University of Pennsylvania Museum of Archaeology and Anthropology.

Berlin, Heinrich
    1958   "El glifo 'emblema' en las inscripciones mayas." *Journal de la Société des Américanistes* 47: 111–19.

Bronson, Bennet
    1978   "Angkor, Anuradhapura, Prambanan, Tikal: Maya Subsistence in an Asian Perspective." In *Pre-Hispanic Maya Agriculture*, edited by Peter D. Harrison and Billie Lee Turner, pp. 255–300. Albuquerque: University of New Mexico Press.

Coe, Michael D.
    1961   "Social Typology and the Tropical Forest Civilizations." *Comparative Studies in Society and History* 4: 65–85.
    1989   "The Hero Twins: Myth and Image." In *The Maya Vase Book: A Corpus of Rollout Photographs of Maya Vases,* Volume 1, by Justin Kerr, pp. 161–84. New York: Kerr Associates.

Coe, Michael D., and Justin Kerr
    1998   *The Art of the Maya Scribe*. New York: Harry N. Abrams.

Dahlin, Bruce
    2002   "Climate Change and the End of the Classic Period in Yucatan: Resolving a Paradox." *Ancient Mesoamerica* 13: 327–40.

Demarest, Arthur Andrew
    1992   "Ideology in Ancient Maya Cultural Evolution: The Dynamics of Galactic Polities." In *Ideology and Pre-Columbian Civilizations*, edited by Arthur Andrew Demarest and Geoffrey W. Conrad, pp. 135–57. School of American Research Advanced Seminar Series. Santa Fe: School of American Research Press.
    2004   *Ancient Maya: Rise and Fall of a Rainforest Civilization*. Case Studies in Early Societies 3. Cambridge: Cambridge University Press.

Drucker, Philip; Robert F. Heizer; and Robert J. Squier
    1959   "Excavations at La Venta, Tabasco, 1955." *Bureau of American Ethnology Bulletin* 170.

Eliade, Mircea
    1964   *Shamanism: Archaic Techniques of Ecstasy*. Bollingen Series 76. New York: Bollingen Foundation.

Estrada-Belli, Francisco
    2006   "Lightning Sky, Rain, and the Maize God, the Ideology of Preclassic Maya Rulers at Cival, Peten, Guatemala." *Ancient Mesoamerica* 17: 57–78.

Fields, Virginia M.
    1989   The Origins of Divine Kingship among the Lowland Classic Maya. Ph.D. dissertation, University of Texas, Austin.

Fields, Virginia M., and Dorie Reents-Budet
    2005   "Introduction: The First Sacred Kings of Mesoamerica." In *Lords of Creation: The Origins of Sacred Maya Kingship*, edited by Virginia M. Fields and Dorie Reents-Budet, pp. 21–27. London: Scala; Los Angeles: Los Angeles County Museum of Art.

Freidel, David A.
    1979   "Culture Areas and Interaction Spheres: Contrasting Approaches to the Emergence of Civilization in the Maya Lowlands." *American Antiquity* 44: 36–54.
    1986   "Terminal Classic Maya: Success, Failure and Aftermath." In *Late Maya Civilization: Classic to Postclassic*, edited by Jeremy A. Sabloff and E. Wyllys Andrews, pp. 409–30. School of American Research Advanced Seminar Series. Albuquerque: University of New Mexico Press.
    1992   "The Trees of Life: Ahau as Idea and Artifact in Classic Lowland Maya Civilization." In *Ideology and Pre-Columbian Civilizations*, edited by Arthur Andrew Demarest and Geoffrey W. Conrad, pp. 115–33. School of American Research Advanced Seminar Series. Santa Fe: School of American Research Press.
    2000   "Mystery of the Maya Facade." *Archaeology* 53: 24–28.

Freidel, David A., and Stanley Guenter
    Forthcoming "Shaman Kings and Priestly Princes: Official Religion in Ancient Maya Civilization."

Freidel, David A., and Vernon L. Scarborough
    1982   "Subsistence, Trade, and Development of the Coastal Maya." In *Maya Subsistence: Studies of Memory of Dennis E. Puleston*, edited by Kent V. Flannery, pp. 131–55. Studies in Archaeology. New York: Academic Press.

Freidel, David A., and Linda Schele
    1988a   "Kingship in the Late Preclassic Lowlands: The Instruments and Places of Ritual Power." *American Anthropologist* 90: 547–67.
    1988b   "Symbol and Power: A History of the Lowland Maya Cosmogram." In *Maya Iconography*, edited by Elizabeth P. Benson and Gillett G. Griffin, pp. 44–93. Princeton: Princeton University Press.

Freidel, David A.; Linda Schele; and Joy Parker
    1993   *Maya Cosmos: Three Thousand Years on the Shaman's Path*. New York: William Morrow.

Freidel, David A., and Justine Shaw
    2000   "The Lowland Maya Civilization: Historical Consciousness and Environment." In *The Way the Wind Blows: Climate, History, and Human Action*, edited by Roderick J. McIntosh, Joseph A. Tainter, and Susan Keech McIntosh, pp. 271–300. Historical Ecology Series. New York: Columbia University Press.

Freidel, David A., and Charles K. Suhler
    1995   "Crown of Creation: The Development of the Maya Royal Diadems in the Late Preclassic and Early Classic Periods." In *The Emergence of Lowland Maya Civilization: The Transition from the Preclassic to the Early Classic (Conference at Hildesheim,*

November 1992), edited by Nikolai Grube, pp. 137–50. Acta Mesoamericana 8. Möckmühl: A. Saurwein.

1999   "The Path of Life: Toward a Functional Analysis of Ancient Maya Architecture." In *Mesoamerican Architecture as a Cultural Symbol*, edited by Jeff Karl Kowalski, pp. 250–75. New York: Oxford University Press.

Freidel, David A.; Charles K. Suhler; George J. Bey III; F. Kent Reilly III; Travis W. Stanton; Tara Bond-Freeman; and Fernando Robles Castellanos

n.d.   "Early Royal Accession Platforms at Yaxuna, Yucatan, Mexico: Possible Evidence of Direct Olmec-Maya Political Interaction."

Gill, Richardson Benedict

2000   *The Great Maya Droughts: Water, Life, and Death*. Albuquerque: University of New Mexico Press.

Grube, Nikolai, editor

2001   *Maya: Divine Kings of the Rain Forest*. Cologne: Könemann Verlagsgesellschaft.

Grube, Nikolai, and Werner Nahm

1994   "A Census of Xibalba: A Complete Inventory of Way Characters on Maya Ceramics." In *The Maya Vase Book: A Corpus of Rollout Photographs of Maya Vases,* Volume 4, edited by Justin Kerr and Barbara Kerr, pp. 686–715. New York: Kerr Associates.

Guenter, Stanley

n.d.   "Waka' Emblem Decipherment." *Mesoweb*.

Guernsey, Julia

2006   *Ritual and Power in Stone: The Performance of Rulership in Mesoamerican Izapan-Style Art*. Austin: University of Texas Press.

Hansen, Richard D., and Stanley P. Guenter

2005   "Early Social Complexity and Kingship in the Mirador Basin." In *Lords of Creation: The Origins of Sacred Maya Kingship*, edited by Virginia M. Fields and Dorie Reents-Budet, pp. 60–61. London: Scala; Los Angeles: Los Angeles County Muesum of Art.

Helms, Mary W.

1993   *Craft and the Kingly Ideal: Art, Trade, and Power*. Austin: University of Texas.

Houston, Stephen D., and David Stuart

1996   "Of Gods, Glyphs and Kings: Divinity and Rulership among the Classic Maya." *Antiquity* 70: 289–312.

Jackson, Sarah, and David Stuart

2001   "Aj K'uhun Title: Deciphering a Classic Maya Term of Rank." *Ancient Mesoamerica* 12: 217–28.

Jones, Christopher, and Linton Satterthwaite

1982   *Monuments and Inscriptions of Tikal*, Part A: *The Carved Monuments*. Tikal Report 33; University Museum Monograph 44. Philadelphia: University Museum, University of Pennsylvania.

Joyce, Rosemary A.

2000   "High Culture, Mesoamerican Civilization, and the Classic Maya Tradition." In *Order, Legitimacy, and Wealth in Ancient States*, edited by Janet E. Richards and Mary Van Buren, pp. 64–76. New Directions in Archaeology. Cambridge: Cambridge University Press.

Kappelman, Julia Guernsey

1997   Of Macaws and Men: Late Preclassic Cosmology and Political Ideology in Itzapan-style Monuments. Ph.D. dissertation, University of Texas at Austin.

Klein, Cecilia; Eulogio Guzman; Elisa C. Mandell; and Maya Stanfield-Mazzi

2002   "The Role of Shamanism in Mesoamerican Art: A Reassessment." *Current Anthropology* 43: 383–419.

Lounsbury, Floyd

1973   "On the Derivation and Reading of the 'ben-ich' Prefix." In *Mesoamerican Writing Systems (Conference at Dumbarton Oaks, 30–31 October, 1971)*, edited by Elizabeth P. Benson, pp. 99–144. Washington, D.C.: Dumbarton Oaks Research Library and Collections.

Marcus, Joyce

1973   "Territorial Organization of the Lowland Classic Maya." *Science* 180: 911–16.

1976   *Emblem and State in the Classic Maya Lowlands: An Epigraphic Approach to Territorial Organization.* Washington, D.C.: Dumbarton Oaks.

2002   "Comment on Klein et al. 'The Role of Shamanism in Mesoamerican Art: A Reassessment.'" *Current Anthropology* 43: 383–419.

Martin, Simon

1997   "The Painted King List: A Commentary on Codex-style Dynastic Vases." In *The Maya Vase Book*, edited by Justin Kerr, pp. 846–67. New York: Kerr Associates, 1997.

Martin, Simon, and Nikolai Grube

2000   *Chronicle of the Maya Kings and Queens: Deciphering the Dynasties of the Ancient Maya.* London: Thames & Hudson.

Mathews, Peter

1991   "Classic Maya Emblem Glyphs." In *Classic Maya Political History: Hieroglyphic and Archaeological Evidence*, edited by T. Patrick Culbert, pp. 19–29. School of American Research Advanced Seminar Series. Cambridge: Cambridge University Press.

Mathews, Peter, and Linda Schele

1974   "Lords of Palenque: The Glyphic Evidence." In *Primeria Mesa Redonda de Palenque*, Volume 1 *(Conference on the Art, Iconography, and Dynastic History of Palenque, Palenque, Chiapas, Mexico, 14–22 December 1973)*, edited by Merle Greene Robertson, pp. 63–76. Pebble Beach: Robert Lewis Stevenson School and Pre Columbian Art Research.

McKillop, Heather Irene

2002   *Salt: White Gold of the Ancient Maya.* Maya Studies. Gainesville: University of Florida Press.

2005   *In Search of Maya Sea Traders.* Texas A & M Anthropology Series 11. College Station: Texas A & M University Press.

Miller, Mary Ellen, and Simon Martin

2004   *Courtly Art of the Ancient Maya.* New York: Thames & Hudson; San Francisco: Fine Arts Museums of San Francisco.

Miller, Mary Ellen, and Karl A. Taube

1997   *An Illustrated Dictionary of the Maya Gods and Symbols of Ancient Mexico and the Maya.* New York: Thames & Hudson.

Morley, Sylvanus G.; George W. Brainerd; and Robert J. Sharer

    1983   *The Ancient Maya*. Fourth edition. Stanford: Stanford University Press.

Proskouriakoff, Tatiana

    1960   "Historical Implications of a Pattern of Dates at Piedras Negras, Guatemala." *American Antiquity* 25: 454–75.

    1963   "Historical Data in the Inscriptions of Yaxchilan (Part 1)." *Estudios de cultura maya* 3: 177–201.

    1964   "Historical Data in the Inscriptions of Yaxchilan (Part 2)." *Estudios de cultura maya* 4: 177–201.

Reilly, F. Kent III

    1991   "Olmec Iconographic Influences on the Symbols of Maya Rulership." In *Sixth Palenque Round Table, 1986*, edited by Merle Greene Robertson and Virginia M. Fields, pp. 125–35. Palenque Round Table Series 8. Norman: University of Oklahoma Press.

    2005   "Olmec Ideological, Ritual, and Symbolic Contributions to the Institution of Classic Maya Kingship." In *Lords of Creation: The Origins of Sacred Maya Kingship*, edited by Virginia M. Fields and Dorie Reents-Budet, pp. 30–36. London: Scala Publishers; Los Angeles: Los Angeles County Museum of Art.

Ringle, William; George Bey; and Tomas Gallareta Negron

    1998   "Return of Quetzalcoatl: Evidence for the Spread of a World Religion during the Epiclassic Period." *Ancient Mesoamerica* 9: 183–232.

Robertson, Merle Greene, and Virginia M. Fields

    1991   *Sixth Palenque Round Table, 1986*. Palenque Round Table Series 8. Norman: University of Oklahoma Press.

Sabloff, Jeremy A.

    1990   *The New Archaeology and the Ancient Maya*. Scientific American Library Series 30. New York: Scientific American Library.

Saturno, William A.; Karl A. Taube; and David Stuart

    2005   *The Murals of San Bartolo, El Petén, Guatemala*, Part 1: *The North Wall*. Ancient America 7. Barnardsville: Center for Ancient American Studies.

Schele, Linda, and David A. Freidel

    1990   *A Forest of Kings: The Untold Story of the Ancient Maya*. New York: William Morrow.

Schele, Linda, and Mary E. Miller

    1986   *The Blood of Kings: Dynasty and Ritual in Maya Art*. New York: G. Braziller; Fort Worth: Kimbell Art Museum.

Sharer, Robert J.

    1994   *The Ancient Maya*. Fifth edition. Stanford: Stanford University Press.

Stanton, Travis W., and Traci Ardren

    2005   "The Middle Formative of Yucatan in Context: The View from Yaxuna." *Ancient Mesoamerica* 16: 1–16.

Stanton, Travis W., and David A. Freidel

    2005   "Placing the Centre, Centring the Place: The Influence of Formative Sacbeob in Classic Site Design at Yaxuná, Yucatán." *Cambridge Archaeological Journal* 15: 225–49.

Stuart, David

    1988   "Blood Symbolism in Maya Iconography." In *Maya Iconography*, edited by Elizabeth P. Benson and Gillett G. Griffin, pp. 175–221. Princeton: Princeton University Press.

    2005   *The Inscriptions from Temple XIX at Palenque: A Commentary*. San Francisco: Pre-Columbian Art Research Institute.

Suhler, Charles K.

    1991   "Excavations at Structure 6E-120, a Late Preclassic Ceremonial Building at the Site of Yaxuna, in the Yucatan, Mexico." Paper presented at the 47th Annual International Conference of Americanists.

Tambiah, Stanley

    1977   "The Galatic Polity: The Structure of Traditional Kingdoms in Southeast Asia." *Annals of the New York Academy of Sciences* 293: 69–97.

Taube, Karl A.

    1985   "Classic Maya Maize God." In *Fifth Palenque Round Table, 1983*, edited by Merle Greene Robertson and Virginia M. Fields, pp. 171–81. Palenque Round Table Series 7. San Francisco: Pre-Columbian Art Research Institute.

    2004   *Olmec Art at Dumbarton Oaks*. Pre-Columbian Art at Dumbarton Oaks 2. Washington, D.C.: Dumbarton Oaks Research Library and Collection.

Zender, Marc Uwe

    2003   A Study of Classic Maya Priesthood. Ph.D. dissertation, University of Calgary.

11

HUMAN AND DIVINE KINGSHIP IN EARLY CHINA: COMPARATIVE REFLECTIONS

MICHAEL PUETT, HARVARD UNIVERSITY

At first glance, it may seem odd to have China brought into a discussion focused upon divine kingship. After all, in comparative discussions of kingship, China is often mentioned as the prototypical example of a culture based upon human, as opposed to divine, visions of sovereignty. For one example among many, one can cite Manabu Waida's argument to this effect in the Encyclopedia of Religion:

> The classical Chinese conception of sovereignty took shape in the Ch'in and Han periods (221 B.C.–220 A.D.). While the sovereign adopted the title, connoting supreme power, of *huangdi* (emperor), he was never considered divine, at least while he was alive, nor was he regarded as an incarnation of a divine being. Rather, he was a "unique man" representing Heaven's will on earth and serving as the link between heaven and earth. The Chinese notion of the Son of Heaven in its classical form had nothing to do with the genealogical conception of kingship, such as in ancient Egypt or Japan, that the king was the descendant of a certain god or the god incarnate; the emperor was simply the earthly representative of Heaven or heavenly will (Waida 2005: 5179).

Unlike a view that rulers are divine by descent, the classical notion in China to which Waida refers holds that the ruler is human. Monarchy was hereditary but would only be maintained within a given lineage as long as that lineage was seen to be doing its job properly. When it was not, the lineage would be overthrown and replaced with another. Thus, although referred to as a "Son of Heaven," the ruler was seen not as truly descended from Heaven but rather, as Waida points out, a representative of Heaven who would be kept in office only as long as he performed his duties properly.

Thus, within a framework that defines cultures in terms of the claimed divinity of their rulers, Egypt and Japan would appear as examples of divine kingship, while China would be an example of a distinctly human vision of sovereignty.

Although such arguments have been common in the history of religions, some questions should be raised about the use of such frameworks. In general, it may be misleading to build comparative frameworks in which entire cultures are placed on a single line defined, in this case, by visions of human kingship on one pole and those of divine kingship on the other. A more promising approach may be to build such frameworks by comparing the tensions and competing claims of the cultures in question, with an interest, among other things, in comparing how and why the tensions were defined as they were and in analyzing the historical implications of the ways those tensions have played out in the various cultures in question.

In the case at hand, we will see that claims to divine kingship were extremely strong in early China. Although such claims were always hotly debated, they nonetheless played a crucial role in the development of imperial rulership in China. Comparatively speaking, then, the interesting issue is not that China represents a vision of human sovereignty — since this was only one of the views that can be found in early China. The interesting issue is rather the tension between human and divine forms of kingship — why this tension developed, how the terms were defined, and historically how these tensions played out.

THE SACRIFICES OF HUMANITY

Allow me to begin my discussion with precisely the sorts of claims one finds in early China concerning the inherent humanity of the king — the sorts of claims, in other words, that generated the kinds of comparative readings of China that have become so common in the writings of contemporary scholars. These are from texts dating from probably the fourth through the second centuries B.C.[1] They would later come to be included in the *Book of Rites* (*Liji*), one of the five classics that would become part of the curriculum of educated elites throughout East Asia and would for significant periods of Chinese history be used as the basis for court ritual in the imperial Chinese state. In short, these would become highly influential texts.

In these texts, it is most certainly true that, although a proper king would be called a "Son of Heaven," this involved no claim whatsoever of an inherent genealogical relationship between Heaven and the ruler. In fact, very much the opposite: the ruler was clearly defined as human, and the relationship with Heaven was most definitely not one of divine genealogy.

The explicit concern of the texts is that the cosmos in which humans reside is at least indifferent to humans and is perhaps governed by highly capricious spirits with whom humans have no inherent relationship whatsoever. Humans are not only disconnected from these divine powers, but they are equally disconnected from each other: they regard only members of their biological families as objects of concern. Moreover, when people die, the energies that kept them alive floats up to the heavens, and their souls settle in the earth — neither having a relationship with the living again. In short, the world is one of discontinuity — families separated from others, humans separated from the rest of the cosmos, the living separated from the dead.

The texts in question offer as a solution the practice of certain sets of sacrifices invented in the distant past by sages — human sages. With these sacrifices, the practitioners come to view the remains of dead humans as ancestors, view the ruler as their father and mother, view the ruler as a Son of Heaven, and view other families as linked through their common relationship to the ruler. In all these cases, the figures in question know that there are no actual genealogical links between, for example, Heaven, the ruler, and the populace. But, through acts of sacrifice, practitioners learn to extend their familial feelings to those other entities. Sacrifice, then, ultimately allows disparate families in an (at best) indifferent cosmos to come to think of the entire realm — other families, the ruler, the larger world — as a single family. In short, with sacrifice, one forms genealogical links at the emotional level with entities with whom one knows oneself to be unrelated.

Let us begin with discussions of the deceased:

> Everything that is born will die. When one dies, one returns to the ground. This was called the "ghost." The bones and flesh wither below; hidden, they become the earth of the fields. Their *qi* (energy) is sent out above; it becomes radiant brightness. According with the essence of things, instituting the pivot of action, [the sages] clearly named these "ghosts" and "spirits," taking them as a pattern for the black-haired

[1] I refer in this section to the "Li yun," "Ji yi," "Ji fa," "Ji tong," and "Jiao te sheng" chapters of the *Book of Rites*. For a fuller discussion of these and related chapters, see Puett 2005.

people. The populace was thereby awed, and the myriad people thereby submitted[2] (*Liji*, "Ji yi," 126/25/25–27).

The terms "ghosts" and "spirits" were given by the sages to those portions of the deceased that went into the ground and air, respectively. Although this nomenclature awed the populace, it was still insufficient (presumably for controlling the populace), and the sages thus created temples and ancestral halls:

> The sages took this as still insufficient, so they constructed dwellings and houses, and set up temples and ancestral halls. They thereby differentiated closer and more distant kinship, and closer and farther removed in terms of descent. [The sages] taught the people to turn to the past and look back to the beginning, no longer forgetting where they came from. The populace submitted to this and therefore obeyed with greater urgency (*Liji*, "Ji yi," 126/25/28).

The invention of places of ancestral worship taught the populace to differentiate kinship levels and to understand the degree to which they are dependent upon what came before. The sages then went on to create ancestral sacrifices:

> When these two ends were established, they responded with two rituals. They set up the morning service, burning fat and manifesting it with the radiance of [burning] southernwood. They thereby responded to the *qi*. This taught the populace to return to the beginning. They offered millet and rice, and served liver, lungs, head, and heart, presenting them and separating them into two bowls, and supplementing them with sacrificial wine. They thereby respond to the earthly souls (*po*). This taught the people to love one another, and taught superiors and inferiors to utilize their dispositions. This was the utmost of ritual (*Liji*, "Ji yi," 126/25/29).

The sacrifices set up for the spirits taught the populace to see themselves as linked to what came before, and the sacrifices set up for the earthly souls in the tomb taught the populace to have proper dispositions toward other humans.

In short, ancestral sacrifices allowed humans to connect with the remains of the deceased as ancestors, and thereby to refine their dispositions toward living kin as well.

Similar arguments underlie these chapters' discussions of sacrifices to elements in the natural world. Both heaven and earth are repeatedly presented as natural elements on which humans are fully dependent. But both are indifferent to humanity. Sacrifice allows the givers to forge relationships with them, thus helping the givers to recognize these forces as powers on which humans depend. Several chapters emphasize that sacrifice leads the recipients to view these indifferent powers as spirits.

Thus, we find a discussion of the reasons that certain natural elements were chosen by the ancient sages as objects of sacrifice:

> When it came to the sun, moon, stars, and constellations, they were what the people looked up to; as for the mountains, forests, rivers, valleys, and hills, these were the places from which the people took their resources to use. If they were not of this type, they were not entered into the sacrificial canon (*Liji*, "Ji fa," 123/24/9).

---

[2] My translations here and throughout have been aided greatly by those of James Legge (1885).

Certain natural elements were important for humanity — either because humans looked up to them or because they contained resources that humans used. Thus, they were entered into the sacrificial canon.

Moreover, some of these natural elements appeared to cause strange phenomena. Thus, they were called "spirits":

> The mountains, forests, rivers, valleys, and hills that could send out clouds, make wind and rain, and cause to appear strange phenomena — all were named "spirits" (*shen*) (*Liji*, "Ji fa," 122/24/3).

In other words, the ancient sages made natural elements into objects of sacrifice not because they were already spirits but because naming them as such and creating sacrifices on their behalf allowed the populace to develop a better relationship to them.

Similarly, the "Jiao te sheng" chapter argues that the *she* sacrifice leads humans to think of the way of earth as a spirit:

> The *she* is that by which one makes into a spirit the way of the earth (*Liji*, "Jiao te sheng," 70/11.17/14).

By worshipping the way of earth as a spirit, humans will constantly be reminded of their dependence on the harvests of the earth and thereby maintain a proper relationship with it.

The "Jiao te sheng" chapter goes on to argue that the *jiao* sacrifice illuminates for humans the way of heaven:

> The *jiao* is that by which one illuminates the way of heaven (*Liji*, "Jiao te sheng," 71/11.20/1).

But if forming Heaven, Earth, and other natural objects into recipients of sacrifice allows humans to forge a better relationship with them, then what precisely is this superior type of relationship that humans should seek? The same, it turns out, as one should forge with one's deceased relatives.

As we have seen, one of the reasons one has ancestral sacrifices is that they lead the living to recognize the degree to which they are dependent on those who came before. This is true of sacrifices to elements of the natural world as well. Ritual allows the living, therefore, to see both Heaven and deceased humans as the source from which the living arose. But it also leads humans to think of these elements of the natural world in kinship ways as well — just as they do with the deceased humans.

Accordingly, the sacrifices to one's ancestors and to Heaven are similar, but also need to be distinguished to underline the distinction between human and natural relations. The chapter discusses this in ritual terms:

> If the ox for Di is inauspicious, one uses it as the ox for [Hou] Ji. The ox for Di must stay in a pen for three months; the ox for Ji need only be complete. This is the means by which one distinguishes between serving the spirits of Heaven and serving the ghosts of humans. The myriad things are rooted in Heaven, humans are rooted in their ancestors. This is the reason that it matches the High Di. The *jiao* sacrifice recompenses the root and returns to the beginning (*Liji*, "Jiao te sheng," 71/11.20/1–2).

Two points must be mentioned to explicate this passage. The first is that the Zhou recognized Hou Ji as their ancestor. The second is that, as in many of the texts from early China, the chapter equates Di (the high god) with Heaven. The chapter is therefore arguing that there is a parallel between Heaven and Hou Ji: all things (including humans) are rooted in Heaven, and all humans are rooted in their ancestors. Thus, the sacrifice to Hou Ji must match the sacrifice to Di (the deified form of Heaven). But the two must also be distinguished, since Heaven is the inclusive ancestor of all, whereas Hou Ji is merely the ancestor of the Zhou people. Thus, worship of the spirits of Heaven must be distinguished from the worship of the ghosts of humans. The rituals are parallel, and both involve an ox, but the sacrifice to Di requires an auspicious ox that has been kept separate from the herd for three months, whereas Hou Ji need only receive an ox that is complete.

But the parallel between the two sacrifices has significant implications. By performing these rituals, both Heaven and Hou Ji come to be seen as ancestors from which we descend.

And these same relations should hold among the living as well. Just as sacrifices allow the living to see Heaven and deceased humans in ancestral terms, so should children, through ritual, recognize their parents as their forebears. And here too, the parallels between the rituals allow the practitioners to see Heaven as like a parent, and the parent as like Heaven. The "Ai gong wen" quotes Confucius as stating:

> "Therefore a humane man serves his parents as he serves Heaven, and serves Heaven as he serves his parents" (*Liji*, "Ai gong wen," 136/28.7/16–17).

Indeed, it is the ruler who sacrifices to Heaven, and, as such the ruler becomes the "Son of Heaven":

> Therefore the Son of Heaven sacrifices to Heaven and Earth, the lords of the states sacrifice to the altars of the land and grain (*Liji*, "Li yun," 61/9/10).

And, if the ruler through sacrifice makes himself the "Son of Heaven," so does his reverence in sacrifice help him to be seen as the father and mother of the people:

> If he is not reverent when sacrificing, how can he be taken as the father and mother of the people? (*Liji*, "Ji tong," 133/26/22).

As the "Li yun" argues, the consequence of these various sacrifices — families developing proper filiality through sacrifices to ancestors, the ruler sacrificing to Heaven and thus defining himself as both the Son of Heaven and the father and mother of the people — is that the entire realm comes to function as a single family:

> Therefore, as for the sage bearing to take all under Heaven as one family and take the central states as one person, it is not something done overtly. He necessarily knows their dispositions, opens up their sense of propriety, clarifies what they feel to be advantageous, and apprehends what they feel to be calamitous. Only then is he capable of enacting it (*Liji*, "Li yun," 62/9/22).

In short, sacrifice allows the sage to build his rule by affecting the dispositions of the populace, leading the people to think of the realm as a single family: the living think of pieces of deceased humans as their ancestors and think of the ruler as their father and mother and also as the Son of Heaven. As such, the sage is able to rule effectively, but not (and this is presumably part of the reasons for the effectiveness) overtly.

Making a similar argument, the "Biao ji" chapter states that sacrifice allows for the realm to be controlled without causing the type of resentment that overt domination creates:

> The Master said, "As for the sacrificial victims, ritual, and music being properly ar-
> ranged and flourishing, this is the means by which there is no harm from the ghosts
> and spirits and no resentment from the hundred families" (*Liji*, "Biao ji," 151/33/27).

Thus, these chapters from the *Book of Rites* utilize a vision of ritual that functions by transforming the participants such that they think of themselves as linked in chains of genealogical continuity. Power, then, is built up through the particular dispositions inculcated through the rituals. The goal is to create a society that is hierarchically ranked, defined through the dispositions associated with those of genealogical relationships. In such a system, the ruler is indeed human, but he comes to be seen as both the Son of Heaven and the father and mother of the people — the central figure linking living humans, dead humans, and the spirit world into a genealogical web of relationships. A form of control, but one that is, as we saw above, "not done overtly."

Not only is the Son of Heaven not seen as a true divine descendant of Heaven, but the relationship in effect operates the other way: it is the ruler who connects Heaven, along with other natural forces, capricious spirits, and deceased humans into a web of human, ritualized genealogical relationships. The key is to humanize (in the sense of bring into the links of human genealogical dispositions) the natural and divine powers, just as disparate families also come to be linked to each other by these same relationships. The ruler thus becomes the center of everything: the father and mother of the myriad disparate families as well as the Son of Heaven.

This is most certainly a vision of human, as opposed to divine, kingship. Indeed, it is a remarkably strong form of human kingship, in which the king's relationships to the divine world and to the populace as a whole is explicitly defined as being simply forged through ritual. Without ritual, there would be no substantial links at all between the ruler and the divine world.

So why were these texts making such arguments and who are they arguing against? And, more specifically, how do they fit into the larger set of tensions to which I alluded at the beginning of this paper?

The chapters under consideration here were written in the Warring States and early Han periods — roughly fourth through second centuries B.C. They are arguing for a particular form of governance and social hierarchy, in opposition to the forms of extreme centralized statecraft that were becoming increasingly dominant over this period. The authors are making their argument through a description of a sacrificial system they claim was created by the ancient sages, was practiced throughout the Bronze Age (during the Xia, Shang, and Zhou dynasties) and should now be instituted again.

Although the authors were of course re-interpreting certain elements of those rituals, they were in fact building on certain elements of what we can reconstruct from at least the late Shang (ca. 1200–1050 B.C.) and Western Zhou (ca. 1050–771 B.C.) periods. In order to understand the historical background to what they were doing, a brief discussion of these earlier periods will be helpful.

KINGSHIP AND SACRIFICE IN THE BRONZE AGE

The social world of the late Shang and Western Zhou periods was composed, at the elite level, of several competing lineages, each of which controlled particular aspects of land, with attendant populations, material resources, and sacred sites (Chang 1980, 1983; Keightley

2000, 1978; Campbell 2007). These lineages do not appear to have thought of themselves as having any kind of genealogical relationship with each other.

At any given time, one of these lineages would control the kingship, and the others would continue to rule their domains while giving ritual obeisance to the royal lineage. All positions of power were based upon one's rank in the lineage and the ranking of that lineage vis-à-vis the royal one.

The royal lineage was not seen as having any inherent divine powers, nor did they have any inherent essence greater than other aristocratic families. A successful ruling lineage would instead be one that, through either conquest or suasion, could gain and maintain the allegiance of the other lineages. When that allegiance could no longer be maintained, it would be overthrown by another lineage that would then take over the royal title of king (*wang*). Hence the dynastic cycle, of one lineage being overthrown by another, with the winner always attempting to control the other families and divine powers.

The lineage in control would always seek the support of the highest divinity — Di (for the Shang) or Heaven (for the Zhou).[3] There was, however, a problem. One of the views that prevails throughout early China is that the more a divine power is removed from earth and earthly forms, the stronger that divine power is, and the less pliable it is by human ritual. Thus, Heaven/Di is not only extremely powerful, but also extremely difficult to sway with human ritual.[4] Even the spirits of long-deceased humans were powerful, but, insofar as they were far removed from the living, they too were difficult humans to control (although not nearly as difficult as Heaven/Di).

To effect change on divine powers, therefore, one would always begin with the most recently deceased. These are the least powerful, but also the ones most pliable by living humans. The goal was to use sacrifice to transform the recently deceased (and usually highly capricious) spirits into ancestors, who could then be called upon to act in support of their descendants. As David Keightley has convincingly demonstrated, Shang sacrificial practice was aimed at "making ancestors" (2004). Building upon Keightley's reading, I have argued:

> The concern, in short, was to transform a capricious and potentially antagonistic spirit world into a hierarchical pantheon of ordered genealogical descent interested in its living descendants' welfare (Puett 2002: 198).

For the royal lineage, then, the goal was to transform the spirits of the deceased into ancestors who would then be called on to ascend and serve the highest divinity, Heaven/Di. Thus, for example, when King Wu of the Zhou conquered the Shang, he called upon his deceased father, King Wen, to serve the high god. One finds in the Tianwang *gui*,[5] a bronze inscription that dates to the reign of King Wu:

> The greatly illustrious deceased father King Wen serves and pleases the Di on high. (Shirakawa 1.1:1)

---

[3] The Zhou also assimilated the Shang god Di to their own high god Heaven. As a result, Zhou texts refer to the high god as either Heaven or Di. As we saw above in our discussion of the *Book of Rites*, this practice of using Heaven and Di interchangeably continued thereafter.

[4] Indeed, the Shang do not appear to have ever sacrificed to Di directly.

[5] Also known as the Da Feng *gui*.

In *Book of Poetry* one finds a similar reference to King Wen serving the high god:

> King Wen is above,
> How glorious he is in Heaven.
> Although Zhou is an old state,
> Its mandate is new.
> Are the rulers of Zhou not illustrious,
> Was the mandate of Di not timely?
> King Wen ascends and descends,
> Residing to the right and left of Di (*Shi*, Mao #235).

This same process would continue with each passing generation: sacrifices would be given to the most recently deceased ancestors, who would then be called upon to serve the next highest in the lineage, all the way up to those ancestors who would be called upon to serve Heaven.

It is certainly true, therefore, that Heaven/Di and the ruler were not understood to have an inherent genealogical relationship. In fact, the only significant access the ruler had with Heaven was through his own ancestors — the deceased being made into ancestors, who would then be called upon to serve the high god and (hopefully) maintain its support.

In such a sacrificial system, however, there was a built-in inevitability of decline. Just as maintaining the allegiance of the other lineages grew progressively more difficult over time, so was there an inherent sense of degeneration from the sacrificial system itself: since it was defined genealogically, each subsequent generation would grow ever more distant from the ancestors serving Heaven. This process can be traced quite well for the Zhou, for whom we have ample documentation. One example can be seen in the Maogong *ding*, a late vessel, perhaps dating to the reign of King Xuan:

> Bright Heaven is sickening and awesome. In succeeding, I, the young man, cannot be up to it. How will the direction of the state be auspicious? In chaos are the four quarters, greatly licentious and untranquil. *Wuhu*! Worried am I, the young man. The family is submerged in difficulty, and eternally (I) fear the former kings (Shirakawa 30.181:637).

Although some scholars read lines such as these from the end of the Western Zhou as indicative of a growing social crisis, one can equally well read them as simply the inevitable ritual statements of later kings, who do, according to the logic of the sacrificial system, see themselves as dangerously distant from the founding ancestors. But, of course, these two readings are directly related. As the reigning kings grow ritually weaker, rival claimants from powerful lineages inevitably begin seeking allegiances that would allow them to overthrow the king and begin a new dynasty.

In short, the late Shang and Western Zhou were characterized by the politics of lineages that do not appear to have seen themselves as connected. The ordering of the political and divine realm would be undertaken by the lineage that could take and maintain the allegiance of the other lineages and the divine powers, and its eventual fall was inevitable — the genealogical ordering of the realm ensured that the dynasty would be seen as weakening over time. The result was a dynastic cycle, in which the rulership would change hands from one lineage to another every few centuries.

EMPIRE

However, as the Zhou declined, no other clan was able to succeed in overthrowing it. The realm gradually fell into disunity, and finally into a system of de facto independent states vying for dominance (Hsü 1965; Lewis 1999, 2006; Falkenhausen 2006). By the fourth and third centuries B.C. one begins to see the formation of centralized forms of statecraft in several of these states. The key is that these centralized institutions were explicitly aimed at undercutting the power of the aristocratic lineages that had dominated political life during the Bronze Age. The goal was to create military and bureaucratic systems that would promote those born beneath the aristocracy — precisely to push the aristocracy from power.

These trends reached their extremity in 221 B.C., when one these states, Qin, succeeded in conquering the others and declaring the emergence of the first unified empire in Chinese history.

To mark his distinction from the dynasties that came before, the Qin ruler invented a new title: "Huangdi," which means literally "august god" (*Shiji*, 6.236). The ruler also proclaimed himself the "First August God." He was to be followed by the "Second August God," and then the third, and so on for the next ten thousand generations (*Shiji*, 6.236). The speech in which this claim appeared was recorded by the historian Sima Qian over a century later, so its historical validity is impossible to verify. But the interpretation that Sima Qian gives certainly makes sense: the use of the prefix "first" implies that the ruler is expected to be only the first in a very long line. The sense would appear to be that the Qin was not simply another dynasty supplanting the Zhou, in turn to be supplanted by another lineage. It was rather intended to be an empire that would continue forever.

To make good on this goal, the Qin ruler began an overt policy of undercutting the power of the lineages throughout the realm. To begin with, the Qin created a military commandery system: the realm was divided into thirty-six commanderies, each of which was controlled by officials appointed directly by the central court (*Shiji*, 6.239). Instead, therefore, of having the land and resources controlled by potentially rival lineages, the Qin emperor would maintain direct control himself. The goal, clearly, was to prevent the empire from simply being like one of the ruling lineages during the Bronze Age — a lineage ruling only until one of the other lineages grew to sufficient strength to stage an overthrow.

As a further measure to undercut the power of rival lineages, the First Emperor forced the powerful families of the realm to move to the First Emperor's capital (*Shiji*, 6.239).[6] Thus, not only did the central court take direct control of the land, but the families themselves were removed from their centers of power.

As might be expected given these goals, the First Emperor went on to shift the sacrificial system dramatically. Instead of basing the sacrificial system on a genealogical vision, the goal was to do the precise opposite. The First Emperor would travel to every local area (previously controlled by the regional lineages) and personally offer the sacrifices to the local spirits (*Shiji*, 28.1377). This of course entailed the First Emperor's direct control over the local areas, instead of a yielding to the local lineages. Moreover, the goal does not appear to be one of bringing the spirits into a pantheon with the ruling lineage on top (as we saw in the Zhou). The claim appeared to be that the ruler was personally strengthened by these encounters with the spirits. Thus, an endless expansion of the empire was necessary to take control of more and

---

[6] I follow the convention of referring to the "First August God" as the "First Emperor." Although this is not a literal translation, it does accurately capture the distinction with the earlier title *wang*, translated as "king."

more such sites so that the ruler could be ever more strengthened by the spirits he encountered. The result of such a procession would be the gradual divinization of the ruler and his ultimate ascension into the heavens as a god. And, as a god, he would not be dependent on the sacrifices of the living to transform him into an ancestor, nor would he be pliable by the entreaties of the living. Moreover, the empire would not be dependent upon him serving Heaven and calling upon Heaven to preserve the ruling lineage, since, as a god, he could intervene directly on behalf of those below.

In short, the First Emperor was indeed asserting a form of divine kingship. But note that it was not a form that claimed any kind of divine descent. Indeed, at the beginning, the ruler would be fully human, but he would transform himself into a divine immortal through the sacrificial process (*Shiji*, 6.245, 252, 258, 263, 28.1377). Once done, the ruler would be completely autonomous from the system of genealogical relationships that defined the Zhou form of governance.

And his empire, of course, could last forever. The sacrificial system of the First Emperor would have ended such an inherent tendency toward degeneration. If, in the previous sacrificial order, the founding king would die and thereafter be made into an ancestor who would serve Heaven until he was replaced by a new founder, the system of the First Emperor would result in the founder — the First Emperor himself — ascending to the heavens and residing there permanently. The empire he founded would then be ruled by his descendants for eternity: since the ritual system would not be based upon moving the sacrifices up the lineage to the founder, the reigning monarch would not become increasingly removed from the founder, and the dynasty would not become progressively weaker. Thus, the founder would never lose his position in the heavens, and he, like the empire he founded, would never be displaced. Thus, the divinity of the ruler provided the longevity that the previous Bronze Age sacrificial system had denied.

In short, a claim of divine sovereignty was also a claim of complete autonomy from the constructed world of lineage relations that defined the Zhou, as well as from the inevitable genealogical weakening that underlies a system based on the dynastic cycle.

But note that this form of divine kingship did require the ruler's ascension into the heavens. As mentioned above, in early China everything on earth was seen as dying, so gods by definition had to reside in the heavens. Thus, for the First Emperor to become divine required his ascension to the heavens and thus also required a second emperor, and a third, and on down to reside on earth.[7] But if the First Emperor himself would not be a god on earth, he would be a god in the heavens, and his empire would last for ten thousand generations.

But if this was the goal of the First Emperor, he failed completely. The Qin fell only a few years after the death of the First Emperor. And, tellingly, it was destroyed precisely by the major families that the First Emperor had tried to undercut (*Shiji*, 6.273). In short, the Qin failed dramatically to end the earlier lineage system on which the previous dynasties had thrived.

Nonetheless, the centralized imperial system and the sacrificial system of the Qin were revived by Emperor Wu of the succeeding Han dynasty. Like that of the First Emperor, the sacrificial system put in place under Emperor Wu involved a divinization of the ruler, resulting in his ultimate ascension, as well as a strong symbolic claim for the personal control that the

---

[7] Thus, unlike Polynesian rulers who, as Sahlins (1985) has argued, became living gods on earth, there was always a cosmological limit in China: the earth consists of forms, which are transitory. Gods are beyond forms, and thus reside in the heavens. For a ruler to become a god, therefore, he had to ascend into the heavens.

emperor should exercise over all sacrificial sites and the territories in which they were found (*Shiji*, 28.1389–96; see also Puett 2002).

Over the subsequent decades, however, the state suffered dramatically from imperial over-reach, and several voices emerged calling for a scaling back of the empire. In particular, the system came under attack during the 30s B.C. by figures such as Kuang Heng and Zhang Tan, who argued that the ritual system introduced by Emperor Wu "differs from the regulations of antiquity" (*Hanshu*, 25B.1254). Explicit calls were made to return to the ritual system of the Zhou. And one of the main texts they turned to was the *Book of Rites*, chapters of which were discussed above.

The appeal of these chapters is that they called for a weakening of the imperial institutions, a strengthening of the lineage systems, and a return to a sacrificial and institutional system based upon lineage and genealogy. Once again, rulers would be defined as human, and the goal of a ruler was not to become divine and thereby take direct control over the populace but rather to build out a set of genealogical relationships that would ultimately allow the ruler to control covertly — but hopefully much more effectively. As we have seen above, the texts put forth a vision of sacrifice clearly based upon (although re-interpreted from) that dominant in the courts of the late Shang and Western Zhou: making the recently deceased into ancestors and then using that as a basis for defining the ruler's relationship to the other families and to the high god in ritually defined genealogical terms.

Ultimately, these voices won. In 31 B.C., the ritual system created by the First Emperor and consolidated by Emperor Wu was overthrown, and a new system based upon a particular reading of the *Book of Rites* was put in place (Loewe 1974; Kern 2001; Puett 2002). The ruler was defined as human and was again referred to as a "Son of Heaven" — defined in ritual terms, not as descent. The emphasis turned again to a form of control based upon a decentral-ized form of governance using ritual claims of constructed genealogies to gain support.

These ritual reforms marked the first point in which the *Book of Rites* became a basis for court ritual. The text would ultimately become highly influential and be defined, as mentioned above, as one of the Five Classics and as one of the key normative works for defining court ritual (Zito 1997; Wilson 2002). It is here that we see the crucial steps taken for defining the "classical form" of Chinese kingship discussed above by Manabu Waida: the ruler as human, as a ritual Son of Heaven, ruling within a royal lineage until a rival lineage could successfully take over and declare a new dynasty.

HUMAN AND DIVINE KINGSHIP

From this brief history it is already clear that the emergence of divine claims of kingship occurred together with the rise of empire. Although these claims were ultimately rejected, they were to remain a crucial part of the repertoire of potential sovereignty claims available to later courts. Indeed, the two systems that were forged at this time — the one based upon constructed genealogical claims, the other on claims of divinity and on a complete autonomy from such claims — operated as almost perfect mirror images of each other, with the strength of each resting in part on its opposition to the other. In the former, the central model is of a lineage-based system, with the ruler as central figure in a web of extended, ritually defined ge-nealogical relations. The ruler becomes the father and mother of the people, as well as the cen-tral sacrifier to the ancestors. In the latter, the ruler himself becomes a god, removed from all genealogical constraints, with direct control over (ideally) everything. The success of each to a significant degree relied on its rejection of the other. Part of the initial appeal and later hatred of the First Emperor no doubt emerged from his successful opposition to the powerful lineages of the day and the entire political and sacrificial system built upon them, and much of the appeal of the subsequent calls to return to a re-interpreted version of the Zhou system of sacrifice lay precisely in its calls for a return to power of dominant lineage organizations.

And this pattern would continue. Later figures who played the extreme forms of divine rulership seen in figures like the First Emperor and Emperor Wu — I am thinking here of figures like Song Huizong and Mao — would work precisely to destroy lineage organizations, and those periods that would emphasize the genealogically based systems of sacrifice would instead appeal to a decentralized form of governance strongly reliant upon the lineage organizations kept (it was hoped) not quite as strong as the ruling family. A further pattern is that those claiming divine rulership have tended to be figures claiming to found a new order that would last longer than the genealogically based lineage systems, and in all cases their calls for complete autonomy have in fact led to political systems that faltered soon after their own deaths.

Even outside of such extreme moments of history, however, notions of divine emperorship were to continue in later Chinese history. If the main court rituals were often modeled upon the *Book of Rites*, visions of divine rulership continued to underlie later Daoist rituals. And both sets of rituals were often sponsored by the courts, thus allowing rulers to shift back and forth between human and divine claims.

In short, the interplay between these two mirror-image visions of sovereignty would continue to play a crucial role throughout later Chinese history.

CONCLUSION

In China, the interplay of human and divine forms of kingship has been crucial in the development of and reaction to the imperial state. In terms of comparative work, these points do not of course completely reject the standard view that in China sovereignty is based upon a notion of human kingship: even the divine claims to kingship assume a human king who is then gradually divinized through sacrificial practice, and the opposition to such divine claims certainly involves an extraordinarily strong assertion of the human nature of rulers. But hopefully the demonstration of this interplay between human and divine claims will allow the Chinese material to be brought into comparative discussions in a more helpful way than just the contrastive framework of placing China on one side of a pole and Egypt and Japan on another.

The more exciting comparative implications of this material would instead encourage further analyses of the ways in which the tensions we have sketched here — between lineage organizations and centralized institutions, human claims to kingship and divine ones, genealogical definitions of sacrifice and theomorphic ones — have played out in China and the degree to which comparable tensions have played out in the histories of other cultures. The comparative focus could then be on the ways in which these tensions have been defined in different cultures and the implications of the nature of these tensions for the histories of the cultures in question.

BIBLIOGRAPHY

Campbell, Roderick

2007   Blood, Flesh, and Bones: Kinship and Violence in the Social Economy of the Late Shang. Ph.D. dissertation, Harvard University.

Chang, Kwang-chih

1980   *Shang Civilization*. New Haven: Yale University Press.

1983   *Art, Myth, and Ritual: The Path to Political Authority in Ancient China*. Cambridge: Harvard University Press.

von Falkenhausen, Lothar

2006   *Chinese Society in the Age of Confucius (1000–250 B.C.): The Archaeological Evidence*. Ideas, Debates, and Perspectives 2. Los Angeles: Cotsen Institute of Archaeology.

Hsü, Cho-yun

1965   *Ancient China in Transition: An Analysis of Social Mobility, 722–222 B.C.* Stanford Studies in the Civilizations of Eastern Asia. Stanford: Stanford University Press.

Keightley, David N.

1978   "The Religious Commitment: Shang Theology and the Genesis of Chinese Political Culture." *History of Religions* 17.3,4: 211–12.

2000   *The Ancestral Landscape: Time, Space, and Community in Late Shang China (ca. 1200–1045 B.C.)*. China Research Monograph 53. Berkeley: University of California, Berkeley and Center for Chinese Studies.

2004   "The Making of the Ancestors: Late Shang Religion and Its Legacy." In *Religion and Chinese Society*, Volume 1: *Ancient and Medieval China*, edited by John Lagerwey, pp. 3–63. Hong Kong: The Chinese University of Hong Kong.

Kern, Martin

2001   "Ritual, Text, and the Formation of the Canon: Historical Transitions of wen in Early China." *T'oung Pao* 87.1–3: 43–91.

Legge, James

1885   *Li Chi: Book of Rites*. 2 volumes. The Sacred Books of China, Texts of Confucianism 3–4. Oxford: Oxford University Press.

Lewis, Mark Edward

1999   "Warring States: Political History." In *The Cambridge History of Ancient China: From the Origins of Civilization to 221 B.C.*, edited by Michael Loewe and Edward L. Shaughnessy, pp. 587–650. Cambridge: Cambridge University Press.

2006   *The Construction of Space in Early China*. State University of New York Series in Chinese Philosophy and Culture. Albany: State University of New York Press.

Loewe, Michael

1974   *Crisis and Conflict in Han China: 104 B.C. to A.D. 9*. London: Allen & Unwin.

1996   *Liji (Book of Rites)*. Institute of Chinese Studies, Ancient Chinese Text Concordance Series. Hong Kong: The Commercial Press.

Puett, Michael J.

2001   *The Ambivalence of Creation: Debates Concerning Innovation and Artifice in Early China*. Stanford: Stanford University Press.

2002   *To Become a God: Cosmology, Sacrifice, and Self-Divinization in Early China*. Harvard-Yenching Institute Monograph Series 57. Cambridge: Harvard University Asia Center.

2005   "The Offering of Food and the Creation of Order: The Practice of Sacrifice in Early China." In *Of Tripod and Palate: Food, Politics, and Religion in Traditional China*, edited by Roel Sterckx, pp. 75–95. New York: Palgrave Macmillan.

Sahlins, Marshall D.

1985   *Islands of History*. Chicago: University of Chicago Press.

Shaughnessy, Edward L.

1991   *Sources of Western Zhou History: Inscribed Bronze Vessels*. Berkeley: University of California Press.

Shirakawa, Shizuka

1962–1984   *Kinbun tsûshaku*. Fifty-six volumes. Hakutsuru Bijutsukan shi 1–56. Kobe: Hakutsuru Bijutsukan.

Sima, Qian

1995   *Shiji*. Beijing: Zhonghua shuju.

Waida, Manabu

2005   "Kingship: Kingship in East Asia." In *Encyclopedia of Religion*, Volume 8, edited by Lindsay Jones, pp. 5178–81. Second edition. Detriot: Macmillan Reference Books.

Wilson, Thomas

2002   "Sacrifice and the Imperial Cult of Confucius." *History of Religions* 41.3: 251–87.

Zito, Angela

1997   *Of Body and Brush: Grand Sacrifice as Text/Performance in Eighteenth-Century China*. Chicago: University of Chicago Press.

12

THE ROLE OF RELIGION IN ACHAEMENIAN IMPERIALISM*

BRUCE LINCOLN, UNIVERSITY OF CHICAGO

I

There was a time when sacred kingship was a fashionable topic among historians of religions, who thought they were able to find confirmation of Frazerian theories in the patterns of myth and ritual attested throughout the ancient Near East. For some, including Sir James George himself, identifying countless examples of dying and rising gods, ritual regicide-cum-deicide, priest-kings with magic control over vegetation and symbolic links to the cycle of the seasons, all served to advance a rationalistic critique of Christian beliefs as yet one more variant on a familiar set of primitive superstitions.[1] For others, and here one thinks of Jessie Weston, T. S. Eliot, and other romantic souls, the same kinds of material and theory served entirely opposite purposes. In their constructions, it was the loss of myth and ritual, declining faith in priests, kings, magic, and the sacred — in short, the same disenchantment of the world that progressive rationalists celebrated — that produced the worst ills of modernity.[2]

The variegated, almost protean utility of Frazerian theory helps explain the breadth of its popularity, although the exoticism of Frazer's examples, the imperial reach of his knowledge, the breathless verve of his descriptive prose, and the skillful way he positioned himself as heir to both Tylor and Robertson Smith also contributed significantly to his success and reputation. Like all grand theorists, however, and especially those of the armchair variety, he was guilty of distortion, pretentiousness, procrusteanism, selective blindness, cultural condescension, and a host of other failings. As each of his errors was identified, his project slowly deflated, with the result that his theories not only lost their power to transport, they began to look a bit pathetic. Although staunch devotees of the "Myth and Ritual School" continued to espouse Frazerian positions even into the 1960s,[3] his serious influence had evaporated long before, the crucial turning point having been Bronislaw Malinowski's Frazer Memorial Lecture of 1924, which some regard as an act of ritual regicide, with Sir James George in attendance, cast as outgoing King of the Wood (Malinowski 1954). At present, Frazer stands alongside Friedrich Max Müller as one of the ancestors remembered with more embarrassment than gratitude, let alone reverence, by the several interrelated disciplines that once hailed him as one of their founders (anthropology, folklore, history of religions).

Assyriologists familiar with the Babylonian *akitu*-festival, Egyptologists steeped in the drama of Osiris, Horus, and Seth, certain students of the Hebrew Bible, and those disposed to

---

* I would like to acknowledge the kind assistance I received from Matthew Stolper in dealing with the Elamite and Akkadian texts treated in this paper.

[1] On Frazer, see Smith 1978: 208–39; Ackerman 1987; Lanwerd 1993; Stocking 1995: 124–51.

[2] For Eliot's use of Frazer in "The Waste Land," and more broadly on Eliot's views concerning myth, religion, politics, culture, and the failings of modernity, see Manganaro 1992 and Carpentier 1998. As Eliot acknowledged, he read Frazer via the mediation of Weston 1920. See also Vickery 1973 and Fraser 1991.

[3] Among the last true believers was Theodore Gaster (1961 and 1969).

221

situate Jesus as a dying-and-rising deity of the ancient Near East were among the most enthusiastic supporters of the Frazerian paradigm, alongside the Cambridge ritualists.[4] In general,
Iranists invested less heavily in the Frazerian model.[5] Those who concerned themselves with
kingship were generally quick to note that the relevant texts construe the royal office as a gift
bestowed upon rulers by Ahura Mazdā ("the Wise Lord"), which is to say that the king himself was not regarded as magic, divine, or priestly. At best, we have a legitimating ideology
couched in a religious idiom, not a sacred kingship recognizably Frazerian in nature (Frye
1964; Schmitt 1977; Root 1979; Duchesne-Guillemin 1979; Frei and Koch 1984; Gnoli 1984;
Kuhrt 1984; Ahn 1992; Lincoln 2007, 2012).

Given the paucity of evidence that might fit their patterns and suit their purposes, enthu-
siasts of *The Golden Bough* thus came to focus their energies on a single Iranian datum. This
is the set of relief sculptures adorning the steps of the Apadāna, an enormous reception hall in
the palace complex of Persepolis. In these images (fig. 12.1), they thought they saw evidence
of a New Year's festival involving the ritual enactment of mythic dramas, through which kingship and the cosmos itself were annually renewed as the king slew dragons, overcame chaos,
and revitalized the earth, crops, and seasons.[6] Some adherents of the theory went so far as to
describe Persepolis as a ritual city, whose sole raison d'être was the annual performance of this
ceremony.[7]

Heady stuff, but very little supported by any evidence of the Achaemenian period. To
compensate for this inconvenient fact, adherents of the thesis relied on comparative materials
(especially the *akitu* ritual) and anachronistic testimonies (especially al-Beruni's description of the Sassanian Now Rōz) to constitute the Apadāna reliefs as one more example of the
patterns they knew so well from elsewhere. For a time, they succeeded in getting their ideas
taken seriously, but the hearing they obtained brought with it critical evaluation, in the wake of
which the Frazerian balloon deflated that much further.[8]

II

Subsequent scholarship has made clear that the Apadāna reliefs depict a procession of
tribute-bearers drawn from every province of the empire bringing gifts to the Achaemenian
king (fig. 12.2; Walser 1966; Hinz 1969: 95–114; Schmidt 1970: 108–20; Tilia 1972; Root
1979: 227–84; Shahbazi 1978; Jacobs 1982; Trümpelmann 1983; Koch 1983; Stronach 1985;
Cahill 1985; Jamzadeh 1992; Hachmann 1995). Although most contemporary authors would
grant that the payment of tribute had a certain ceremonial aspect, few would explain this via

[4] For Frazerian influence in studies of the ancient Near East, see Hooke 1933, 1935, 1958. Also relevant are such works as Langdon 1914; Labat 1939; Engnell 1943; Frankfort et al. 1946; Frankfort 1948; Gadd 1948; Kramer 1969; Jacobsen 1976. Among the writings of the Classicists influenced by Frazer who styled themselves "Cambridge Ritualists," note Harrison 1912, 1922; Murray 1912. Also useful are Ackerman 1991; Segal 1996, 1998.

[5] The chief exception is Geo Widengren, whose sense of Iranian sacred kingship was strongly influenced by Frazer, but mediated by Dumézil 1924, 1929. See, for instance, Widengren 1953: 201–09, 1955: 51–55, 1959,

1965: 41–49, 1974, and 1983. Less important, but worth noting. is Richards 1979.

[6] Crucial to this view was interpretation of a relief sculpture from Persepolis in which a lion overcame a bull as having calendric and zodiacal significance denoting the New Year as the moment when the constellation Leo succeeded that of Taurus. Such was argued by Herzfeld 1941: 251; Pope 1957a: 128; Hartner and Ettinghausen 1964, but is quite unlikely, as shown by Nylander 1974: 141–44.

[7] This was argued by Pope 1957a–b; Ghirshman 1957; Erdmann 1960; and Fennelly 1980.

[8] The most telling critiques are Nylander 1974; Calmeyer 1980, 1985–86; and Sancisi-Weerdenburg 1991.

a discourse of sacred kingship and rituals of renewal, rather than one of imperial protocol, for example.[9] There are alternatives, however, to the abuses of Frazerian comparatism on the one hand, and a principled — but anachronistic — insistence on treating ancient political institutions as wholly secular in nature. For in antiquity, neither kingship, nor tribute, nor much else for that matter, can be properly understood without some reference to religion, insofar as all ideology tended to be couched in a religious idiom. For it is only with the Enlightenment that religion came to be viewed and organized as one cultural system among others (politics, economy, literature, art, philosophy, fashion, etc.), all of which enjoy relative independence. Previously, religion was constituted as a uniquely privileged transcendent system of culture that encompassed, structured, disciplined, and permeated all others. And, as a result of the extent to which those other systems were informed, even controlled by the religious, none of them can be understood as secular in the modern sense.

On general principles, I am thus inclined to think the tributary practices depicted in the Apadāna reliefs had a certain religious significance, although not of the sort normally associated with Frazerian models of sacred kingship. To demonstrate this, however, depends on close consideration of the Achaemenian evidence, most important of all the reliefs themselves and the four inscriptions placed on the south retaining wall of Persepolis (original site of entry to the palace complex). As has been generally recognized, the physical placement of these inscriptions suggests they were meant to form a coherent set, and this is also evident in their use of language. For although most Achaemenian inscriptions are trilingual (Old Persian, Elamite, and Akkadian), the same three languages are distributed among these inscriptions, such that reading left to right, the first two are in Old Persian (DPd and DPe), the third in Elamite (DPf), and the last in Akkadian (DPg). As a set, they thus make a statement about unity and diversity, while also describing linguistic and political relations at the central core of the empire. Three different languages and peoples cooperate in the central administration, but one — the Persian rulers and their native tongue — outrank the others, as marked by both number and sequence (although it may be that the two inscriptions in Old Persian are meant to represent the Persians first and then the Medes).[10]

For our purposes, the most convenient point of departure is the inscription known as DPg, written in Akkadian, which begins with an account of the world's creation. This is not unusual, for 70% (23/33) of the Achaemenian inscriptions that contain more than two paragraphs begin in the same fashion. In all cases, however, the cosmogonic narratives are brief, stereotyped, and highly formulaic.[11] In its opening passage, DPg conforms closely to the standard formulae, but as it continues, it develops in ways that are unique and highly significant. The vast majority of variants attribute five distinct acts of creation to the Wise Lord (Ahura Mazdā), four of which occurred at the dawn of time, before history proper. In its treatment of these primordial events, DPg follows conventions, as is apparent when one compares it to other variants for which we have good Akkadian versions (table 12.1).[12]

[9] To date, discussions of tribute have not paid particular attention to their religious dimension, but have been understandably concerned with issues of political economy. See, above all, Koch 1980; Briant 1982, 1986; Descat 1985; Briant and Herrenschmidt 1989; and Sancisi-Weerdenburg 1998.

[10] On these inscriptions, their placement, and their coherence as a set, see Shahbazi 1985: 15–16; Herrenschmidt 1990; Lecoq 1997: 97–98; Schmitt 1999: 27–36, 2000:

56. On the extent to which the Achaemenian inscriptions use a language that makes use of both Median and Persian forms, see Lecoq 1974.

[11] The fullest study of these formulaic texts is Herrenschmidt 1977.

[12] For the most part, the Old Persian variants are identical in content to the Akkadian versions presented here, but for the purposes of precise analysis, it is preferable to compare DPg to variants written in the same language.

Table 12.1. The Four Primordial Creations, as Narrated in Four Variants of the Cosmogony
Written in Akkadian

Darius, *Persepolis (DPg)*	*Darius,* *Elvend*	*Darius,* *Naqš-i Rustam*	*Xerxes,* *Persepolis (XPa)*
Great is the Wise Lord, who is the greatest of all the gods,	A great god is the Wise Lord	A great god is the Wise Lord	A great god is the Wise Lord
who made sky	who created this earth	who made sky	who created this earth
and earth,	who created that sky,	and earth,	who created that sky,
who made people,	who created people,	and who made people,	who created humanity
who gave all happiness to people living therein.[13]	who created all abundance for people.[14]	who created happiness for people.[15]	who created happiness for humanity.[16]

The contents here are quite consistent and require little commentary. For our purposes, it suffices to mention a few points only. First, three of the four primordial creations are denoted in the singular (heaven, earth, and happiness~abundance). Second, as regards the remaining item, usage varies. While DPg, DE, and DNa speak of "people" in the plural, XPa speaks of "humanity" in the singular (*amelûtú*). In general, the Akkadian versions of the Achaemenian cosmogony tend to employ the plural here, but on this point XPa follows the Old Persian variants, which consistently use the singular (*martiya* "man, mankind") and do so to make an important point. For within pan-Iranian mythic traditions, the human species makes its original appearance in a single, prototypical individual who encompasses within his being all the possibilities later distributed among different members of the species. (The same is true for plants and animals in Zoroastrian accounts.) Diversity, then, enters only at a later stage of cosmic history, when the demonic force the Achaemenians referred to as "the Lie" (Old Persian *drauga*, Akkadian *pirṣātú*) assaulted the world and caused its fragmentation.[17]

The Lie's assault disrupted the primordial peace, beauty, and "happiness" (Old Persian *šiyāti*, Akkadian *dumqu*) of creation, introducing strife, corruption, and death into existence. It also marked the beginning of history proper, history being the finite time when the Wise Lord and the Lie struggle for supremacy, with the world as their battleground. The two cosmic powers do not grapple with one another directly, however. Instead, people — now differentiated morally and in other fashions — become foot soldiers on either side, while the forces of good are placed under the leadership of a trusted individual. It is in this context that the cosmogonic accounts narrate the Wise Lord's fifth act of creation, temporally removed from the first four, as a response to the crisis provoked by the Lie's invasion. It is on this precise point that the

[13] DPg §1: *Urumazda rabi ša rabû ina muḫḫi ilāni gabbi, ša šamê u erṣiti ibnû u nišê *ibnû, ša dumqi gabbi iddinuma nišī ina libbi balṭū.* Text in Weissbach 1911: 85. I am grateful to Matt Stolper for his help in translating this inscription.

[14] DE §1 (Babylonian): *ilu rabû Aḫurumazdā, ša qaqqaru agâ iddinu ša šamê annûtu iddinu ša ummānāti (?) iddinu ša gabbi nuḫšu ana ummānāti (?) iddinu.* Text in Weissbach 1911: 101.

[15] DNa §1: *ilu rabû Aḫurmazdā ša šamê u erṣeti [ib]nû u nišī ibnû ša dumqi ana nišī iddinu.* Text in Weissbach 1911: 87.

[16] XPa §1: *ilu rabû Aḫurumazdā ša qaqqaru agâ iddinu ša šamê annûtu iddinu ša amēlūtu iddinu ša dumqi ana amēlūtu iddinu.* Text in Weissbach 1911: 107.

[17] The Zoroastrian variants are most extensively narrated in the *Greater Bundahišn* 1–18, the *Selections of Zād Spram* 1–3, and *Dādestān ī Dēnīg* 36.

originality of DPg becomes evident, for it describes the Wise Lord's fifth creation in much more elaborate fashion than do any of the other variants (table 12.2).

Table 12.2. The Fifth Act of Creation, as Narrated in Four Variants of the Cosmogony
Written in Akkadian

Darius, Persepolis (DPg)	Darius, Elvend	Darius, Naqš-i Rustam	Xerxes, Persepolis (XPa)
who made Darius king	who made Darius king	who made Darius king	who made Xerxes king
	one over the previously existing kings, one over the previously existing rulers.[18]	of many kings.[19]	one over many kings, one over many rulers.[20]
and gave King Darius kingship over this broad earth,			
which has many lands-and-peoples in it:			
Persia, Media, and other lands-and-peoples			
with other languages,			
with mountains and plains,			
on this side of the ocean (lit., the bitter river) and the far side of the ocean,			
on this side of the desert (lit., the land of thirst) and the far side of the desert.[21]			

---

[18] DE §1: ša ana Dāriamuš šarru ibnû, ištēn ina šarrāni maḫrûtu, ištēn ina mute'imē maḫrûtu. Text in Weissbach 1911: 101.

[19] DNa §1: [ša] ana Dāriamuš šarru ša šarrāni mādūtu ibnû. Text in Weissbach 1911: 87.

[20] XPa §1: ša ana Ḫišîarši šarru ibnû ištēn ina šarrāni mādūtu ištēn ina mute'imē mādūtu. Text in Weissbach 1911: 107.

[21] DPg §1: ša ana Dariamuš šarru ibnû u ana Dariamuš šarri šarrūtu iddinu ina qaqqar agâ rapšātu ša mātāti madetu ina libbišu Parsu Mādaya u mātāi šanêtima lišānu šanītu, ša šadî u mātu ša aḫanā agâ ša nār marratu u aḫulluâ ullî ša naru marratu, ša aḫanā agâ ša qaqqar ṣumāma'itu u aḫulluâ ullî ša qaqqar ṣumama'itu. Text in Weissbach 1911: 85.

Obviously, all these texts are concerned to represent the King as possessing a divine charisma in the most literal sense. Called by the Wise Lord, he serves as the instrument through which divine purpose is to be accomplished on earth. Somewhat less obviously, the same passages also address the issue of unity and diversity, for they implicitly acknowledge that as a result of the Lie's action, humanity has fractured into multiple groups, each of which produces its own leaders who style themselves as kings, and this situation produces the possibility of competition, rivalry, warfare, bloodshed, disorder, and terrible suffering. The solution to this, as suggested by the phrases that name Darius "one king over many kings, one ruler over many rulers," is for the many to be encompassed by the one, as all other kings (and all other peoples) accept the leadership of God's chosen: the Achaemenian monarch.

Whereas all other variants signal this set of (complex and tendentious) ideas with a single well-chosen phrase, DPg alone develops the issues at length. It thus announces that the Wise Lord conferred not just kingship on Darius, but universal kingship: "kingship over this broad earth" and, going further, it reflects on the relation of unity and diversity within his domain by specifying that the "broad earth" over which the king rules has "many lands-and-peoples in it." And here, it is relevant to note that the standard royal titulary ended by naming Achaemenian rulers "King of lands-and-peoples, King in this earth," with the further understanding that the term translated as "earth" (Old Persian *būmī*) also denoted the empire (Herrenschmidt 1976).

DPg then offers a set of binary oppositions that organize the categories into which lands and peoples have been divided: the divisions to be overcome, if primordial unity and perfection are to be restored. As regards peoples, the primary division is that between those of the absolute center (Persians and Medes), as opposed to all others, with language as the chief index of diversity. As regards lands, three interrelated binaries are introduced: high/low (mountains and plains), wet/dry (sea and desert), near/far (this side and that side of the sea or desert). Implicitly, these also encode a hierarchy of values, suggesting that the ideal terrain is neither high nor low, neither so wet as to be chaotic (the sea), nor so dry as to be arid (the desert), but a land that is moist and fertile. Presumably, it was understood that this was the situation of the earth as it was originally created, and that the diversity introduced by the Lie's assault was a diversity of inferior forms, for each separate terrain came to achieve its unique identity only in the degree to which it deviated from primordial perfection, becoming a bit more dry, a bit more moist, a bit more high and rocky, a bit more low and swampy, etc., as a mark of its fallen state.

Fragmentation of original unity thus produced multiple different lands, each with its own distinctive people, speaking their own language, and differing from all others in its institutions, habits, character, and culture. What is more, each land — by virtue of its different climate and terrain — was capable of supporting different forms of plant and animal life, while the earth itself harbored different minerals, ores, and other resources. Some areas were richer, others more poor, but none possessed everything, and insofar as all lands and peoples lacked certain goods (understanding "goods" not only in an economic sense, but also with broader moral, aesthetic, and religious implications), general well-being and contentment were compromised. Alternatively, one could say that the unified, perfect, primordial happiness that the Wise Lord created for humanity as the last of his original acts had been fractured and pieces of it distributed across the now-diversified globe. It is this situation that the fifth act of creation was meant to redress, and the continuation of DPg — which is unparalleled in any other inscription — describes how this might be accomplished.

> King Darius proclaims: Under protection of the Wise Lord, these are the lands-and-peoples who made this (palace) that is made here:[22] Persia, Media, and other lands-and-peoples, with other languages, with mountains and plains, on this side of the ocean and on the far side of the ocean, on this side of the desert and the far side of desert, according to the order I gave them.[23]

What Darius describes is the reunification of peoples across all the lines that divide them. At his command, all assemble at Persepolis and the palace itself is the product of their coordinated, cooperative, unified-and-unifying labor.[24] But how was this accomplished? The other inscriptions that accompany DPg on the city's south wall help address that question.

III

DPe also signals its interest in the problem of unity and diversity, albeit in subtle fashion. Thus, whereas the Achaemenian ruler is always given the title "King of lands-and-peoples," only DPe calls him "King of lands-and-peoples, *of which there are many.*"[25] Like many other inscriptions, it follows the royal titulary with a list of the numerous lands-and-peoples (Old Persian *dahyāva*) that, to date, have been encompassed within the empire. Unlike the others, however, it specifies the instrument through which this has been accomplished (table 12.3).

---

[22] Weissbach (1911: 85) read *ip-ḫu-rum*, and his reading was accepted by the *Chicago Assyrian Dictionary* in its listing for *akanna* "here," which cites him and translates the relevant phrase "these are the nations which *gathered* here." After studying the text once again in situ, George Cameron revised Weissbach on this and other points. His translation appeared in Schmidt (1953: 63), where the same phrase is rendered "these (are) the countries which *did this which was done* here." Schmidt (1953: 62 n. 20) stated that Cameron had prepared a new transcription of the text that ought to be separately published, but apparently this was never done. Matt Stolper informs me (pers. comm., 9 January 2007) that having consulted all published photographs of the inscription, he takes the text to be defective, but believes that Weissbach's *ip-ḫu-rum* (from the verb *paharu*, "to gather [intransitive]") is impossible, given details of the epigraphy evident in

Schmidt's plate 7b. Possible and preferable is *ep-šú*, from the verb *epešu* "to make, do, build"; also possible is *ib-nu*, "they made/built." Presumably, this is what Cameron also concluded.

[23] DPg §2: *Dāriamuš šarru iqabbi ina ṣilli ša Urumazda aganētu mātātī, ša agâ īpušā, ša akanna epšu Parsu Madāya u mātāati madêtu šanêtima lišanu šanītu, ša šadî u mātu ša aḫanā agâ ša nār marratu u aḫulluā ullî ša nār marratu, ša aḫanā agâ ša qaqqar ṣumāma'ītu u aḫulluā ullî ša qaqqar ṣumāma'ītu libbû ša anāku ṭēme aškunušunu.*

[24] DSf, DS, and DSaa describe the palace Darius built at Susa as the result of a similar process, and do so in some detail. See further Lincoln 1996.

[25] DPe §1: *xšāyaθiya dahyūnām tayaịšām parūnām.* Text in Schmitt 2000: 61.

Table 12.3. Introductory Formulae Preceding Lists of Lands-and-Peoples under Achaemenian Rule

Darius, Persepolis	Darius, Bisitun	Darius, Susa	Darius, Susa and Naqš-i Rustam; Xerxes, Persepolis
Proclaims Darius the King:	Proclaims Darius the King:	Proclaims Darius the King:	Proclaims Darius the King:
		The Wise Lord bestowed the kingship/ kingdom that is great, whose people are good, on me. He made me king in this earth/ empire.	
By the Wise Lord's will,	These lands-and-peoples, which came to me by the Wise Lord's will,	By the Wise Lord's will,	By the Wise Lord's will,
these are the lands-and-peoples		these are the lands-and-peoples	these are the lands-and-peoples
that I took hold of	I was king of them.[26]	over which I became king.[27]	that I seized far from Persia.
with this Persian army.			
They feared me		I ruled over them.	
and bore me tribute.[28]			They bore me tribute.[29]

If all the inscriptions consistently and obsessively proclaim the king as God's chosen instrument, DPe is unique in acknowledging the Persian army as the instrument through which that king subjugated other lands-and-peoples. In its closing paragraph, this text goes further still as Darius advises his successors on how they can complete the divinely-enjoined project he began.

[26] DB §6: θati Dārayavauš xšāyaθiya: imā dahyāva, tayā manā patiyāi̯ ša, vašnā Auramazdāha adamšām xšāyaθiya āham. Text in Schmitt 1991: 49.

[27] DSm §2: θāti Dārayavauš XŠ AMmaiy xšaçam frābara taya vazṛkam taya umartiyam, mām xšāyaθiyam ahyāyā būmiyā akunauš, vašnā AMhā imā dahyāva tayaišām adam xšāyaθiya abavam. Text in Kent 1953: 145.

[28] DPe §2: θāti Dārayavauš xšāyaθiya: vašnā Auramazdāhā imā dahyāva, tayā adam adarši hadā anā Pārsā kārā, tayā hacāma atṛsa, manā bājim abara. Text in Schmitt 2000: 61.

[29] DSe §3 = DNa §3 = XPh §3: θāti Dārayavauš xšāyaθiya: vašna Auramazdāha imā dahyāva, tayā adam agṛbāyam apataram hacā Parsā; adamšam patiyaxšayai̯; manā bājim abaraha. There follows one other phrase before the list commences ("That which was proclaimed to them by me, that they did. My law — that held them" tayašām hacāma aθanhya, ava akunava; dātam taya manā avadis adāraya). Texts in Schmitt 2000: 29, 91; Kent 1953: 141.

> Proclaims Darius the King: If you should think thus: "May I feel no fear from any
> other," then protect this Persian army. If the Persian army should be protected, happi-
> ness will be undestroyed for the longest time.[30]

As this passage makes clear, the issue is not just conquest or pacification in a narrowly military
sense, but the restoration of primordial happiness and the accomplishment of God's will for
humanity. Thus, Old Persian *šiyāti*, which means "happiness," occurs twenty-three times in the
corpus of Achaemenian inscriptions. All twenty-two of the other occurrences are in variants of
the cosmogonic account, where it always denotes the last of the Wise Lord's original creations:
"happiness for mankind" (*šiyāti ... martiyahyā*).[31] Considering DPe §§2 and 3 together, we
come to understand that the Persian army was responsible for three interrelated accomplish-
ments: (1) it inspired fear in all other lands-and-peoples; (2) this led those lands and peoples
to pay tribute (*bāji*) to the Persian king; (3) this led to the restoration of a happiness that "will
be undestroyed for the longest time," that is, an enduring happiness that comes with the establishment of a Pax Persiana, imposed by military force, but opening onto a final eternity whose
bliss and perfection mirror those of the era before the assault of the Lie.

IV

If DPg describes the unity of the original cosmos, fresh from the Wise Lord's hand, and
contrasts this with the lacerated state that characterizes existence in historic time, DPe speaks
of the way to reverse this fall from perfection, pointing to the Achaemenian king and the Persian army as prime agents in the process. DPd pursues the argument further still, indicating
why this role fell to the Persians and identifying the obstacles they had to overcome in order to
fulfill their mission.

As regards the former point, the assertion is simple enough:

> Proclaims Darius the King: This land-and-people Persia, which the Wise Lord be-
> stowed on me, is good. Possessed of good horses, possessed of good people, by the
> will of the Wise Lord and of me, Darius the King, it feels no fear of any other.[32]

Three points are worth making. First, the adjective *naiba*, which here modifies Persia, is a religiously charged term that connotes a moral, aesthetic, and ethical status attuned to the divine.[33]
Although the word occurs eight times, only Persia and the Persian kingship (or kingdom, the
semantic range of *xšaça* encompasses both) are said to be *naiba* by nature.[34] Uniquely gifted,
Persia possess animate resources — good men and good horses — that give it an advantage
over all other lands-and-peoples, but insofar as these are a gift of God, they bring with them a

---

[30] DPe §3: *θāti Dārayavauš xšāyaθiya: yadi avaθā
maniyāhai̯: hacā aniyanā mā tr̥sam, imam Pārsam
kāram pādi; yadi kāra Pārsa pāta ahati, hayā duvaištam
šiyātiš āxšatā.* Text in Schmitt 2000: 61.

[31] On the semantics of this highly significant term, see
Herrenschmidt 1991; Kellens 1995: 34–38; Piras 1994–
95; and Lincoln 2003.

[32] DPd §2: *θāti Dārayavauš xšāyaθiya: iyam dahyāu̯š
Pārsa, tayām manā Auramazdā frābara, hayā
naibā uvaspā umartiyā, vašnā Auramazdāhā manacā
Dārayavahau̯š xšāyaθiyahyā hacā aniyanā nai̯ tr̥sati.*
Text in Schmitt 2000: 58.

[33] On the semantics and significance of Old Persian
naiba, see Kent 1953: 192; Herzfeld 1938: 266–67, with
comparison to Ossetic (Iron) *nōib* "holy."

[34] Note also DSp §1: "The great Wise Lord is the greatest
of the gods. He created Darius (as) king. He bestowed
the kingship/kingdom on him, which is good (*naibam*),
whose chariots are good, whose horses are good, whose
people are good." *Auramazdā vazr̥ka haya maθišta
bagānām hau̯ Dārayavaum XŠyam adā hau̯šai̯ xšaçam
frābara taya naibam taya uraθam uvaspam umartiyam.*
Text in Kent 1953: 146.

divine responsibility. Everything else described as "good" (*naiba*) becomes so only as the result of some constructive action undertaken by the Persian king, as in the following examples.

> Proclaims Darius the King: When the Wise Lord made me king in this earth/empire, by the Wise Lord's will, I made everything good (*naibam*).[35]

> Proclaims Xerxes the King: By the Wise Lord's will, I made this colonnade of all lands-and-peoples. Much other good (*naibam*) was made in Persepolis: that I made and my father made it. That which is made that seems good (*naibam*), all that we made by the Wise Lord's will.[36]

> Proclaims Darius the King: Much that was ill-done, that I made good (*naibam*). The lands-and-peoples were seething (in rebellion), one smote the other. This I did by the Wise Lord's will, so that one does not smite the other any more.[37]

Having been given a good land from which to work, a land blessed with good men and horses — who in turn will fill his armies — the Persian king works to make other things good. And because this task is divinely ordained, neither he, nor his army, nor his people need feel fear of any other. Rather, they cause others to fear, submit, obey, and bear tribute.

Immediately after commenting upon the fearlessness of the Persian land-and-people, DPd proceeds to identify the three greatest forces that cause fear and disrupt the state of happiness God intended for humanity. To recover the primordial state of unity, wholeness, and bliss, it is thus necessary to vanquish these dangers.

> Proclaims Darius the King: May the Wise Lord bear me aid, together with all the gods, and may the Wise Lord protect this land-and-people from the enemy army, from famine, from the Lie.[38]

Although this triad of ills has often been studied as a set, it is also important to understand them as a sequence.[39] Logically (and chronologically) first is the menace that is named last in the text: the Lie, whose entry into creation caused the loss of unity. Thus, whereas there is only one Truth, falsehood by nature implies duplicity in the most literal sense, that is, a deceptive duality that plays on the difference between the way things are and the way one's speech makes them seem to be. The Lie thus manifests itself in countless ways, all of them corrosive of morality, harmony, decency, and order. Where true speech — in the form of promises, contracts, treaties, vows, oaths, solemn pledges, honest testimony, sincere acts of self-disclosure, and the like — binds people together, building trust and creating the basis for future cooperation, false speech does precisely the opposite, sowing mistrust, confusion, suspicion, hostility, envy, resentment, and hate. False speech — in such forms as perjury, heresy, slander, fraud,

---

[35] DSi §2: *θāti Dārayavauš XŠ yaθā AM mām XŠyam akunauš ahyāyā BUyā vašnā AMha visam naibam akunavam.* Text in Kent 1953: 144.

[36] XPa §3: *θāti Xšayaṛšā xšāyaθiya: vašnā Auramazdāhā imam duvarθim visadahyum adam akunavam; vasai aniyašci naibam kṛtam anā Pārsā, taya adam akunavam utamai taya pitā akunauš; tayapati kṛtam vainatai naibam, ava visam vašnā Auramazdāhā akumā.* Text in Schmitt 2000: 68.

[37] DSe §4: *θāti Dārayavauš XŠ: vasi taya duškartam āha, ava naibam akunavam. dahyāva ayauda, aniya ani-*

yam aja. ava adam akunavam vašnā Auramazdāhā yaθā aniya aniyam nai jati cinā. Text in Kent: 141.

[38] DPd §3: *θāti Dārayavauš xšāyaθiya: manā Auramazdā upastām baratu hadā visaibiš bagḁbiš, utā imām dahyāum Auramazdā pātu hacā haināyā, hacā dušiyārā, hacā drauḡā.*

[39] The older analysis of Benveniste 1938 now must be modified in light of Panaino 1986. See also Herrenschmidt 1991.

breach of contract, deceit, seduction, beguilement, treason, sedition, and so forth — not only produces concrete harm, it also breeds mistrust and resentment, driving people apart and leading them to resolve their differences, not through speech (which has proven untrustworthy), but through violent action.

The Lie thus gives rise to war, or at least to the threat described as the "enemy army." Here, it should be noted that the term translated in this fashion (Old Persian *hainā*) had the most sinister connotations and was used only for non-Persian troops.[40] In pointed contrast, the much more benign term *kāra* was reserved for the Persian army or, more precisely for the Persian people-in-arms, since this word could also be used of the same men when they turned their energies to peaceful occupations (Benveniste 1969: 111–12). The threat of an enemy army (*hainā*) forced them to put down their tools of productive labor and pick up weapons, with the consequence that when the *kāra*-at-peace became the *kāra*-at-arms, the herds, fields, and crops were abandoned. Which is to say, once the Lie had manifested itself so powerfully as to cause war, the threat of the enemy army subsequently led to famine.

Clearly enough, the triple scourges were to be confronted and overcome by their opposites. It was not sufficient, however, for the Persian army to vanquish the enemy army, fighting on the defensive. Rather, the Persian army had to fight on behalf of Truth, had to conquer not only its military foes, but also the Lie that inspired them, and had to do so not just in one battle or on one terrain, but had to triumph over falsehood everywhere. Only then could all people return to peaceful activities, generating prosperity and surpluses sufficient to obviate all threat of famine. It is this situation — conclusive defeat of the Lie by the Truth, the triumph of the Persian army over all others, and the production of enduring global abundance — that Darius anticipated in DPe §3, when advising his successors "If the Persian army should be protected, happiness will be undestroyed for the longest time." [41]

V

This brings us to DPf, the last of the set to be considered. After listing Darius's royal titles, the text continues as follows.

> Says Darius the King: On this terrace, here where this palace (or: fortress) is built, previously there was no palace built here. By the Wise Lord's will, I built this palace. The Wise Lord and all the gods desired that this palace be built and I built it. I built it solid and beautiful, just as I desired it.

> Says Darius the King: May the Wise Lord protect me, together with all the gods, and this palace, *and also those assembled here on this terrace.*[42]

---

[40] The *daēvic* nature of Old Persian *hainā* and its Avestan cognate *haēnā* has been recognized since Bartholomae 1904: 1729. On the systematic opposition of demonic (*daēvic*) and divine (*ahuric*) vocabularies in Iranian languages, see Güntert 1914.

[41] DPe §3: *yadi kāra Pārsa pāta ahati, hayā duvaištam šiyātiš āxšatā.* Text in Schmitt 2000: 61.

[42] DPf: §1: *ak Dariamauš sunkir nanri kat hima mur halmarriš hi kušika appuka hima halmarriš inni kušik zau-min Uramazdana hi halmarriš u kušiya ak Uramazda hi zila tukminina nap marpepda idaka appa hi halmarriš kušika ak u kušiya kutta kušiya tarma ak šišni kutta šillak hi zila sap u tukmana. Ak Dariamauš sunkir nanri u Uramazda un nuškišni nap marpepda idaka ak kutta halmarriš hi kutta šarak kat hi ikka kappaka.* I am grateful to Matt Stolper for his kind assistance in the interpretation of this passage.

In contrast to the three other inscriptions with which this one is grouped, DPf has an immediacy and an almost deictic quality to it. It speaks of the very place on which it is inscribed and of the people assembled on that place.[43] Nothing in this inscription addresses the question of who these people are, what brings them to Persepolis, or what is their relation to the building and the king. All those questions, however, do receive oblique attention in the inscription placed right beside DPf: DPg, the text with which we began.

> Under the protection of the Wise Lord, *these are the lands-and-peoples who made this (palace) that is made here:* Persia, Media, and other lands, with other languages, with mountains and plains ... etc.[44]

Although Darius states in DPf that he himself built the palace, while giving credit to all the diverse lands-and-peoples of the empire in DPg, there is no contradiction between the two texts. Rather, construction of the capital city is ultimately credited to the Wise Lord, who works through the king, just as the king works through the labor force that he assembled. Of particular note, however, is the international nature of that labor force, which came from every part of the empire — "Persia, Media, and other lands, with other languages" — bringing distinctive skills, tools, and materials with them. The palace is thus construed as something like the inverse image of the Biblical Tower of Babel, that is, the product of international collaboration, where human difference, as measured by language, was dissolved, rather than created. Or, to put the point back into an Iranian frame of reference, the construction of the palace constituted the reversal of the Lie's primordial assault and the reunification of a previously sundered humanity.

Ongoing use of the palace also served to reunite peoples and goods, through the ceremonial presentation of tribute. One gets a better sense of how this act was theorized, however, when one realizes that the tribute bearers depicted on the Apadāna stairs bore *con*-tributions of things that had been *dis*-tributed as the result of the Lie's assault, and the *con*-centration of those goods — also of those peoples — at the imperial center was the means of reversing the fragmentation and strife that had characterized existence ever since.

The relief sculptures depict delegations representing twenty-three lands-and-peoples as they bring tribute to the Persian king. Each of these delegations is led toward him by a Persian or Median official, and the order of the march reflects geographic distance from the Persian center. There is, however, no Persian delegation, as Persians were exempt from tribute (Herodotus 3.97; Wiesehöfer 1989). The first delegation is that of the Medes, led in by a Persian, after which follow Elamites, Armenians, Babylonians, and others, down to Libyans and Ethiopians at the end of the file.

Each delegation is quite distinct from the others in their physiognomy and clothing, and the artists were so concerned to depict national, racial, and cultural difference that the reliefs have been called a veritable ethnographic museum (Dandamaev and Lukonin 1989: 251). Painstaking attention was also given to the different animals each delegation brought with it and the material objects they conferred, down to the containers in which these were carried

---

[43] Other prayer formulae ask the Wise Lord to protect the King, his household, the Persian land-and-people, the kingship/kingdom, and all that the King has built (AsH §2, DPd §3, DPh §2, DNa §5, DSe §6, DSf §4, DSj §3, DSn, DSs, DSt §2, DH §2, XPa §4, XPb §3, XPc §3, XPf §5, XPg, XPh §5, XSc §2, XV §3, A¹Pa §3, A²Sa, A²Sd §2, A²Ha §2, A²Hc §3, A³Pa §4, D²Sa). No other variant, however, seeks divine protection for the empire's subject peoples. Here, once again, DPf is unique.

[44] DPg §2: *ina ṣilli ša Urumazda aganētu mātāti ša agâ īpušā ša akanna epšu Parsu Madāya u mātāti madêtu šanêtima lišānu šanitu ša šadî u mātu ....*

(figs. 12.3–4). So much so that it is easy to misread the relief in naïve democratic fashion as a celebration of diversity.

One must carefully note, however, that the relief captures all these people, animals, and objects as they mount the stairs, which is to say, in their very last moment of existence in the state of fragmentation and diaspora that has marked history since the assault of the Lie. Directly they stand assembled upon the platform of the Apadāna itself, all of them — animate and inanimate — will have left their provincial identities behind and been absorbed (or dissolved) into the imperial whole. At that moment, the state of wholeness, totality, and "happiness for mankind" that the Wise Lord made the crown of his original creation will have been restored, at least at the imperial center: a microcosm, where representatives of all the lands-and-peoples stand assembled, so the Great King can call God's blessing upon them. Later, as surplus of all goods accumulates at the center, this can be returned to the peripheries. At that point, the entire world becomes happy, prosperous, peaceful, and whole once again, as history ends and a state of eschatological perfection opens onto eternity, thanks to the work of the Achaemenian king, the Persian army, and the tribute bearers of every land-and-people.

Or so the ideologists of empire believed and wished to believe. Not quite Frazer's model of sacred kingship, nor a secular model of political economy, but — if I am not mistaken — something that might legitimately be understood as a theology of empire, in which the king is theorized as God's chosen, who reunites the world and restores its perfection by processes that other, lesser-minded types might describe as conquest, domination, and tribute.

Figure 12.1. A Portion of the Relief Sculptures on the Apadāna Steps, Persepolis. Nine of the Twenty-three Delegations that Fill the Staircase Appear in this Photo (Walser 1966: pl. 3)

Figure 12.2. Relief Panel Initially Placed at the Summit of the Apadāna Stairs, Showing an Enthroned Darius, as He Receives the First Delegation of Tribute Bearers (Oriental Institute Museum P.57121)

Figure 12.3. Apadāna Reliefs, Detail. Contrast the Babylonian Delegation Above (led by a Mede) with the Assyrians Below (led by a Persian). Difference Is Marked at Every Level: Hats, Robes, Shoes, Beard and Hair, Facial Features, Animals, Vessels, and Gifts (Oriental Institute Museum P.29002)

Figure 12.4. Last and Most Exotic of the Delegations, That of the Ethiopians (led by a Mede). Note the Giraffe and the Ivory Tusk that the Third Man in Line Carries on His Shoulder (Oriental Institute Museum P.28981)

BIBLIOGRAPHY

Ackerman, Robert

    1987   *J. G. Frazer: His Life and Work.* Cambridge: Cambridge University Press.

    1991   *The Myth and Ritual School: J. G. Frazer and the Cambridge Ritualists.* Theorists of Myth 2. Garland Reference Library of the Humanities 1282. New York: Garland.

Ahn, Gregor

    1992   *Religiöse Herrscherlegitimation im Achämenidischen Iran: Die Voraussetzungen und die Struktur ihrer Argumentation.* Acta Iranica 31; Textes et mémoires 17. Leiden: Brill.

Bartholomae, Christian

    1904   *Altiranisches Wörterbuch.* Berlin: Walter de Gruyter.

Benveniste, Émile

    1938   "Traditions indo-iraniennes sur les classes sociales." *Journal asiatique* 230: 529–49.

    1969   *Le vocabulaire des institutions indo-européennes.* 2 volumes. Paris: Éditions de Minuit.

Briant, Pierre

    1982   *Rois, tributes et paysans: Études sur les formations tributaires du Moyen-Orient ancien.* Annales littéraires de l'Université de Besançon 269; Centre de recherches d'histoire ancienne 43. Paris: Les Belles Lettres.

    1986   "Guerre, tribut, et forces productives dans l'empire acheménide." *Dialogues d'histoire ancienne* 12: 33–48.

Briant, Pierre, and Clarisse Herrenschmidt, editors

    1989   *Le tribut dans l'empire perse* (Actes de la table ronde de Paris, 12–13 December 1986). Travaux de l'Institut d'études iraniennes de l'Université de la Sorbonne nouvelle 13. Paris: Peeters.

Cahill, Nicholas

    1985   "The Treasury at Persepolis: Gift-giving at the City of the Persians." *American Journal of Archaeology* 89: 373–89.

Calmeyer, Peter

    1980   "Textual Sources for the Interpretation of Achaemenian Palace Decorations." *Iran* 18: 55–63.

    1985–86   "Dareios in Bagestana und Xerxes in Persepolis: Zur parataktischen Komposition achaimenidischer Herrscherdarstellungen." *Visible Religion* 4–5: 76–95.

Carpentier, Martha C.

    1998   *Ritual, Myth, and the Modernist Text: The Influence of Jane Ellen Harrison on Joyce, Eliot, and Woolf.* Library of Anthropology 12. Amsterdam: Gordon & Breach.

Dandamaev, Muhammad A., and Vladimir G. Lukonin

    1989   *The Culture and Social Institutions of Ancient Iran.* Cambridge: Cambridge University Press.

Descat, Raymond

    1985   "Mnésimachos, Hérodote et le système tributaire acheménide." *Révue des études anciennes* 87: 97–112.

Duchesne-Guillemin, Jacques

    1979   "La royauté iranienne et le xvarenah." In *Iranica,* edited by Gherardo Gnoli, pp. 375–
                86. Series minor, Istituto universitario orientale, Seminario di studi asiatici 10. Na-
                ples: Istituto universitario orientale.

Dumézil, Georges

    1924   *Le festin d'immortalité: Étude de mythologie comparée indo-européenne.* Annales du
                Musé Guimet, Bibliothèque d'études 34. Paris: Librairie Orientaliste Paul Geuthner.

    1929   *Le problème des centaures: Étude de mythologie comparée indo-européenne.* Annales
                du Musée Guimet, Bibliothèque d'études 41. Paris: Librairie Orientaliste Paul Geuth-
                ner.

Engnell, Ivan

    1943   *Studies in Divine Kingship in the Ancient Near East.* Uppsala: Almqvist & Wiksell.

Erdmann, Kurt

    1960   "Persepolis — Daten und Deutungen." *Mitteilungen der Deutschen Orient Gesell-
                schaft* 92: 21–47.

Frankfort, Henri

    1948   *Kingship and the Gods: A Study of Ancient Near Eastern Religion as the Integration
                of Society and Nature.* Oriental Institute Essay. Chicago: University of Chicago Press.

Frankfort, Henri; H. A. Groenewegen-Frankfort; John A. Wilson; Thorkild Jacobsen; and William
Andrew Irwin

    1946   *The Intellectual Adventure of Ancient Man: An Essay on Speculative Thought in the
                Ancient Near East.* Chicago: University of Chicago Press.

Fennelly, James

    1980   "The Persepolis Ritual." *Biblical Archaeology* 43: 135–62.

Fraser, Robert, editor

    1991   *Sir James Frazer and the Literary Imagination: Essays in Affinity and Influence.* New
                York: St. Martin's Press.

Frei, Peter, and Klaus Koch

    1984   *Reichsidee und Reichsorganisation im Perserreich.* Orbis Biblicus et Orientalis 55.
                Göttingen: Vandenhoeck & Ruprecht.

Frye, Richard N.

    1964   "The Charisma of Kingship in Ancient Iran." *Iranica Antiqua* 4: 36–54.

Gadd, C. J.

    1948   *Ideas of Divine Rule in the Ancient East.* Schweich Lectures 1945. London: Oxford
                University Press.

Gaster, Theodore H.

    1961   *Thespis: Ritual, Myth, and Drama in the Ancient Near East.* Anchor Books A230.
                Garden City: Doubleday.

    1969   *Myth, Legend, and Custom in the Old Testament: A Comparative Study, with Chap-
                ters from Sir James George Frazer's Folklore in the Old Testament.* New York:
                Harper & Row.

Ghirshman, Roland

    1957   "Notes iraniennes VII: à propos de Persépolis." *Artibus Asiae* 20: 265–78.

Gnoli, Gherardo

    1984   "Note sullo xvarenah." *Acta Iranica* 23: 207–18.

Güntert, Hermann

    1914   *Über die ahurischen und daēvischen ausdrücke im Awesta: Eine semasiologische stu-die*. Sitzungsberichte der Heidelberger Akademie der Wissenschaften, Philosophisch-historische Klasse 5. Heidelberg: C. Winter.

Hachmann, Rolf

    1995   "Die Völkerschaften auf den Bildwerken von Persepolis." In *Beiträge zur Kulturge-schichte Vorderasiens: Festschrift für Rainer Michael Boehmer*, edited by Uwe Fink-beiner, Reinhard Dittmann, and Harald Hauptmann, pp. 195–223. Mainz am Rhein: Philipp von Zabern.

Harrison, Jane Ellen

    1912   *Themis: A Study of the Social Origins of Greek Religion*. Cambridge: University Press.

    1922   *Prolegomena to the Study of Greek Religion*. Cambridge: Cambridge University Press.

Hartner, Willy, and Richard Ettinghausen

    1964   "The Conquering Lion — The Life Cycle of a Symbol." *Oriens* 17: 161–71.

Herrenschmidt, Clarisse

    1976   "Désignation de l'empire et concepts politiques de Darius Ier d'après ses inscriptions en vieux perse." *Studia Iranica* 5: 33–65.

    1977   "Les créations d'Ahuramazda." *Studia Iranica* 6: 17–58.

    1990   "Nugae Antico-Persianae." *Achaemenid History* 4: 54–60.

    1991   "Vieux-perse šiyāti." In *La religion iranienne à l'époque achéménide* (Actes du col-loque de Liège, 11 December 1987), edited by Jean Kellens, pp. 13–21. Iranica Anti-qua Supplément 5. Ghent: Iranica Antiqua.

Herzfeld, Ernst

    1938   *Altpersische Inschriften*. Archäologische Mitteilungen aus Iran 1. Berlin: Dietrich Re-imer.

    1941   *Iran in the Ancient East: Archaeological Studies Presented in the Lowell Lectures at Boston*. London: Oxford University Press.

Hinz, Walther

    1969   *Altiranische Funde und Forschungen*. Berlin: Walter de Gruyter.

Hooke, Samuel Henry, editor

    1933   *Myth and Ritual: Essays on the Myth and Ritual of the Hebrews in Relation to the Culture Pattern of the Ancient East*. London: Oxford University Press.

    1935   *The Labyrinth: Further Studies in the Relation between Myth and Ritual in the An-cient World*. London: Society for Promoting Christian Knowledge.

    1958   *Myth, Ritual, and Kingship: Essays on the Theory and Practice of Kingship in the An-cient Near East and in Israel*. Oxford: Clarendon Press.

Jacobs, Bruno

    1982   "Persepolisdelegationen und Satrapienordnung." *Acta Praehistorica et Archaeologica* 13–14: 75–84.

Jacobsen, Thorkild

    1976   *The Treasures of Darkness: A History of Mesopotamian Religion*. New Haven: Yale University Press.

Jamzadeh, Parivash

    1992   "The Apadāna Reliefs and the Metaphor of Conquest." *Iranica Antiqua* 27: 125–47.

Kellens, Jean

    1995   "L'âme entre le cadavre et le paradis." *Journal asiatique* 283: 19–56.

Kent, Roland G.

    1953   *Old Persian: Grammar, Texts, Lexicon*. American Oriental Series 33. New Haven: American Oriental Society.

Koch, Heidemarie

    1980   "Steuern in der achämenidischen Persis?" *Zeitschrift für Assyriologie* 70: 105–37.

Koch, Klaus

    1983   "Die Völkerrepresentänten auf den Reliefs von Persepolis und den achaimenidischen Gräbern." *Zeitschrift der deutschen morgenlandischen Gesellschaft, Supplement* 5: 290–300.

Kramer, Samuel Noah

    1969   *The Sacred Marriage Rite: Aspects of Faith, Myth, and Ritual in Ancient Sumer*. Bloomington: Indiana University Press.

Kuhrt, Amélie

    1984   "The Achaemenid Concept of Kingship." *Iran* 22: 156–60.

Labat, René

    1939   *Le caractère religieux de la royauté assyro-babylonienne*. Paris: Librairie d'Amérique et d'Orient.

Langdon, Stephen

    1914   *Tammuz and Ishtar: A Monograph upon Babylonian Religion and Theology*. Oxford: Clarendon Press.

Lanwerd, Susanne

    1993   *Mythos, Mutterrecht und Magie: Zur Geschichte religionswissenschaftlicher Begriffe*. Berlin: Dietrich Reimer.

Lecoq, Pierre

    1974   "La langue des inscriptions achéménides." *Acta Iranica* 3: 55–62.

    1997   *Les inscriptions de la Perse achéménide*. L'Aube des peuples. Paris: Gallimard.

Lincoln, Bruce

    1996   "Old Persian fraša and vašna: Two Terms at the Intersection of Religious and Imperial Discourse." *Indogermanische Forschungen* 101: 147–67.

    2003   "À la recherché du paradis perdu." *History of Religions* 43: 139–54.

    2007   *Religion, Empire, and Torture: The Case of Achaemenian Persia*. Chicago: University of Chicago Press.

    2012   *'Happiness for Mankind': Achaemenian Religion and the Imperial Project*. Acta Iranica 53. Louvain: Peeters.

Malinowski, Bronislaw

    1954   "Myth in Primitive Psychology." In *Magic, Science and Religion, and Other Essays*, edited by Bronislaw Malinowski, pp. 93–148. Doubleday Anchor Books A23. Garden City: Doubleday.

Manganaro, Marc

    1992   *Myth, Rhetoric, and the Voice of Authority: A Critique of Frazer, Eliot, Frye, and Campbell*. New Haven: Yale University Press.

Murray, Gilbert

    1912   *Four Stages of Greek Religion: Studies Based on a Course of Lectures Delivered in April 1912 at Columbia University.* Columbia University Lectures. New York: Columbia University Press.

Nylander, Carl

    1974   "Al-Beruni and Persepolis." *Acta Iranica* 1: 137–50.

Panaino, Antonio

    1986   "Hainā-, dušiyāra-, drauga-: Un confronto antico-persiano avestico." *Socalizio glottologico Milanese* 27: 95–102.

Piras, Andrea

    1994–95   "A proposito di antico-persiano šiyāti." *Studi Orientali e Linguistici* 5: 91–97.

Pope, Arthur Upham

    1957a   "Persepolis as a Ritual City." *Archaeology* 10: 123–30.

    1957b   "Persepolis Considered as a Ritual City." In *Proceedings of the Twenty-Second Congress of Orientalists Held in Istanbul, 15–22 September 1951*, Volume 2: *Communications,* edited by Ahmed Zeki Velidi Togan, pp. 58–66. Leiden: Brill.

Richards, John W.

    1979   "Sacral Kings of Iran." *Mankind Quarterly* 20: 143–60.

Root, Margaret Cool

    1979   *The King and Kingship in Achaemenid Art: Essay on the Creation of an Iconography of Empire.* Acta Iranica 19; Textes et mémoires 9. Leiden: Brill.

Sancisi-Weerdenburg, Heleen

    1991   "Nowruz at Persepolis." *Achaemenid History* 7: 173–201.

    1998   "Bājī." *Achaemenid History* 11: 23–34.

Schmidt, Erich F.

    1953   *Persepolis*, Volume 1: *Structures, Reliefs, Inscriptions.* Oriental Institute Publications 68. Chicago: The Oriental Institute.

    1970   *Persepolis*, Volume 3: *The Royal Tombs and Other Monuments.* Oriental Institute Publications 70. Chicago: The Oriental Institute.

Schmitt, Rüdiger

    1977   "Königtum im alten Iran." *Saeculum* 28: 384–95.

    1991   *The Bisitun Inscriptions of Darius the Great: Old Persian Text.* Corpus Inscriptionum Iranicarum 1. London: School of Oriental and African Studies.

    1999   *Beiträge zu altpersischen Inschriften.* Wiesbaden: Reichert Verlag.

    2000   *The Old Persian Inscriptions of Naqsh-i Rustam and Persepolis.* Corpus Inscriptionum Iranicarum 2. London: School of Oriental and African Studies.

Segal, Robert A., editor

    1996   *Ritual and Myth: Robertson Smith, Frazer, Hooke, and Harrison.* Theories of Myth 5. New York: Garland.

    1998   *The Myth and Ritual Theory: An Anthology.* Malden: Blackwell.

Shahbazi, Ali Shahpur

    1978   "New Aspects of Persepolitan Studies." *Gymnasium* 85: 487–500.

    1985   *Old Persian Inscriptions of the Persepolis Platform.* Corpus Inscriptionum Iranicarum 1. London: Lund Humphries.

Smith, Jonathan Z.

> 1978   "When the Bough Breaks." In *Map Is Not Territory: Studies in the History of Religions*, edited by Jonathan Z. Smith, pp. 208–39. Studies in Judaism in Late Antiquity 23. Leiden: Brill.

Stocking, George W.

> 1995   *After Tylor: British Social Anthropology, 1888–1951.* Madison: University of Wisconsin Press.

Stronach, David

> 1985   "The Apadāna: A Signature of the Line of Darius." In *De l'Indus aux Balkans: Recueil à la mémoire de Jean Deshayes*, edited by Jean-Louis Huot, Marguerite Yon, and Yves Calvet, pp. 433–45. Paris: Recherche sur les civilisations.

Tilia, Ann Britt

> 1972   *Studies and Restorations at Persepolis and Other Sites in Fars.* Reports and Memoirs 16. Rome: Istituto Italiano per il Medio ed Estremo Oriente.

Trümpelmann, Leo

> 1983   "Zu den Gebäuden von Persepolis und ihrer Funktion." In *Kunst, Kultur und Geschichte der Achämenidenzeit und ihr Fortleben,* edited Heidemarie Koch and D. N. MacKenzie, pp. 225–37. Archäologische Mitteilungen aus Iran, Ergänzungsband 10. Berlin: Dietrich Reimer.

Vickery, John B.

> 1973   *The Literary Impact of the Golden Bough.* Princeton: Princeton University Press.

Walser, Gerold

> 1966   *Die Völkerschaften auf den Reliefs von Persepolis: Historische Studien über den sogenannten Tributzug an der Apadānatreppe.* Teheraner Forschungen 2. Berlin: Mann.

Weissbach, Franz H., editor

> 1911   *Die Keilinschriften der Achämeniden.* Vorderasiatische Bibliothek 3. Leipzig: J. C. Hinrich.

Weston, Jessie L.

> 1920   *From Ritual to Romance: An Account of the Holy Grail from Ancient Ritual to Christian Symbol.* Cambridge: Cambridge University Press.

Widengren, Geo

> 1953   *Religionens Värld: Religionsfenomenologiska studier och översikter.* Stockholm: Svenska Kyrkans Diakonstyrelses.
> 1955   *Stand und Aufgaben der iranischen Religionsgeschichte.* Leiden: Brill.
> 1959   "The Sacral Kingship of Iran." In *La Regalità sacra: Contributi al tema dell'VIII Congresso Internazionale di Storia delle Religioni (Rome, April 1955),* pp. 242–57. Studies in the History of Religions 4. Leiden: Brill.
> 1965   *Die Religionen Irans.* Die Religionen der Menschheit 14. Stuttgart: W. Kohlhammer.
> 1974   "La royauté de l'Iran antique." *Acta Iranica* 1: 84–89.
> 1983   "Die Neujahrsfest im alten Iran." *Iranzamin* 2: 35–42.

Wiesehöfer, Josef

> 1989   "*Tauta gar en atelea*: Beobachtungen zur Abgabenfreiheit im Achaimenidenreich." In *Le tribut dans l'empire perse* (Actes de la table ronde de Paris, 12–13 December 1986), edited by Pierre Briant and Clarisse Herrenschmidt, pp. 183–92. Travaux de l'Institut d'études iraniennes de l'Université de la Sorbonne nouvelle 13. Paris: Peeters.

13

DIVINITY AND POWER IN ANCIENT ROME

GREG WOOLF, ST. ANDREWS UNIVERSITY*

Debates over ruler cult in ancient Rome have taken a different course from those in Oriental Studies. Attention was at one time focused on the precise question of whether or not Roman emperors were considered gods. There is now a near consensus that it is more profitable to explore a wide variety of associations of the divine with political power in a more nuanced fashion, one that incorporates ceremonial, imagery, sacral functions, and titulature and does not treat "god" as a concept that can be easily translated from one cultural system to another. There is certainly a danger that this broader program of exploration will become less focused than older paradigms, but this paper hopes to show the advantages of the approach. In particular, it argues that, viewed in a suitably broad context, the old problem of "How did Romans and Greeks really come to accept a human being as a god?" is to be replaced with the question "How did the ancient Mediterranean manage without divine kings for so much of the last millennium B.C.?" This paper argues that this apparent absence is in fact a product of the way we have posed the question of divine kingship.

ROME WITHOUT RULER CULT?

Ruler worship is not generally considered characteristic of Roman society in the Republican period (conventionally 509–31 B.C.), a period during which the polity developed from a conventional city-state to a regional hegemon and finally a territorial empire controlling the entire Mediterranean basin and its immediate hinterlands. Properly speaking, the cult of the emperors extended from the accession of the first emperor, Octavian/Augustus (conventionally dated to 31 B.C.) to the conversion to Christianity of the emperor Constantine in A.D. 312. Framed in these terms, divine kingship in Rome is a phenomenon limited to the early empire, commonly termed the Principate. Yet there are good reasons to nuance this picture.

First, Romans believed that they had been ruled by kings for two and a half centuries before the foundation of the oligarchic republic. Many of the traditions about the regal period were negative, and many of the stories recall those told by Greeks about their own age of tyrants. But there was also a positive tradition about the kings of Rome, especially the founders, and some of these positive traditions concerned cult (cf. Fears 1977: 85–119). The creation of much of the Roman religious system was ascribed to the second king, Numa, who was said to have had the nymph Egeria as a lover. His predecessor Romulus was believed to be the son of Mars, and to have been taken up to heaven at the end of his reign. He was subsequently worshipped as Quirinus. A more distant founder figure, the Trojan refugee Aeneas, was the son of Venus. Even before Aeneas, tradition had it, Hercules had visited the future site of Rome.

* Conversations with other participants at Chicago not only broadened my perspective on these issues, but also helped me see how differently the Roman case is debated when compared to scholarship on the ancient Near East. I am grateful to all my fellow participants and in particular to Nicole Brisch for the invitation to attend. Some of my comments on the cult of the *divi* would be even less coherent were it not for conversations with Gwynaeth Macintyre, whose current work on the subject will eventually make it even clearer. My thanks to all.

Cult was paid to him from a very early period at the Ara Maxima near the Tiber port. He too was believed to have been deified after his death. Even during the Republic a number of ritual functions were carried out by the *rex sacrorum* (literally the King of Rituals). This strongly suggests an original sacral role for the kings.

Second, religious authority of various kinds was concentrated in the hands of the aristocratic oligarchy that replaced the kings. Divine ancestry was claimed — how seriously we cannot say — by many of the oldest aristocratic families. The Julian gens, for example, claimed descent from Venus via Aeneas and his son Iulius. Religious authority in Republican Rome seems to have rested with the Senate, a council made up of ex-magistrates who served for life, subject to them satisfying a property qualification. It was a decree of the Senate issued in 186 B.C., rather than a law passed in the assemblies, which set restrictions on the cult of Bacchus throughout Italy. Portents were reported to the Senate. New cults were authorized by the Senate, and were often introduced on the recommendation of a priestly college that was periodically sent in times of crisis to consult the oracular Sybilline Books. Senators monopolized membership of this and the other major priestly colleges. Some priesthoods — that of the *flamen Dialis* (the priest of Jupiter), for instance — were restricted to an inner circle of families, the patriciate, who claimed descent from those who had been senators in the regal period. A group of prominent rituals involved members of the innermost elite "play-acting" the role of actual deities. Most famous is the triumph in which a victorious general was allegedly carried motionless through the City, his face rouged with ochre to resemble a terra-cotta cult statue, wearing robes borrowed from the cult statue of Jupiter on the Capitol. Other rituals of this kind were performed by the Vestals, unmarried women chosen from aristocratic families. On other occasions, statues of the gods processed around the City or attended banquets with members of the Roman aristocracy. It has been recently argued that it was the cumulative religious authority of the Senate rather than any constitutional pre-eminence, that maintained their ascendancy in Rome over the wide citizen body (North 1990).

Third, Roman hegemony expanded into a world in which ruler cult, understood widely, was already present in many forms. Relatively little is known of the belief systems of the pre-conquest populations of Europe north of the Alps, of the Iberian peninsula nor of north Africa. East of the Adriatic, however, Romans encountered varieties of ruler cult descended in the first instance from the religious fusions created by Alexander the Great and the generals who succeeded him. Those fusions had been created from a combination of Macedonian kingship, with a system of honors developed in Greek cities, with Greek iconography and rituals and with Achaemenid ritual, which itself incorporated elements of Egyptian, Babylonian, and other religious traditions. That Hellenistic matrix is naturally susceptible to the same sort of questions as the Roman one that supplanted it. The Achaemenid emperors were not gods, but wove a web of relations between themselves and a whole series of gods in their subject territories (Kuhrt 1987). Achaemenid court ceremonial, when adopted by Alexander, seemed to some Greeks to demand honors greater than should be paid to any man. Yet Greeks first, then Romans, soon learned to use these and new rituals to domesticate monarchy within their different religious and political understandings of the world. As first aristocratic Roman magistrates and generals, and later emperors and their relatives moved through this world, local communities and corporations received them with customary honors. A dossier can be compiled from the last two centuries B.C. of Roman magistrates receiving god-like honors (*isotheoi timai*) as well as royal insignia by the public vote of Greek communities (Price 1984b: 40–47). Roman emperors in Egypt were, like their royal Macedonian predecessors, treated as pharaohs. Cult of the personification Roma is attested in the eastern Mediterranean area from the beginning of the second century B.C. Cult was even paid to the Roman Senate. It seems quite probable that some similar processes were taking place in the west, despite the relative paucity of the epigraphic and iconographic record. The main indications of this are anecdotes surrounding the treatment of Republican generals: Sertorius in Spain was apparently believed to be advised by a deity in the form of a deer, and a relic of Julius Caesar was revered in a Gallic temple as late as A.D. 69. These apparent transformations of local religious idioms to accommodate Roman invaders may be compared to cargo cults. Equally, the immediate popularity of ruler cult in the western provinces has suggested to some a receptivity based on local tradition. Many scholars have thought they could detect pre-conquest "survivals" in the local forms that Roman imperial cult took in these regions. Ruler cult has also been explained as a response to a collapse of local religious systems. These explanations are not exclusive.

Specifically Roman forms of imperial cult were created both in the subjected provinces and in the city of Rome itself. Many decisions were apparently taken at a local level about what kinds of honors were acceptable when offered by provincial subjects. A mass of testimony refers to ostentatious refusals, on the part of the emperors, of certain honors, often linked to acquiescence in others. So Augustus circulated a decree accepting worship from the association of the Greek cities of the province of Asia (roughly the western part of Anatolian Turkey) but instructed associations of Roman citizens in the province to worship the deified Julius and the goddess Roma. Tiberius, the second emperor, accepted honors voted to himself, along with his mother Livia and the Senate by the Asian cities, but he declined similar honors offered by Spanish communities (Tacitus *Annales* 4.37–38). The fourth emperor, Claudius, wrote to the citizens of Alexandria in Egypt agreeing to statues of himself and his immediate family and that his birthday should be treated as a sacred day, but declining a high priest and temples (P.Lond 1912 = Select Papyri 212). One approach has been to attempt to combine this sort of testimony with evidence for imperial religious foundations, to try to map out an implicit Roman "theology" of the imperial cult, or indeed to trace the evolution of such an entity. But it is now more widely accepted that these highly publicized refusals were in fact performances designed to demonstrate the eminence of the emperors (who else could refuse such honors?) at the same time as their sensitivity to civic sentiment (Charlesworth 1939; Millar 1973). It has also been pointed out that if the emperors did strive to control provincial manifestations of ruler cult, they were markedly unsuccessful in doing so. Octavian/Augustus refused, on visiting Egypt, to pay the Apis bull the homage traditionally performed by pharaohs. Nevertheless, images of him doing so, in traditional pharaonic regalia, were carved on the temple walls at Edfu. As he was identified by a cartouche, it is unlikely that any non-Egyptian audience was intended for this representation. Equally, cities in north Africa had cults of the second emperor, Tiberius, who had ostentatiously refused such cult in his lifetime and was not recognized as a *divus* through the ceremony of *consecratio* after his death as both Caesar and Augustus had been.

The second front on which forms of ruler cult were developed was Rome itself. Like the nobilities of other Italian city-states, the Roman elite had been engaged since at least the third century B.C. with the cluster of literary, representational, and social forms usually termed Hellenism. The reasons why Greek cultural products beguiled so many societies from Parthia to Etruria cannot be considered here. But in Rome, as in all Mediterranean societies undergoing similar encounters, this took the form of debates over what should be accepted, what rejected, and how what was accepted should be best subordinated to local forms and values. Religious practices and ideas were affected as much as anything else. Indigenous forms of ancestor cult are well attested — if not often given that name. Noble families kept images of prominent ancestors along with cult statues of the Lares and Penates, deities given domestic cult. A famous account of Roman noble funerals written in the second century B.C. by the Greek historian Polybius describes a procession that included actors dressed in masks to act out the parts of prominent deceased ancestors. At an annual festival, the *parentalia*, meals were eaten at the graves of the dead and shared with them. The combats fought to the death at the funerals of noble Romans by gladiators have also been regarded by many as tantamount to human sacrifice (although Romans themselves never considered them in this light). All these traditions combined with Greek eschatological debates during the last century of the Republic, at the same time as the most prominent aristocrats were receiving royal and god-like honors from Greek embassies in the east (and occasionally in Rome, too). The best documented instance of these local arrangements concerns the honors paid to Julius Caesar during the last years of his life while he ruled as dictator. His effigy was to be carried in processions like the statues of the gods, he would have a *flamen* (like the priests of Jupiter, Mars, and Quirinus), his statue was placed in the temple of Quirinus, alongside the cult statues of the god, and a temple to his clemency was decreed. His desire for divine honors is often cited as one reason for his assassination, yet similar and greater honors were decreed to his heir Octavian, including the title Augustus and in his case these cults are often regarded as providing legitimacy for the new regime.

Perhaps it is a little artificial to distinguish debates over divine rulers at Rome from those in the provinces. After all, Rome's provinces were not particularly distant. A distinguishing feature of Roman imperialism was the absence of creole administrations or remote provincial satrapies. Roman generals and governors moved back and forth between the metropole and the provinces every few years, there was a steady stream of embassies, and the imperial capital had a huge population drawn from all over the empire. The level of connectivity between Mediterranean communities throughout antiquity and the middle ages has recently been stressed (Horden and Purcell 2000); at no time were levels of trade and migration as high as in the late Republican and early imperial periods. The great monumentalization of Rome during precisely these periods involved the architectural incorporation of Egyptian obelisks and Hellenistic theaters, while domestic luxury looked to styles of ornament and luxury developed in central Italy where Greek, Italian, and Punic technologies and traditions had mingled since the second century B.C. As Rome reached its ancient demographic apogee of around a million, there can have been few deities from the ancient Mediterranean and Near East who did not have worshippers in the capital. A great horde of gods is attested, and many were incorporated into the public cults of the City.

It is, however, important to emphasize the local Italian and Roman roots of ruler cult, owing to a key feature of ancient and modern historiography of the subject. These processes have often been presented in terms of a progressive orientalization of Roman civic cult and political culture. There is support for this in some Roman texts. Some categories of Greek ritual are represented by Roman writers as *superstitio*. (*Superstitio* generally denoted excessive practices, sometimes connected to magic, often to private and illegitimate cult, and contrasted to *religio* which was proper, usually collective, civic cult.) Emperors like Caius and Domitian were attacked, admittedly in texts written after their respective assassinations, for appropriating divine titles and prerogatives. These ancient debates parallel earlier protests at Alexander the Great's appropriation of Achaemenid royal ceremonial. Together they supported an ancient discourse of orientalism, in which easterners were soft, feminized, servile, and fit only to be ruled by tyrants. The transmission of these ideas via classical education made them one of the roots of the much studied nineteenth-century discourses focused on Arab culture and the Ottoman empire. This approach to Roman ruler cult seems to me, however, fundamentally misleading.

Looking across the ancient Mediterranean world as a whole, it is very striking that the kinds of observations made above about early Rome can be replicated wherever there is sufficient testimony. Many Greek cities too had a tradition of kings, many of them allegedly descended from gods. A heroic age was remembered in which mortal kings and deities encountered each other more frequently on the earth than in later periods. Many of these kings were connected with oracular shrines or cult places. There were stories too about Phoenician royalty and Etruscan kings and heroes, and these too had supernatural elements. It is, naturally, possible that some of these stories imitate Near Eastern models, just as some see the Roman stories about Aeneas and Romulus as calques on Greek myth. But it seems just as reasonable to regard these as parallel formations. Athens had a *basileus archon* — a King Magistrate — just as Rome had its *rex sacrorum*. Even if we leave aside the uncertain nature of Bronze Age Aegean kingship, it is very striking that the city-state cultures of the classical Mediterranean commonly associated monarchy with the divine.

Since Fustel de Coulanges (1864), classicists have been accustomed to think of the ancient city-state as a religious as well as a political community. It was in this respect above all that ancient citizenship differed from the notions of citizenship that followed the French and American revolutions. Indeed, those revolutionary appropriations of the Roman Republic have (along with Aristotle and his philosophical successors) created a potentially misleading notion of the ancient city-state as essentially a political community through which rights and duties were distributed among a citizen body, subject to laws and institutions analogous to those of modern nation-states. Common cults were central to participation in the ancient city. Priesthoods were generally — not just in Rome — monopolized by the political elite and aristocratic families. Religious authority tended to reside alongside political, that is with the Senate of the Roman Republic, and with the people in the Athenian democracy. Religious calendars ordered civic life, and civic festivals like the Ludi Romani or the Greater Dionysia at Athens provided occasions for enacting the civic order. Phoenician, Greek, Etruscan, and Roman cities tended to have not exactly patron deities, but a group of deities who were believed to have special fondness for the city. Romans summoned out the greatest gods of cities they were about to attack with the ritual of *evocatio* and built them temples in the City. One way of expressing this relationship has been to say that in some sense the gods were regarded as forming part of the citizen body, sharing in its victories and celebrations, joining with mortal citizens in the commensality that followed blood sacrifice.

What I am suggesting is that if the Greek world before Alexander, or Rome before Augustus, seem to be worlds without ruler cult, this is in part a result of us defining the latter in a rather narrow form. Rather than islands of rationality that anticipated or intimated the secular civil societies of the Enlightenment nation-state, these ancient communities as they became civic had incorporated the divine into political and social institutions. The return of monarchy across the Mediterranean in the Hellenistic and Roman periods resulted in an easy re-adjustment. This was not an orientalization so much as the end of a relatively brief (and anomalous) period in which monarchic elements were, as it were, distributed throughout the City. Hobbes' notion of the sovereign as an artificial monarch, as a sort of robot autocrat, is useful here. Ruler cult existed then in the archaic and classical Mediterranean... so long as by ruler we understand the political hegemony of the city and the social dominance of ancient aristocracies.

This does not mean, naturally, that civic elites did not find the religious consequence of the return of monarchy difficult to negotiate (cf. Levene 1997). The diffidence of the first emperors expressed their own sensitivity to these feelings, and perhaps also their own nervousness at the sudden precipitation of godhead in their persons. Yet the period in which these awkwardnesses are most evident extended only until the middle of the first century A.D. Vespasian reputedly joked on his death bed that he was becoming a god. Tacitus may have complained in the early second century about *graeca adulatio,* but his contemporary Pliny developed a panegyrical form suffused with religious language. Augustus had favored an iconography that emphasized his sacerdotal role and advertised his restoration of ancient cults and temples to traditional deities. By the early second century A.D. the cult of the deified emperors hardly seems to have provoked any reaction. The city of Rome was becoming as filled with their temples as were its provincial colonies.

RULER CULT IN ITS ROMAN CONTEXTS

Historians of ancient Rome have evolved a variety of vocabularies with which to describe what orientalists term divine kingship. Imperial cult and *culte impérial* are effective synonyms for *Herrscherkult,* Ruler Cult, *Kaiserkult,* and the *culte des souverains.* All these terms emphasize the centrality of the *person* of the emperor.

Recently there has been some discussion of *Reichsreligion* or "the religion of the empire" (e.g., Cancik and Rüpke 1997; Rives 1999; Ando 2003). Formulations of this kind are a shorthand for various attempts to delineate a set of religious norms, rules, institutions, and/or beliefs that can justly be considered to be shared by the entire empire, a sort of common imperial religious culture. Yet none of these conceptualizations are entirely satisfactory.

It is true that Roman polytheism was anything but tolerant. Roman hegemony inevitably encouraged some religious forms and discouraged others in the many societies they ruled. Human sacrifice, for example, was feared and associated with magic and it was largely banned. Mutilation of the body was despised and eventually prohibited. There was clearly also a distrust of models of priesthood that were very different from those of Roman and Greek city-states. So Egyptian priesthoods were bound into the administrative framework of the province, Druidism was discouraged and eventually apparently abolished. A strong preference for anthropomorphic representations of deities made itself felt in many regions. New iconographies were created in the north and west, where very few pre-conquest images of the gods are known. Egyptian gods lost their animal heads, first when exported outside Egypt as Isis was during the Hellenistic period, and eventually within Egypt itself. Betyls survived in some parts of the Near East, but anthropomorphic alternatives were devised and widely used. All the same, convergence on some norms of practice and representation stopped a long way short of religious uniformity.

Equally, the empire provided (as some early Christians recognized) a good matrix for the spread of new religious forms. A few of these were now religions in the modern sense of worshipping traditions shared by groups who had nothing else in common (North 1992). These had hardly existed before the Hellenistic and Roman empires and had been completely subordinated to cult embedded in social institutions, above all in those of the city-state. Several factors explain why the empire facilitated religious exchanges. Communications were in general made easier by peace, and improved roads and ports. Latin and especially Greek texts provided media through which local bodies of religious knowledge came into contact. So Judaism and Platonism found new correlations in the philosophy of Philo in the first century A.D., while in late antiquity Chaldaean astronomy and the Egyptian magical tradition known as Heremetica all contributed to a new intellectual paganism, in Greek. Urbanization and military service created environments of intense culture contact. Personal travel was available to many and resulted in overlapping commercial and cultural diasporas of Italians, Greeks, Syrians, and

Jews. Migrations were even imposed on particular sectors including slaves, soldiers, prisoners of war, and some displaced provincial populations, and the empire organized several colonization movements of different kinds. Finally, the structures of the city-state were loosened and undermined in many different ways.

Yet there were no official lists of permitted and forbidden cults (Millar 1973). The emperors created no centralized organizations for the oversight of cult. It was not until the third century A.D. — by which stage most free inhabitants of the empire were in fact Roman citizens — that emperors seem to have felt able to legislate about religious matters, whether enjoining universal cult or issuing universal edicts of persecution or toleration (Rives 1999). Until then, Roman authorities tended to discourage more often than they banned particular cults or rituals. Generally, oversight of cult was left to local communities. For most regions this meant that civic authorities organized the most prominent cults and had authority over all cultic action in the territories they administered. In Egypt and Judaea the high priests were in different ways integrated into provincial government. In Asia the sanctuaries were subordinated to local civic authorities, and so on.

Fragmentation was the rule. Roman religion properly speaking comprised the public cults (*sacra publica*) of the city of Rome and its citizens. Budding out from this model, as it were, were the cultic practices of various notionally autonomous citizen groups: first of all were the cults of the citizen colonies, modeled on those of Rome but often incorporating pre-Roman cults and managed by local priestly colleges and magistrates. There were the cults run by associations of Roman citizens found in many provinces. Public cult was paid by Roman magistrates and governors on behalf of their provinces. There were collective "Roman" cultic traditions for each detachment of the citizen army, but none of the army as a whole since no unitary military version of Roman religion existed (Herz 2001). Not only were all these versions of Roman religion slightly different — magistrates had relatively more authority than priests in *coloniae*, military hierarchies replaced the civic order in the camps, and so on — there was also no central authority governing all citizen cult. Around these were communities of non-citizens — Greek and Punic city-states, priestly hierarchies in Judaea and Egypt, municipalized tribes in Spain and Gaul, and many others — each also running their own cults, in different ways. So the great sanctuaries were more autonomous in Asia than in Egypt, there were some supra-civic religious associations in the Greek world, but fewer in the west except those set up by Roman governors and so on. Romans serving outside Italy in an official capacity seem never to have completely resolved how far their authority extended over the cultic activity of the non-citizens under their supervision. There are some eloquent letters of the governor Pliny on the subject, and some interesting but inconclusive discussions among those legal writers named jurists. Typically, Roman authorities only became involved when public order was at stake. Almost all the examples of which we know involved religious communities that were not organized on civic lines — notably worshippers of Bacchus or Isis, Jewish, and Christian minorities — coming into conflict with civic authorities. No pagan Roman emperor, with the possible exception of Julian, who was himself raised as a Christian, seems to have envisaged organizing all the cults of the empire into a single system governed by one authority.

Understanding the place of ruler cult in the Roman empire depends crucially on understanding the empire as a mosaic of notionally autonomous religious systems. The worship of the emperors was ordered separately within each of these systems (Hopkins 1978: 207–09). Even within any one society, it often took the form of a bundle of cults rather than a unitary whole. One might reasonably argue that the notion of *the* imperial cult is a modern invention, a convenient taxonomic category that groups together a mass of discrete occasions on each of which the name and image of the emperor, and sometimes also those of his relatives and ancestors, were given a place in essentially local rituals, temples, hymns, and prayers (cf. Bickerman 1973 with following discussion).

Even the public cults of the city of Rome illustrate this (Gradel 2002; Beard, North, and Price 1998). Consider for example the public cult of members of the imperial household deified after their deaths, the *divi* and *divae*. By the end of the first century A.D. the list of those deified apparently included Julius Caesar, the emperors Augustus, Claudius, Vespasian and Titus along with Livia the wife of Augustus, Drusilla, the sister of Caligula, Claudia, the daughter of Nero, Poppaea, the wife of Nero, Domitilla, the wife of Vespasian, Flavius Vespasianus and Caesar, the sons of Domitian, and Julia, the daughter of Titus (Cagnat 1914: 169–74). To become a *divus* or *diva* it was necessary to undergo post-mortem *consecratio*. Like sanctification in the Roman Catholic Church today, this process seems to have been taken as a recognition of an objective reality about the deceased, as well as the simple authorization of public cult. Witnesses to the ascent of the soul of the deceased gave testimony, and in the case of Caesar the portent of a comet was observed and formed a key part of the subsequent iconography. Decisions over *consecrationes* were formally taken by the Senate. But in practice the view of the reigning emperor was paramount. The absence from the list of the emperors Tiberius, Caligula, Nero, and Domitian largely reflects their successors' attitudes to them. Likewise, the deification of imperial relatives (some of them quite obscure) reflects the wishes (and interests) of the reigning emperor. No inconsistency was apparently felt in the fact that the children of Domitian were deified in his lifetime but that following his assassination he was not, nor that Nero's wife had been deified although he had not been.

The rule looks clear enough, but it conceals an evolving use of the terms and rituals involved. The first *divus* had been Julius Caesar. The title had originally been a synonym for *deus*, the more usual term for god — there had been scholarly debates in Caesar's lifetime about the difference — but he seems to have resolved it in favor of the sense that a *divus* was a god who had once been a man (like the god Quirinus, who as a man had been known as Romulus, that is). It now seems clear that Caesar had already planned to take this title during his lifetime (North 1975), but was forestalled by his assassination. The *consecratio* went ahead after his death, because his immediate successors — at war first with his assassins and then with each other — each needed to bolster their credentials as his heir by promoting the priesthood of the new god and building his temple in the center of the City. There are signs that the cult of *Divus* Julius was being extended to the provinces in the early 30s B.C. It acquired a new significance for Octavian/Augustus after victory in 31 B.C. made him sole ruler. He was able to make cautious claims for his own divine legitimacy by declaring himself *Divi filius*, son of the deified (Julius), and by promoting that cult in the provinces. From this point on it became common for emperors in Rome to associate themselves with their deified predecessors, but not to seek worship in their own lifetimes. Augustus was deified after his death, making his adopted stepson Tiberius *Divi filius*. Caligula seems to have sought worship in his lifetime (Simpson 1996), but his assassination encouraged his successor, Claudius, to revert to the Augustan model. Not being a descendant of any of the existing *divi*, he engineered a *consecratio* of his dead grandmother, Augustus' wife Livia. Nero, Claudius' adopted son, had Claudius deified to give himself a similar title. And so on. The ceremonial of *consecratio* at Rome, drawing heavily for symbols on the funerals of Republican aristocrats, was to become a central component of the succession rituals of Roman emperors (Price 1987).

The consecration of imperial relatives, begun by Caligula, needs to be understood in a different sense. Publicly they offered emperors opportunities for ceremonial display, great public occasions that involved all citizens in the sorrows of the imperial house, just as they were involved in celebrations of birthdays, of the occasions when imperial princes took on the *toga* of manhood and so on. As on those occasions, social rank determined the degree and kind of involvement. Foregrounding the immediate family in ceremonial and imagery was a key part of early imperial style (Rowe 2002). But it might be too cynical to dismiss these *consecrationes* entirely in those terms. The republican senator Cicero, grief stricken at his daughter's death, had contemplated creating a temple to her.

The cults of minor relatives did not, by and large, continue to be remembered, although the practice of consecrating relatives did (Gradel 2002). The emperor Trajan had his father, his sister, and his niece consecrated. By the end of the first century A.D., it was the cult of dead emperors that really mattered. The magistrates of Republican colonies, when they had to take certain oaths, had sworn oaths by Jupiter and the Penates, the household gods of Rome. A law issued to a late first-century A.D. *municipium* adds to this list the *Divus* Augustus, the *Divus* Claudius, the *Divus* Vespasianus, the *Divus* Titus, and the *genius* of the current emperor Domitian. Domitian also built a Porticus of the Divi on the Field of Mars in Rome. It seems to have housed temples to and statues of his father Vespasian and his brother Titus. The evolution of *consecratio* is evident. The etiquette is clear — swear by the *genius* of the living emperor and also by his deified predecessors. Other deified relatives (and Julius Caesar) have been quietly dropped from this list, although in the City, Domitian used *consecratio* to honor other dead relatives.

The cult of the *divi* did not exhaust divine kingship in Rome. Domitian also dedicated the small house on the Quirinal, where he had been born, as a Temple of the Flavian Clan (his family that is): in Hadrian's reign it still functioned as a kind of memorial that might be visited (Suetonius *Titus* 1). Annual vows were made for the emperor's safety by the Arval Brethren, an aristocratic priesthood whose feasts and rituals are minutely documented in the epigraphy of the shrine of Dea Dia (Scheid 1990). Regular sacrifices were also paid to the *genius* of the reigning emperor by local neighborhood associations. There were 265 of these local districts in the City, and during the Republic their cult activity had been focused on the Lares Compitales (the tutelary deities of the crossroads). Augustus reorganized the cult into a worship of the Lares Augusti along with the Genius Augusti. The associations were led by *vicomagistri*, often former slaves, who were allowed to wear the same ceremonial costume as state magistrates as they presided over games, sacrifices, and festivals which they paid for themselves. Cult to the emperor's *genius* was also paid by some households as part of the collective cult of a family, one that also included the household Lares. The official calendar of the City included numerous festivals marking the rites of passage of emperors and other members of the imperial house. The seventeenth of January, for example, had been decreed a perpetual holiday by the Senate to commemorate Tiberius Caesar having dedicated an altar to his father, the deified Augustus. Some sacral roles came to be reserved for emperors and their relatives: celebrating a triumph, for example, was a ritual no longer available to those outside the imperial household. Then there were instances in which the emperor was insinuated into great cults. The most famous example is the Temple of Mars the Avenger, originally vowed to the god by Octavian and Mark Antony as they waged war on Caesar's assassins. When finally built, it was located in the vast Augustan Forum, at the center of which stood a statue of Augustus on a four-horse chariot. On the pediment of the temple were images of *Divus* Iulius, Mars, and Venus, the three gods from whom Augustus claimed descent. A complex program of statues celebrated the kings of Rome, Augustus' adopted clan, the *gens Iulia,* and a succession of Roman heroes. This forum was not reserved for the cult of Mars, nor just for public display. The Senate met here to meet embassies from foreign peoples and to debate (with strict guidance from the emperor) whether or not to declare war. Great families also visited the forum when young men took on the toga of manhood (Zanker 1987).

Religious authority under the Roman Republic had been characterized by its extreme dispersal among the aristocratic elite. A very large number of senators were members of one or another priestly college. Equally, the number of discrete cults and temples was enormous: there were large numbers of holidays (*feriae*) and games (*ludi*), perhaps taking up a third of the year by the end of the Republic. The streets and squares of the City were thronged with hundreds of temples. In one way or another, the emperors entered into a great proportion of these cults. Yet this was far from a free-for-all. The rules, rituals, membership, and formulary prayers of each one of these associations were tightly regulated, indeed the minute regulation of cult was a central part of the activity of Roman priestly colleges. This survived the transition from political pluralism to monarchy at the end of the Republic. Emperors simply fitted in wherever a chance appeared. But it is difficult to detect any *co-ordinated* plan for the creation and ordering of what we call imperial cult.

Where should we draw the limits of the imperial cult in the city of Rome? Should we include all the other devices by which emperors gathered religious legitimacy (Gordon 1990a)? Emperors all held the quasi-religious title Augustus granted to the first emperor by the Senate. Every emperor held the senior priesthood — *pontifex maximus* — and he was a member of all the senior colleges of priests (Stepper 2003). Augustus listed his priesthoods as *pontifex maximus, augur, quindecimvir sacris faciundis, septemvir epulonum, frater arvalis, sodalis Titius*, and *fetialis*. This was an unparalleled accumulation. During the Republic there seems to have been a normal convention against multiplying priesthoods. Not only was he a member of all the colleges that counted, but as *pontifex maximus* he also had some authority over a number of other priests, including the *flamen* of Jupiter and the Vestals. Every emperor dedicated and repaired temples in the City. Many initiated new religious festivals such as the Capitoline Games set up by Domitian or the Saecular Games celebrated by several emperors. All regularly presided over the central religious celebrations of the City, the great games above all. The iconography of emperors included scenes of them performing sacrifice, celebrating triumphs, and ascending to heaven after their deaths. Poets and orators addressed them as gods and declared their god-like characteristics (Levene 1997). There was no body in Rome with any religious authority of which the emperor was not a member. Statues of the emperors were everywhere.

There were, nevertheless, some limits of what was deemed acceptable. No sacrifices, for example, were performed to living emperors. When Tacitus described how, after the death of Augustus, all prayers (*preces*) turned to Tiberius it was a way of expressing the servility of the Senate. A consistent language emerged. The gods were *dei* and *deae*, those emperors and their relatives who had undergone *consecratio* were *divi* and *divae*, the reigning emperor might be *divi filius*, one might sacrifice to his *genius*, refer to communications from him as *sacrae litterae* (sacred letters), but he was positioned quite precisely in relation to gods and men. As far as we can see, these conventions did not derive from a single edict nor were they the work of a single authority. Rather, a consensus about what was acceptable emerged from and was communicated by a series of imperial initiatives — like remodelling the cult of the Lares Compitales in 7 B.C., or the dedication of an altar to the emperor's *numen* by his recently adopted stepson (and heir designate), probably in A.D. 5 or 6. Those innovations gave the lead for imitation. On occasion, we might imagine approval was sought for some new cult. This is more obvious in the case of provincial requests to build temples to deified or living emperors, several of which are documented. In the provinces too we occasionally glimpse the Roman governor quietly giving advice on what forms of cult would be most acceptable (Price 1984a). This is not to retreat to a vague notion of ruler cult springing up spontaneously. It originated in complex negotiations in which the center always had the upper hand. But that is not the same as saying there was a Roman concept of ruler cult, nor that its totality was carefully planned, and certainly not that its implementation was prosecuted from the imperial palace.

RULER CULT IN NON-ROMAN COMMUNITIES

In other religious systems in the empire quite different rules might be applied. By far the best studied in relation to the imperial cult are the cults of that part of what is now western Anatolia that formed the Roman province of Asia (Price 1984a). The cult of Roma is well attested in the Republic, and after the transition to monarchy it was directed by Greek communities to the living emperor. The list of emperors honored is, as a result, rather different from the canonical list of the *divi*. Greeks had, it seems, no native notion that corresponded to *divus*, although they encountered the term in Roman usage and occasionally translated it (Price 1984b). Instead, the living emperor was worshipped as a god. Very early on a tradition emerged in which the Greek cities of the province collectively built a provincial temple for each individual living emperor. The emperor might sometimes be associated with other deities. Pergamum had a temple to Rome and Augustus, Smyrna had one to Tiberius, Livia, and the Senate, and so on. The City which hosted the temple then took on the title *neokoros* (lit., "temple warden") and hosted an annual festival to this emperor (Burrell 2004). Competition for neocorates was intense, requiring negotiation among the cities of the province and the approval of Senate and emperor. The rich epigraphic record of this part of the empire makes it possible to track particularly closely the dynamics of co-operation and rivalry that were articulated through the creation and maintenance of cult at the provincial level. Competition between cities meshed with competition *within* each city for local priesthoods of the imperial cult, and also with a competition for the provincial priesthood, the position of Asiarch. Priests of the imperial cult presided over great games, games at which gladiators — a Roman innovation — fought. The priests wore headdresses decorated with portrait busts of the emperors, and statues of civic nobles often immortalize them in this costume. Civic coinages bore, among other motifs, images of the temples of the emperors and their legends proclaimed each city's neokorates. Occasionally a temple was reassigned to a new imperial dedicant, especially when an emperor fell from favor, a risk that faced Greek cult of living rulers in a way it did not face Romans who awaited postmortem consecrations.

Again, these cults did not exhaust what we might call imperial cult. There were oaths to the emperor, conducted from the reign of the first emperor. Also from Augustus' reign are inscriptions recording a competition established by the *Koinon* (the association of Greek cities in the province) for the best honor for Augustus: it was won by the Roman governor who suggested a synchronism of all the civic calendars of the province so that each began their year on Augustus' birthday. Then there were the local decisions to place the statue of the emperor in the temples of major deities like Artemis of Ephesus. Busts of the emperors were everywhere. The great Bath-Gymnasium complex at Sardis had a *Kaisersaal*, a room apparently devoted to images of the Caesars. Portraits of reigning emperors also appeared on the reverses of base metal civic coins, as they did on the imperial silver issues that circulated in the same region.

From Asia too it is possible to see how the emperors interacted with these cults. It seems that the provincial Koinon felt it was prudent, or possibly was required, to submit proposals to emperors before cults were established. Augustus, we are told by a much later source

(Dio Cassius 51.20.6–9), required the Roman citizens of Asia and the neighboring province of Bithynia to set up precincts to *Divus* Julius in the cities of Ephesus and Nicomedia respectively, and at the same time consented to cult being paid to himself in association with Roma in the cities of Pergamum and Nikaea by the Greek cities of the two provinces. Formally these were two different kinds of interaction. The status of cult paid by associations of Roman expatriates remained unclear to Romans: they were not exactly *sacra publica*, since they were not conducted on Roman soil nor by the Roman state, and in any case in 29 B.C. Octavian/Augustus had no real religious authority (he did not become *pontifex maximus* until 12 B.C.). But he was certainly in a quite different relation to embassies from provincial subject approaching him as de facto representative of the Roman state. When his heir Tiberius was approached with similar requests he received the embassies in the Senate. But if there was productive ambiguity in how these different forms of cult were related to each other, each made perfect sense within their own religious system. In each province, Roman citizens gathered to worship the dead *divi* in one city, while the Greek cities worshipped his living successor. We should presume the rituals too, like the languages employed, were quite different.

Greeks and Romans did not together comprise the entirety of the population of the province of Asia. There were other expatriate communities, such as the Diasporan Jewish communities in the heart of all the major Greek cities. They did not participate in imperial cult, although they made vows for the safety and well-being of the emperor (Williams 1998: 91–92). And then there were the rural populations, mostly ruled by Greek cities, but speaking a scatter of other languages. A much later inscription recording the establishment of a great Greek-style festival in Oenoanda — once Carian, but now thoroughly Hellenized by Hadrian's reign when the events in question took place — shows how the surrounding villages were drawn into celebrations that had a place for imperial cult (Wörrle 1988). Villagers were to contribute sacrificial beasts and could presumably attend the festivities. The rhetorical and musical contests in Greek cannot have impressed them much. All the same, they would be present at sacrifices to the emperor.

The province of Asia is unusual only in the extent of the documentation available and the quality of recent studies based on it. In every part of the empire we encounter similar bundles of cult acts and images, usually in the idiom of the pre-existing religious system of the place and people concerned. So in Egypt the emperors took their place alongside Ptolemies and earlier pharaohs in the iconography of traditional temples, while their statues were placed next to those of the gods in Greek-style temples. A series of Caesarea were built dedicated to their worship in the main cities. Following ethnic violence in Alexandria, the Jewish population was accused by their Greek enemies of not participating in the worship of Caligula. They responded that they sacrificed prominently on his behalf (but to their own god of course). There was no Egyptian form of *the* imperial cult, but the emperors were present in every religious tradition represented in the province.

Everywhere, there were also many ways of incorporating the emperor into local religion that stopped short of a public cult with its own priest, temple, and festival. It was common to set up a statue of an emperor alongside the cult statue of another deity inside his or her temple. The title *theos sunnaos* denoted such cohabitation in the Greek world. The statue of an emperor might be carried alongside those of other gods in a procession through a Roman or Greek city, his name added to a hymn or a prayer. It is not always easy to see where cult ends and something else — homage? honor? — begins. Are the collections of portrait busts of emperors in public baths an aspect of emperor worship? What about the near-ubiquitous habit of putting the emperor's head on the back of a coin, even for local coinages? What about dedications to gods with titles like *Mercurius Augustus*? Treating these as all part of the imperial cult seems to empty out the concept of much precise meaning. On the other hand, it is difficult to set a limit that is not arbitrary. An analogous problem faces archaeologists of early imperial cities. It is unusual in the extreme for cities not to have prominent temples and statues to emperors and sometimes to their relatives as well, usually in the central public space. A number of scholars now write of imperial cult utterly transforming the civic landscape, especially of the new cities of the west (e.g., Trillmich and Zanker 1990). But these were fast evolving cityscapes in any case, and to show the worship of the emperors had a place within them is not the same as attributing to it the driving force.

Ubiquity is not the same as uniformity. For this reason I find it hard to see the imperial cult giving the empire any "symbolic unity" (Hopkins 1978) other than that created by multiple connections between local bodies and the center. If imperial cult had been a sacred scandal, an alien intrusion into every religious system of the empire and a brutal innovation, then perhaps it might have been recognized as a new and unifying force. But the cults I have been discussing grew naturally within open systems, drawing in each locality on ancient resources of ritual and cosmological thought. The person of the emperor was a common focus, but no more. If all cults led to Rome, it was hardly a well-ordered road network.

How did imperial cult come to be so ubiquitous and so quickly? On the face of it, it is easier to explain any ubiquitous and broadly synchronous phenomenon in terms of central initiative or organization. But this was apparently not the case. It is clear that many of the above examples emerged from local initiatives, even if, when it is possible to follow the creation of a cult in detail, there is often a sense that preliminary conversations had gone on beforehand between all parties. Ruler cult has been represented as an example of gift-exchange, a rather special case of the reciprocal relations between gods and humans that seem implicit in much ancient religion (Price 1984a). There were certainly occasions when representatives of the center did organize cult, even for non-Roman communities. A series of great monumental altars were set up in the reigns of Augustus and Tiberius, some in Rome — some in the western provinces — at which collective cult was to be paid by various groups. The imperial prince Drusus set up one of these at Lyon in Gaul to be the focus of a sanctuary where representatives of every tribal community would gather every year to elect an annual priest (a *sacerdos*) of Rome and Augustus who would then pay for extravagant games. This is pretty clearly modeled on the Asian Koinon. But it rapidly came to serve local ends and took local forms. All over the Roman world, the various forms that divine kingship took reflected local traditions and also the balance of power within local communities. A rash of cities named after Caesar or Augustus were created, many founded by client kings and friends of the new Roman monarch. Festivals connected with the emperors gave local elites everywhere marvellous opportunities to associate themselves with the "theodicy of good fortune" that declared the emperor's rule just and divinely ordained as well as absolute (Gordon 1990b).

What we should imagine is a densely interconnected Mediterranean world through which ideas spread rapidly. It was a world used to religious innovation and used to parallel convulsions of politics and cult. That world shared a long heritage of interaction, often at the cultic level, and was more recently united by the common traumas of conquest and civil war. When autocracy emerged (or re-emerged) from the convulsions, all parties participated in formulating religious responses. An essential precondition was the readiness of so many local communities to consider such a move. This paper began by arguing that the archaic and classical Mediterranean was not ruled by secular republics, and that something like ruler cult was already dispersed among the magistrates, priests, and institutions of the city-state. As a result, there were few if any communities who did not find some place for the emperors in their ritual lives. The professions of Christian apologists, like their Jewish predecessors, that they prayed *for* the emperor even if not *to* him, makes perfect sense as the incorporation of the emperor into their rituals.

OF GODS AND MEN

Unlike some Near Eastern writing systems, neither Latin nor Greek had an unambiguous sign to differentiate gods from men. Indeed a creative and suggestive ambiguity often seems one of the hallmarks of Roman navigation in these tricky theological waters. Many historians have found it difficult to imagine sane rational Romans mistaking a fellow human being for a god. How could the greatest Roman aristocrats who shared the emperor's table (and some-times his bed), who plotted against and with him, and perhaps hoped one day to succeed to the throne, regard the Roman *princeps* as really divine? Many scholars were tempted to regard ruler cult as politics, not religion, and its rituals as homage, not worship, seeing the imperial cult as a pantomime performed for the benefit of easily duped masses. That view is no longer tenable. Titles, images, temples, altars, and rituals allow no distinction between these rites and those paid other deities. There is a widespread agreement that Christianizing assumptions about the category "god" and the centrality of belief (as opposed to practice) have confused the issue. One view is that the emperor was a god like any other (e.g., Clauss 1999). But for many of the religious cultures of the empire it is preferable to imagine a continuum stretching from men to the greatest creator deities. Emperors were the lowest of the gods, and the greatest of men. They were the greatest of priests and the least of all those beings that were paid cult.

Ruler cult in the Roman world represented, I have argued, a re-emergence in the region of a very widespread tendency to focus worship on powerful individuals. That tendency is visible in the Bronze Age, in traditions of archaic kingship, and for that matter in the cults of civic founders, heroes, and savior figures even in the last millennium B.C. The return of monarchy following first Alexander's conquests and then the end of the Roman Republic was accom-panied by the return of divine kingship. It was as if divinity was precipitated in the person of emperors as part of the complex chemical reactions that transformed the ancient world at the end of the last millennium B.C.

That divine kingship in Rome was never centralized, and never submitted to an orthodoxy or disciplinary apparatus, is not so strange. For a start, no other public cults were policed in this way in Rome. Nor was Augustus the first emperor to draw religious legitimacy from a range of sources. The Achaemenids sponsored Marduk in Babylon, rebuilt the temple of Yawheh in Jerusalem, protected the gardens of Apollo at Magnesia-on-the-Maeander without relinquishing the claim that they owed everything to the aid offered by Ahura Mazda. Perhaps it made little difference in practice whether a monarch claimed the mandate of Heaven, or to be a living god, or a man who might reasonably expect post-mortem deification. When pagan polytheism collapsed across much of the Old World during the fourth to seventh centuries A.D., we might have expected this to be a body-blow to the prestige of divine emperors and divinely favored kings alike. With that collapse were carried away all the imperial cults of the Roman world, so closely tied were they into the religious traditions within which they had grown up. Yet the emperors of Byzantium, the caliphs of Baghdad, and the barbarian kings of the west seem hardly to have broken pace. Instead they found new ways to stand between their subjects and the heavens.

BIBLIOGRAPHY

Ando, Clifford
    2003   "A Religion for the Empire?" In *Flavian Rome: Culture, Image, Text,* edited by Anthony J. Boyle and William J. Dominik, pp. 323–44. Leiden: Brill.

Athanassiadi, Polymnia, and Michael Frede, editors
    1999   *Pagan Monotheism in Late Antiquity.* Oxford: Oxford University Press.

Beard, Mary; John A. North; and Simon R. F. Price
    1998   *Religions of Rome.* 2 volumes. Cambridge: Cambridge University Press.

Bickerman, Elias
    1973   "Consecratio." In *Le culte des souverains dans l'empire romain: 7 exposés suivis de discussions,* edited by Willem den Boer, pp. 2–37. Entretiens sur l'antiquité classique 19. Vandoeuvres-Geneva: Fondation Hardt.

Burrell, Barbara
    2004   *Neokoroi: Greek Cities and Roman Emperors.* Cincinnati Classical Studies, New Series 9. Leiden: Brill.

Cancik, Hubert, and Konrad Hitzl, editors
    2003   *Die Praxis der Herrscherverehrung in Rom und seinen Provinzen.* Tübingen: Mohr Siebeck.

Cancik, Hubert, and Jörg Rüpke, editors
    1997   *Römische Reichsreligion und Provinzialreligion.* Tübingen: Mohr Siebeck.

Cagnat, René
    1914   *Cours d'épigraphie latine.* Fourth edition. Paris: Fontemoing et cie.

Charlesworth, Martin Percival
    1939   "The Refusal of Divine Honours: An Augustan Formula." *Papers of the British School at Rome* 15: 1–10.

Clauss, Manfred
    1999   *Kaiser und Gott: Herrscherkult im römischen Reich.* Stuttgart: Teubner.

Etienne, Robert
    1958   *Le culte impérial dans la péninsule ibérique d'Auguste à Dioclétien.* Bibliothèque des écoles françaises d'Athènes et de Rome 191. Paris: Éditions de Boccard.

Fears, J. Rufus
    1977   *Princeps a diis electus: The Divine Election of the Emperor as a Political Concept at Rome.* American Academy in Rome Papers and Monographs 26. Rome: American Academy.

Fishwick, Duncan
    1987–2005   *The Imperial Cult in the Latin West: Studies in the Ruler Cult of the Western Provinces of the Roman Empire.* 3 volumes. Études préliminaires aux religions orientales dans l'Empire romain 108; Religions in the Graeco-Roman World 148. Leiden: Brill.

Fustel De Coulanges, Numa Denis
    1864   *La cité antique: Étude sur le culte, le droit, les institutions de la Grèce et de Rome.* Paris: Durand.

Gordon, Richard

    1990a   "From Republic to Principate: Religion, Priesthood and Ideology." In *Pagan Priests: Religion and Power in the Ancient World,* edited by Mary Beard and John A. North, pp. 179–98. Ithaca: Cornell University Press.

    1990b   "Religion in the Roman Empire: The Civic Compromise and Its Limits." In *Pagan Priests: Religion and Power in the Ancient World,* edited by Mary Beard and John A. North, pp. 235–55. Ithaca: Cornell University Press.

Gradel, Ittai

    2002   *Emperor Worship and Roman Religion.* Oxford Classical Monographs. Oxford: Clarendon Press.

Herz, Peter

    1978   "Bibliographie zum römischen Kaiserkult (1955–1975)." In *Aufstieg und Niedergang der römischen Welt* II.16.2, edited by Hildegard Temporini, pp. 833–910. Berlin: Walter de Gruyter.

    2001   "Das römische Heer und der Kaiserkult in Germanien." In *Religion in den germanischen Provinzen Roms*, edited by Wolfgang Spickermann, pp. 91–116. Tübingen: Mohr Siebeck.

Hopkins, Keith

    1978   "Divine Emperors, or the Symbolic Unity of the Roman Empire." In *Conquerors and Slaves,* edited by Keith Hopkins, pp. 197–242. Sociological Studies in Roman History 1. Cambridge: Cambridge University Press.

Horden, Peregrine, and Nicholas Purcell

    2000   *The Corrupting Sea: A Study of Mediterranean History.* Oxford: Blackwell.

Kuhrt, Amélie

    1987   "Usurpation, Conquest and Ceremonial: From Babylon to Persia." In *Rituals of Royalty: Power and Ceremonial in Traditional Societies,* edited by David Cannadine and Simon R. F. Price, pp. 20–55. Past and Present Publications. Cambridge: Cambridge University Press.

Levene, David

    1997   "God and Man in the Classical Latin Panegyric." *Proceedings of the Cambridge Philological Society* 43: 66–103.

Millar, Fergus

    1973   "The Imperial Cult and the Persecutions." In *Le culte des souverains dans l'empire romain: 7 exposés suivis de discussions*, edited by Willem den Boer, pp. 143–75. Entretiens sur l'antiquité classique 19. Vandoeuvres-Geneva: Fondation Hardt.

North, John

    1975   "Praesens Divus: Review of Weinstock (1971)." *Journal of Roman Studies* 65: 171–77.

    1990   "Democratic Politics in Republican Rome." *Past and Present* 126: 3–21.

    1992   "The Development of Religious Pluralism." In *The Jews among Pagans and Christians: In the Roman Empire,* edited by Judith Lieu, John A. North, and Tessa Rajak, pp. 174–93. London: Routledge.

Price, Simon R. F.

    1984a   "Gods and Emperors: The Greek Language of the Imperial Cult." *Journal of Hellenic Studies* 104: 79–95.

1984b   *Rituals and Power: The Roman Imperial Cult in Asia Minor.* Cambridge: Cambridge University Press.

1987   "From Noble Funerals to Divine Cult: The Consecration of Roman Emperors." In *Rituals of Royalty: Power and Ceremonial in Traditional Societies,* edited by David Cannadine and Simon R. F. Price, pp. 56–107. Past and Present Publications. Cambridge: Cambridge University Press.

Rives, James

1999   "The Decree of Decius and the Religion of the Empire." *Journal of Roman Studies* 89: 135–54.

Rowe, Greg

2002   *Princes and Political Cultures: The New Tiberian Senatorial Decrees.* Ann Arbor: University of Michigan Press.

Scheid, John

1990   *Romulus et ses frères: Le collège des Frères Arvales, modèle du culte public dans la Rome des empereurs.* Bibliothèque des écoles françaises d'Athènes et de Rome 275. Rome: Ecole française de Rome.

Simpson, C. J.

1996   "Caligula's Cult: Immolation, Immortality, Intent." In *Subject and Ruler: The Cult of the Ruling Power in Classical Antiquity,* edited by Alistair Small, pp. 63–71. Journal of Roman Archaeology Supplementary Papers 17. Ann Arbor: Journal of Roman Archaeology.

Small, Alistair, editor

1996   *Subject and Ruler: The Cult of the Ruling Power in Classical Antiquity* (Papers from a Conference to celebrate the 65th Anniversary of Duncan Fishwick in Alberta, 13–15, 1994). Journal of Roman Archaeology Supplementary Series 17. Ann Arbor: Journal of Roman Archaeology.

Stepper, R.

2003   "Der Kaiser als Priester: Schwerpunkte und Reichweite seines oberpontifikalen Handelns." In *Die Praxis der Herrscherverehrung in Rom und seinen Provinzen*, edited by Hubert Cancik and Konrad Hitzl, pp. 157–87. Tübingen: Mohr Siebeck.

Trillmich, Walter, and Paul Zanker, editors

1990   *Stadtbild und Ideologie: Die Monumentalisierung hispanischer Städte zwischen Republik und Kaiserzeit* (Colloquium in Madrid, 19–23 October 1987). Abhandlungen/ Bayerische Akademie der Wissenschaften, Philosophisch-Historische Klasse, Neue Folge 103. Munich: Verlag der Bayerischen Akademie der Wissenschaften.

Weinstock, Stefan

1971   *Divus Julius.* Oxford: Clarendon Press.

Williams, Margaret

1998   *The Jews among the Greeks and Romans: A Diasporan Sourcebook.* Baltimore: Johns Hopkins University Press.

Wörrle, Michael

1988   *Stadt und Fest in kaiserzeitlichen Kleinasien: Studien zu einer agonistischen Stiftung aus Oinoanda.* Vestigia 39. Munich: C. H. Beck.

Zanker, Paul

1987   *Augustus und die Macht der Bilder.* Munich: C. H. Beck.

14

DIVINE KINGSHIP IN MESOPOTAMIA, A FLEETING PHENOMENON

JERROLD S. COOPER, JOHNS HOPKINS UNIVERSITY

Not long after the middle of the third millennium B.C., Eanatum, ruler[1] of Lagash, whose realm in Sumer extended from Girsu southeastward through Lagash and Niŋen (Nina) to Guaba on the Persian Gulf, was portrayed in the text of his famous Stele of the Vultures as sired, suckled, named, and appointed king by the gods, a superman who measured over nine feet at birth.[2] Not long before the middle of the first millennium B.C., Ashurbanipal, king of an Assyrian empire that stretched from Iran to Egypt, was, we are told, suckled at the four breasts of Ishtar of Nineveh.[3] Neither ruler, however, claimed divinity in his own right; both were content, as were the vast majority of Mesopotamian sovereigns, to be mediators between their subjects and the gods. As several contributors have noted, kingship in Mesopotamia was always sacred, but only rarely divine.

The first Mesopotamian ruler to be deified was Naramsin of Akkade, sometime after the middle of the twenty-third century B.C., but the practice sputtered out under his son,[4] only to be revived in the twenty-first century B.C. by the second king of the Third Dynasty of Ur (Ur III). It continued under his successors, and the successor dynasty of Isin as well as peripheral successor dynasts, sporadically and with diminishing force through the time of Rimsin and Hammurabi (see Michalowski and Reichel, this volume, for details). Three important questions arise with regard to this phenomenon:

1. What impelled Naramsin and Shulgi to break with the traditional model of kingship and become gods?

2. How did divine kingship differ from traditional kingship and traditional divinity?

3. Why was divine kingship such a fleeting phenomenon in the millennia-long history of ancient Mesopotamia?

Addressing the first question, both Michalowski and Winter stress that unlike kings in Egypt, Mesopotamian kings were not inherently divine. Rather, divine kingship in Mesopotamia was a historically contingent phenomenon. So far, so good, but when it comes to defining what the specific contingencies may have been in each case, our results tend to be rather banal or, if more specific, shots in the dark. As Michalowski points out, our sole native explanation of king becoming god comes from Naramsin's Bassetki inscription, where we are told that "his city" requested that the major deities make him a god because "he secured the foundations of his city in times of trouble," and that a temple was built for him in the city Akkade. Scholars assume that the "times of trouble" refers to the Great Rebellion against Naramsin, when armies

---

[1] I subscribe fully to Michalowski's assertion above that en, lugal, and ensí are "just different local words for" ruler, used at Uruk, Ur, and Lagash respectively.

[2] Frayne 2007: 129f.

[3] Livingstone 1997: 476.

[4] Michalowski states that the son "did not aspire to divine status," but immediately provides evidence to the contrary. Our sources' testimony regarding Sharkalisharri's divine kingship is ambivalent, as he himself may have been.

of both southern and northern Babylonia were arrayed against Akkadian forces, and Naramsin emerged victorious only after chasing his foes over the entire Mesopotamian landscape, as far as the Jebel Bishri in Syria.[5] Yet we cannot probe more deeply, since, as Michalowski tells us, the chronology of Naramsin's reign is so uncertain. The most we can do is point to a series of innovations in his reign and count his deification as another.[6] To say that it is historically determined, while certainly the case, is begging the question.

Naramsin is also the only king to be represented with the horned crown of a deity, both on the justly famous stele that bears his name,[7] and on a spectacular — if genuine — unprovenanced stone mold.[8] The former shows Naramsin triumphant over enemies in mountainous terrain, and the latter portrays the king seated with Ishtar, holding a ring retaining nose ropes attached to two tribute-bearing mountain gods, and two bound prisoners, each standing on an architectonic pedestal set against a stylized mountain. Both representations, then, commemorate victories in the eastern mountains, not the defeat of Babylonian rebels. The horned crown is the visual analogue of the divine determinative that precedes the names of gods in Sumerian and Akkadian cuneiform,[9] and that determinative is preposed to Naramsin's name on the stele's inscription. But the determinative is absent in the Bassetki inscription,[10] as well as in several other inscriptions that mention the defeat of the Great Rebellion.[11] It has been restored for the inscription on the Pir Hüseyn stele,[12] where, however, Naramsin is not wearing a horned crown. If the restoration is correct, we can reconstruct a process whereby the deification explicitly set forth in the Bassetki inscription was initially not manifest in visual or inscriptional representations, then appeared first in inscriptions with the use of the divine determinative (Pir Hüseyn) and only later in visual imagery (the horned crown on the stele and mold). The horned crown thus is possibly a considerably later component of Naramsin's representation as god, which would explain why our only two examples of its use are on monuments that do not refer to the original motivation for his deification.

Shulgi became a god by the middle of his long reign, but no explicit justification of this transformation has survived. As with Naramsin, his deification is just one of many innovations associated with his rule, and specifically with its midpoint.[13] As Michalowski tells us, the year names of Shulgi's first twenty years are primarily concerned with cultic matters, but from his twenty-first year on, we hear mainly about military expeditions. This suggests that after two relatively peaceful decades, Shulgi had to mount a vigorous two-decade long response to external threats. If his deification was one response to these threats, then, like Naramsin, and as Michalowski suggests, Shulgi was proclaimed divine not as the culmination of a successful reign, but in the wake of near fatal collapse. In both cases, what may have been portrayed as a reward for valiant defense of the homeland might really have been part of an attempt to reconstitute a more robust notion of kingship, or, in Michalowski's terms, a reinvention of the state. Unfortunately, we have no preserved commemorative monuments of Shulgi or of his deified

---

[5] Wilcke 1997.

[6] Westenholz 1999.

[7] See the references given by Winter, and her figure 1.

[8] That the stele is a masterpiece should not blind us to the fact that other Naramsin monuments may have been more ordinary, as is his fragmentary monument from Pir Hüseyn. The mold (Hansen 2002) reminds us of the great difficulties in authenticating unique unprovenanced

works, and how much information is lost when objects are looted rather than properly excavated.

[9] Cf. Winter, above.

[10] Frayne 1993: E2.1.4.10.

[11] Frayne 1993: 116.

[12] Frayne 1993: E2.1.4.24.

[13] Sallaberger 1999; Michalowski, above.

successors, so we can't say if divine kingship was expressed visually in the Ur III period by portraying the ruler wearing a horned crown.[14]

What were the perks of divine kings? What difference did it make in how the ruler perceived his role vis-à-vis his subjects, and how those subjects perceived and behaved toward the ruler? Here, on the one hand, we can cite the evidence for an actual royal cult, complete with temple, discussed most thoroughly by Reichel, or the effusive hymns written to deified kings, or Shulgi's ascent to heaven following his death, or the possibility — joining danger to pleasure — of bedding the goddess Inana/Ishtar in the sacred marriage. On the other hand, Selz's discussion of the category "god" in ancient Mesopotamia is most useful. Within that category, the divine king is hardly the prototype that springs to mind. Rather, and despite our great distance from the ancients in every respect, it is safe to say that a Babylonian would sooner think of one of the great gods or perhaps a personal god as the prototypical member of the category. In that category's hierarchy, the divine king would probably rank higher than most of the deified objects and offices mentioned by Selz, but it is not certain where among the lesser deities he might rank, or even if he would rank above, say, the emblem of an important god.

The changes wrought by deification of the ruler seem purely ideological, designed to bolster the notion of king as god, but changing the practice of kingship little if at all. The strong ruler gained no additional power from his godship, so it seems, nor was a weak ruler like Ibbisin protected by it. After the middle of the second millennium, there were great and mighty kings in Mesopotamia whose power was in no way constrained by their ordinary mortality. The two examples in the first paragraph of this response bracket the enormous chronological range of the Mesopotamian rulers who claimed participation in some aspect of the divine without actually proclaiming themselves god. Here we must invoke Selz's fuzzy category boundaries: the king is not god but partakes of the divine, and is human, but without many of the limitations of the prototypical human being.

Winter has pointed out that even the Stele of Naramsin expresses a certain ambivalence toward royal divinity,[15] and we might say that the ascription of near-divine qualities and abilities to kings who are not deified expresses a certain ambivalence toward royal mortality. Yet despite this latter ambivalence, none of the great and powerful rulers of Mesopotamia after the time of Hammurabi of Babylon became god. Ashurbanipal and Nebuchadnezzar ruled empires of roughly comparable size, yet, as Ehrenberg emphasizes, both the written and visual manifestations of their kingship could not be more different. If we can understand that Neo-Babylonian monarchs, who portray themselves as humble servants of the gods, would be very unlikely to consider self-deification, the resistance of the Neo-Assyrian kings, who styled themselves both visually and in writing as mighty warriors and deputies of the gods, is more difficult to comprehend.

---

[14] Canephore figurines of Ur III rulers would not be appropriate vehicles for displaying the horned crown, and other statuettes are acephalous. That large Ur III narrative commemorative monuments once existed is certain from the descriptions accompanying the Old Babylonian copies of inscriptions on the monuments of Shusin (Frayne 1997: E3/2.1.4.1–9). The statue of the Ur III contemporary Puzur-Ishtar of Mari seems to show him wearing a horned crown, but the inscription on the statue does not prepose the divine determinative to his name (Frayne 1997: E3/2.4.5). If this practice — horned crown without divine determinative — is modeled on the practice of the rulers of Ur, they, too, must have been

portrayed horned. But unlike the rulers of Ur, Puzur-Ishtar does not use the divine determinative, so that the practice on this statue is opposite to that on Naramsin's Pir Hüseyn monument, described above (but cf. Blocher 1999, who argues that Puzur-Ishtar's horns were added only in the Neo-Babylonian period).

[15] Similar ambivalence appears on the stone mold, where, facing the goddess Ishtar, Naramsin in horned crown sits holding a ring to which are tethered defeated enemies and their gods. Ishtar holds the wrist of the hand in which Naramsin holds the ring, and the ropes pass from the ring through the goddess's other hand before reaching the captives.

Resistance to transgressing the fuzzy boundary between human and divine is not a marker of first-millennium kingship only. It had been there from the beginning — so, Eanatum, super-sized divine progeny, remained a mortal — was responsible for the detectable ambivalence toward divine kingship during the relatively short period of experimentation with the idea, and led to its permanent demise thereafter, persisting through regimes and dynasties with varied conceptions of kingship. We can't say much more, except that since divine kingship cross-culturally seems to be the exception rather than the rule, there could well be some basic human cognitive resistance to pushing any living mortal fully into the category of the divine.

BIBLIOGRAPHY

Blocher, Felix

    1999   "Wann wurde Puzur-Eštar zum Gott?" In *Babylon: Focus mesopotamischer Geschichte, Wiege früher Gelehrsamkeit, Mythos in der Moderne*, edited by Johannes Renger, pp. 253–69. Berlin: Deutsche Orient-Gesellschaft.

Frayne, Douglas

    1993   *Sargonic and Gutian Periods, 2334–2113 B.C.* Royal Inscriptions of Mesopotamia 2. Toronto: University of Toronto Press.

    1997   *Ur III Period, 2112–2004 B.C.* Royal Inscriptions of Mesopotamia 3/2. Toronto: University of Toronto Press.

    2007   *Presargonic Period (2700–2350 B.C.).* Royal Inscriptions of Mesopotamia 1. Toronto: University of Toronto Press.

Hansen, Donald

    2002   "Through the Love of Ishtar." In *Of Pots and Plans: Papers on the Archaeology and History of Mesopotamia and Syria Presented to David Oates in Honour of His 75th Birthday*, edited by Lamia al-Gailani Weir et al., pp. 91–112. London: NABU.

Livingstone, Alasdair

    1997   "A Late Piece of Constructed Mythology Relevant to the Neo-Assyrian and Middle Assyrian Coronation Hymn and Prayer (1.146)." In *The Context of Scripture*, Volume 1: *Canonical Compositions from the Biblical World*, edited by William W. Hallo, pp. 476–77. Leiden: Brill.

Sallaberger, Walther

    1999   "Ur III-Zeit." In *Mesopotamien: Akkade-Zeit und Ur III-Zeit*, edited by Pascal Attinger and Markus Wäfler, pp. 121–390. Orbis Biblicus et Orientalis 160/3. Freiburg: Universitätsverlag; Göttingen: Vandenhoeck & Ruprecht.

Westenholz, Åge

    1999   "The Old Akkadian Period: History and Culture." In *Mesopotamien: Akkade-Zeit und Ur III-Zeit*, edited by Pascal Attinger and Markus Wäfler, pp. 17–120. Orbis Biblicus et Orientalis 160/3. Freiburg: Universitätsverlag; Göttingen: Vandenhoeck & Ruprecht.

Wilcke, Claus

    1997   "Amar-girids Revolte gegen Naram-Suen," *Zeitschrift für Assyriologie* 87: 11–32.

15

WHEN GODS RULED: COMMENTS ON DIVINE KINGSHIP

KATHLEEN D. MORRISON, UNIVERSITY OF CHICAGO

While there is probably no form of political power which exists entirely independent of structured belief systems, the institution of divine kingship is surely one of the most extreme manifestations of the entanglement of religion and rule. Although it might seem that kings who were not only, in Winter's (this volume) words, "infused with the divine," but who had actually achieved divinity themselves would always be the most powerful political leaders, in fact, historical analysis suggests certain ambiguities and difficulties in the exercise of political power, difficulties not always erased by an assumption of godhead. As the papers in this volume illustrate, there is no simple relationship between the effective exercise of power and what might be glossed as the degree of divinity, though they also show a consistent pattern of *striving* toward political power that seems often to accompany claims of divine kingship.

What this formulation implicitly suggests, of course, is that "political power" is somehow different from religious position — more material, secular, even more "real." Clearly, both binaries — "religion" and "power" — could be destabilized to positive effect and indeed in most of the cases considered in this volume, the boundaries between these categories are diffuse. What models of the state such as Geertz' (1988) Theater State, Tambiah's (1976) Galactic Polity, and Stein's (1980) Segmentary State (after Southall 1956) point out, albeit in different ways, is the importance of seeing ritual power *as* political, with theorists such as Geertz going so far as to see the ritual action of the state as fully constituting the state itself. It is, however, not necessary to adopt this perspective to realize that religion, ritual, and belief need to be an integral part of the theorization of politics, that religion is as "real" a component of the state as are resource flows.

Whether or not we wish to conceive of religion as a kind of Marxian veil over material relations of power is, to some extent, a matter of taste, but clearly, an understanding of the potential significance of the repeated recurrence of divine kingship in many times and places needs to take into account both the specifics of local belief systems as well as the strategies of rulers and flows of resources and personnel. Are there consistent contexts in which such claims are made, accepted, or rejected? Are particular religious traditions more amenable to claims of divinity by sitting or deceased rulers? How about particular political forms, such as incorporative empires? The authors in this volume consider these (and other) questions primarily in light of detailed analyses of specific cases, including instances in which attempts to delineate a divine kingship never got fully established (China), kings marked as divine were relatively uncommon (Mesopotamia), kings are always divine but not powerful (contemporary Akwapim), divine and powerful (Egypt, Maya), semi-divine (Rome), and so on. Such a range of case studies makes this book a critical resource for answering these general questions.

Moving from a more generic notion of religion to specific concepts of divinity and indeed from a general notion of power to specific ideas of sovereignty highlights some of the variability in these concepts evident historically and geographically. Most critical, perhaps, for the authors in this volume, is the issue of the partibility of both divinity and sovereignty — can either be shared? If so, how fungible might they be and how expansive? Woolf (this volume) considers the "dispersal" of divinity during both the Republic and the Roman empire, a situation in which the sharing and spreading of divinity was apparently seen as reasonable. In his discussion of China, Puett (this volume) analyses several competing claims about the nature of kingship with the hindsight of long-term historical experience, making the critical point that even within an apparently unified context, there existed multiple viewpoints and contested formulations, a point also stressed by Winter (this volume). Puett's account points to a situation in which the establishment of a system of divine kingship was thwarted, an important counterexample to the other case studies presented here.

Using Foucault as a springboard, Bernbeck's paper (this volume) considers how it might be possible to "close the gap" between humans and the divine in situations where the distance seems great, such as the relatively closed monotheistic programs of Christianity and Islam, as well as in instances where humans and the divine are not so widely separated. While all the papers in this volume pose critical questions, such as how kingship was understood, how sovereignty was realized in courtly life, and how concepts of divine kingship emerged, fewer take up the broader comparative issues Bernbeck's paper addresses. Building on Battaglia's (1997) notion of "ambiguation," that is, either a concealment or revelation of agency that creates ambiguity in human and divine relationships and roles, Bernbeck proposes ambiguation as a political strategy leading to divine kingship. This provocative analysis, of course, also invites response. While Bernbeck's discussion opens up consideration of religion and the divine as well as of political power, a factor perhaps insufficiently explored in the papers as a whole, his (perhaps implicit) framework of probabilities for deified kingship seems somewhat exception prone. For example, while the fungibility of human and divine attributes is extremely high in Hindu religious traditions, in fact truly deified rulers are rare in South Asia. In India, in particular, both shared divinity and shared sovereignty were the norm and, despite persistent royal strategies such as symbolic associations with the ideal god-king Rama, kings themselves were generally not regarded as gods. Certainly, political leadership was (and is) consistently infused with the divine, a fact clearly seen in the recent political success of several film stars famous for their depictions of gods and religious leaders in the cinema. In Hinduism's exported variants in Southeast Asia, however, deified rulers were common, suggesting that more than simply the structural possibilities of religious systems are at issue, as indeed Bernbeck is well aware.

On what is perhaps the other end of the spectrum, one might imagine that Islamic or Christian traditions would completely exclude any possibility for divine kings. This is not entirely untrue, though one thinks immediately of the Mughal emperor Akbar who, although Muslim, developed a kind of syncretic royal religion, Din-I-Ilahi, which included elements of ruler deification. Admittedly, this did not outlast him, but as Woolf notes (this volume), even post-pagan Roman rulers "found new ways to stand between their subjects and heaven" notwithstanding the great distance between god and man in Christian traditions. All this makes us aware that there are no simple relationships between structures of belief and the entanglements of religion and power; indeed, the contributors to this volume make the important point that such relationships are generally both contested and recursive. At the same time, the lack of a simple relationship does not mean the lack of any relationship at all — clearly, we have some way to go in understanding the range of forms, past and present, presented by actually existing systems of power and religion, to say nothing of the causal interrelationships between these factors.

Several papers in this collection also raise critical questions about the actual practices of divine kingship, what one might think of as the practical, logistical issues of living with and relating to a god on earth. One senses that divine kings lived in a world hedged with ritual and elaborate protocol, separated from human society, an existence perhaps very trying and not as glamorous as one might first imagine. Gilbert's (this volume) descriptions of contemporary Akwapim divine kings in Africa reveal a ruler curiously non-agentive, a ceremonial object apparently limited as much as empowered by his own divinity.

Friedel (this volume), further, reminds us of the material as well as managerial responsibilities of divine kings. Maya kings, associated with the maize god, had to actually assure that there was maize to eat by producing good harvests on a regular basis. Close identification with nature can indeed present a problem when nature misbehaves, especially if we insist on the secular view that even divine kings did not *actually* have supernatural powers. Friedel notes that although Maya kings were clearly divinized, divinity did not necessarily translate into unchecked power, noting that the entire system of divine kingship appears to have collapsed following a period of sectarian wars, droughts, and crop failures. As Puett and Lincoln also demonstrate, the assumption of divine status provides no assurance of total control nor indeed of the perpetuation of the institution of divine kingship itself. As Gilbert explains, the divine king carries on his shoulders a dreadful responsibility, with her description of the de-stooling of the Akwapim king relatively benign in contrast to the many examples of regicide she cites, the crime which so fascinated Frazier.

Rather than assuming a binary opposition between the sacred and the profane, it may indeed be useful to consider deification in terms of degree rather than fixed identity (admittedly, the nature of the evidence makes this difficult in many instances, as in the much-discussed case of Shulgi in ancient Mesopotamia). Woolf notes, for example, some of the limits to emperor deification in Rome. No sacrifices were made to living emperors and emperors and their relatives who had undergone *consecratio* were clearly distinguished linguistically from both gods and humans. Indeed, more general cultural-religious strategies for the construction of intermediate categories of divinity — saints, heroes, prophets, and other agents of the divine — might be key to understanding explicitly *political* strategies of rule which, to varying degrees, reference, share in, or even co-opt the divine realm entirely.

Finally, let us consider the inverse, or perhaps close relative of the divine king — the ruling god. Winter brings to our attention the prevalence of the ancient Near Eastern concept of gods as kings, a pattern also evident in pre-colonial South Asia, where Hindu deities were often represented as being the actual rulers of a kingdom, with the king and his family the God's (or Goddess') chief devotees. Clearly, human relationships and understandings of human society constitute powerful metaphors for both natural and supernatural worlds. Gods may have families, children, disagreements, social positions, and they may rule or even be deposed.

Even when the natural world is represented as the inspiration for understanding human politics — Aesop's fables, the *Panchatantra*, even the "law of the fishes" — animal models provide a transparent medium for distinctly human moral lessons.[1] Animals live in "kingdoms" and have "kings," a role usually filled by an apex predator such as the lion or jaguar, though

---

[1] The *Panchatantra* is a collection of stories, perhaps already quite old, made between the third and fifth centuries A.D. Much like Aesop's fables, they teach simple moral lessons using tales of animals and magic. In Sanskrit literature, the "law of the fishes" (the larger fish eats the smaller, and so on, quite similar to the notion of the "law of the jungle") represents an apology for the institution of kingship. Without kings, the natural order of things would ensure that the strong rule the weak and disharmony would prevail. Kings, however, protect their subjects and bring an ordered existence out of anarchy (e.g., Smith 2003).

other animals also variously enjoy royal associations. Like humans, some animals are more equal than others. Human rulers, as various contributors to this volume note, freely borrow the power and energy of their "peers," whether those are gods, lions, elephants, or neighboring dynasts. This riot of political opportunism, in a cynical reading, or, somewhat less cynically, participation in historically and culturally rich languages of power and authority, seems to be a general strategy of rule, an effort which only at some times and places resulted in divine kings. While depictions of kings overcoming lions and other powerful beasts, as well as those of defeat and humiliation of human enemies, appear as almost stock images in the cases discussed in this volume, contests between gods and humans appear to be less overt. Perhaps it is generally too risky to overthrow a god (or commission a sculpture of yourself doing so), a more prudent strategy being, "if you can't beat them, join them." This limitation (though the followers of problematic divine competitors always seem to be fair game) indeed makes the ability of both the political and belief systems to accommodate shared divinity, and perhaps shared sovereignty, critical, as Bernbeck points out. Divine kingship, rather than representing a strange, isolated, and somewhat exotic category, an intellectual legacy carried down to us from Frazier, may represent simply one (or really several) potential outcome of more general strategies of rule that can be observed elsewhere. Indeed, the cases discussed in this volume, with the interesting exception of Egypt, suggest that the institution of divine kingship may be a rarely achieved, often unstable form, albeit one in which the diverse worlds of humanity, nature, and the supernatural come together in a kind of orgy of ambiguation, creating openings for new understandings of what it means to be human and, indeed, divine.

BIBLIOGRAPHY

Battaglia, D.

    1997   "Ambiguating Agency: The Case of Malinowski's Ghost." *American Anthropologist* 99/3: 505–10.

Choudhury, Makhan Lal Roy

    1997   *The Din-I-Ilahi, or, The Religion of Akbar*. New Delhi: Munshiram Manoharlal.

Geertz, Clifford

    1980   *Negara: The Theatre State in Nineteenth-century Bali*. Princeton: Princeton University Press.

Smith, Brian K.

    2003   "Hinduism." In *God's Rule: The Politics of World Religions*, edited by Jacob Neusner, pp. 185–212. Georgetown: Georgetown University Press.

Stein, Burton

    1980   *Peasant State and Society in Medieval South India*. New Delhi: Oxford University Press.

Tambaiah, Stanley J.

    1976   *World Conqueror and World Renouncer: A Study of Buddhism and Polity in Thailand against a Historical Background*. Cambridge: Cambridge University Press.